READING COLORADO

A LITERARY ROAD GUIDE

READING COLORADO

A LITERARY ROAD GUIDE

PETER ANDERSON

Foreword by
THOMAS "DR. COLORADO" NOEL

BOWER
HOUSE

DENVER

www.BowerHouseBooks.com

Designed by Margaret McCullough
Cover map art by Brian Billow and Michele Scrivner, www.bbmsart.com
Interior maps by Rebecca Finkel, F + P Graphic Design

Printed in Canada

Library of Congress Control Number: 2023930623

Paperback ISBN: 978-1-917895-19-4
Ebook ISBN: 978-1-917895-20-0

10 9 8 7 6 5 4 3 2 1

For Chris Ransick

TABLE OF CONTENTS

THE FIRST WAVE 141

WESTERN SLOPE CENTRAL:
COLORADO AND GUNNISON RIVERS

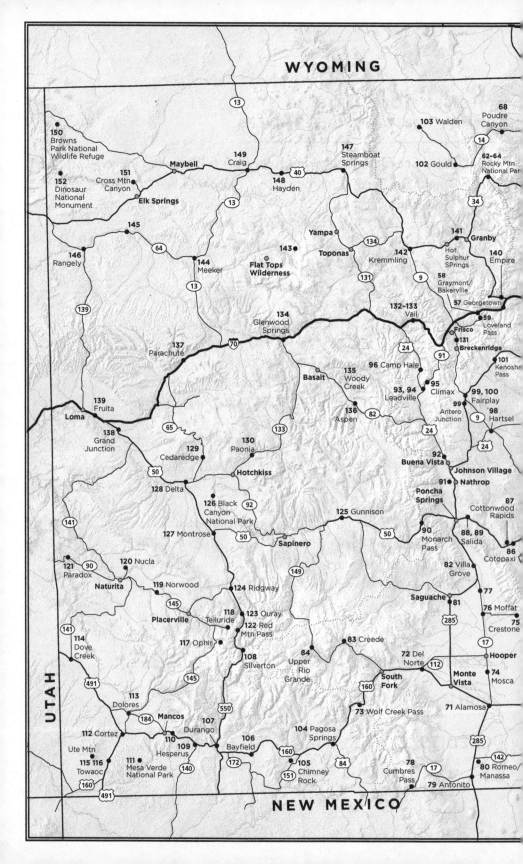

WYOMING

150 Browns Park National Wildlife Refuge

152 Dinosaur National Monument

151 Cross Mtn Canyon

Maybell

149 Craig

148 Hayden

147 Steamboat Springs

103 Walden

68 Poudre Canyon

102 Gould

62-64 Rocky Mtn National Par

Elk Springs

145

146 Rangely

144 Meeker

143 Flat Tops Wilderness

Yampa

Toponas

134 Kremmling

142 Kremmling

141 Granby

Hot Sulphur SPrings

140 Empire

58 Graymont/ Bakerville

57 Georgetown

134 Glenwood Springs

131

132-133 Vail

59 Loveland Pass

131

Breckenridge

137 Parachute

96 Camp Hale

101 Kenosha Pass

139 Fruita

Loma

Basalt

135 Woody Creek

93, 94 Leadville

95 Climax

99, 100 Fairplay

99 Antero Junction

98 Hartsel

138 Grand Junction

136 Aspen

65

133

129 Cedaredge

130 Paonia

Hotchkiss

92 Buena Vista

Johnson Village

91 Nathrop

87 Cottonwood Rapids

50

128 Delta

126 Black Canyon National Park

92

125 Gunnison

50

90 Monarch Pass

88, 89 Salida

86 Cotopaxi

141

127 Montrose

50

Sapinero

82 Villa Grove

121 Paradox

90

120 Nucla

149

Naturita

119 Norwood

124 Ridgway

Saguache

81

77

76 Moffat

75 Crestone

145

118 Telluride

123 Ouray

122 Red Mtn Pass

83 Creede

285

114 Dove Creek

117 Ophir

108 Silverton

84 Upper Rio Grande

72 Del Norte

112

17 Hooper

141

145

73 Wolf Creek Pass

South Fork

71 Alamosa

74 Mosca

Monte Vista

113 Dolores

Mancos

107 Durango

106 Bayfield

104 Pagosa Springs

160

285

112 Cortez

110 Hesperus

109 Hesperus

105 Chimney Rock

84

78 Cumbres Pass

80 Romeo/ Manassa

142

Ute Mtn

111 Mesa Verde National Park

140

172

151

17

79 Antonito

115 116 Towaoc

NEW MEXICO

UTAH

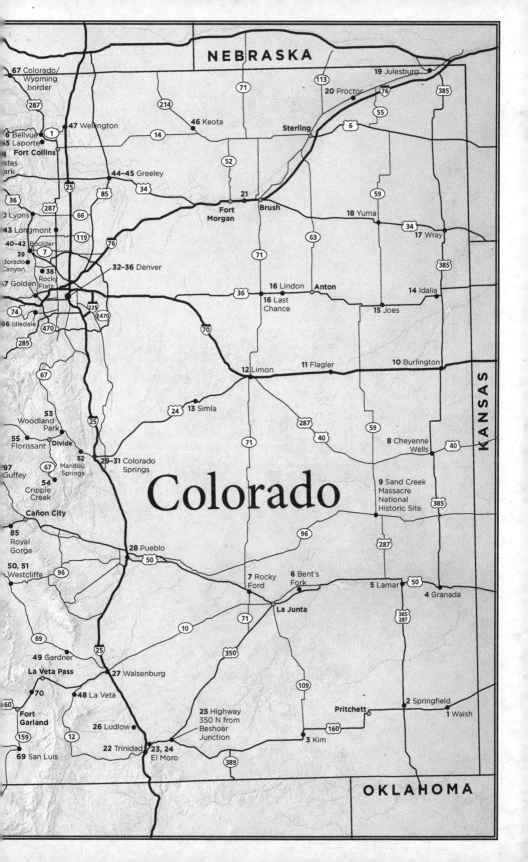

FOREWORD
Tom "Dr. Colorado" Noel

In the long run, often it is eloquent writers who keep a place memorable. Where would Troy be without its Homer? In this crackerjack anthology, Peter Anderson has assembled passages from writers who have put places on Colorado's literary map. Your favorites are probably here, but Anderson also introduces us to lesser-known writers and poets.

Just skimming these literary locales should leave you looking forward to more from authors who have elevated the highest state with their words. Native American voices like Linda Hogan (Chickasaw) and Regina Lopez-Whiteskunk (Ute) are found in these pages as are so many of the place names inherited from this region's earlier inhabitants. George Bird Grinnell, one of the first to write sympathetically about Colorado's Native Americans, explores Bent's Fort (now reconstructed by the National Park Service) as that relatively harmonious gathering place for Indians and palefaces alike. But we are reminded too, by way of powerful eye-witness accounts from Captain Silas Soule and Lieutenant Joseph Kramer, of the unprovoked early morning raid on a peaceful settlement of Cheyenne and Arapaho that took place at Sand Creek in nearby Kiowa County.

Hispanic voices—including Luis Alberto Urrea, philosopher Reyes Garcia, and Antonito mayor Aaron Abeyta—are represented here, as is San Luis, the oldest town in Colorado, in Fred Baca's "Little Bethlehem." Featured women include Isabella Bird, a strong seller to this day, with her ascent of Long's Peak in *A Lady's Life in the Rocky Mountains*. Helen Hunt Jackson, that great defender of Native Americans, shows up here scrutinizing and praising her beloved Colorado Springs. Under Leadville, newspaper editor Carlyle Channing Davis is followed by Victorian artist and writer, Mary Hallock Foote. An excerpt from Wallace Stegner's novel *Angle of Repose,* which was based on Foote's letters and won a Pulitzer Prize, describes a harrowing journey up the Mosquito Pass road between Fairplay and Leadville.

· Mother Jones, shows up in Trinidad to support striking coal miners. Upton Sinclair explores coal mining around Walsenburg in his novel *King Coal.* Rare insight into the underground world of mining men comes from Harriett Fish Backus's coverage of Telluride, whose mining trams have evolved into ski lifts. Despite a humble self-assessment in the title of her book, *Life of an Ordinary Woman,* Anne Ellis was an extraordinary Colorado author who describes turn-of-the-century life in the mining town of Bonanza. Nearby, Cy Warman edited the *Creede Candle* newspaper and immortalized that mining town with a poem whose first stanza is:

> Here's a land where all are equal—
> Of high or lowly birth—
> A land where men make millions,
> Dug from the dreary earth.
> Here the meek and mild-eyed burro
> On mineral mountains feed—
> It's day all day, in the day-time,
> And there is no night in Creede.

Baca County in the state's southeastern corner is covered by Sanora Babb, who gives us a little girl's perspective of growing up on a harsh, windblown, and sand-blasted prairie farm. Colorado's High Plains have also inspired fine work from Kent Haruf, represented here with an excerpt from his acclaimed novel *Plainsong,* and Hal Borland, the pioneer environmental writer for the *New York Times,* who writes about his hometown of Flagler. Novelist and historian Sandra Dallas, who has also reviewed Colorado fiction and nonfiction in *The Denver Post* since 1961, portrays a woman homesteader in an entry from *The Diary of Mattie Spenser.* In that book (and some of her other novels) Sandra covers incest, rape, and the abuse women have long suffered—horrors that historians have not thoroughly explored.

Bayard Taylor, one of the first (1866) nationally noted authors to tour Colorado, described Hot Sulphur Springs, helping to make it one of the state's first tourist targets. Walt Whitman, an early celebrity tourist in Colorado, writes about its landscape wonders on a railroad trip to Kenosha Pass. Colorado's former poet laureate, Thomas Hornsby Ferril, shows up in these pages with his poem—"Here is a Land Where Life is Written in Water"—that welcomes visitors to the State Capitol rotunda.

Among the recently departed included herein is Hunter Thompson, the legendary gonzo journalist from Woody Creek, as well as Ed Quillen, the sage of Salida. Voices representing the Western Slope include Willa Cather on Mesa Verde, David Lavender on Paradox, and Peter Decker on Ridgway, where this former Colorado Secretary of Agriculture ran his ranch. On the eastern side of the Divide, John Fante writes about Boulder and John Williams describes the historic Smoky River route into Colorado. Author and *New York Times* columnist Timothy Egan recreates the Dust Bowl hardships of the "dirty thirties" around Springfield.

Some of these writers made history as well as writing it. Enos Mills, the great naturalist, wrote about the Rocky Mountains and did more than anyone to celebrate them with a national park. In Georgetown, James Grafton Rogers wrote *My Mountain Valley* and spearheaded creation of the Georgetown Loop Historic Mining and Railroad Park which today carries some 170,000 passengers a year into the past. Dalton Trumbo, who fictionalized Grand Junction in his novel *Eclipse*, and whose career survived the blacklists of the 1940s and 50s, now sits on Main Street in a life-size sculpture soaking in his bathtub while writing Hollywood scripts. Vail is described by Peter Seibert, the founding father of what now claims to be North America's largest ski resort. Poets Corky Gonzales and Lalo Delgado not only wrote as Chicano activists in Denver, they also spearheaded the movement.

Offbeat writers also await you. Jack Kerouac takes a memorable nap on the grass fronting a Longmont gas station in *On the Road*. Neil Cassady recalls a down-and-out childhood in Denver. Ken Kesey revisits his Eastern Colorado stomping ground in *Sometimes a Great Notion*. Anne Waldman and Allen Ginsberg bring words of protest to Rocky Flats.

The best seller of all Colorado authors is James Michener, whose novel, *Centennial*, remains a fine, fictional overview of our state's history starting with the dinosaurs. Here he reminisces about the area around Greeley and the High Plains town of Keota.

In an excerpt from *Roughing It*, the greatest American writer of them all, Mark Twain, is on the road to California when he passes through the crossroads town of Julesburg. In these pages you will find a wonderful range of writers to accompany any road trip as you explore Colorado communities and the words they have inspired.

—Tom "Dr. Colorado" Noel

Tom is the co-author or author of fifty-three books on Colorado.

A FEW GEOGRAPHICAL
AND LITERARY NOTES

When I lit out from my home on the eastern edge of the San Luis Valley in August of 2019, the old Chevy had about 120,000 miles on it, but it also had good tires, fresh oil, and a recently tuned engine—a decent enough rig for hauling a pop-up camper back and forth across the Divide a few times. My plan was to spend a couple of months driving the major routes through Colorado. For starters, I would head north and east into the Arkansas Valley and South Park, north across Middle Park and North Park, and then west along the Yampa River to Dinosaur. From there, I'd turn south toward the San Juans. I wanted to drive the western slope during the waning weeks of summer. As fall came on, I planned on heading for the Plains. Other than visiting some old pals and a few favorite haunts along the way and driving a few roads I had never driven, the purpose of the trip was twofold: to revisit the geography of Colorado and to gather material for this anthology in local libraries, museums, and various visitor centers throughout the state.

Thirty-five hundred miles and a few months later, I came home with folders full of maps, brochures, and many pages of copied excerpts for this book, not to mention lots of snapshot-sized memories, or "neurochromes," of various scenes along the way—shooting stars over Gore Pass, nighthawks at dusk along the Green River in Brown's Park, a high plains dome of blue sky over Baca County. I have heard Colorado described as "the land of the long look." Driving south over Poncha Pass, that seemed about right as the great expanse of the San Luis Valley welcomed me home.

As far as gathering literary materials was concerned, I was open to any genre—letters, journals, memoir, history, fiction, poetry, journalism—as long as the writer knew about a particular part of the state and had something of interest to say about it. Later on, I made a decision to limit the poetry entries to those of a more historical nature. Part of the issue had to do with the sheer quantity of material I was accumulating. Part of it had do with a wonderful community of contemporary poets in Colorado whose work, it seemed to me, deserved its own book—an atlas of Colorado poets and places perhaps. The material I had gathered for this book included a wide range of voices. Some writers were long-time residents; others were just passing through. Some were famous, others had never been published. Literary credentials didn't matter; what mattered was that a writer had a story or a few good lines that might "deepen the map" for readers wanting to know this place.

I also came home with a renewed sense of Colorado's geographical and cultural landscape...how for example, one might sense traces of neighboring states—a stronger Mormon presence out toward the Utah border, the libertarian cowboy ethos of Wyoming in the north, hard-scrabble agrarian histories from Nebraska, Kansas, and Oklahoma in the east, traces of older ways and traditions from New Mexican villages and pueblos to the south. What people referred to as an "arroyo" in the southern part of the state, might be known as a "wash" somewhere up north. The word "awesome" might mean one thing to a snowboarder in Breckenridge and something else to an old timer in Limon who had seen a few tornados. While I had no intention of trying to put together a comprehensive anthology of Colorado literature, I did want to represent, as best I could, the diverse, if not eclectic, constellation of voices who had something to say about this state.

And I wanted to present those materials in a geographical context: place by place, road by road, region by region. When it came to the prospect of determining regions within the state, especially in the mountains, I chose to hew pretty closely to watershed boundaries. But in some areas, most notably the eastern part of the state which geographers (and historians) often divide into sub-regions determined by the Arkansas and South Platte rivers, the material seemed to fit a broader category—The Eastern Plains—as did the literature from the meeting place of plains and mountains—The Corridor—which also contains the most densely populated parts of the state. Coloradoans often use the name Front Range generically to describe both the urban corridor and

*the eastern edge of the mountains that run along a north-south axis
throughout the state, but the Front Range, as a geological entity, only
extends a little farther south than Pikes Peak. The transition from the
plains into the high country, referred to in this book as The First Wave,
includes the Front Range and the first wave of mountains between
Pikes Peak and New Mexico.*

*Moving west, the watershed boundaries became more import-
ant in describing high country areas along the eastern side of the
Continental Divide, which are covered in the High Parks and Valleys
section of the book. The term "park" in this case is not a government
designation setting aside a place of interest, it is a geographical term
referring to a wide treeless basin bordered on all sides by mountains;
east of the Divide, those areas are the San Luis Valley (once known as
San Luis Park), South Park, and North Park. The word valley in this
category refers to the Upper Arkansas region; though not as broad
an expanse, it borders the Divide and gathers eastern slope water
into a significant river (The Arkansas) as do each of the three parks
(San Luis—The Rio Grande, South Park—The South Platte, and North
Park— the North Platte).*

*Although, the western slope is a term universally applied to the
territory in Colorado west of the Continental Divide, all of which
eventually drains into the Colorado River (except for that water that
is diverted, much to the chagrin of Western Slopers, to points east of
the Divide) it is also a wide-ranging region that encompasses lots of
geographical and cultural variation. For that reason, and for the sake
of organizing the material in this book, it became useful to think about
the western slope as three different subregions. As is so often the case
throughout the west, major transportation routes follow the water. Most
of the traffic crossing the western slope follows the I-70 corridor, which
also parallels the Colorado River. US 50, the other east-west artery
carrying the most traffic through the center of the western slope, parallels the Gunnison River. Taken together, these two rivers and roads
encompass the central portion of the western slope. Major east-west
thoroughfares in the north and south, Highway 40 and Highway 160,
respectively, correspond with the two major watersheds: The Yampa in*

the north and the San Juan in the south. Those rivers and roads shape the other subregions.

    Roads and the rivers they so often follow are the bones of this book, which travels from south to north and east to west. If you were to read straight through, you would be moving in the same direction as earlier waves of non-native settlers who came into Colorado. Geography largely determined the way those populations settled here, as it influenced the lifeways of earlier residents whose words still name many of the places on the map. Similarly, our experience of this land generates words and stories, which influences our experience of the land, which invites more words and stories, and round and round the cycle goes, like water moving through this place called Colorado.

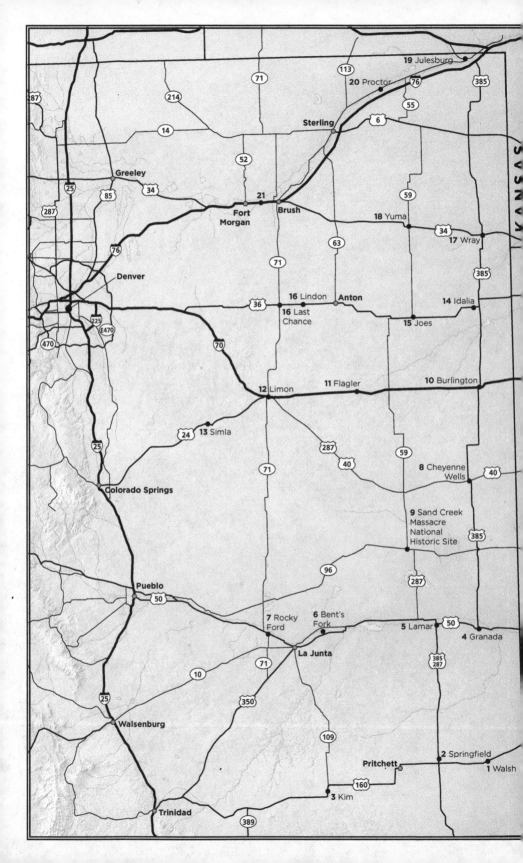

THE EASTERN PLAINS

Those who are obsessed with vertical landscapes will tell you that Eastern Colorado, the other Colorado from their point of view, is nothing but flatland, a description that holds true only if you aren't paying attention. Though more subtle than the mountain geography to the west, the Eastern Plains region, where short grass prairies and vast stretches of agricultural land dominate the landscape, also has its canyons, washes, swales, and rolling mesas; there are sand hills, buttes, arroyos and wide-ranging river valleys.

The high plains of eastern Colorado welcome the waters of the Arkansas and South Platte, as well as lesser known rivers like the Purgatoire, or the "Picketwire" as some have called it, and the Apishipa, which also carry the runoff from distant mountains. Then there are rivers that begin in the higher reaches of the plains themselves like the Cimarron, the Smoky Hill, the Republican, and the Arikaree; and where there are rivers, there are also cottonwoods, which harbor owls, hawks, and magpies, as well as a host of other winged residents, some of whom are locals and some of whom are only passing through.

The Comanche, Arapaho, Cheyenne, and Pawnee found shelter along these high plains waterways, as did later waves of immigrants who came west along thoroughfares like the Santa Fe, Smoky Hill, and South Platte trails, seeking land, gold, or just a new beginning. Shelter is scarce, water is limited, the sun is strong, and the wind can be fierce—making a home here requires some resilience. But for those who stay, there are rewards, not the least of which is an immense dome of sky and an accompanying sense of freedom and possibility.

Highway 160
Colorado-Kansas line west to Trinidad

1. Walsh
from *An Owl on Every Post* by Sanora Babb

For almost a half a century beginning in the 1860s, much of the territory in this part of Eastern Colorado was open range cattle country. That began to change in the 1880s as new waves of homesteaders, or nesters, as the cattlemen liked to call them, moved into the area. One of the most popular homesteading crops around Baca County towns like Walsh was broomcorn, a type of sorghum which grew in tall corn-like stalks, the panicles of which were used to make brooms.

Sanora Babb was six years old when she moved with her family from Oklahoma to the Two Buttes area northwest of Walsh. Her father, following the example of his father, settled 320 acres with the intent of raising broomcorn. Babb's novel, An Owl on Every Post, *was based on her life experiences in the vast spaces of her new home. "Its loneliness stretched my soul," she wrote. Whether or not her encounter with an otherworldly horse in the following excerpt actually happened is left for you, the reader, to decide, but the details in her description of this prairie night are impeccable.*

There was nothing in sight on the open prairie. The high clear air shimmered with moonlight. The silence deepened into a sound of itself, a palpable atmosphere through which we walked to what destination I did not know. In this unpeopled place what destination could there be? An intensely felt but not understood part of me was being stretched in every direction to the circular horizon and upward to that immense field of stars. I was aware of my hunger then, a hunger that stirred me to living life, a knowledge that I was more than myself, that self of the hours of day and night, that the unknown answer lay all about me, that everything spoke to me and yet I could not understand. I wanted to be alone with this new feeling, but I was overcome with such a loneliness that I dared to run ahead and slip my hand into Grandfather's. His dry fingers bent to enclose my hand that sought his finite touch and comfort. We walked like this until we neared the length of prairie that broke off at a precipice, a long high cliff following the creekbed far below. He let go my hand and walked more slowly, scuffing over the grass here and there, feeling for button cactus. He sat down, raised his knees, and let his arms rest upon them. A sigh came out of his slackened body. He motioned for me to sit near him and for Bounce to lie down at his feet. We sat looking into the nothingness of night. We listened to baby coyotes yipping over a kill their parents had brought them.

I supposed that soon we would continue our ramble or turn back, and found nothing unusual in Grandfather's silence as he rarely spoke unless he had something particular and necessary to say. I did not pester him with questions when he was "studying about things," as he called serious thinking.

Bounce whined very low and started up.

"Down!" Grandfather said in a hushed voice. Bounce obeyed reluctantly, pressing against my bare legs. I pulled him back across my lap, keeping my fingers in his thick coat. He was trembling, wanting to whine or bark, but he understood his master's command.

"There's a horse!" I could not help my exclamation as a young bay trotted up near us out of nowhere.

Grandfather turned his head and looked at me in rather a surprised way, but he was not at all surprised by the horse. Then he did a strange thing. He nodded a thoughtful yes. I did not know what he meant. We turned back to watching the horse.

"Let him be," Grandfather said. "That's Daft."

"Who is Daft?" I whispered.

"Never mind now."

Daft was a dark bay with the short head of a mustang. His coat gleamed in the moonlight as if his owner curried him every day and combed out his long black mane and tail. He was very frisky. Apparently he had been grazing and suddenly felt an urge to play. He nipped a little grass, then capered about, arching his neck, kicking his hind legs out, stopping dead still, then throwing his head back and smelling the air with pleasure. It was great fun to watch him, and I knew that Grandfather had brought me to share his entertainment. I wondered for a moment how on this vast plain Grandfather knew exactly where to find Daft at this summer-night play. We had crossed no fences but our own, we had seen no lighted windows or farmhouse, but farms were distant from one another and I had not expected to see one. This walk proved once again how well Grandfather knew this unmarked land.

Bounce was trembling more and whining under his breath as if he would burst if not allowed to run and bark. I held him and stroked his head, but he was not consoled.

Daft whinnied. Grandfather said, "Hear that?"

"Yes."

"Well, I'll declare."

Suddenly, I saw Daft's forelegs curve, his black hoofs lift, and he galloped away in his own thunder, his mane and tail flying beautifully. He ran in utmost delight, swerved back, and raced by us at frightening speed, swiping us with a stream of cold night air. He was running toward the cliff. We leaped up. At the last dangerous moment, he stopped short with legs stiffened, braking his motion.

"Thank God!" Grandfather said. He touched me. "Let's go home now."

At once Daft galloped away over the plain, farther this time, and thundered back in the direction of the cliff. Grandfather put an arm around my shoulders and tried to press my face against his side, but I pulled away. Bounce jerked free of my hand and ran after the horse, barking madly. Daft streaked past us like a cold wind, ears back, nostrils wide open, and his eyes wild. He headed straight for the precipice. Beyond it, suspended for an instant in the empty air, he fell, screaming all the way down. The horror of an echo came back to us from the rock wall of the cliff.

In the awesome quiet after, we waited stunned, and then I began to cry for Daft.

"I'm sorry, child. I brought you just to see Daft play."

We began our anguished long walk home. Grandfather let me cry awhile, to comfort me, and when I could listen to him, he said, "Don't cry anymore, don't grieve, and I'll try and tell you why Daft is all right. We'll come back again and you'll see."

"No! How can I see him again when he is killed?"

"I can't very well explain that when I don't know myself. There are many strange things we don't yet understand, but that doesn't mean you need to be afraid of something you don't understand, does it?"

"I guess not."

"Then I'll tell you this. I wanted to see if you could *see* Daft. You saw him first. Now Daft ran over that cliff and killed himself two years ago. I felt mighty bad. Daft was my horse, my favorite, but he got to eating locoweed and he was ruined."

"Was he loco?"

"Yes, he was loco. I didn't know it at first, and I named him Daft because he acted so daft."

"I know about locoweed."

"But we don't know all the rest. After Daft was killed, I had only one horse for a time, and one day I rode over to see an artesian well come in, and I rode home after dark. That was the first time I saw Daft. It scared me, I can tell you, but I got over that. I've seen that horse many times. I'd walk over there on fair nights just to watch him play. He hardly ever jumps off the cliff. He just plays. I thought he had quit doing that or I wouldn't have taken you there."

"I might go again," I said.

"We'll talk about that later."

"I'd like to see him because he isn't real."

"That's the pure self of Daft," he said.

I was bewildered by this, but Grandfather said, "Never mind," so I knew he was talking to himself....

"...I have told no one about seeing Daft, but several others have seen him too. I just keep still."

"Why?"

"Because I don't understand it, and I don't like talking a lot of nonsense. Therefore, I am asking you to keep this a secret with me."

"Even from Mama and Papa?"

"Yes."

"I promise." I felt proud and glad that he trusted me and wished me to share such a marvelous secret.

After that we walked in silence, and I longed for the sound of Daft's screaming to go out of my head. I wanted to see him again if I could be sure that he wouldn't jump off the precipice. I couldn't bear it again. I was thinking so hard about all that had happened that I stumbled and fell against Bounce. He growled, and he had never growled at me before. I got to my feet, and there was Daft standing a little way off looking at us in a peaceful, browsing way. I began to shudder, and no matter how gently his large dark eyes looked at me, my skin was cold with terror and I felt all my pores rise. It was almost impossible to take my gaze away, but I made the effort to lift my face toward Grandfather. He was smiling at the pure self of Daft.

"Thank you, lad," Grandfather said to him, and the terror let go my body....

...Bounce, his tail now lifted high from between his shivering legs, wandered ahead of us in his customary good humor. We were all part of the luminous night, Grandfather, myself, Bounce, and Daft.

2. Springfield
from *The Worst Hard Time* by Timothy Egan

Imagine these skies darkened by towering mountains of wind-driven dust, some of them rising to altitudes of 10,000 feet. In the 1930s, there were days here in southeastern Colorado, and all across the southern Great Plains, when you couldn't see your hand in front of your face. During the "dirty thirties," people wore respiratory masks when they went outside. They rubbed Vaseline inside their noses to filter out the dust. They hung wet sheets on their windows to protect themselves from rolling clouds of dirt. One of the few redeeming qualities of dugouts, the burrow-like homes that homesteaders excavated on the prairie, was that the wind wouldn't carry them away. The Black Sunday winds that devastated this region in April of 1935, took just about everything else.

In The Worst Hard Time, *a book about the dust bowl years on the Great Plains, author and New York Times columnist Timothy Egan describes the aftermath of Black Sunday here in Baca County: "Baca,*

so heavily plowed in the 1920s, was one of the most blown-away coun-
ties in the heart of the Dust Bowl; more than 1.1 million acres were so
eroded they probably would never support a crop again, in the view
of the government men....It wasn't considered a weakness to get help
from somewhere else, because the land itself had given up."

If the land itself had given up, how were the residents of this
region supposed to carry on? Some stayed put and eked out a living
with the help of government assistance until they were able to get back
on their feet or sell out. Others were forced to leave their homes and
seek employment elsewhere.

Along with eight brothers and sisters, Ike Osteen had grown up on
320 acres of marginal farmland, which his parents had homesteaded
outside of Springfield. Even during the good years when the rains
came, life on the farm had never been easy; his father had died at the
age of forty-one. After a few years of weathering the big dust storms,
his mother gave up on the farm and moved her daughters into town,
leaving the place for Ike and his brother Oscar to manage. They knew
that this diminished land would not support them both. What they
didn't know was any other way to make a living in this area at the time.
As it turned out, Ike's hunch that he might be able to hire on with the
railroad eventually proved up, but his destiny was more than a little
uncertain the day he left the farm.

... Later in the year, Ike's mother turned her back on the dugout for the
last time and moved into town with the two girls. The other children
were gone, drifted away. She said the boys could split the homestead if
they wanted it or sell it to the Resettlement people. Do whatever. After
giving a quarter century of her life to raising nine children on the High
Plains, she was done with the hole in the ground.

Ike took up the homestead topic with his brother.

"You want it?"

Oscar shrugged. "I don't have no other place to go."

"You're staying, then?"

"I guess. But I can't see how this could support two families. It ain't
like it was in Daddy's day."

"Then it's yours," said Ike. "The place is yours."

"You want something for your half?"

"Nope. It's yours, Os."

"Well, all right then."

A few days later, Ike packed a bag with some dried meat, a couple of biscuits, a canteen of water. He walked one last time over the dirt floor of the dugout, looked in disgust at the muck clinging to the browned sheets over the windows, at the stove that had kept him warm through so many nights, fueled by cow turds. Above ground, the place was nearly buried. The fence line formed a barrier of snagged tumbleweeds and dust.

"What you gonna do, Ike?"

"Don't know."

"You leaving, then?"

"Yep."

"For good?"

"Don't know."

"Where you going?"

"Don't know. Not far, probably. Gotta find some work." He had heard there was a job in Springfield, on the railroad line by the Cimarron River.

"I'll see ya, then."

"Yeah. See ya."

Ike walked away from the homestead with just the clothes on his back and his bag of food and water, waded through the dunes, past the nearly covered outhouse, the barn with the wall of sand on one side, the windmill and its crackling static, the muddied trough of the stock tank, past the lone surviving tree—*goodbye to all that*—and out to the open country, the land that had been so full of ancient mystery, these secrets of the conquistadors, these Indian burial grounds, this place of ghost grass and ghost bison. He just kept walking.

3. Kim
Poems by Bruce Kiskaddon

*Between 1790 and 1890, a place was officially designated unsettled or
frontier if it had a population density of less than two people per square
mile. As of the 2000 census (and it hasn't changed much since then), the
population density of Baca County averaged two people per square mile.*

*It is less than that outside of Kim, where sixth generation rancher
Floyd Beard lives and works, and that suits him just fine as he says in a
poem called "I Ain't No Recluse": "Neighbors are scarce where I come
from.../ I like folks best when they are scattered some." Beard carries on
a time-honored tradition in this part of the state, not only as a working
cowboy, but also as someone who writes poems and songs about his way
of making a living, in which he highlights some of the chores familiar
to the ranching residents of this area: "A calf gets roped, a cow heads
out, they cut 'er back on a dime, / Those cattle country rituals, a western
branding time."*

*In 1918, another cowboy, who later took to writing verse, came here
from Pennsylvania. Bruce Kiskaddon spent the first ten years of his
cowboying career chasing cattle over the short grass prairie between
Kim and the canyon country along the Purgatoire (or Picketwire, as it
was known in cowboy parlance) River. Some years later, he described his
experience in this excerpt from a poem called "Cowboy Days":*

Can you recollect the country that we knew in days gone by
Where the prairie met the sunrise and the mountains met the sky.
Where you rode through rugged canyons and o'er rolling mesas wide
Or you crossed the wind swept prairie on a long and lonely ride.

How your bits and spurs would jingle and the only other sound
Was the creaking of your saddle and the hoof beats on the ground.
Almost any where you landed there was something you could do
You were happy in that country with the people that you knew.

*Kiskaddon was adept at evoking some of the trials and travails of a
cowboy's working life, and he often did it with a sense of humor, as in
this excerpt from* "Ridin' Fence."

Ridin' along at a easy walk with your steeples and hammer and pliers.
Keepin' a watch fer the tracks of stock or the
weeds blowed up on the wires.

You'll find some sign of coyotes, too, and plenty of rabbit tracks.
And down in the wash some calves crawled thru
and scraped the hair off their backs.

You must fix the gate on the other side along where the road goes through.
The past'rs big. It's a good long ride and they's allus a heap to do.
You find a place where a big old bull went through in a patch of oak.
They's a picket out and some steeples pulled
and a couple of wires broke... .

Fence ridin' jobs ain't allus snaps. I never did call it fun.
The worst thing about it is perhaps that yore never exactly done.
But any feller that's got good sense can figger the whole affair.
If nothin' went wrong with a string of fence, he wouldn't be needed there

Or in this poem called "Drinkin' Water"

.When a feller comes to pond or a tank,
It is better to ride out a ways from the bank.
For the water is clearer out there as a rule,
And besides it is deep and a little more cool.
And out toward deep water, you notice somehow,
You miss a whole lot of that flavor of cow.
You can dip up a drink with the brim of yore hat,
And water makes purty good drinkin' at that.
You mebby spill some down the front of yore shirt,

But any old waddy knows that doesn't hurt.
There may be some bugs and a couple insecks
But it all goes the same down a cowpuncher's neck.
I know there is plenty of folks would explain
Why such water had ort to be filtered or strained.
Sech people as that never suffered from thirst,
Or they'd think of it later and drink it down first.

Highway 50

Colorado-Kansas Line West to Pueblo

4. Granada
from *Gasa Gasa Girl Goes to Camp* by Lily Nakai

Shortly after the attack on Pearl Harbor in December of 1941, a rising tide of prejudice led Franklin Delano Roosevelt to issue a proclamation forcing West Coast residents of Japanese descent, most of whom were American citizens, into relocation camps. One of those camps was located west of Granada and south of Highway 50. The Granada Relocations Camp, later renamed Amache after the Cheyenne wife of a prominent early settler, housed more than 7500 men, women, and children in a military-style facility surrounded by gun towers and barbed wire fences. It is true that Amache had a school and other "amenities," including ten thousand acres of farmland which supported the community. Still, residents were incarcerated and living in primitive dormitories, which left them more exposed to the elements than their neighbors in Granada. In winter, the cold north wind scoured the camp, which was perched on a bluff above the Arkansas River. In the summer, a relentless sun beat down on shadeless barracks. In between, frequent dust storms were so bad it was often hard to breathe.

So much for the milder climate of southern California where Lily Nikai came from. She was ten years old when her family was forced to move to Granada. In her memoir, Gasa Gasa Girl Goes to Camp, *she revisits her life in a "tar-papered barrack, gazing out at the nightly searchlight. She wondered if anything would ever be normal again." She recalls moments of beauty and wonder in the midst of all the hardship. Nevertheless, the fence was always there. The high plains beyond the barbed wire suggested freedom, which was something, as a young girl on the wrong side of the fence, that she could only know by way of her imagination.*

I wore a jacket when mornings turned crisp and donned boots when it rained. I splashed into the iridescent puddles shimmering at the entrance of the bus maintenance shed on the way to school. I jumped into those green and purple puddles. The colors fractured into stars: red, gold, blue. I hopped into another little lake. Tiny rainbows swirled insanely like drunken bugs. Raindrops pocked the oily surface, then bounced off as flecks of light. I squatted and smeared the edge of a puddle oozing with tarry liquid. My finger smelled of dirt and gas.

Winter in Amache was sometimes gentle, often brutal, but always amazing. The first winter began with a chill suspended in the air. The sky was gray and featureless ... a studied watercolor wash. A few small snowflakes flitted in midair, dancing as if unable to make up their minds, then floated to the ground. The flakes, weightless, melted instantly on my palm. I glimpsed a fleeting crystal on the back of my hand. The flakes wavered before they touched the ground and disappeared. As I stood there, they fell faster, clung to my clothes, and feathered the sagebrush.

Soon the snow fell in clusters. I went inside and watched snow temper the angles of the barracks and glaze the windows. A gentle wind sculpted the snow into soft mounds. The desert was transformed into wispy cotton candy, swollen *mochi*, bloated meringues. The monotonous gray was layered with a soft sheen muted by the golden reflections of a late-afternoon sun trying bravely to push aside the clouds.

I whipped at the snow with my feet to the end of our block and looked toward the vastness of Kansas, smothered by the same white blanket. Jackrabbits hopped through the barbed-wire fence, oblivious to the armed guards, nibbling at the scraps the mess cook had left for them. I crept closer and tried to coax one near. For a second, it looked at me, then scampered away. "Come on," it seemed to say, "follow me." I watched as it tracked black prints in the snow.

"I envy you Mr. Rabbit," I told him. "You're free. You can hop to Kansas if you want." I yearned for this place I had never seen and barely knew about, but it lay beyond the barbed wire, beyond the reaches of the searchlights. It symbolized nirvana, the Promised Land.

The glimpse of Kansas heaven had to wait almost sixty years before it became real. In 1998 there was an Amache camp reunion. My son and I went two days before the official celebration to visit the camp. In our rental car, we stopped at the entrance....

"I used to stand by the barbed-wire fence and wish I could squeeze through like the rabbits and make my way to Kansas," I told Michael.

"The state line is only about fifteen miles away," he said and turned the car around.

We drove away from Amache and soon spied a sign displaying a huge sunflower. "Welcome to Kansas," it beckoned. I stepped out on the side of the road.

"You've been to Kansas now," Michael said.

What could I reply? "Thank you" wasn't enough.

5. Lamar
"The Confession of William Dargy" by Priscilla Waggoner

Priscilla Waggoner is a writer, playwright, screenwriter, and former editor of the Kiowa County Independent newspaper in which the following story first appeared. The story is also included on a website about the canyons and plains of southeastern Colorado which she and other local writers and artists created. On that website, Waggoner describes William Dargy as a taciturn Scotsman and an early settler up near the Kiowa/Prowers county line. "Although the handful of Scots in the area raised sheep, William Dargy chose to raise cattle...," she writes. "He preferred keeping to himself, working on his ranch and watching it begin to prosper." If he needed to "spend a little time with others, he attended one of the Masonic fraternity meetings in nearby Lamar." In other words, he wasn't the kind of person who needed much company but, as it turned out, he wasn't opposed to it either. In those days, many people came west on the Santa Fe Trail seeking out a new beginning. One such person turned up at Dargy's ranch.

One day, a young man came to his ranch looking for work. Young man was a bit of a stretch, he was hardly more than a boy. But Dargy respected anyone willing to work hard and agreed to give him a try. He quickly discovered that the boy had a good character and was devoted to his duties. He was unusually quiet, even for Dargy, but when he spoke, it was in an articulate and educated way.

So, they worked together for the next few days. If the boy found the work difficult, he didn't complain. In fact, he managed to keep step with Dargy, which was no easy task. The long days ended with quiet conversations in the evening, a pastime Dargy realized he'd been missing. The boy was a good listener and often asked good questions, reflecting his intelligence. But Dargy couldn't help but notice that the boy spoke very little of his own life and, when asked, would change the subject to something else. Later, when he looked back on things, Dargy remembered one night when the young man sat by the fire writing a letter only to stop and stare off into space, an expression of deep sorrow on his face. The old Scot never asked about the letter or anything else for that matter. The way he viewed it, if the boy wanted to share his thoughts, he would.

Dargy grew accustomed to the company and convinced the boy to prolong his stay. He had to admit he felt a growing affection for the lad. Once or twice, he even allowed himself to think that this must be what it felt like to have a son. But he didn't allow those thoughts to linger for long. Dargy was a Scotsman. He practiced economy in everything, even in his thoughts. Besides, he had no illusions of the boy staying permanently; the sorrow that Dargy had seen in his eyes suggested that this young man would eventually leave to finish whatever unfinished business still called to him.

So Dargy decided to set aside a small sum of extra pay to help him whenever that day came, which, of course, it did. The boy received a letter and whatever it said caused him great distress. He told Dargy he must be on his way that very same day. Dargy didn't ask why. It wasn't his question to ask. But when he gave him the money he had set aside, he was embarrassed at the emotion that overcame them both. His gruffness returned, deliberately so, and only faded when he could no longer see the boy walking away.

It took a while for Dargy to adjust to the boy's absence. He berated himself for such foolishness, but eventually the old routine soothed his loneliness.
Time passed and he stopped wondering about the young man's fate.

Then one day, he got a telegram from Denver, asking him to come at
once. A person in the hospital was dying and wanted to see him. More
curious than anything else, Mr. Dargy took the very next train, having no
idea who the person might be.

When he was ushered into the hospital room, he was introduced to a
refined young woman who, sadly, was ill beyond any hope of recovery. It
was not until she spoke and held out her hand that he realized the young
woman before him was his former ranch hand. She introduced him to her
husband who was standing at her bedside—Dargy had never seen someone so heartbroken—and she told him why she'd assumed the appearance
of a man. Her husband had been convicted of a crime while in a position
of great honor and trust. She'd been shunned, dismissed and disgraced to
such an extent that she headed west to lose herself among strangers who
knew nothing of her past.

Later, her husband, who had been cleared of the crime, received the
letter she had written him and came to find her. They were only reunited
for a brief time before the onset of her illness. The hardships she had
endured after leaving her home were more than her body could take, and
the damage done, as it turned out, was irreparable.

"I asked to see you so that I might thank you for your kindness," she
said, "and to apologize for my deceit. Had I not met you ... I think I
would have been lost forever." Dargy simply shook his head and grasped
her hand a little tighter. He stayed with her until she fell asleep.

For many years, William Dargy kept this story to himself. The day
before he left for a visit home to Scotland, a trip from which he would
never return (as he too succumbed to a fatal illness), he told his tale to a
man he barely knew. As a result, his story remained with this land and
the people who live here. And maybe that's the way that Dargy would
have wanted it.

6. Bent's Fort
from *Bent's Fort and Its Builders* by George Bird Grinnell

*The Santa Fe Trail, one of the major routes for explorers, traders, and
settlers headed into the American Southwest, paralleled the Arkansas
River between the Kansas line and La Junta, as does Highway 50. As
teenagers, William Bent (1809-1869), who would become a major
presence on the Santa Fe Trail, and his brother Charles, traveled
west from St. Louis trapping beaver. In the early 1830s, William,
Charles, and their partner Ceran St.Vrain built an adobe fort along
the Arkansas River, which became the only major trading post on the
Santa Fe Trail between Missouri and the territory that eventually
became New Mexico. William Bent ran the fort from 1833 until 1849,
when the Cheyenne and other Indian residents of the regions were
especially hard hit by a cholera outbreak.*

*Over the years, Bent developed a good rapport with many of the
Plains Indians in the region, especially the Cheyenne. Early on, he
won the confidence of leaders like White Thunder when he rescued
several Cheyenne from some Comanche marauders. Later he married
Owl Woman, White Thunder's daughter, who became the mother of his
first four children. Owl Woman didn't care for their noisy quarters
next to a blacksmith's shop inside of the fort, so she usually spent the
night in a nearby camp that she preferred and Bent often joined her
there. Shortly after Owl Woman died giving birth to their fourth child,
Bent married her sister, Yellow Woman, with whom he had an additional child.*

*Other tribes came and camped near the fort for trading purposes,
but the Cheyenne were more welcome inside of the fort because of
their connection with Bent. That connection benefitted both parties
at times, as when Bent took sick and was attended to by a Cheyenne
medicine man. An account of that incident (originally recorded by
W.M. Boggs) was included in historian George Bird Grinnell's book,*
Bent's Fort and its Builders, *which he wrote for the Kansas Historical
Society in 1923.*

"William Bent had contracted a severe cold and sore throat ... and
it became so bad that he had ceased to swallow and could only
talk in a whisper, until his throat closed and his wife fed him with
broth ... through a quill which she passed down his throat. I went into
his lodge to see how he was, and he told me, by writing on a piece of
slate that he had with him, that if he did not get relief in a very short
time he was bound to die, and that he had sent for an Indian doctor
called 'Lawyer,' and was expecting him every hour. The Indian came
while I was there, a plain-looking Indian without any show or orna-
mentation about him. He proceeded at once to examine Bent's throat
by pressing the handle of a large spoon on his tongue just as any other
doctor would do, and on looking into Bent's throat he shook his head,
got up and went out of the lodge and returned very soon with a handful
of small sand burs. They were about the size of a large marrowfat pea,
with barbs all around, as sharp as fishhooks and turned up one way.
They were so sharp that by pressing them they would stick to one's
fingers. He called for a piece of sinew and a lump of marrow grease.
He made five or six threads of the sinew and tied a knot in one end
of each, took an awl and pierced a hole through each bur and ran the
sinew through it down to the knot, then rolled the bur in marrow grease
until it completely covered over the barbs of the bur; took a small, flat
stick about like a China chopstick, cut a notch in one end, wrapped one
end of the sinew around his finger and placed the notched stick against
the bur, and made Bent open his mouth, and he forced that bur or ball
down Bent's throat the length of the stick and drew it out of the throat
and repeated that three or four times, drawing out [on the barbs] all the
dry and corrupt matter each time and opened the throat passage so that
Bent could swallow soup. In a day or two, Bent was well enough to eat
food. And he told me that he certainly would of [sic] died if that Indian
had not come to his relief...

"The Indian was laughing while he performed the operation ... He
was the most unassuming Indian I saw among the Cheyennes, but was
considered by all the whites that knew him the shrewdest doctor belonging to the tribe. No medicine would of had any effect in removing these
obstructions in Bent's throat. It had become as dry as the bark on a tree,

and but for this simple remedy Bent would of died. No one but an Indian would ever of thought of resorting to such a remedy."

7. Rocky Ford
from *Sometimes a Great Notion* by Ken Kesey

During the Dust Bowl years of the 1930s, Ken Kesey's family went west from Arkansas, Oklahoma, and Texas. His mother's parents settled in La Junta for a while. While visiting them, Kesey's father found a job at a local creamery and moved into a nearby farmhouse. The view out front was nothing special, just a yard filled with discarded farm equipment. Behind their house, on the other hand, was a rich pasture where horses grazed through patches of wildflowers. This was the home that author Ken Kesey would know for the first seven years of his life and which he would later recall with some fondness. He remembered gathering wildflower bouquets for his mom out in the pasture. There were days, he said, when he would wander with his dog out into the prairie and imagine distant rumbles of thunder as the sound of horses chasing one another out across the plains.

A month or two short of Ken's eighth birthday, and a year after his father had joined the Navy, the Kesey family relocated to the Willamette Valley where his mother's parents had already moved. That part of Oregon would be home for the rest of his life, but in Sometimes a Great Notion, *Kesey revisits the territory of his early boyhood by way of his character, Hank Stamper. Stamper, who has just finished a hitch with the military and has a pocket full of cash, buys a motorcycle on the east coast and is riding it home to Oregon. When he comes wheeling across the eastern plains of Colorado, he sees a sign advertising the annual Watermelon Fair in Rocky Ford—"Free Melons"—which is reason enough to stop. A few too many beers later, he gets into a fight with a big guy "about three sheets gone and me about the same," and ends up spending the night in jail. But this cloudy occasion has a silver lining. The next day, just before he gets out of jail, he realizes that one of the jailkeepers is an attractive young woman who*

*seems to have taken notice of him during his short residency. Later in
the story, this young woman will become his wife, but in this passage,
he describes their initial meeting. Shortly after he gets out of jail, he
finds her at home just outside of town, a place not unlike the one that
Kesey knew as young boy. Almost instantly their flirting morphs into
some romance under the prairie stars.*

"Listen sweetheart; I'm serious. Tell me, oh ... what you want out of life?"

"What I want," she sounded amused. "Now, do you really care? I
mean come on, there isn't any need, really; it's fine just being a man and
a woman; it's fine...." She rolled her face toward him, pulling her hair
back so he could see her dim smile.

"... Do you really want to know what I want out of life?"

"Yeah," Hank said slowly, beginning to mean it. "Yes, I think I do."

She rolled again to her back and crossed her hands behind her head.
"Well ... of course I want a home and some kids and like that, all the
usual things... "

This time she waited a while before he spoke. "I guess... " she said
slowly, "I want somebody. All I mean to my uncle and aunt is help at the
jail and the fruit stand. I want a lot of other unusual things too, like a
page-boy cut, and a good sewing machine and a German roller singing
canary like I remember my mother had—but mostly, I guess, I want to
really mean something to somebody, something to somebody more'n just
a jail cook and a watermelon weigher."

"Like what? What do you want to be?"

"Whatever this Somebody wants, I guess." Not sounding at all like
she was guessing.

"Dang, now; that don't sound like much of an ambition to me. What
if this Somebody just happens to want a cook an' a melon tender, then
where'd you be?"

"He won't," she answered.

"Who?" Hank asked with more concern in his voice than he intended.
"Who won't?"

"Oh, I don't know." She laughed, and again answered his unspoken
question. "Just the Somebody. Whoever he someday turns out to be."

Hank was relieved. "Boy, if you ain't a case: waiting someday to be a something to a Somebody you don't even know yet. And, yeah, how about that? How will you know this Somebody when you come across him?"

"I won't know... " she said, and sat up to slide over to the side of the pick-up, with the quiet and lazy speed of a cat; she stood in the wet sand of the ditch bank, coiling her hair into a loose knot at the back of her head, "... he will." And turned her back to him.

"Hey. Where are you going?"

"It's all right," she answered in a whisper, " just in the ditch," then stepped into the water so delicately that the frogs across the ditch continued singing undisturbed .... .

There was no moon, but the night was bright and clear and the girl's naked body seemed almost to glow she was so pale. How in the world could she keep so white, Hank wondered, in a country where even the bartenders are baked brown?

The girl began humming again. She turned facing the pick-up and stood for a moment facing him, ankle-deep in the pond full of stars and cottonwood fluff, then, still humming, began walking slowly backward. Hank watched her pale body dissolve from the feet upwards into the dark as the water grew gradually deeper—her knees, her trim hips made feminine only by a trimmer waist, her stomach, her dots of nipple—until only her face flickered bodiless there under the cottonwood. The sight was incredible. "Suck egg mule," he whispered to himself, "if she ain't something."

"I like the water," the girl remarked matter-of-factly, and disappeared altogether without a ripple and with an effect so eerie that Hank had to argue with his impulses reminding himself that the ditch was only four feet or so at the deepest. He stared transfixed at the circling water. He'd never felt himself so hooked by a girl; and while she remained under water he wondered, half amused and half frightened, just which of them had been doing the hustling.

And the sky, he noticed, no longer seemed made of tinfoil.

He stayed over the next day, meeting the girl's aunt, who was married to the cop. He read detective magazines while he waited for her to return from her cleaning chores at the jail. He still wasn't able to pin her down

about her age or background or anything, though he found out from the
wire-haired aunt that her parents were dead and she lived most of the
time at a fruit stand out on the highway. They spent another night in the
pick-up, but Hank was becoming uneasy. He told the girl he had to leave
at dawn, be back later, okay? She smiled and told him that it had been
very fine, and when he kicked his motorcycle to noisy life in the gray
plains dawn she stood on the hood of the pick-up and waved as he pulled
a great plume of white dust down the road out of sight.

Highway 40

Kansas-Colorado line to Limon

8. Cheyenne Wells
from *Butcher's Crossing* by John Williams

*Butcher's Crossing, unlike so many of the shoot-'em-up horse op-
eras associated with the genre, was a serious western—serious not
only in terms of craft and style but also because author and Denver
University professor John Williams was attentive to the real-life
details of western life underneath all the usual mythologies. Butcher's
Crossing, along with a subsequent novel called Stoner (a very different
story exploring the psyche of a midwestern professor) contributed to
Williams's reputation for writing great books which, at first anyway,
were largely overlooked. As friend and fellow author Dan Wakefield
put it, "he was almost famous for not being famous."*

*Butcher's Crossing tells the story of William Andrews, a young
Harvard man headed west for adventure, who helps finance a business
venture and expedition to hunt buffalo from one of the last known
herds in Colorado. To get there, he is dependent on an old mountain
man named Miller who knows where the herd is and knows—at least,
he says he knows—how to get there. His route-finding abilities come
into question shortly after his party follows the Smoky Hill Trail onto
the high plains of Colorado. The Smoky Hill Trail was a shorter route
to the Rockies and all the resources they contained, but additional
challenges made up for that as Andrews and the other members of
this caravan soon find out. Beyond the headwaters of the Smoky Hill
River near Cheyenne Wells, the route was harder to follow, and water
became increasingly scarce.*

The party turned to the flat land upon which they could see neither
tree nor trail to guide them, and went forward upon it. Soon the line of
green that marked the Smoky Hill River was lost to them; and in the flat

unbroken land Andrews had to keep his eyes firmly fixed on Miller's back to find any direction to go in.

Twilight came upon them. Had it not been for his tiredness, and the awkward, shambling weariness of the horses beneath the weight they carried forward, Andrews might have thought that the night came on and held them where they started, back at the bend of the Smoky Hill. During the afternoon's drive he had seen no break in the flat country, neither tree, nor gully, nor rise in the land that might serve as a landmark to show Miller the way he went. They camped that night without water.

Few words were exchanged as they broke the packs from their horses and set up the night's camp on the open prairie. Charley Hoge led the oxen one by one to the back of the wagon; Miller held the large canvas receptacle erect while the oxen drank. By the light of a lantern he kept careful watch on the level of water; when an ox had drunk its quota, Miller would say sharply: "That's enough," and kick at the beast as Charley Hoge tugged its head away. When the oxen and the horses had drunk, the tank remained one-fourth full.

Much later, around the campfire, which Charley Hoge had prepared with wood gathered at their noon stop, the men squatted and drank their coffee. Schneider, whose tight impassive face seemed to twitch and change in the flickering firelight, said impersonally: "It's about a fourth full."

Schneider nodded. "We can make one more day on that, I figure. It'll be a mite dry, but we should make one more day."

"If we don't come across some water," Schneider said.

"If we don't come across some water," Miller agreed.

Schneider lifted his tin cup and drained the last dreg of coffee from it. In the firelight, his raised chin and throat bristled and quivered. His voice was cool and lazy. "I reckon we'd better hit some water tomorrow."

"We'd better," Miller said. Then: "There's plenty of water; it's just there for the finding." No one answered him. He went on. "I must have missed a mark somewhere. There should have been water right along here. But it's nothing serious. We'll get water tomorrow, for sure."

The three men were watching him intently. In the dying light, Miller returned each of their stares, looking at Schneider at length, coolly. After a moment he sighed and put his cup carefully on the ground in front of Charley Hoge.

"Let's get some sleep," Miller said. "I want to get an early start in the morning, before the heat sets in."

Andrews tried to sleep, but despite his tiredness he did not rest soundly. He kept being awakened by the low moaning of the oxen, which gathered at the end of the wagon, pawed the earth, and butted against the closed tailgate that protected the little store of water in the open canvas tank.

Andrews was shaken from his uneasy sleep by Miller's hand on his shoulder. His eyes opened on darkness, and on the dim hulk of Miller above him. He heard the others moving about, stumbling and cursing in the early morning dark.

"If we can get them going soon enough, they won't miss the watering," Miller said.

By the time the false light shone in the east, the oxen were yoked; the party again moved westward.

"Give your horses their heads," Miller told them. "Let them set their own pace. We'll do better not to push any of them till we get some water."

The animals moved sluggishly through the warming day. As the sun brightened, Miller rode far ahead of the main party; he sat erect in his saddle and moved his head constantly from one side to another. Occasionally he got off his horse and examined the ground closely, as if it concealed some sign that he had missed atop his horse. They continued their journey well into the middle of the day, and past it. When one of the oxen stumbled and in getting to its feet gashed at its fellow with a blunt horn, Miller called the party to a halt.

"Fill your canteens," he said. "We've got to water the stock and there won't be any left."

Silently, the men did as they were told. Schneider was the last to approach the canvas tank; he filled his canteen, drank from it in long, heavy gulps, and refilled it.

Schneider helped Charley Hoge control the oxen as, one by one, they were led to the rear of the wagon and the open tank of water. When the oxen were watered and tethered at some distance from the wagon, the

horses were allowed to finish the water. After the horses had got from
the tank all that they were able, Miller broke down the saplings that gave
the canvas its shape, and with Charley Hoge's help drained the water that
remained in the folds of the canvas into a wooden keg.

Charley Hoge untethered the oxen and let them graze on the short
yellowish grass. Then he returned to the wagon and broke out a package
of dried biscuits.

"Don't eat too many of them," Miller said. "They'll dry you out."

The men squatted in the narrow shade cast by the wagon. Slowly and
delicately, Schneider ate one of the biscuits and took a small sip of water
after it.

Finally he sighed, and spoke directly to Miller: "What's the story,
Miller? Do you know where there's water?"

Miller said: "There was a little pile of rocks a piece back I think I
remember. Another half-day, and we ought to hit a stream"

Schneider looked at him quizzically. Then he stiffened, took a deep
breath, and asked, his voice soft: "Where are we, Miller?"

"No need to worry," Miller said. "Some of the landmarks have
changed since I was here. But another half-day, and I'll get us fixed."

Schneider grinned, and shook his head. He laughed softly and sat
down on the ground, shaking his head.

"My God," he said. "We're lost."

"As long as we keep going in that direction," Miller pointed away
from their shadows, toward the falling sun, "we're not lost. We're bound
to run into water tonight, or early in the morning."

"This is a big country," Schneider said. "We're not bound to do
anything."

"No need to worry," Miller said.

Schneider looked at Andrews, still grinning. "How does it feel, Mr.
Andrews? Just thinking about it makes you thirsty, don't it?"

Andrews looked away from him quickly, and frowned; but what he said
was true. The biscuit in his mouth felt suddenly dry, like sun-beat sand.

9. Sand Creek Massacre National Historic Site
The letters of Captain Silas Soule
and Lieutenant Joseph Cramer

*Highway 287, which heads south from Highway 40 near the town of Kit
Carson, and subsequent county roads will eventually bring you to the
Sand Creek Massacre National Historic Site, a landscape as stunning
as its history is tragic. Here one finds cottonwood groves in a shallow
valley under a very wide sky. The US Park Service facility is simple
and straightforward—a few interpretive signs, some outbuildings, a
trailer where well-informed rangers are available to answer questions.
A lonely trail heads west from the visitor center leading eventually to an overview of the lowlands where the massacre took place.
Sometimes less is more.*

*The history of the Sand Creek Massacre is beyond the scope of this
introduction to fully explain, but the following is a very brief summary
of the basics from the US Park Service. "The seeds of the Sand Creek
Massacre lay in the presence of two historically discordant cultures
within a geographical area that both coveted for disparate reasons, an
avoidable situation that resulted in tragedy." As was often the case in
the West, settlement pressures precipitated in part by the discovery
of gold—the rush to Denver began after a discovery on Cherry Creek
in 1859—led waves of newcomers to travel through hunting grounds
favored by the Cheyenne, the Arapaho, and other native people of the
plains. Conflicts were inevitable, although there were those from both
cultures who were intent on fostering peaceable co-existence wherever
it was possible. Colonel John M. Chivington, an overzealous military
man who led an unprovoked early morning raid on a peaceful settlement of Cheyenne and Arapaho, was not one of them. It is a dark irony
at best that Chivington's name, with which nearby settlers chose to
identify their community, lingers to this day on the Colorado map.*

*Powerful testimonies bearing witness to Colonel Chivington's
actions at Sand Creek on November 29, 1864, were written by two
dissenting cavalry officers—Captain Silas Soule and Lieutenant
Joseph Cramer—in the form of letters to their former Fort Lyon*

*commander, Major Edward (Ned) Wynkoop. Prior to the massacre at
Sand Creek, both men had attended peace talks with Wynkoop and
various Cheyenne and Arapaho leaders. The following excerpts from
their letters say the rest:*

Fort Lyon, C.T.
December 14, 1864

Dear Ned:

Two days after you left here the 3rd Reg. with a Battalion of the
1st arrived here, having moved so secretly that we were not aware
of their approach until they had Pickets around the post, allowing
no one to pass out! They arrested Capt. Bent and John Vogle
and placed guards around their houses. Then they declared their
intention to massacre the friendly Indians camped on Sand Creek.
Major Anthony gave all information, and eagerly joined in with
Chivington and Co. and ordered Lieut. Cramer with his whole
Co. to join the command. As soon as I knew of their movement
I was indignant as you would have been were you here, and went
to Cannon's room, where a number of officers of the 1st and 3rd
were congregated and told them that any man who would take
part in the murders, knowing the circumstances as we did, was
a low lived cowardly son of a bitch. Capt. J. J. Johnson and Lieut.
Harding went to camp and reported to Chiv, Downing and the
whole outfit what I had said, and you can bet hell was to pay in
camp. Chiv and all hands swore they would hang me before they
moved camp, but I stuck it out, and all the officers of the post,
except Anthony backed me.
     We arrived at Black Kettle and Left Hand's Camp at day light.
Lieut. Wilson with Co.s "C", "E" & "G" were ordered to advance
to cut off their herd. He made a circle to the rear and formed a
line 200 yds. from the village, and opened fire. Poor old John
Smith and Louderbeck ran out with white flags but they paid
no attention to them, and they ran back into the tents. Anthony

then rushed up with Co's "D" "K" & "G," to within one hundred
yards and commenced firing. I refused to fire and swore that
none but a coward would. For by this time hundreds of women
and children were coming towards us and getting on their knees
for mercy. Anthony shouted, "kill the sons of bitches." Smith
and Louderbeck came to our command, although I am confident
there were 200 shots fired at them, for I heard an officer say that
Old Smith and any one who sympathized with the Indians, ought
to be killed and now was a good time to do it. The Battery then
came up in our rear, and opened on them. I took my comp'y
across the Creek, and by this time the whole of the 3rd and the
Batteries were firing into them and you can form some idea of
the slaughter. When the Indians found that there was no hope for
them they went for the Creek, and buried themselves in the Sand
and got under the banks and some of the Bucks got their bows
and a few rifles and defended themselves as well as they could.
By this time there was no organization among our troops, they
were a perfect mob—every man on his own hook. My Co. was
the only one that kept their formation, and we did not fire a shot.

Yours,
(signed) S.S. Soule

*Here is an excerpt from Lieutenant Cramer's letter, written on
December 19, 1864, which does not spare any graphic details.*

Dear Major:

...I swore I would not burn powder and I did not. Captain Soule
the same. It is no use for me to try to tell you how the fight was
managed, only that I think the Officer in Command should be
hung, and I know when the truth is known it will cashier him.
    After the fight there was a sight I hope I may never see again.
Bucks, women, and children were scalped, fingers cut off to get

the rings on them, and this as much with Officers as men, and
one of those Officers a Major, and a Lt. Col. Cut off Ears, of all
he came across, a squaw ripped open and a child taken from
her, little children shot, while begging for their lives (and all the
indignities shown their bodies that was ever heard of) (women
shot while on their knees, with their arms around soldiers a
begging for their lives) things that Indians would be ashamed to
do. To give you some idea, squaws were known to kill their own
children, and then themselves, rather than to have them taken
prisoners. Most of the Indians yielded 4 or 5 scalps. But enough!
For I know you are disgusted already. Black Kettle, White
Antelope, War Bonnet, Left Hand, Little Robe and several other
chiefs were killed. Black Kettle said when he saw us coming that
he was glad, for it was Major Wynkoop coming to make peace.
Left Hand stood with his hands folded across his breast, until he
was shot saying, "Soldier no hurt me—soldiers my friends...."

  After all the pledges made by Major A-to these Indians and
then take the course he did .... He has a face for every man he
talks. The action taken by Captain Soule and myself were under
protest .... Col. C was going to have Soule hung for saying there
were all cowardly Sons of B----s; if Soule did not take it back,
but nary take a back with Soule. I told the Col. That I thought it
murder to jump them friendly Indians. He says in reply; Damn
any man or men who are in sympathy with them. Such men as
you and Major Wynkoop better leave the U.S. Service....I expect
Col. C—and Downing will do all in their power to have Soule,
Cossitt and I dismissed. Well, let them work for what they damn
please, I ask no favors of them. If you are in Washington, for
God's sake, Major, keep Chivington from being a Bri'g Genl.
Which he expects ....

Very Respectfully
Your Well Wisher
(signed) Joe A. Cramer

Interstate 70

Colorado-Kansas line to Denver

10. Burlington
from "Flight Pattern" by Joanne Greenberg

Joanne Greenberg, who lives on Lookout Mountain near Golden, Colorado, may be best-known for her novel, I Never Promised You a Rose Garden *(1964), but that came relatively early in a long list of accomplishments which includes eleven other novels and four collections of short stories, teaching at Colorado School of Mines (anthropology and fiction writing), and serving for thirteen years as a volunteer firefighter and emergency medical technician.*

"Flight Pattern," one of her many short stories, take us out onto the plains of Eastern Colorado, a landscape whose openness, depending on the observer, may be boring, exhilarating, intimidating, maybe even otherworldly. Here, on the interstate west of Burlington, she describes a young hitchhiker named Ben who is desperate for a ride. Hitchhiking may have been an adventure at one time, but now that he is also a cocaine smuggler, it is an exhausting ordeal, each ride nothing more than a means of transport across a foreboding geography. That is, until his next ride comes along and "foreboding" becomes "surreal."

Now there was something off in the distance. A car. He began to hope fervently, almost to pray that this one would stop for him ... .

There seemed to be something wrong with the car. It was listing, unless the road wasn't even, a dusty Buick, '38 or '39 the kind that was sure to be carrying an old rancher and his tired wife toward town. That kind never picked up hitchhikers. Too dangerous. He leaned toward the road as the car came close seeking the driver's eye—it was a man, he saw, alone and not old. The car began to slow and stopped about fifty feet ahead of him. Then, to his surprise, it courteously backed up as he ran toward it. He got in quickly and thanked the driver.

"You going to Burlington?" the driver asked.

"Yes, sir, I am."

They started up with a little shudder, but the ride was surprisingly smooth. Ben did not perceive the list he thought he had seen. "It's a mighty bad stretch," the driver said. "When I travel this road I'm usually the only one on it." Ben looked at him. He was about thirty-five, and ordinary looking.

"I guess I've been waiting for three hours or so. I almost gave up hope."

"It's really been a little over two hours," the driver said, "but I can imagine your nervousness, seeing as how you're carrying all that cocaine."

There seemed to be a stopping in Ben of every function except fear. He felt the blood falling from his brain; he didn't or couldn't speak or reason. His hands hung, his feet went heavy. He could only sit im-mobilized. The driver, after watching the road for a minute, turned to him again affably and continued. "Of course, it's worth a good deal of money—more than you've ever made before at one time. Oh, by the way, Lawrence is in jail."

"Lawrence?" He was surprised that he was able to push out the single word. Maybe there was still hope. He didn't know anyone named Lawrence. The driver continued pleasantly, "You call him Grog. Didn't you know his real name? Apparently the long wait for your return was too much for him. He saw life passing him by—he scored some cocaine downtown in K.C. and went back uptown to sell it. He cuts such an unprepossessing figure that the only buyer he had in three hours of dedicated hustle was Lujean Adams, a narcotics officer. Off duty. Lujean arranged another buy, and in two hours Lawrence was being read his rights."

"Is this—are you a cop?"

"No."

"Who are you, then?"

"I'm not a policeman. Definitely not."

"Are you ... someone from the Mob?"

"The Mob!" The driver laughed. It was a surprisingly musical laugh. Ben's terror deepened. He had not known that fear could go so deep.

"For God sakes," he said very quietly, "don't ...don't..."

"Don't *you*," the driver said stiffly. "Of all the emotions there are and all the combinations of emotion, fear is the one I least understand. The lack is mine, no doubt, but your terror is affecting the air around you, and because I am sitting so close, I am being upset by it. Ordinarily, it wouldn't matter, but in serious cases my vision gets extremely short, and while driving I might—"

"What are you talking about?"

"I'm sorry but before I go stone-blind as a result of your terror I'm going to have to pull over."

There was no shoulder, no fence in the vast flatness. Ben had already begun to grieve for himself at this moment of his death, coming so suddenly and so unfairly. He felt a terrible loss for the body he already saw lying in these spaces, covered and uncovered by blowing snow, torn by coyotes and dried to half-rotted leather by the sun and wind. "I don't want to die," he murmured. "I'll do anything I have to do, but I don't want to die."

The driver laughed again. "We'll deal with that when we come to it."

The car had stopped. Absently Ben looked out the window and saw with sudden and surprising clarity as though for the first time, the prairie at the roadside. What an intricate, complex ecology there was. Tiny crickets and beetles struggled through small clumps of grass, and their dozen shades of green, olive, and brown proclaimed themselves to his eye. Here and there the tiniest of flowers opened starry umbels to him; small mosses hid purple blooms of incomparable beauty. How had he ever seen this plain as empty! His hands were trembling. It had never seemed so important that he live—continue to live. "Listen to me," the driver said at his side. "I'm trying to talk to you." Ben tore his eyes from the patch of ground at which he had been staring.

"I've been trying to tell you," the driver said, "that you are a fool. Fools, though you probably don't know it, are of particular importance in the universe. They test the limits of everything....Whenever the lord has been convinced to widen his mercy or extend his patience it has been at the behest of a fool. You are such a fool...."

"Who are you?" Ben demanded. "I mean, who the hell are you!"

"I'm a *malakh*," the driver said. "You have forgotten your Hebrew, but in English they call it an angel. I'm not using the English meaning, but the Hebrew one."

"Come on, if you're from outer space I can believe it—you don't have to lie to me. I know you're not from here, from … us. Are you someone sent to make contact?"

"Why is it so much more likely that I am from another planet than that I am what I say I am?"

"I don't believe in any of that."

"Irrelevant," the driver said. "What is relevant is my being, and my being here.…"

11. Flagler
from *Country Editor's Boy* by Hal Borland

Hal Borland was ten years old in 1910 when he moved with his family from Nebraska to Brush, Colorado. There, his dad did some occasional newspaper work while staking out a homestead claim on the prairie further south. Borland wrote about his family's homesteading years in the book, High, Wild, and Lonesome. *Later, his father bought and ran the newspaper in Flagler, the town where Borland finished high school. Those were also formative years during which he helped his father print the newspaper, joined his high school football team, and became the projectionist at Flagler's first movie theater. He wrote about all of this, as well as his explorations in and around his hometown, in a book called* Country Editor's Boy.

It didn't take long for Borland to find friends in Flagler who enjoyed the adventures available to them in a small prairie town. With his new pals, he walked up railroad tracks past the big red water tank and into the cottonwood groves, rode his bike out past the grain elevator and the stockyards, past sod houses on the edge of town, past farms and ranches, and out to the swales and hollows looking for frogs and snakes, all the while taking in his surroundings which he later wrote about in wonderful detail. Here, excerpted from Country Editor's Boy, *is his description of spring coming to the high plains around Flagler.*

The winter passed, the snow began to melt, and April came to the High Plains. April, on those plains, can be a season all by itself. Mild air begins to flow up from the south, all the way from the Gulf of Mexico and across the whole of Texas. The melt begins. Spring rains come. Melt and rain combine to create shallow ponds in every upland swale and hollow. You go out and feel that air and see that water and you know it was worth enduring the winter just to emerge into this. Ducks come winging in, ducks that really shouldn't be there at all, so far from real lakes and running water. But there they are, huge rafts of them on those shallow ponds, resting, feeding, quacking loudly for a few days, maybe as long as a week, before they move on north, only to be followed by more mallards, more canvasbacks, more teal. That's the way it used to be, the way it was that spring. And here and there were geese, mostly the big Canadas but occasionally snow geese with their coal-black wing tips. Honking as they came over, with a gabble that made you think of a pack of small, feisty dogs chasing a rabbit out at the edge of town. The geese, too, stayed a few days at the big shallow ponds, then went on. And in those days there were other strangers such as snipe and curlew and upland plover, to make our remote inland pools as exotic as the bayous of Texas. And then our own birds come back, the meadow larks and the doves and the prairie falcons, and the bullbats, the night hawks that yeeped and soared and made roaring dives in the quiet evening sky. The half-dozen robins that nested in the Lavington cottonwoods returned and sang all day long. And our horned larks, most of which had never gone far away, sang again, spiraling like the storied skylarks that sang so beautifully in English poetry. Our larks sang beautifully, too, and in reality, not in poems that used verbs like *wert* and *wingest*. Sand lilies bloomed, little white stars in the tentative new grass. Here and there, in specially favored places, were violets, more yellows than purples. Wild onions shot up, greener than the new grass, green-hungry cows ate them, and for several weeks the milk was so rank of onions you couldn't drink it and even the cream stations in town had an aroma of mild garlic. On the cactus flats, prickly pear and grizzly-bear freshened, their broad pads fattened as they stored moisture for the dry weeks of midsummer, and the first small nubbins of flower buds appeared. Buffalo grass turned the brown winter hills a tawny greenish tan as its first new shoots appeared.

By mid-April it began to feel like spring, to look like spring. You could feel it in the air, feel it underfoot right through the soles of your shoes. You could hear it in people's voices, see it in their eyes.

12. Limon
from *A Place to Call Home* by Lyle Miller

Out on the Eastern Plains, lack of topography and vegetation allows for more sky in one's perspective. Sometimes the sky feels especially close at hand. It is hard to imagine the level of vulnerability one must experience in a high plains tornado. Reading Lyle Miller's description of the tornado that decimated Limon on Wednesday June 6, 1990 may be as close as anyone would want to come to that experience. As he points out in A Place to Call Home, *living through such an experience and rebuilding a life afterwards demands plenty of resilience from long-term residents of prairie communities like Limon. The tornado he describes in the following excerpt injured fourteen people. Miraculously, there were no fatalities.*

"It all began at Jack's Place," according to the Ranchland News. Shortly before 8 p.m., a tornado touched down at the Horner Ranch, six miles southwest of town. The wind was blowing and swirling around the house—and then there was a lull. Jack Horner went outside. He could hear the roar but could see nothing. As he stepped back into the house the violent winds returned and blew a tree past the window. The family ran to the basement to wait out the storm. When it seemed safe, Jack went to check on his parents who lived nearby. His wife, Robyn, called the State Patrol office in Limon and alerted the town to the oncoming storm. Just then another twister headed north appeared. State Patrol dispatcher Pete Holmstedt sounded the emergency siren.

A fierce thunderstorm was pelting the community with hail at such force that it drowned out the siren for many who were only a few blocks away. The police drove up and down the streets sounding their car sirens to warn those in remote regions of town. The people understood there was an emergency. The policy was to sound the warning siren for five minutes and at 8:05 the siren stopped; at 8:06 the tornado hit.

The storm stirred things up in South Limon, especially the feedlots, then crossed the Big Sandy and tumbled a few cars on the railroad tracks. Pieces of sheet metal torn from the nearby grain storage units smashed into the Love Funeral Home at F Avenue and Second Street. The twister then jumped across the street to destroy most of the city hall and the police and fire station. It ripped off the front of the First National Bank on E Avenue, and then unleashed its fury on Limon's commercial district. The storm ravaged the plumbing shop, blew windows out of the video store, and took the marquee from the Lincoln Theatre. It lifted the roof from the *Limon Leader* building across the street and set it back in place after destroying the majority of the showroom and wrecking the production area of the local newspaper office. Main Street and Riverdale's Bar were the next victims. Manager Joe Clements and several patrons hid in the beer cooler while the walls around them crumbled.

The tornado made a right turn at the stoplight, "almost like it was supposed to," remarked county sheriff LeRoy Yowell. Julie Beyeler was closing Limon Super Foods store for the night. She and two clerks sought shelter in the basement when the roof disappeared. Super Foods was damaged so badly it left the community without a grocery store.

Vivian Lowe and guests at the Midwest Country Inn at the corner of D Avenue and Main Street fled to the basement. The damage to the establishment was extensive but the solid building fared better than neighboring structures. Guests at the Lariat Motel further east on Main Street sought shelter in the bathtub in their room and huddled under a mattress taken from the bed.

The tornado then headed northeast towards the vulnerable Vista Village mobile home park. Homes were blown apart, tumbled on their sides, or were thrown against one another. Grace Swanson sought shelter in the bedroom between twin beds. When the trailer stopped moving, she crawled out from under a mattress and stepped across what was actually the ceiling. She looked out the window directly into the window of the adjourning home ... .

The Limon Office of the State Patrol could not be contacted as their radio communications had been severed. Several patrol cars in the garage had been damaged as the roof caved in. Nevertheless, the Limon office at First Street and C Avenue became the local command post for emergency help almost immediately. By 10:30 pm the front office and reception area were crowded with groups such as the El Paso County Sheriff's Office and the Boy Scouts.

Governor Roy Romer flew to Limon by helicopter spending the night and part of the next day with little sleep. He surveyed the damage by air and on the ground. He was able to offer some state disaster aid. Getting Federal aid would be more difficult ... .

Some twisters wander randomly but this one cut swaths entire blocks wide. Sixteen single-family dwellings and thirty-one mobile homes were completely destroyed and major damage was inflicted on twenty-eight homes and three motor homes. Fifty-six businesses were either destroyed or received substantial damage. Buildings on two blocks in the storm path were destroyed or damaged. The tornado was spawned by a Super Cell with a powerful updraft and cloudbank that grew into a towering anvil 70,000 feet high. The National Center for Atmospheric Research called it one of the largest recorded in Colorado up to that time. It was rated at a category F3 to F4. A number of Limon residents walked the streets that night overwhelmed by the damage.

Highway 24
Limon to Colorado Springs

13. Simla
from *Tenderfoot Bride* by Clarice E. Richards

In the late 1890s, Clarice E. Richards met her husband Jarvis while visiting a friend in Nebraska. She was not as widely traveled as Jarvis, who had been a pastor at several congregational churches in Vermont and South Dakota, and had also been the manager of his brother's ranch in the sandhills of Nebraska. Originally from Dayton, Ohio, Clarice was new to ranching life when, as a newlywed bride in 1900, she came to the place that her husband had purchased northwest of Simla, Colorado.

She later put together a collection of tales from her life on that ranch called Tenderfoot Bride. *As historian Maxine Benson writes in the introduction, "the book portrays turn-of-the-century 'cowpunchers' and other diverse characters who would soon disappear forever." In other words, the "frontier" West was changing into a place that was slightly more settled and pastoral. Clarice E. Richards was also in transition. Her story traces "the evolution of a woman," writes Benson, "from a tenderfoot to a died-in-the-wool westerner." In this excerpt, she describes, in great detail, some of the skills required of a cowpuncher at that time.*

After the Government had awarded a contract to furnish "150 horses of a dark bay color for cavalry use" our life became dramatic, with the riders cast in the leading roles.

The stage-setting consisted of a large circular corral, twelve feet high, built of heavy pitch-pine posts and three-inch planks with a massive snubbing post set in the center. Since there was a "standing room only," cracks were at a premium.

The dramatis personae were two tall, slender-waisted cow-punchers who walked with a slightly rolling gait, due to extremely high-heeled boots, much too small for them. In their right hands they carried a coiled rope swinging easily. Their costumes were composed of cloth or corduroy trousers, dark-colored shirts, nondescript vests of some sort, dark blue or red handkerchiefs knotted loosely about their necks, expensively-made boots, the tops of which were covered by the legs of the "pants"; spurs, of course; high-priced Stetson hats, the crown creased to a peak, and frequently encircled by the skin of a rattle-snake, and exceedingly soft gauntlet-gloves. It was my observation that the old-time cow-puncher wore gloves at all times. He did remove them when eating, and, I presume, before going to bed, but they were always in evidence.

The "Star" is a frightened, snorting "broncho," or unbroken horse which for the five or six years of its life had been running loose. Now it was to be "busted." It is cut out from the bunch and run into the corral and the gate securely fastened.

One of the men stands near the post, the other does the roping. Facing the men, the broncho stands still, his head high, his eyes wild and full of fear. An abrupt motion by one of the riders starts him on a frantic run around and around in a circle. A sudden throw of the rope and both front feet are in the loop. Quick as lightning the man settles back on it, both front legs are pulled out from under the horse and he falls on his side; the helper runs to his head, seizes the muzzle and twists it straight up, thrusts one knee against the neck and holds the top of the head to the ground. The roper puts two or three more loops above the front hoofs, passes the rope, now doubled forming a loop, between the legs, to one of the hind feet, then pulls on the end that he has all the time held. This action draws all three feet together. One or two more loops about them, a hitch and the horse is tied so that it is impossible for him to get up. While the broncho lies helpless, the saddle and bridle are put on, a large handkerchief passed under the straps of the bridle over the eyes and made fast. The rope is taken off. Feeling a measure of freedom, he staggers to his feet and stands. The cinches are drawn very tight, the rider mounts, gives a sharp order to "let him go," the man on the ground pulls the handkerchief from the eyes of the horse, and jumps aside.

For a moment the broncho stands dazed, then jumps, throws his head between his front legs almost to the ground, squeals, humps his back and pitches around and around the corral in a vain attempt to rid himself of the fearsome thing on his back. The circular corral, limited in space, gives little opportunity to succeed; the rider has the advantage. The horse stops pitching and runs frantically about the corral, at length tiring himself out. Dripping with sweat, trembling from fear and excitement, he comes to a slow trot. The gate is thrown open. Making a dash for freedom, he plunges through the outside corrals, the horseman or "circler" close beside him, trying to keep between the half-crazed broncho and any object he might run into. The horse bolts out into the open; his is the advantage now, and he makes the rider ride. He bucks this way and that, twisting, turning, jumping and running, the man on his back so racked and shaken it seems incredible that his body can hold together. They tear out over the prairie in a wild race, far off over the hills, out of sight now. After a time they come back on a walk. The broncho has been busted— the act has ended.

Highway 36

Colorado-Kansas Line to Byers/I-70

14. Idalia
from *The Diary of Mattie Spencer* by Sandra Dallas

North of Idalia, just beyond the Arikaree River, are some of the only known sod buildings that remain from Colorado's homesteading era. These sod buildings, originally constructed in 1909 by Walter and Anna Zion, were maintained and eventually plastered over with a mixture of limestone and concrete by their descendants and are currently under the care of the Idalia Vision Historical Foundation. The Zion family initiated their farming operation forty years or so after the earliest wave of homesteaders took out claims here in Yuma County.

In her novel, The Diary of Mattie Spenser, *Sandra Dallas imagines life on an earlier homestead in northeastern Colorado from a woman's point of view. In May of 1865, her character Mattie Spenser travels west from Iowa with Luke, her new husband, to settle a homestead that he has already seeded with wheat. As a newlywed, she experiences all the hazards of the overland journey. Now, as a homesteader and a new mother, she grapples with all the uncertainties of farming as well as the gritty realities of daily life in a sod house where she is often left alone with her newborn. Her diary becomes a way of coping with the challenges of such a life, not the least of which is loneliness. Here is an entry from that fictional diary.*

July 14, 1866.
Prairie Home

I knew there would be little time to attend to my journal. Still, I had not meant to neglect it for so many weeks. There is no leisure for Self these days. When Baby is asleep, Luke is underfoot, and when Luke is busy elsewhere, why then Baby demands attention.

He frets a great deal, due to the heat, I believe. When he finishes nursing, his face must be pulled from my breast, making a great sucking sound, as his little mouth is glued to my skin with his perspiration.

It is so hot in the soddy that I think my milk must sour, but I am loath to go outside with Johnnie for fear of rattlesnakes, more numerous even than last year. Mr. Bondurant brought me a stout buffalo-hair rope to lay on the ground in a circle about the cradle, saying the snakes will not cross it. Perhaps not, but they come close, and I have killed seven this summer. I fancy that by chopping off their heads with a hoe, I even the score a little for Mother Eve!

I suffer much this summer with headaches and lack of sleep, and I think back on my wedding trip to Colorado Territory, with all its dangers, as a carefree time. Last summer, Emmie Lou confessed she was so weary, she could sell her soul to the Devil for a night's sleep. I thought the remark blasphemous, but now that I am awake much of the night with Johnnie, I believe it a passable bargain. If Lucifer would agree to give me a real bath in the bargain, then my soul would indeed be in jeopardy.

Of course, no one suspects my despair, for I endeavor to keep a cheerful countenance around Luke and friends and tell my real thoughts only to my journal. Confiding them renews my strength, even if the listener is only a blank page.

There is much for which I am grateful. With Baby to keep me busy, I am not so lonely for the dear ones in Fort Madison. Like Luke, I enjoy the violent sunsets of an evening, although they do not thrill my soul as they do his. After a year, they still frighten me because they set the sky on fire, and I think they will consume me. Perhaps someday I shall come to love Colorado, but not yet.

Luke works harder than any man I ever saw, and I have no complaints on that score. He is quieter, more critical, since his return. Perhaps the reason is that he is now an old family man with responsibilities for Son, as well as Wife, but sometimes, I think I understand Luke even less today than I did when we were wed. I have learnt little about men in fourteen months of marriage.

Luke is the most indulgent of papas, playing with Baby in the evenings and showing him off to all who visit. Luke is right pleased with his "seed."

He is pleased, as well, with the turkey red seed for hard winter wheat that he brought back from Fort Madison. (Luke would be shocked with this little joke, but I intend to write it to Carrie, who will find it funny. I wonder, do men know we women talk about such things, just as they do?) It not only resists drought but also thrives under the hot winds. Our wheat does better than any in the neighborhood, and I believe my husband will leave his mark as an agrarian.

Mr. Bondurant's pack mule was loaded down with farm necessities when Luke returned from Fort Madison. Still, knowing my sweet tooth, he found room for a little gift of chocolate. I am not so wanton with it as I was last year, using small amounts now, and only on special occasions. Luke brought other favors, including photographs of loved ones. Carrie's precious Wee Willie is every bit as splendid as my own Johnnie, which means he is very handsome indeed. Carrie also sent a purse she embroidered with ferns and heartsease, which is displayed upon the wall, as the neighbors would accuse me of putting on airs were I to carry such a fine item. I shall save it for the day I am in *real* society again.

I have resumed my marital duties. At first, I held off, for *Dr. Chase's Recipes* warns about too quick a resumption of relations. Besides, I do not care to follow Emmie Lou's example and pop out babies as if I were shelling peas in a pod. But as a nursing mother, I believe I am safe from conception, and since Luke was so insistent, I gave in. I am rewarded each time with his kind attention for a day. I think men benefit from the act, and women from their husband's gratitude.

15. Joes
from *East of Denver* by Gregory Hill

Author and musician Gregory Hill grew up in Joes, Colorado, which
is still "his favorite place in the world." His appreciation of small
town life on the eastern plains, and an understanding of the region's
agricultural roots, inform his first novel, East of Denver. *The story he*
tells, as is true with the other two titles in his Stratford County trilogy,
is also offbeat and quirky. When Shakespeare Williams returns to his
family's farm in eastern Colorado to bury his dead cat, he finds out
that a local banker has taken advantage of his widowed and senile
father who is now living in squalor. So Shakespeare hatches a plan,
along with his father and an eccentric gang of former high school
classmates, to rob the bank that has stolen his family's future. In this
excerpt, Hill evokes the pathos of an all too common scene on the east-
ern plains where farmers struggle to hang on and where sometimes
they are unable to do so.

Dad was watching TV. I brought him his shoes. Tennies with Velcro
straps. He used to wear boots.

I shut off the tube. "Father, let's have a look at the estate."

"It's hot out there."

"It's hot in here."

We surveyed the farm on foot. Three hundred acres, half a square
mile. A few acres were set aside for the house (built 1930) shed (built
1976), grain bins (1978, '81, '82), and two buildings from the old days:
the granary (1899) and well house (1912).

We walked out to the runway. The overgrown runway. It had never
been much more than a strip of mowed weeds. Now, you couldn't tell it
from the rest of the prairie. All around was pasture that used to be wheat
fields until the government started paying Dad not to farm. The wheat
fields Dad had farmed for fifty years were full of rabbits, mice, and
badgers all citied among the bunchgrass.

We walked past a stand of juniper trees that we'd watered by hand
once a week until their roots got deep enough to survive on their own. It

took years to teach those trees to live off the land. Most of them were still alive, but they had the twisted, dusty look that things get when they're not where they belong.

Every farm has a row of equipment, lined up and ready to mangle dirt. We inspect our holdings. The John Deere 4020 tractor, with three flat tires. A drill, which is a wheat planter. Dad had apparently failed to clean it out the last time he used it; little wheat plants were growing out of the hoppers. A disc, which is a weed killer, now obsolete in the low-till era. The ancient combine, which harvested wheat, with the windshield busted out. Everything had thistles growing up to the axles.

Farmers like their landscapes well kept. Dad had always made sure that the area around the house was mowed. The ditches and everything, acres of it. Mowing was my job. Hours and hours bouncing on the seat of a riding lawn mower. I hated mowing. It was all sneezing and flies and dust stuck to the sweat on your forehead.

The farm hadn't been mowed for at least two years. The place looked like shit, like one of those abandoned homesteads you see.

We stood in front of the grain bins, the giant, corrugated galvanized tubs that city folks mistake for silos.

Under our feet was a slab of crumbling concrete, the last remnant of the original sod house built by my great-grandparents a hundred and twenty years ago. I used to play inside that house. One day, Dad knocked it over with a bulldozer and shoved it into a hole in the ground. When I cried, he said, "It was ready to fall down. I didn't want it to fall on you. Anyway, it was ugly."

We stood on that foundation, scratched weeds with our heels.

"This is our dominion," I said.

"Hard to believe," said Pa.

"Hard not to."

16. Lindon / Last Chance
"The Last Chance, Colorado Tornados" by William Reid

"Tornado season in Eastern Colorado is generally considered to be mid-May through June," writes climatologist William Reid. "The jet stream is typically too far north of the state during July and August for storms such as these." But any weather-watcher knows that the weather is never entirely predictable. It was on July 21, 1993, that Reid and fellow stormchaser Charles Bustamante were able to film the so-called "Lindon Tornados," which are among the largest tornados ever seen and photographed in Colorado.

Along with some other stormchasers, they had been driving county roads in pursuit of the storm. After witnessing some impressive funnel clouds, they spotted one that ran all the way to the ground in an approaching tornado. Here is an excerpt from William Reid's account of what happened that day. The full story is available on his website, www.stormbruiser.com.

At 6 p.m. the storm was just north of Last Chance, Colorado. It had moved only 30 miles east in three hours! One could have chased this storm on foot, though he would have been a good target for lightning and dusty outflow winds ....

Finally, a good-looking funnel cloud formed a few miles northeast of Last Chance, beneath a rotating updraft. It never appeared to touch the ground, but there were several other small and weak "dust-nados" underneath the grayish/white updraft. We had three storms to watch now—the primary storm, slipping into darkness to the northeast; a nice bell-shaped-based updraft to the northwest, and a developing cell to our southwest.

Charlie and I left the others and headed a few miles north and east, somewhat undecided about where to go, but trying to keep the base of the original storm in sight. The other storm to the northwest was weakening, and the one northeast of us looked less organized. What surprised me at this point was that the low clouds above were streaming to the southwest—towards the newest updraft! We observed that the base of this

storm, perhaps 15 miles away and back near Last Chance, was issuing
some very suspicious shapes.

It was off to the races: south to U.S. 36, west a couple of miles to
Road U (two miles east of Lindon), and south again five more miles.
While we videotaped and zig-zagged ever closer to the storm, the obvious shape of a tornado gradually appeared. Anticipation, anxiety, and
exhilaration reached new heights for Charlie and me—this was our first
real tornado: it wasn't a wimpy landspout or funnel-less dust whirl. For
a few seconds two tornados were observed, side-by-side. We turned west
off of Road U onto Road 7. A few miles, dead ahead, was a huge tornadic
wedge, maybe more than one-half mile wide, churning the farmland. We
could not believe what we were seeing!

Charlie and I were awestruck as we cautiously drove another mile
west. We passed a farmhand who was working with some equipment
by the road. I honked, as it appeared he had no idea of the impending
calamity swirling a few miles away. At Road T a combination of fear
and common sense came over us (this is close enough!), and we stopped
to set up the tripods. It was 8:00 p.m.—still about 15 minutes before
sunset. We both felt that we would not be able to linger long at this site.
Though the tornado was not moving forward very quickly, we thought
that we were in its path. We were contemplating escape routes: Road T,
unfortunately, only went north—into an increasingly black and noisy
thunderstorm, surely filled with hail. The car was left running and
pointed east down Road 7.

Charlie's camera clicked away and I monitored the camcorder as the
tornado slowly approached. We had an excellent view: there was nothing
to obscure this grand vision. Sunlit skies framed the black and ominous
wedge as it decreased a little in size and moved slowly to the left from
our perspective. After about six minutes the tornado was twice as close
as when we had stopped, but we felt much less threatened, as it was now
southwest of us and moving east-southeast. (We became more concerned
with the hollow-sounding crashes of thunder just to our north.)

An amazing sequence of events was about to transpire. The wide
condensation funnel began to dissipate near the surface, so that the
entire rotation (front and back) could be seen. Just when I thought that

the tornado was going to end, a very thin condensation "needle" formed inside of the larger circulation. The needle rapidly expanded—and our large, black wedge had become a rather narrow, gray column. Less than a minute later the column's bottom portion began to disappear, but another narrow tube quickly reformed. The tornado now had a more classic, slender-looking funnel shape. During the next couple of minutes the gray tornado again assumed a more-columnar shape; to our south-southwest it stood nearly stationary in "Tower-of-Pisa"-like formation.

About ten minutes after we had stopped to set up, the tornado rapidly roped-out for good, leaving behind a cloud of dust and two happy people. How fortunate could two storm-chasers be? We were provided with a large, slow-moving tornado from a relatively tranquil, obstruction-free viewing site with great backlighting. All cameras worked, the car continued to run, and lightning lurked but did not strike us.

A farmer, Philip Scott, and his wife, Lois, drove up to us only a minute or so after the tornado vanished. Their home was the farmhouse one-quarter mile west. Mrs. Scott said that she had seen us along the road from the house and wondered if we were stuck or something. Then she looked west and fled for the basement. Her husband had watched the storm from another part of his farm. The Scott's home was spared because of the "right-moving" tendency of tornadic storms. We learned later that the tornado had injured some animals and damaged some farm equipment on its six-mile trek.

The supercell spawned another tornado around 8:30 p.m., which wrecked a farmstead. Charlie and I were content to watch the storm from the Scott's place, and we did not see that tornado. I was concerned for our safety and the body of the car, as lightning increased and golf-ball-sized hail sprinkled our vicinity. The farmland beneath the rotating supercell's incredibly low base, only a couple of miles to the southeast, was awash in a murky-white haze. Who knew how large the hail was underneath that behemoth? What senseless soul would dare test the fury of this airborne maelstrom? Well, we could see who—a Denver TV-NEWS crew!

I called Channel 4 in Denver, and we met their news van at Byers at 10 p.m. Our tornado video was seen on the Denver news that night.

Charlie and I began the drive home. It was not until we reached Los
Angeles the next evening, exhausted but still exhilarated, that we learned
that our last chance chase—our Last Chance tornado—had been shown
over and over again on The Weather Channel.

Highway 34
Colorado-Kansas line to US 76 in Brush

17. Wray
from "Colorado Romance" by Sureva Towler

Sureva Towler has written plenty of copy about her home in Steamboat Springs, both in book form and as a columnist for newspapers, including The Denver Post. But she also likes to get out on the road. "Windshield time is good for the soul," she writes. In an essay called "Colorado Roadtrips," which appears in a book called, The Boys at the Bar: Antics of a Vanishing Breed of Cowboys and Hellions, *she offers other road-trippers the following advice: "Travel slowly. Explore country where a community is judged by the size of its grain elevator, and guys not only know what sorghum is, they keep close tabs on its market price. Search for a place ... where everyone can recite the 4-H pledge. Read every historic marker, eat at the greasy spoon and visit with someone driving a tractor." In other words, keep an eye out for places like Wray, Colorado. You never know what you may find there.*

Nobody says "I love you" more convincingly than a prairie chicken. Mockingbirds sing, peacocks strut, bowerbirds build elaborate nests, egrets grow feathers, but prairie chickens do it best. They dance and croon at dawn and dusk. They lean forward, puff up their throat and ear feathers, drop their wings, and fan their tails. The sound of air rushing from their inflated, bright-orange neck sacs makes a booming sound as they stomp their feet and strut around in circles, not unlike a Bronco quarterback after a touchdown.

The best place to watch the mating dance of greater prairie chickens is in the grassy sandhills, north of Wray, where eighty percent of Colorado's ten thousand chickens hang out, near the Kansas and Nebraska state lines. The numbers come close to matching the people population in Yuma County, which issued only seventy-three marriage licenses last year, suggesting that prairie chickens may have far more fun courting in the cornfields than do the locals.

Their eerie sounds and aerial leaps are generating economic development for the Wray Chamber of Commerce and East Yuma County Historical Society that, from mid-March until mid-May, haul voyeurs to the booming grounds. There, squinting into the cold and dark, bird watchers and snoops can spy on rooster and hens cavorting on the lek under the educated eyes of Division of Wildlife yentas. The ruckus attracts females from five miles away and tourists from around the globe.

Like good men, prairie chickens are hard to find. They hide in the brush, claim a territory, and protect it from other males. They fight frequently but most face-offs are bluffs. The most dominant bird claims the center of the booming grounds, a hilltop meadow with a good view of any approaching predators. When a hen enters the lek, the males run toward her and, ignoring territorial boundaries, position themselves to stomp, boom, cackle, jump, and bow. It looks a lot like the Corral Club at closing time.

Mating is chauvinistic and promiscuous. After booming, the Casanovas return to the lek and continue to display. In winter they flock up because there's safety in numbers, but while females migrate long distances, males remain near the booming grounds, not unlike the Boys at the Bar who, unless some hen pries them off, can perch on the same bar stool for twenty years.

Scholars have always been interested in how men troll for women. They devoted a decade to discovering that giardia have a sex life, but only recently did a pair of anthropologists move their research on the mating behavior of apes into bars, not a quantum leap. In a recent article in a learned journal on evolution and behavior, these researchers concluded that guys attract gals with macho male body language, by stroking their beards, punching their male friends, or sprawling across furniture with legs akimbo. The key to scoring, they explained, lies in males shooting repeated glances at females, and average of thirteen times in a half hour for those who landed dates. Because the study was not federally funded, it failed to examine the impact of jewelry, furs, yachts, and cars on courting.

The best place to witness human mating rituals is when the last call sounds down at the local watering hole. That's when the Boys at the Bar begin to preen, strut, and squawk. They convince themselves that, with just one more round, they can slay dragons, swim moats, and survive duels. They attempt to persuade any damsel within earshot that only she can feel the pea under the mattress, spin flax into gold, and remain beautiful forever.

After enough brewskis they are ready to round up twelve goats, the tail of a white sheep, or some dried dove's tongues. Truth be told, Harry is worn out from running around the countryside looking for a lost slipper, and Agnes is tired of kissing frogs, so they agree to exchange e-mails.

Nowadays, love is found in cyberspace, defined in a pre-nuptial agreement, and consummated with a glacier-sized rock. The rules of catch-and-release have changed. The search for keepers now takes place in gourmet groceries and continuing ed classes, at museums and libraries, on trips up ski lifts and the Himalayas. Hanging out at the hardware stores and airport baggage claim roundabouts are proving some of the best modern booming grounds.

Today, the fanciest courting may occur not in Colorado's fifteen thousand bars, but on the state's seven hundred leks, where prairie chickens, once endangered, are demonstrating how to perpetuate the species without benefit of cards and candy.

18. Yuma
from *Plainsong* by Kent Haruf

Holt, Colorado, thanks to Kent Haruf, author of many best-selling novels including Plainsong, Eventide, Benediction, *and* Our Souls at Night, *may be one of the most widely recognized small towns in the northeastern part of the state. But you won't find it on the map, because Holt is a fictional composite of towns like Holyoke, Wray, and Yuma where Haruf went to elementary school and where his father was a Methodist minister.*

Though it is a fictional place, Haruf's descriptions of Holt may remind readers of other prairie towns "where the houses were painted blue or yellow or pale green and might have chickens in the back lots

in wire pens and here and there dogs on chains and also car bodies
rusting among the cheetweed and redroot under the low-hanging
mulberry trees." And the country outside of Holt—"all flat and sandy
again, the stunted stands of trees at the isolated farmhouses, the grav-
el section roads running exactly north and south like lines drawn in
a child's picture book and the four-strand fences rimming the barrow
ditches," may sound familiar to those who live in or have traveled
through this part of Colorado. Further down the road, there may be
"cows with fresh calves in the pastures behind the barbed-wire fences
and here and there a red mare with a new-foaled colt, and far away
on the horizon to the south the low sandhills ... as blue as plums," and
those who know Haruf's books may see an isolated farmhouse nearby
and imagine it as the residence of Harold and Raymond McPheron—
brothers, bachelor farmers, and two of Haruf's most beloved charac-
ters—whose lives are forever changed when they decide to help out a
young woman in need of shelter. Here, in an excerpt from Plainsong, *is*
the conversation that led to that momentous decision.

Later, when the sun had gone down in the late afternoon, after the sky
had turned faint and wispy and the thin blue shadows had reached across
the snow, the brothers did talk. They were out in the horse lot, working at
the stock tank.

The tank had frozen over with ice. The shaggy saddle horses, already
winter-coated, stood with their back to the wind, watching the two men
in the corral, the horses' tails blowing out, their breath snorted out in
white plumes and carried away in tatters by the wind.

Harold chopped at the ice on the stock tank with a wood axe. He
flailed at it and finally broke through into the water below, the head of the
axe sunken helve-deep out of sight and suddenly heavy, and he pulled it
out and chopped again. Then Raymond scooped out the ice chunks with
his cob fork and flung the ice away from the tank onto the hard ground
behind him where it landed among other frozen blocks and pieces. When
the tank was clear they lifted the lid from the galvanized watertight box
that floated in the water. Inside the box was the tank heater. When they
looked inside they could see that the pilot light had blown out. Harold

took off his gloves and withdrew a long firebox match from his inside
pocket, popped it on his thumbnail and cupped the little flame and held
it down into the box. When the pilot light took he adjusted the flame
and drew his arm out, and Raymond wired the lid tight again. Then they
checked on the propane bottle that was standing out of the way. It looked
all right.

So for a while they stood below the windmill in the failing light. The
thirsty horses approached and peered at them and sniffed at the water
and began to drink, sucking up long draughts of it. Afterward they stood
back watching the two brothers, their eyes as large and luminous as
perfect round knobs of mahogany glass.

It was almost dark now. Only a thin violet band of light showed in the
west on the low horizon.

All right, Harold said. I know what I think. What do you think we do
with her?

We take her in, Raymond said. He spoke without hesitation as though
he'd only been waiting for his brother to start so they could have this out
and settle it. Maybe she wouldn't be as much trouble, he said.

I'm not talking about that yet, Harold said. He looked out into the
gathering darkness. I'm talking about – why hell, look at us. Old men
alone. Decrepit old bachelors out here in the country seventeen miles
from the closest town which don't amount to much of a good goddamn
even when you get there. Think of us. Crotchety and ignorant. Lonesome.
Independent. Set in all our ways. How you going to change now at this
age of life?

I can't say, Raymond said. But I'm going to. That's what I know.

And what do you mean? How come she wouldn't be no trouble?

I never said she wouldn't be no trouble. I said maybe she wouldn't be
as much trouble.

Why wouldn't she be as much trouble? As much trouble at what? You
ever had a girl living with you before?

You know I ain't, Raymond said.

Well, I ain't either. But let me tell you. A girl is different. They want
things. They need things on a regular schedule. Why a girl's got purposes you and me can't even imagine. They got ideas in their heads you and

me can't even suppose. And god-damn it, there's the baby too. What do you know about babies?

Nothing. I don't even know the first thing about em, Raymond said.

Well then?

But I don't have to know about any babies yet. Maybe I'll have time to learn. Now, are you going to go in on this thing with me or not? Cause I'm going to do it anyhow, whatever.

Harold turned toward him. The light was gone in the sky and he couldn't make out the features on his brother's face. There was only this dark familiar figure against the failed horizon.

All right, he said. I will. I'll agree. I shouldn't, but I will. I'll make up my mind to it. But I'm going to tell you one thing first.

What is it?

You're getting goddamn stubborn and hard to live with. That's all I'll say. Raymond, you're my brother. But you're getting flat unruly and difficult to abide. And I'll say one thing more.

What?

This ain't going to be no goddamn Sunday school picnic.

No, it ain't, Raymond said. But I don't recall you ever attending Sunday school either.

Highway 76
West from Julesburg to Denver

19. Julesburg
from *Roughing It* by Mark Twain

From its earliest days as a trading post in the 1850s, Julesburg has always been a waystation of one kind or another: for trappers and pioneers on the Overland Route, for Pony Express riders, for passengers on the Union Pacific Railroad, and for motorists on the Lincoln Highway and eventually the interstate. As such, it has seen its share of noteworthy characters, two of whom almost immediately had it out for one another.

In 1858, a French-Canadian trapper named Jules Beni set up a small trading post on the South Platte River, which became a rendezvous point for trappers, traders, adventurers, and desperados. In the summer of 1859, the Jones and Russell Stagecoach Line hired Beni to manage a station there. After that company failed and was reorganized as the Central Overland, California and Pikes Peak Express Company, Joseph "Jack" Slade was hired as the superintendent of the Sweetwater section of the line, which included Beni's station. Notorious for laying down the law (his law) with ne'er-do-wells and anyone else who got in his way, Slade saw Beni as an incompetent and corrupt station manager, and so he fired him. Right away there was bad blood between the two men. After Slade confiscated some horses, which he claimed Beni had taken from the Overland Stage, Beni swore vengeance, which he later got, leaving Slade riddled with the contents of both a revolver and a shotgun. Somehow Slade survived, and later he would be the one to walk away from the showdown.

Even before July 30, 1861, when Mark Twain arrived in Julesburg, he had heard tales about Slade. In Roughing It, *the book he later wrote about his travels out west to Nevada and California, Twain offered this assessment of Slade's reputation: "A high and efficient servant of the Overland, an outlaw among outlaws and yet their relentless scourge,*

Slade was at once the most bloody, the most dangerous and the most
valuable citizen that inhabited the savage fastnesses of the mountains."
Who knows whether or not the final showdown between Slade and Beni
came down as laid out in the following description? Mark Twain was
known to include a few embellishments for the sake of a good story.

In the fulness of time Slade's myrmidons captured his ancient enemy
Jules, whom they found in a well-chosen hiding-place in the remote
fastnesses of the mountains, gaining a precarious livelihood with his
rifle. They brought him to Rocky Ridge, bound hand and foot, and deposited him in the middle of the cattle-yard with his back against a post.
It is said that the pleasure that lit Slade's face when he heard of it was
something fearful to contemplate. He examined his enemy to see that
he was securely tied, and then went to bed, content to wait till morning
before enjoying the luxury of killing him. Jules spent the night in the
cattle-yard, and it is a region where warm nights are never known. In the
morning Slade practiced on him with his revolver, nipping the flesh here
and there, and occasionally clipping off a finger, while Jules begged him
to kill him outright and put him out of his misery. Finally Slade reloaded,
and walking up close to his victim, made some characteristic remarks and
then dispatched him. The body lay there half a day, nobody venturing to
touch it without orders, and then Slade detailed a party and assisted at the
burial himself. But he first cut off the dead man's ears and put them in his
vest pocket, where he carried them for some time with great satisfaction.
That is the story as I have frequently heard it told and seen it in print in
California newspapers. It is doubtless correct in all essential particulars.

But even before the execution of Jules Beni as Twain heard it told,
Slade's reputation was well established on the stage line circuit.

... from the hour we had left Overland City, also known as Julesburg, we
had heard drivers and conductors talk about only three things—"Cali-
forny," the Nevada silver mines, and this desperado Slade. And ... most
of the talk was about Slade. We had gradually come to have a realizing
sense of the fact that Slade was a man whose heart and hands and soul

were steeped in the blood of offenders against his dignity; a man who awfully avenged all injuries, affront, insults or slights, of whatever kind—on the spot if he could, years afterward if lack of earlier opportunity compelled it; a man whose hate tortured him day and night till vengeance appeased it—and not an ordinary vengeance either, but his enemy's absolute death—nothing less.

Given everything he had heard about the man, it comes as no surprise that Mark Twain was wary of doing anything that might offend Mr. Slade, who he happened to meet during a stage stop breakfast. It is unlikely that Slade had killed as many men as some stories suggest, including the following; but from Twain's uneasy perspective sitting next to him that day, he might as well have. Here is that story as only Mark Twain could tell it:

In due time we rattled up to a stage-station, and sat down to breakfast with a half-savage, half-civilized company of armed and bearded mountaineers, ranchmen and station employees. The most gentlemanly-appearing, quiet and affable officer we had yet found along the road in the Overland Company's service was the person who sat at the head of the table, at my elbow. Never had a youth stared and shivered as I did when I heard them call him SLADE!

Here was romance, and I sitting face to face with it!—looking upon it—touching it—hobnobbing with it, as it were! Here, right by my side, was the actual ogre who, in fights and brawls and various ways, had taken the lives of twenty-six human beings, or all men lied about him! I suppose I was the proudest stripling that ever traveled to see strange lands and wonderful people.

He was so friendly and so gentle-spoken that I warmed to him in spite of his awful history. It was hardly possible to realize that this pleasant person was the pitiless scourge of the outlaws, the raw-head-and-bloody-bones the nursing mothers of the mountains terrified their children with. And to this day I can remember nothing remarkable about Slade except that his face was rather broad across the cheek bones, and that the cheek bones were low and the lips peculiarly thin and straight.

But that was enough to leave something of an effect upon me, for since
then I seldom see a face possessing those characteristics without fancy-
ing that the owner of it is a dangerous man.

The coffee ran out. At least it was reduced to one tin-cupful, and
Slade was about to take it when he saw that my cup was empty.

He politely offered to fill it, but although I wanted it, I politely de-
clined. I was afraid he had not killed anybody that morning, and might be
needing diversion. But still with firm politeness he insisted on filling my
cup, and said I had traveled all night and better deserved it than he—and
while he talked he placidly poured the fluid, to the last drop. I thanked him
and drank it, but it gave me no comfort, for I could not feel sure that he
would not be sorry, presently, that he had given it away, and proceed to kill
me to distract his thoughts from the loss. But nothing of the kind occurred.
We left him with only twenty-six dead people to account for, and I felt a
tranquil satisfaction in the thought that in so judiciously taking care of No.
1 at that breakfast-table I had pleasantly escaped being No. 27. Slade came
out to the coach and saw us off, first ordering certain rearrangements of
the mail-bags for our comfort, and then we took leave of him, satisfied that
we should hear of him again, some day, and wondering in what connection.

20. Proctor
from *Roughing It* by Mark Twain and
Colorado Without Mountains:
A High Plains Memoir by Harold Hamil

In July of 1861, when Mark Twain crossed the South Platte in a
"mud-wagon," he was less than impressed with the river:

We came to the shallow, yellow, muddy South Platte, with its low banks
and its scattering flat sand-bars and pigmy islands—a melancholy stream
straggling through the centre of the enormous flat plain, and only saved
from being impossible to find with the naked eye by its sentinel rank
of scattering trees standing on either bank. The Platte was "up," they
said—which made me wish I could see it when it was down, if it could

look any sicker and sorrier. They said it was a dangerous stream to cross, now, because its quicksands were liable to swallow up horses, coach and passengers if an attempt was made to ford it. But the mails had to go, and we made the attempt. Once or twice in midstream the wheels sunk into the yielding sands so threateningly that we half believed we had dreaded and avoided the sea all our lives to be shipwrecked in a "mud-wagon" in the middle of a desert at last.

For Mark Twain who had spent much of his life around the Mississippi, the South Platte wasn't much of a river. Over the years, others have dismissed it as "a mile wide and an inch deep" or "too thick to drink and too thin to plow." Still, for residents of the arid eastern plains, like Harold Hamil, who grew up in the tiny town of Proctor, this humble river was still a major presence. Hamil writes about the South Platte in Colorado Without Mountains: A High Plains Memoir.

The overgrown river area was like a strip of African jungle to plains-bred youngsters exploring it on summer days. The trees and bushes shut off the incessant winds at ground level, making it easier to hear the whispering of the cottonwood leaves 20 or 30 feet above. The insect life and, to some extent, the bird life were different from what one saw and heard in the neighboring hay meadows, alkali flats and sandhills. The rasping soliloquy of the cicada came from countless tree trunks. Magpies swept low over open spaces, killdeers strutted on the wet sand. And here and there a red-winged or yellow-headed blackbird sang from a perch in the undergrowth. The moist air was heavy with the smell of cottonwood sap and wild rose.

Now and then a carp could be spooked from a hole along a bank and sent squirming into shallow water for easy catching. Ducks and geese landed in the river in the fall, and in those few years when the dryland corn made a decent crop the ducks stayed in the neighborhood for weeks, shuttling between the river and these new-found feeding grounds. There were prairie chickens in the hay meadows adjacent to the river in the days of my earliest recollections, but they had disappeared by 1920....

There were places along the edge of the valley from which one could trace the line of trees from horizon to horizon, a distance of a dozen

miles or more. This was especially true in the spring when the green
willows and cottonwoods stood against the dull grays and browns of
bared fields and pastures. Because vistas were long and unobstructed
from most any point in the valley or along its edges, the South Platte was
an overwhelming presence....

It is the central explanation of an excavation in the plains which in
some places is more than 20 miles from rim to rim. Not the least of the
distinctions of this strip of terrain are the sandhills that rise in folds form
the valley floor to the level of the divide on the south and east for all of the
river's course through the county. The river gets credit for having washed
in the sand which the winds of countless centuries blew into dunes and the
patience of other natural forces finally cloaked with grass ... .

This river ... dictated the course of the Union Pacific tracks from
Julesburg to Denver ... . Seven settlements grew up along the reach of
the railroad through the county. The first to attain any size became the
county seat, Sterling. Others were Merino, Atwood, Iliff, Crook, Red
Lion, and Proctor, which was our town...destined never to count as many
as hundred persons in its population. But it was at this pinpoint on the
map that I began to sense man's historic relationship with rivers, even
the small unspectacular ones, the ones which sometime run dry in the
summer, as did the South Platte.

21. Brush / Fort Morgan
from *Stygo* by Laura Hendrie

*For some young people who have grown up in small towns, especially a
small town where they have been unable for whatever reason to fit in or
find their passion, dreams of being elsewhere can be seductive—even
more so with a busy highway nearby. Colorado author Laura Hendrie
set her novel,* Stygo, *in an agricultural, sugar beet town, where most of
the jobs were either in the field or at the local sugar plant. At one time,
sugar beets were a dominant force in the local economy here in Morgan
County. There is still a sugar refining factory in Fort Morgan. And the
South Platte, though it may not look at times like it has the water to do*

so, still irrigates hundreds of farms in this area (though now they are more likely to grow wheat, hay, melons, or vegetables). Hendrie said that the fictional town in her book was a composite of towns like Brush and Fort Morgan as well as other farming communities in eastern Colorado. In her town, Tom Go is young and restless, working a dead-end job at the Sugar Beet Café. For that reason, dreams of faraway places, one in particular, helps him get through the day.

When Tom Go set out to become a man, he carried a Rand-McNally map everywhere he went. He was a thin, embattled-looking boy with white skin and fire-red hair who ran the Sugar Beet Café during the day and played pinball at the Rockeroy Bar at night. Because he was shy around girls his own age, he had not yet found one to love. He believed, from the look in the eyes of the men who waited at the bar at night for Willa Moon, that he would put women altogether out of his life.

"They just hold you down," he liked to tell the group who gathered on the porch of the Sugar Beet in the afternoons to watch the cars pass. "When I leave here, I'll leave no regrets." Whether or not his listeners asked for it, Tom Go would then stand up to tick off the reasons on his fingers, one by one, talking as much to himself as to anyone else.

"I'm no good at the restaurant business, I don't like farming, I can't stand heat, I'm allergic to dust and the only other choice I've got is to just sit here and take it. That or play pinball the rest of my life. Plus, I hate it to death that nobody around here seems to remember what happens from one year to the next anymore. Which in my book," he'd say, stabbing himself hard in the chest, "adds up to getting out."

Whenever Tom Go got on the subject of travel, something lit up his heart and it was hard for him to stand still. Forgetting his shyness, he would leave the café and wander up and down the street, scowling at women and pouncing on any man who looked as if he had the time to listen. Frank Stiles, who had more or less looked after Tom Go since the death of his parents, said it was nothing to worry about. Walking the dog, he called it, pulling the bill of his cap down and tilting his chair back on two legs. "Just like his pap and his grandpap before him. He'll outgrow it ... ."

Some white-hot-afternoons when the dust had settled and the street
was quiet and the only customers in the Sugar Beet were flies, Tom could
feel the need to leave spreading through him as surely as if he were
coming down with a fever.

His friends tried to help. Oren Whatly said San Diego was Tom's
best bet, Jake Loper said he had heard Florida was nice, and Harley
Barrows suggested he and Tom go on a spree through Mexico. Frank
Stiles held out for Rock Island and even offered Tom his station wagon.
But Tom felt his whole life before him and if he was ever to feel the
wonder of it, there was only one solution. He had discovered it while at
the arcade one Saturday in Mason City, an Arctic parka hanging in the
window of the Army Navy store across the street. One sleeve was torn
and the other smelled of grease, but the thing fit him like a fat glove,
with wide pockets for supplies and a dog-ruff hood that closed around
his face like a periscope. Looking at himself in the mirror, Tom Go felt
his future before him coiled and aimed like a harpoon. "Alaska," he
whispered. He bought the coat on credit, and from then on, whenever
he had to drive to Mason City for supplies, as convinced of his luck as
any sourdough bound for the Klondike, he stopped at the Army Navy to
search the winter camping aisles.

He also always bought two dollars' worth of lottery tickets at the
Discount Center. For reasons of his own, he usually kept these in his
wallet until he was back home and seated again at the café. "I guess I'm
different from most people around here," he'd say, pouncing on Sam
Waters and his wife Edie when they came in for lunch after seeing Edie's
doctor. "That's why I can't stay here much longer. I gotta go someplace
wild where nothing's settled yet and nothing's easy. I'll just never belong
here, I guess." Sam Waters would wave the boy off, but it never stopped
Tom. Astride an idea with luck in his pocket, Tom Go was invincible. "I
know what you're thinking. I don't know what Alaska's like, right? I
don't even know what I've got to face. But that's the point. I don't know
anything except that I got to try myself. It's what I'm good for." And later
when he was working at the bar, he'd mutter, "Look at them," jamming
another dime into the pinball machine. "Talk, talk, talk. Nobody believes
anything anymore. Nobody cares."

Tom Go traced the Alkan Highway on his Rand-McNally until holes appeared in Canada. He read books about the beauty of the wilderness and what happened when a man went into it. Hypothermia, the importance of matches, the danger of sleep. "Alaska," he whispered, turning his back on his customer to scratch the silver off his lottery tickets.

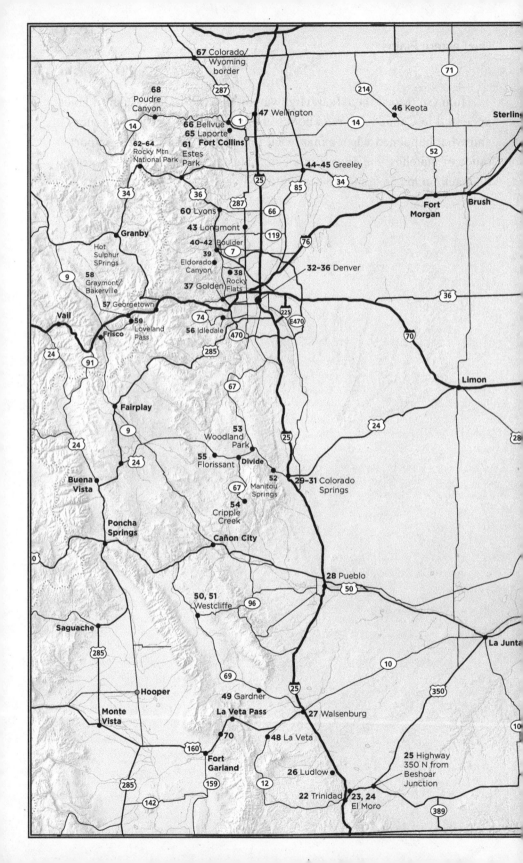

THE CORRIDOR

The horizontal and vertical worlds of Colorado meet in a geographical corridor along the eastern edge of the mountains and the western edge of the prairie. This north-south corridor offers shelter from more extreme weather to the west and the wide-open aridity of the high plains to the east. Interstate 25 parallels this ecological edge, or ecotone, where the flora and fauna of both regions overlap. Indigenous hunters were here as early as 12,000 years ago, as were the Utes who settled in around 1500—wintering at the base of the mountains and hunting in the higher elevations during the summer months. Plains Indians, like the Arapahoe, arrived in these edge lands later on, as westering waves of settlement encroached on their favored hunting grounds.

In the 1860s, when Charles Goodnight and Oliver Loving formed a partnership to deliver Texas Longhorns to western markets via railheads in Denver and Cheyenne, they trailed their herds along this edge where water sources were more reliable and the weather less severe. From the hustle and bustle of Denver and other urban areas that sprang up along the edge later on, entrepreneurs went west into the mountains and launched their gold and silver dreams, as did the railroad builders who followed them. In the late nineteenth century, waves of newcomers came for the sunshine and fresh air that promised a cure for various respiratory ailments. As a long history of urban growth along the corridor suggests, this part of Colorado has continued to attract successive waves of newcomers, all of whom arrive with their own desires and expectations.

Interstate 25

from New Mexico to Denver

22. Trinidad
from The Autobiography of Mother Jones
by Mary G. Harris "Mother" Jones

Incorporated in 1876, Trinidad became the supply and transportation hub for the coal mining industry in this part of Colorado. Colorado Fuel and Iron Company (CFI), one of the largest coal operators and most powerful corporations in the West during the early twentieth century, employed as many 7000 miners. At first, CFI management was successful in preventing miners from forming unions. One of their tactics was to hire immigrants, many of them from southern Europe, who were unable to communicate with one another and organize because of language barriers. Later, after the unions had been established, CFI's management, now in the hands of the powerful Rockefeller family, hired strike breakers from Mexico to disrupt labor protests.

In September of 1913, miners in the area called for an expanded strike. Seventy-five-year-old Mary G. Harris Jones, a former schoolteacher and dressmaker and an itinerant labor activist known to miners and other workers all over the country as Mother Jones, arrived in Trinidad to support their cause. Getting there had not been easy. Elias Ammons, the governor of Colorado and an ally of the Rockefellers, was determined to keep her out of Colorado coal country where she had been known to galvanize laborers in the past. As she wrote in her autobiography, The Autobiography of Mother Jones *(eventually published in 1925), she wasn't one to shy away from such a challenge: "I was in Washington, DC at the time of the great coal strike against the Rockefeller holdings in southern Colorado ... . One day I read in the newspaper that Governor Ammons of Colorado said that Mother Jones was not to be allowed to go into the southern field where the strike was raging. That night I took a train and went directly to Denver."*

Getting from Denver to Trinidad, however, would require some extra cunning and stealth on her part. Knowing that the authorities were on the lookout for her, she snuck out onto the tracks behind the depot in Denver before daybreak and found a friendly railroader who escorted her to the southbound train before anyone else had boarded. Another railroading ally made sure that she got off at the Santa Fe Crossing, several miles to the north of the Trinidad Station, so that she was able to sneak into town for a meeting with some of the striking miners before the authorities knew she was there. She tells the rest of the story in the following excerpt from her autobiography.

It was very early and I walked into the little town of Trinidad and got breakfast. Down at the station a company of military were watching to see if I came into town. But no Mother Jones got off at the depot, and the company marched back to headquarters, which was just across the street from the hotel where I was staying.

I was in Trinidad three hours before they knew I was there. They telephoned the governor. They telephoned General Chase in charge of the militia. "Mother Jones is in Trinidad!" they said.

"Impossible!" said the governor.

"Impossible!" said the general.

"Nevertheless, she is here!"

"We have had her well watched at the hotels and the depots," they said.

"Nevertheless, she is here!"

My arrest was ordered.

A delegation of miners came to me. "Boys," I said, "they are going to arrest me but don't make any trouble. Just let them do it."

"Mother," said they, "we aren't going to let them arrest you!"

"Yes, you will. Let them carry on their game."

While we were sitting there talking, I heard footsteps tramping up the stairs.

"Here they come," said I and we sat quietly waiting.

The door opened. It was a company of militia.

"Did you come after me, boys?" said I. They looked embarrassed.

"Pack your valise and come," said the captain.

They marched me down stairs and put me in an automobile that was waiting at the door.

The miners had followed. One of them had tears rolling down his cheeks. "Mother," he cried, "I wish I could go for you!"

We drove to the prison first, passing cavalry and infantry and gunmen, sent by the state to subdue the miners. Orders were given to drive me to the Sisters' Hospital, a portion of which had been turned into a military prison. They put me in a small room with white plastered walls, with a cot, a chair and a table, and for nine weeks I stayed in that one room, seeing no human beings but the silent military. One stood on either side of the cell door, two stood across the hall, one at the entrance to the hall, two at the elevator entrance on my floor, two on the ground floor elevator entrance.

Outside my window a guard walked up and down, up and down, day and night, day and night, his bayonet flashing in the sun. "Lads," said I to the two silent chaps at the door, "the great Standard Oil is certainly afraid of an old woman!" They grinned.

My meals were sent to me by the sisters. They were not, of course, luxurious. In all those nine weeks I saw no one, received not a letter, a paper, a postal card. I saw only landscape and the bayonet flashing in the sun. Finally, Mr. Hawkins, the attorney for the miners, was allowed to visit me. Then on Sunday, Colonel Davis came to me and said the governor wanted to see me in Denver.

The colonel and a subordinate came for me that night at nine o'clock. As we went down the hall, I noticed there was not a soldier in sight. There was none in the elevator. There was none in the entrance way. Everything was strangely silent. No one was about. A closed automobile waited us. We three got in.

"Drive the back way!" said the colonel to the chauffeur.

We drove through dark, lonely streets. The curtains of the machine were down. It was black outside and inside. It was the one time in my life that I thought my end had come; that I was to say farewell to the earth, but I made up my mind that I would put up a good fight before passing out of life!

When we reached the Santa Fe crossing I was put aboard the train. I felt great relief, for the strike had only begun and I had much to do.

Mother Jones was escorted to the governor's office in Denver, where he told her, in no uncertain terms, that she would not be returning to the coalfields. She thought otherwise.

"Governor," said I, "if Washington took instructions from such as you, we would be under King George's descendants yet! If Lincoln took instructions from you, Grant would never have gone to Gettysburg. I think I had better not take your orders."

I stayed on a week in Denver. Then I got a ticket and sleeper for Trinidad.

As it turned out, Mother Jones only got as far as Walsenburg where she was once again taken into custody, but not before sharing a few inspiring words with the coal miners and others who came out to meet her train there.

23. El Moro
just north of Trinidad
from *Essays of an American Peasant* by Tomas Mariano

Not all the immigrant families who settled in this region remained dependent on the coal mining industry for their livelihood. Some families sought out agricultural opportunities. Tomas Mariano's family raised alfalfa and whatever else they needed to get by on their land near El Moro. Mariano, who was born in 1914, recorded some of his early experiences on that farm in a number of books, one of which is called Essays of an American Peasant.

In my early life on the farm, the Sabbath meant nothing, and work came before the commandments of the Lord; Sunday was just another day, the same as any other day of the week.

Father was on the board of directors on the irrigation ditch company from which we received our irrigation water, and if anything was wrong, but could be put off until later, the directors met on Sunday morning at some designated persons' diversion box. There the problems would be

discussed and many times resolved and corrected, but at such meetings
the secretary never took minutes, nothing was recorded, and the decisions of the day were left to the good faith, credibility and honor of the
participants.

Father left shortly after breakfast on one particular Sunday morning
in mid-summer for such a meeting. The sun was shining bright, with
every indication of a clear hot day to come.

Father took off across the fields on horseback, and I asked, "Why not
the car?" He explained to me that he would rather have the horse so he
could ride to different places they would be inspecting along the ditch
bank. He also told me he would be back early, not later than noon. He
trotted his horse away with his stub cigar in his mouth, and his feet in his
irrigation boots.

My duty for the forenoon was to gather the remains of an alfalfa
harvest of some 250 bales of hay from one particular field. True to form,
it turned out to be a hot summer day with the sun beating down on me
as I bucked bales onto the truck, and unloaded them into the barn. I was
almost finished unloading my last load before noon, when I spotted the
horse my father rode off on, and father following close behind. They
were at the far end of the farm, more than a mile away.

Jimmy was a good saddle horse, but he was smart, tricky, stubborn
and very contrary, especially if he knew he was able to outsmart his
rider. So it happened on this particular day, that after Father reached his
destination and dismounted, he dropped the bridle reins to the ground expecting to be able to pick them up and mount his horse when it was time
to go home. The horse remained in one spot until after the meeting, but
when my father went to pick up the reins and mount, the horse bounded
away for several yards and kept an arm's length distance from my father
all the way to the corral. The comedy accelerated as they came into
hearing distance, and I watched my father drag his heavy hot irrigation
boots across the hot fields as he cast curse after curse on the horse and
associated every saint in the heavens with every curse upon the animal.

At one point when he knew he was in my hearing distance he commanded me to "Go get the gun, I'm gonna shoot that damned horse!" The
horse went straight to the barn where I unsaddled and fed him. When I

entered the house and sat at the dinner table, Father was over his anger and had forgotten all about the gun.

There are many expressions about horse power, speed, and gait, but the best one is that of horse sense. Now no one really believes horses can match wits with human beings, but they do. This same horse was used at times to go for a few items at the grocery store at El Moro, two miles up the road. The family tried to put the three youngest girls on the horse for that errand, but this horse carried them the exact distance of one mile to the curve of our neighbors, the Buccolas.

Here Jimmy stopped and would not take one step further. The girls would get off and try to lead him past the curve, but he would brace his feet and pull back on the reins as though he had learned the Italian Army's battle cry of Piave, "Di Qui non si passa" (at this point you will not pass). Mary and Angelina accepted his decision and most of the time sent Bertha home with the horse, while they proceeded afoot to the store and back.

24. El Moro
from *Drop City: The First Hippie Commune and the Summer of Love* by John Curl

In 1965, four art students and filmmakers from the University of Colorado and the University of Kansas bought a seven-acre tract of land several miles north of Trinidad with the intention of setting up an experimental community and art colony. John Curl was at loose ends when he met two of Drop City's founders—Gene Bernofsky (Curly) and Joanne Bernofsky (Jo)—while they were visiting a mutual friend in New York City. He liked what he heard about Drop City, which sounded like the kind of place that might enable him to pursue a more creative life. So, a few months later, having made the necessary arrangements, he hitchhiked across the country and took them up on their invitation to come visit.

In the prologue to his memoir, Drop City: The First Hippie Commune and the Summer of Love, *Curl offers this overview of the community: "I lived at Drop City for three years, participating in its precipitous rise and the events that followed ... it quickly became a*

crucible of the time, a hotspot of creative ferment and radical ideas,
a countercultural crossroads stop for numerous seekers traversing
America on their way to some better future. Drop City provided some
of the earliest form and image to some of the ideas bubbling out of the
ferment of related movements for social change during the Sixties ... .
The media portrayed it as a center of the drug culture, but Drop City
is where I and a lot of others stopped taking drugs. Because something
important happened there, the name Drop City still rings in our deep
cultural memory over forty years later."

    In the following excerpt, Curl describes the scene as he found it
when he first came to Drop City.

Most of the land looked barren—cactus, low shrubs and brush. A couple
of trees down by the A-frame dome. A few tents and a shed. Some chickens scratching. A dog. A woman with a baby walked down a trail from
the dome on the hill, across a narrow bridge spanning a run-off furrow.
Looked like Jo. She disappeared inside the A-frame dome. There were a
few regular houses in sight and a large adobe building directly across the
gravel road. I slung my pack over my shoulder and crossed onto the land
near the large open structure.

    "Hey!" I looked up. A guy with no shirt, pudgy, wild kinky hair,
sunglasses, about twenty feet above me. It was Curly. "Throw me up that
hammer lying there, okay?"

    I slipped through the open struts into the dome. "Curly! Remember
me? Kugo's friend. We met in New York. I wrote you a letter."

    "I can see it's you, man. Throw me up that hammer, OK?"

    I picked up an old hammer with a cracked and taped handle, and
tossed it up. He let it sail past its apex, then snatched it from the air on
the way down. "Good catch."

    "I'm an expert. Now, you see them bolts and washers lying there?
Stuff a few in your pocket, grab that socket wrench, come on up here
and help me. We got to get this done before dinner." I cautiously climbed
the structure made from two-by-fours bolted to sections of plastic pipe.
I don't like heights. "I thought you were coming last week," he said. "I
almost gave up on you, man."

"It was always my plan to get here about now."

"Last week, this week. I keep losing track of time. Out here it all fades together into a big pile of time." He chortled. "Chuck me one of them bolts."

I helped him align and screw in the struts. I could see a panorama from the top of the dome. About a half mile away a band of trees snaked through the desert. To the south was a small town, must be Trinidad. The sun slipped beyond the western peaks. The light was fading fast.

"Is that a river?" I pointed

"The Purgatoire. Ain't that perfect?"

"You mean, like Purgatory?"

"That's really its name. Beautiful Drop City, near the banks of the beautiful Purgatoire." We had a good laugh.

"So who's living here now?"

"Well, me of course and Jo and the fattest baby you ever seen."

"I saw Jo carrying her. Congratulations."

"T'anks," he replied in an exaggerated New York accent. "And Clard (Clark Richert) and Lard (Richard Kallweit, the other two founders of Drop City)."

"Talking about me again?" A voice from below, a thick midwestern twang.

"I always talk about you behind your back, man," he yelled down. "That's Clard," he said to me. Clard climbed up the dome. A shock of straight blond hair fell across his forehead.

"Anyway," Curly went on, "the other people here are Miss Margarine and Nani and Rabbit." He ticked them off on his fingers. "And Poly Ester and the kids."

"What about Frinki?"

"She's Miss Margarine now. You got here just in time to see her. She's leaving tomorrow."

"Going back to New York?"

"She and the girls got real homesick for her dumb husband."

Clard made his way up to us. "What lies are you telling about me, Curly?"

"That you're afraid of everything except heights."

"That's true."

"This dome's really Clard's baby," Curly said. "Those little domes are a cinch. But building on a grand scale, we didn't know jack shit about it, but he just came out here and started doing it. It was a fucking inspiration."

"A lot of people can live in this dome," I said.

"Nobody's going to live in it," Clard said. The blondness of his eyebrows made his eyes look small and close to his pinched nose. He had a ruddy complexion and wore cowboy boots. "This is going to be our theater. One big painting inside. Total environment. People are going to be immersed, right inside the painting instead of outside looking in. Strobe lights flashing on revolving paintings, films and film loops projected simultaneously, sound speakers scattered all over. Electronic psychedelics. Cut you off from your conditioning, bump you into spiritual enlightenment. Give you constant orgasm."

"Constant orgasm!" I exclaimed. "What a concept!"

"It's not a concept," Clard replied. "It's my everyday reality. Nobody believes me."

"This will be our interface with the world," Curly added. "That's why we're building it here next to the parking lot. Most people will just stay here and leave our little domes alone. When the local vigilantes come out wondering what the fuck we're doing here, we show them the theater, give them a show, they figure we're just crazy artists and put their guns away."

"Good plan," I said.

A gong sounded. I saw Frinki standing inside the screens of the A-frame porch, beating on the gong.

"Chow time," Curly said. As we climbed down, I could see people straggling toward the A-frame from various directions ....

I followed Curly past Rabbit's new foundation, to the far corner of the land, the highest point on the property, strewn with piles of old building materials, lumber, plumbing, sculptures, and painted wooden art construction. "This represents the secret key to Drop City's success. We scavenge everything we can lay our hands on. This area's poor, but the country's so rich that even here it's full of stuff that nobody else is using.

If you went down to Mexico, you wouldn't find good junk like this just laying around. And in twenty years you probably won't here neither. But right now we're on the great cusp, and there's grand pickings. Wherever we go we're on the lookout for it. A lot of people are just glad for us to haul it away."

On the other side of the junkyard was a barbed wire cattle fence, and beyond that, a farm. All property lines in the region were marked by these cattle fences, which a person could easily cross. It felt weird that they were around Drop City. Yet the fences surrounding Drop City were draped and decorated everywhere with works of art, and the art pieces seemed to create a magical space inside, protected from the outside world.

"Do you get along with the neighbors?"

"Like butter. That white frame house down past the kitchen dome, those are the people we bought the land from. Retired couple. Very Anglo, but okay. She brings us cookies." He pointed in a circle. "This guy's Italian. Cattle rancher. A few crops too. Over there's goat farmers. Make cheese. Got a nice setup. I'll take you over there some time."

"How about that big adobe building across the road?"

"El Moro Elementary School. In a weird way, the school's our protection. The school busses bring the local kids here every morning. When they see us, the kids all flash us V-signs. They dig us. They're all on our side. And their parents can see we got nothing to hide."

25. Near El Moro
from "The Road to the Purgatoire" by Doug Holdread

Time spent on the road can alter one's point of view, maybe even encourage a welcome shift in perspective. That was the case for Doug Holdread, writer, artist, and long-time professor at Trinidad State College, whose life took a positive turn after a road trip up Highway 350 northeast of Trinidad. He hadn't left home with any particular destination in mind. He just wanted some diversion, a brief respite from a challenging time in his life. What he found on the road that day was a renewed sense of meaning (and a new project: namely exploring, and recording in word and image,

the path of the Purgatoire River from its confluence with the Arkansas
River to its source in the Sangre de Cristo Mountains).

The emptiness of the prairie filled me with dread as I drove the long,
straight county road east of Trinidad. I had no destination. My twen-
ty-year marriage was crumbling, and I wanted to lose myself in the
sprawling desolation of that windswept landscape for a while.

Headed north on 350, I drove fast: Model-Tyrone-Thatcher-Delhi. An
endless row of gnarly cedar fence posts flashed by in my periphery. The
road stretched out in front of me toward the edge of the earth. Everything
converged upon a receding vanishing point. I needed the emptiness.

What was I hoping for? An epiphany? The cold prairie seemed an
unlikely place for a "mountain top experience." I simply wanted to feel
the relief of a mindless drive upon the powdery dullness, straight toward
that point on the horizon where everything disappears.

The frigid emptiness was almost entirely unbroken excerpt for the distant plume of dust stirred up by a pickup truck—maybe a rancher checking
his cows; the skeletal silhouette of an abandoned homestead; a pronghorn
racing across the horizon; a wayward maverick bawling for its mother on
the other side of a barbed-wire fence. Mostly there was nothing, which is
what I was looking for: a forgiving emptiness. Some time to forget.

After a while, I caught a glimpse of Raton Mesa in the rear-view
mirror and recognized a bend in the road ahead of me that skirted the
contours of the canyon rim above the Purgatoire River. Through the
haze, a curious configuration of buildings took shape. The guard towers
and walls of the Bent County Correctional Facility came into view. I
drove past the place slowly, cautiously, past the sad, gray structure which
housed human beings deemed unfit to move about in society. I thought
of Van Gogh's portrait of himself as prisoner, walking endless circles in
the prison yard, hoping to catch a bit of sunlight, or maybe just feel the
bodily sensations of movement.

A couple hundred yards further down the road, a weathered wooden
sign; "Original grave site, William Bent." I'd heard of Bent, the old
trader who'd built Bent's Fort. Now I was outside of a prison named after
a county in Colorado, named after Bent. The gravestone was a low, flat

marker in the middle of a plowed field. The furrows diverted around the marker in concentric arcs that spread out like ripples on the surface of a pond. It was engraved with the dates of his birth and death." Born, Saint Louis on May 23, 1809. Died, May 19th, 1869. I figured that his stockade home must have been nearby, along the riverbank. The old farmhouse a few hundred yard away seemed a likely spot.

A lone crow floated overhead, adjusting its wings to the variations of the chilly autumn air. Its undulating shadow flowed across the furrows as it glided above the high security fence. I stood there for a long time, shivering in the cold wind, as if visiting the grave of an old friend. Muffled directives from the prison's public address system were carried off by the wind and absorbed into low, gray clouds. I couldn't understand the words but knew they marked the daily routines of the prisoners' lives. I looked at my hands, turned red by the cold. A droplet formed at the tip of my nose and fell like a diamond on one of the stones at my feet.

I picked up the stone, held it in my hand, this piece of granite that had tumbled for millennia, down from its headwaters in the Sangre de Cristo Mountains, rolling past the coal camps, through the cottonwood grove that would become Trinidad, past the site of a 1960s commune known as Drop City. I thought of it rolling through the Army's Pinon Canyon Maneuvers Site, across the dinosaur tracks at Picketwire Canyon, past the cattle ranches and ephemeral remains of homesteads and Indian camps. I saw it tumbling down, through the centuries, all the way to this place, rounded and worn smooth as the river pushed it along and deposited it here at the confluence of the Purgatoire and Arkansas rivers, this place where William Bent once built his home, and where his sons would eventually dig their father's grave, scooping shovels full of river rock to shield his corpse from the coyotes.

I understood then that I was in need of something more than just a long drive. I was in need of a sacrament. I needed to do something for my soul. I determined, in that moment, that I would carry the stone back up to its place of origin, to the crags where the waters of the Purgatoire seep out of the Blood of Christ Mountains. I was tired of walking in circles. Here, I would begin a long walk upstream, following the meanders of the river as it came down from its source. I would be a riverwalker.

26. Ludlow
from *Ludlow: A Verse-Novel* by David Mason

*In the summer of 1913, 8000 Colorado coal miners went on strike for
better wages and working conditions. In response to their eviction from
company housing—most of them were employed by Colorado Fuel and
Iron Company—they constructed tent villages near the mines where they
were working. In an effort to break up the strike, hired thugs and later the
national guard ran regular raids on the camp. In April of 1914, tensions
on both sides erupted into armed conflict, which led to one of the bloodiest
episodes in American labor history. At least nineteen people were killed,
among them a national guardsman and five miners. Louis Tikas, a union
organizer, was shot three times in the back. Thinking it had largely been
deserted, the National Guard set fire to the camp. The bodies of thirteen
women and children, who had been hiding out in a cellar, were found a
day later. In 1916, the United Mine Workers purchased the land where the
Ludlow tent villages had been and where the subsequent massacre took
place, and in 1918 they built a monument to the miners, their families, and
those who died fighting for better working conditions.*

*On periodic visits to see relatives in Trinidad, former Colorado poet
laureate David Mason passed through this area as a boy. The history
that lingered here, as well as the arid volcanics of this region, so different from the coast of Washington where he grew up, left a lasting impression. Later, in the spirit of revisiting family roots, he came to reimagine
this place which once was Ludlow, and which remains a monument to
those who lived and died here. In a "verse-novel" called* Ludlow, *he
recalls his initial encounters with this landscape.*

I saw this land first in a boyhood dream
made of my father's stories. Colorado,
where the red of earth turned at night to the blue
of moonlit heaven, where coyotes yapped
up the arroyo, and the deer came down
to seek unsullied water in the streams.
It was a fantasy:
cowboys and Indians. *Home on the Range.*

And then I saw it from an uncle's car
on the hot, endless drive from his Boulder home
to Trinidad, before the Interstate
and air-conditioning—in the late fifties.
I, the spoiled middle son of a doctor
asking when we'd get there, where *there* was,
and now *there* seemed so inhospitable
I no doubt longed for my rainy home up north.

A solitary cone of rock rose up
from lacerated land, the dry arroyos,
scars that scuppered water in flood season
down to a river. In dusty summertime
the cottonwoods eked out a living there
in a ragged line below the high peaks.
the ground was a plate of stony scutes that shone
like diamonds at noon, an hour when diamondbacks

coiled on sunbaked rocks ....
We were driving south,
and to the west the heat-waved mountains rose,
abrasive peaks without a trace of snow,
bare rock above a belt of evergreens.
This was my father's home. My father had

a childhood here, so far away from mine,
and knew of mines in the long-vanished towns,
a butte the Mexicans had name "the Orphan,"
and two peaks Indians called the *Huajatollas*,
"Breasts of the Earth," that made me and my brother
giggle, pounding each other's arms. "Ludlow,"
my uncle said and pointed. Father told
of militia men posted in those hills.

The miners camped below. "The bastards fired
machine guns on the miners' tents," he said.
"Yes, and set the tents on fire" – our uncle
told the rest, but I was much too young
to think of soldiers doing any evil,
and yawned these complications out of mind.
An open window of my uncle's car
with dry wind whooshing through it framed my dreams.

*Dreaming into this place many years later, Mason imagined the tent
camp in Ludlow by way of the characters in his narrative, one of whom
is Luisa, a young woman whose parents had come up from New Mexico
to work in the mines. Her mother had died in an outbreak of typhoid
fever; her father, a veteran underground with a little bit of black lung
to show for it, was a firer—a miner in charge of operations involving
dynamite. Luisa knew about the hazards of coal mining as this excerpt
suggests, but what she didn't know was that an underground explosion
would soon take her father's life and leave her orphaned.*

Some nights she waited till the lamps went out
in cabins all along the line, where men
who'd tried to wash the coal dust from their skin
snored and tossed, endured by wives and children,
catching sleep for an early start—from dark
to dark below,

from desert stars to flickering kerosene,
foul air that made the young men think of death.

Luisa waited in the twilit Babel
of miners bedding down – some Mexican
like her late mother, some filling the night
with songs in Welsh, Italian. Some were Greek
and talked of fighting wars against the Turks
and made *bouzouki* strings and *lyras* sing,
their workers' fingers nimble when they played
in high dry air of a Colorado camp.

But some nights she could barely hear the life
around her, hauling water from the creek
and pouring off the clearer part for drinking,
her heart held steady till explosions came
from gaping mines uphill, dull thudding sounds
like the push of air a man's torso made
when other men lit into him with fists.
The mesa sounded like a beaten man,

pinned down and beaten senseless in the night
the way it sometimes happened to a scab
or union organizer or a man
brought in from far away to agitate.
No one who grew up as Luisa had
in coal camps from Trinidad to Pueblo,
watching the typhoid rake through families,
could say she'd never seen a beaten man.

The mines made widows too, when timbermen
or diggers deep inside the earth cut through
to gas and lanterns set it off, or when
the pillared chambers fell. You heard a slump
within, and some poor digger ran out choking
there was thirty boys still trapped in the seam.
And some days all you'd see was bodies carted
down the hill and bosses counting heads.

27. Walsenburg
from *King Coal* by Upton Sinclair

*Beginning in the 1880s, Walsenburg was the hub of a coal mining
district. Coal was plentiful at the base of nearby mountains, new
developments had improved the smelting process, and increasingly
cost-effective railroad shipping led to the development of mining
operations in the area. In the decades that followed, Walsenburg came
to be known as the "city built on coal."*

In the novel King Coal, *which was published in 1917, Upton Sinclair
described the town of Pedro as follows: It "stood on the edge of mountain country; a straggling assemblage of stores and saloons from which
a number of branch railroads ran up into the canyons, feeding the coal-
camps. Through the week it slept peacefully; but on Saturday, when the
miners came trooping down, and ranchmen came in on horseback and
in automobiles, it wakened to a seething life." After a couple of trips
to this region, Sinclair likely modeled the fictional town of Pedro on
Walsenburg. Like the author himself, Hal Warner, the novel's protagonist, is an idealistic young man who comes west to investigate news of
unfair labor practices in the mines around Pedro. The stories he hears
were based on the stories that Sinclair heard when he came to southern
Colorado.*

The second day he made the acquaintance of two other gentlemen of the
road, who sat by the railroad-track toasting some bacon over a fire. They

welcomed him, and after they had heard his story, adopted him into the fraternity and instructed him in its ways of life. Pretty soon he made the acquaintance of one who had been a miner and was able to give him the information he needed before climbing another canyon.

"Dutch Mike" was the name this person bore, for reasons he did not explain. He was a black-eyed and dangerous-looking rascal, and when the subject of mines and mining was broached, he opened up the flood-gates of an amazing reservoir of profanity. He was through with that game—Hal or any other God-damned fool might have his job for the asking. It was only because there were so many natural-born God-damned fools in the world that the game could be kept going. "Dutch Mike" went on to relate dreadful tales of mine-life, and to summon before him the ghosts of one pit-boss after another, consigning them to the fires of eternal perdition ....

Hal took a fancy to this spontaneous revolutionist, and travelled with him for a couple of days, in the course of which he pumped him as to details of the life of a miner. Most of the companies used regular employment agencies...but the trouble was, these agencies got something from your pay for a long time—the bosses were "in cahoots" with them ....

There was another way, Old Mike explained, in which the miner was at the mercy of others; this was the matter of stealing cars. Each miner had brass checks with his number on them, and when he sent up a loaded car, he hung one of these checks on a hook inside. [Coal miners were paid on the basis of coal they dug out and sent up in their cars]. In the course of the long journey to the tipple, someone would change the check, and the car was gone. In some mines, the number was put on the car with chalk; and how easy it was for someone to rub it out and change it! It appeared to Hal that it would have been a simple matter to put a number padlock on the car, instead of a check; but such equipment would have cost the company one or two hundred dollars, he was told, and so the stealing went on year after year.

"You think it's the bosses steal these cars?" asked Hal.

"Sometimes bosses, sometimes bosses' friend—sometimes company himself steal them from miners." In North Valley it was the company, the old Slovak insisted. It was no use sending up more than six cars in one day, he declared; you could never get credit for more than six. Nor was it worthwhile loading more than a ton on a car; they did not really weigh the cars, the boss just ran them quickly over the scales, and had orders not to go above a certain average. Mike told of an Italian who had loaded a car for a test, so high that he could barely pass it under the roof of the entry, and went up on the tipple and saw it weighed himself, and it was sixty-five hundred pounds. They gave him thirty-five hundred, and when he started to fight, they arrested him. Mike had not seen him arrested, but when he had come out of the mine, the man was gone, and nobody ever saw him again. After that they put a door onto the weigh-room, so that no one could see the scales.

The more Hal listened to the men and reflected upon these things, the more he came to see that the miner was a contractor who had no opportunity to determine the size of the contract before he took it on, nor afterwards to determine how much work he had done. More than that, he was obliged to use supplies, over the price and measurements of which he had no control. He used powder [dynamite] and would find himself docked at the end of the month for a certain quantity, and if the quantity was wrong, he would have no redress. He was charged a certain sum for "black-smithing"—the keeping of his tools in order; and he would find a dollar or two deducted from his account each month, even though he had not been near the blacksmith shop.

Let any business-man in the world consider the proposition, thought Hal, and say if he would take a contract upon such terms! Would a man undertake to build a dam, for example, with no chance to measure the ground in advance, nor any way of determining how many cubic yards of concrete he had to put in? Would a grocer sell to a customer who proposed to come into the store and do his own weighing—and meantime locking the grocer outside? Merely to put such questions was to show the preposterousness of the thing; yet in this district were fifteen thousand men working on precisely such terms.

28. Pueblo
from *The World of Damon Runyon* by Tom Clark and
A Gentleman of Broadway by Edwin P. Hoyt

Alfred Damon Runyon worked for a number of Colorado newspapers
during the early stages of his career. Later, he put his writing skills
to use crafting short stories, plays (most famously Guys and Dolls*),*
and screenplays for numerous Hollywood movies. Although he is best
known for the work he did after leaving Colorado, which included his
career as a reporter and columnist covering the New York beat during
the prohibition era, his legacy lives on in Pueblo where an athletic
complex, a repertory theater, and a lake all bear his name.

As Tom Clark writes in his book The World of Damon Runyon, *young*
Al (it wasn't until later on that he went by Damon) likely had ink in his
veins. Newspaper work was a family tradition. His grandfather was a
printer, and his father edited a paper in Manhattan, Kansas. In 1882,
his father sold that paper and moved the family to Pueblo, hoping that
the climate might benefit his ailing wife who eventually died after years
of suffering from diphtheria and tuberculosis. Damon Runyon's sisters
moved back in with Kansas relatives while he stayed on in Pueblo,
dropped out of school, and followed his father's path into the newspa-
per business.

When Young Al grabbed the bottom rung of the newspaper business at
the Pueblo Evening Press in his early teens, it was simply the extension
of a family tradition. He was printer's devil, janitor, and gopher; he
brandished a wet mop and hot type before touching pen or typewriter.
Before long he was writing what would now be called human interest
pieces (about kids and animals)....At fourteen, he received his first
news assignment to cover a lynching in Pueblo. By fifteen he was a
full-fledged news reporter, a chain smoker, and an accomplished barfly.
Red eye and oval Turkish cigarettes were the ice cream and soda pop of
Al Runyan's childhood. He had his own boarding house room, owned a
decent suit of clothes, and diploma or no diploma, he was on his way. He
ran everywhere for his stories and after work, he regaled fellow tipplers

at the Home Café and Bucket of Blood with exaggerated versions of the
exploits. He even toted a six-gun, not so much out of necessity as for the
notoriety it gave him. He wanted to appear a veteran, a man despite his
years. His childhood had not been particularly pleasant; he was impatient
for it to be over.

*Damon Runyon not only followed his mostly absentee father into the
newspaper business, he also emulated some of the old man's other
habits as described in* A Gentleman of Broadway *by Edwin P. Hoyt. By
the time he moved to New York City in 1910, he had quit drinking, but
during his early years, he found some comfort in the saloons of Pueblo.*

From his father he had acquired two tastes: ... he wanted more clothes
than he could wear in a week and so many pairs of shoes that they would
never look worn. He also wanted to stand up at the bar with the men, raise
his glass, and bask in the urbanity of companionship with the men of the
world who haunted the Arkansas Saloon. Runyan's father—the Old Man,
he called him now—possessed an erudite and eloquent tongue. Young Al
was quiet most of the time .... He had no equal in fomenting mischief, and
he was not afraid of the devil, but he had no tongue for ready speech. He
was a listener, a tortured talker who wore his sense of inferiority like a
hair shirt. Except when he drank. The ruddy elixir of the saloons stilled Al
Runyan's anxieties and calmed his fear of making a fool of himself. The
glow of rye whiskey loosened his jaw and brightened his stories. But not at
the Arkansas Saloon. Old man Runyan had no taste for filial companionship in drink; his son went elsewhere to be one of the boys. Al went to the
Bucket of Blood and the Home Café where his status as a regular customer
was announced silently by the bartender's reach for the proper bottle as the
boy walked through the swinging doors. What the hell! He was a full-
fledged reporter, was he not? He was a man among men. He was just over
fifteen years old.

29. Colorado Springs
from *Westward to a High Mountain*
by Helen Hunt Jackson

*Like so many early settlers in the Pikes Peak Region, Helen Hunt
Jackson came west seeking a dry climate, fresh air, and a recovery
from tuberculosis. As many as a third of Colorado Springs residents in
the 1880s had come west for that reason. During the winter of 1873-74,
she took up residence at the Seven Falls Resort, which is where she met
William Sharpless Jackson, a wealthy banker and railroad man whom
she later married.*

*Originally from Amherst, Massachusetts, Helen Hunt Jackson had
developed a friendship with poet Emily Dickinson, but she didn't write
any of her own poetry until after she had moved to Colorado. After
several family tragedies—the loss of her two sons to sickness and
her husband's death in an industrial accident—she turned to writing
for solace. In addition to poetry, she also took up the cause of native
people in her nonfiction,* A Century of Dishonor *(1881) and in a novel,*
Ramona *(1884), which she modeled after* Uncle Tom's Cabin *by Harriet
Beecher Stowe. Her advocacy for native people, the Utes in particular,
was not always well-received by other Coloradans at that time, but she
persisted nonetheless.*

*As in the following essay called "Colorado Springs," which appears
in a collection of her essays called* Westward to a High Mountain,
*Helen Hunt Jackson wrote eloquently, and romantically as was the
style at that time, about the landscapes she encountered out west.
Although she wasn't impressed with Colorado Springs at first, over time
she came to appreciate this area, and Cheyenne Mountain in particular. When her husband rebuilt their house on the corner of Kiowa and
Weber, a few blocks north of what is now downtown Colorado Springs,
he made sure that she had a good view of her beloved mountain.*

I shall never forget my sudden sense of hopeless disappointment at the
moment when I first looked on the town. It was a gray day in November.
I had crossed the continent, ill, disheartened, to find a climate which

would not kill. There stretched before me, to the east, a bleak, bare, unrelieved, desolate plain. There rose behind me, to the west, a dark range of mountains, snow-topped, rocky-walled, stern, cruel, relentless. Between lay the town – small, straight, new, treeless.

"One might die of such a place alone," I said bitterly. "Death by disease would be more natural."

To-day that plain and those mountains are to me well-nigh the fairest spot on earth. To-day I say, "One might almost live on such a place alone." I have learned it, as I learned the human face, by heart; and there can be a heart and a significant record in the face of a plain and mountain, as much as in the face of man....

For myself, therefore, and for those along whom I might possibly win to love Colorado Springs as I love it, I repeat that it is a town lying east of the Great Mountains and west of the sun. Between it and the morning sun and between it and the far southern horizon stretch plains which have all the beauty of the sea added to the beauty of plains. Like the sea they are ever changing in color, and seem illimitable in distance. But they are full of tender undulations and curves, which never vary except by light and shade. They are threaded here and there by narrow creeks, whose course is revealed by slender, winding lines of cottonwood trees, dark green in summer, and in winter of a soft, clear gray, more beautiful still. They are broken here and there by sudden rises of table-lands, sometimes abrupt, sharp-sided, and rocky, looking like huge castles or lines of fortification; sometimes soft, mound-like, and imperceptibly widening, like a second narrow tier of plain overlying the first....

Looking westward, we see only mountains. Their summits are in the skies, ten, twelve, fourteen thousand feet high. Their foot-hills and foot-hill slopes reach almost to the base of the plateau on which the town stands. Whether the summits or the foot-hills are most beautiful one forever wonders and is never sure. The summits are sharp, some of them of bare red rock, gleaming under the summer sunrise like pyramids of solid garnet, yet blue again at sunset,-of a purple blue, as soft as the purple blue of grapes at their ripest. Sometimes in winter, they are more beautiful still, - so spotless white, stately, and solemn that if one believes there is a city of angels he must believe that these are the towers and gates thereof.

The foot-hills are closely grown with grass. In winter they are, like the prairies, brown and yellow and claret, varying in tint and shade, according to the different growths and in every shifting light from sunrise to sunset. No one who has not seen can fancy the beauty of a belt of such colors as these at base of mountains of red and yellow sandstone. The foot-hills lap and overlap and interrupt each other, sometimes repeating in softened miniature the outline of the crowding and overlapping peaks above. Here and there sharp ridges of sandstone rock have been thrown up among them. The spaces between these are so hollowed and smooth-moulded that they look like beautiful terraced valleys, with jagged red walls on either hand. When sunset casts alternate beams of light and shade across these valleys, and the red walls glow redder and redder, they look like veritable enchanted lands; and if one looks up to the snow-topped mountains above the sense of enchantment is only heightened. And this is what Colorado Springs sees, looking east. Are there many spots on earth where the whole rounded horizon is thus full of beauty and grandeur, and where to all the grandeur of outline and beauty of color is added the subtle and indescribable spell of the rarefied air and light of six thousand feet above the sea?

30. Colorado Springs
from *Of Time and Change* by Frank Waters

Frank Waters, who has been referred to as "the grandfather of south-western literature," grew up in the vicinity of what is now downtown Colorado Springs. Waters Park, which the city of Colorado Springs dedicated in his honor in 1991, is located between Bijou and East Platte Street along a creek known as Shook's Run, and across the street from his boyhood house at 435 E. Bijou. Born here in 1902, Waters witnessed the tail end of the early mining days in nearby Cripple Creek, which he later wrote about in several historical novels, collectively known as his Pikes Peak trilogy.

His father, who Waters said was part Cheyenne, passed along his interest in native people and their traditions. Frank wrote extensively

about the native cultures of the southwest in both his fiction and
nonfiction. The indigenous view of the world, as reflected in writings
like The Man Who Killed the Deer *and* The Book of the Hopi, *informed*
his own sense of wonder and mystery. He celebrates an early encounter
with that mystery in this excerpt from his memoir, Of Time and Change,
which was published shortly after his death in 1995.

My grandfather Joseph Dozier was a Southerner who had come west in
the early 1870s. He built a large house for his growing family along the
stream of Shook's Run and became a leading building contractor. My
mother, Onie, was the oldest of his five daughters; and my father, Frank
Jonathon, was a relative newcomer to the region....

My father, with his dark skin and straight black hair, was of a different breed than the Dozier clan. We didn't know much of his background
save that he was part Indian—Cheyenne. National prejudice against
Indians was still prevalent, and my maternal grandmother was never
quite reconciled to accepting him into the family.

One of his best friends was a vegetable huckster named Joe, a
Cheyenne. Father often rode with him on his rounds. Sight of my father
neatly dressed in a suit and polished boots as he sat on the plank seat of a
rickety wagon beside an Indian huddled in a tattered blanket with moc-
casins on his bare feet always disconcerted Mother. She was even more
upset by Father's frequent visits to the Ute encampment on the mesa.

The Utes had been moved to a western reservation; however, a band
of them was permitted to return here to their former homeland every
summer. Their smoke-gray lodges were shunned by respectable towns-
people, but Father often took me there of an evening. He would squat
down cross-legged in the circle of men around the cooking fire. With
the long-bladed knife he always wore, even in church, he would cut off a
pink slice of the steaming haunch and eat it, as did they, in his fingers. I
waited patiently with the women and children for our turn at the table.

The high peak rising above us was the Utes' sacred mountain [which
they referred to as Tava, meaning sun]. Looming prominently in their
creation myth, it always had been a place of power, not only for the
mountain Utes but for Cheyennes and Arapahos who had come in from

the plains to deposit votive offerings at the many mineral springs. Later it became the beacon for white gold-seekers whose wagon sheets were emblazoned with the boast, "Pikes Peak or Bust."

Not until years later, in 1891, was gold finally discovered on the south slope of the fourteen-thousand-foot Peak itself. The "Cripple Creek Cow Pasture," only eighteen miles west and one mile up from sedate Little London, as Colorado Springs was familiarly called, quickly became the world's greatest gold camp. The pharmacist at our corner drugstore rushed up there one Sunday morning. Throwing his hat into a gulch and digging where it fell, he discovered the famous Pharmacist Mine.

Occasionally I was taken up to the gold camp by Grandfather and Father on the spectacular Cripple Creek Short Line Railroad. Cripple Creek was everything that conservative Little London was not. It was a madhouse of activity and extravagant hopes. The muddy streets of Cripple Creek, the largest new town, swarmed with muckers, drillers, promoters and stockbrokers, ladies in long skirts and high button shoes, jostled off the boardwalks by painted prostitutes. Across the whole slope of Pikes Peak rumbled mule-drawn freight and ore wagons. Everywhere surface structures of great mines rose amidst open tunnels and shafts. All this activity, Father told me, was devoted to mining tons of rock from the Peak, grinding it into dust, and extracting a few specks of gold.

One day while playing with a handful of sand on the dump of one of Grandfather's mines, I had a strange experience of a far different nature.

In the bright sunlight every grain stood out with its distinctive shape, color, and texture. Then it happened. In an instant Pike's Peak took on a new and different meaning. I saw that it was composed of all these millions of grains of sand, which were mysteriously and precisely fitted together into one mighty, single whole—a sacred place of power, as the Utes regarded it. This momentary realization prompted the extravagant notion that all the mountains and continents in the world, like the grains in my hand, were also precisely fitted together to make a greater whole whose purpose and meaning were perceived by another world somewhere. The notion frightened me a little, but I never forgot it.

31. Colorado Springs
from *Everybody Welcome: A Memoir of Fannie Mae Duncan and the Cotton Club*
by Fannie Mae Duncan with Kathleen Esmiol

Fannie Mae Duncan was an African American entrepreneur, philanthropist, and community activist in Colorado Springs, best known as the owner of a jazz venue called The Cotton Club, which stood around the corner from the present-day Pikes Peak Center. She began her business life running a soda fountain for black soldiers at Camp Carson during World War II. In the 1950s, she opened the Cotton Club, which showcased musicians like Louis Armstrong, Billie Holiday, Duke Ellington, Count Basie, Lionel Hampton, Mahalia Jackson, Muddy Waters and many others. She hired a multiethnic staff to serve soldiers and their brides who also represented many races. Despite some local resistance to a gathering place with mixed patronage, she persisted, posting a permanent sign in her window that said, "Everybody Welcome."

"Everybody Welcome" is also the title of her memoir, written with Kathleen Esmiol, whose efforts were central, later on, in establishing a tribute and a statue honoring Fannie Mae, which is located downtown in front of the Pikes Peak Center (190 S. Cascade). In the following excerpt, Fannie Mae recalls an experience with baseball star Satchel Paige, one of the many celebrities who came calling at The Cotton Club.

You have to treat your business like you'd treat your sweetheart—with lots of tender lovin' care. I was very attentive to my customers and to all the details you have to keep track of to make sure they're comfortable and enjoyin' themselves. I liked it when the floor show was goin' on. Things finally calmed down, and people were drinkin' faster. That kept the cash register goin'. Just like different recipes, it takes lots of ingredients to create success in the nightclub business.

One thing that's a sure-fire guarantee you're gonna have a big night is when celebrities start showin' up at the most unexpected times. Word gets 'round fast. After runnin' the Cotton Club for so many years I thought I'd seen and heard it all, 'specially where celebrities are concerned. Of course, that was before the night Satchel Paige sauntered into the club.

Satchel was a baseball player of such enormous talent that most everybody still thinks he always played in the major leagues throughout his legendary career. The truth is, he was black and that limited his options for decades—but only in baseball. Satchel seemed to be equally famous as a ladies man … 'though I must confess that I didn't really know his reputation on that 'count when he walked in the club that evenin'. Him and his cronies had been on the road for weeks, and they were real glad for a night on the town.

The military unofficially continued to give me national publicity free of charge. Soldiers were like the dandelions that kids hold up and blow into the air, scatterin' the feathery seeds to the four winds. Every time they were reassigned and sent 'cross the country, they talked me and my nightclub up good. As a result, folks comin' into town came lookin' for the Cotton Club. That's probably why some of Satchel's buddies happened to bring him to the club that night. Of course, a few of 'em knew I was the proprietor and ran the place, but they had their reasons for keepin' Satchel in the dark about who I was.

Every night I made a habit of weavin' through the tables and treatin' my customers just like guests in my home, and I always dressed the part. I was wearin' a long black taffeta gown, cut low in the front and covered with ebony beads arranged in patterns 'cross the top. I was feelin' good, and I was lookin' good, too, if I do say so myself. And I do.

At that point, I hadn't kept up much with baseball, and I didn't know Satchel Paige from Adam, but apparently he had set his sights on me, and he was bankin' on makin' time with me. He was sure of himself and willin' to wager that he would get his way. Bets were runnin' high by the end of the evenin', but Satchel's buddies were bettin' on him losin' the game this time. They decided to let Selena in on their little scam, and of course, she tol' me. I looked over at their table. They were throwin' back drinks and beginnin' to talk loud, so I decided to edge a little closer to hear just what was goin' on.

"You're not gonna get to first base with that one, Satchel. I'm tellin' you. She's not gonna give you the time of day."

"Oh yeah? Just what makes you think so? She gives me the eye every time she passes our table. She's interested in me. I can tell."

"Ya don't see her stoppin', d'ya?"

"She's just checkin' me out. You'll see. I'm the man."

"You got a big imagination. That one's not available. I'm tellin' ya. I've tried. I've been here before."

Of course, that was a lie. I'd never seen the guy in my life, but you know how it goes when men get to braggin' and darin' each other. Satchel was a competitor, and he wasn't gonna let it go.

"I'll lay you money, I'm gonna be walkin' out that door with her tonight... and on to bigger things. Guarantee you. So fellas, what d'ya say? Are we on?"

Satchel stood up for a minute. Reachin' for his leather wallet in the hip pocket of his expensive, grey-pinstriped wool suit, he pulled out a big wad of cash. He acted like he was conductin' a ceremony when he made a show of layin' big bills on the table, one on top of the other. It was an impressive stack.

"You're on!"

I walked to the back of the room. Negotiations were clearly underway. 'Bout closin' time, Satchel just happened to be hangin' 'round still. I could sense he was gettin' ready to make his move. I strolled nonchalantly over to Selena. "Will you close up the club for me tonight?"

Selena was in on the joke, so she turned to the dwindlin' crowd. "Last call everybody. We're just about to close up for the night. Last call. C'mon, fellas. Let's go."

She motioned to Satchel's buddies who were laughin' and slappin' each other on the back as they watched Satchel get up from their table, button his jacket, and straighten his snazzy silk tie. He made a polite remark to Selena, probably thinkin' she owned the place, and he headed straight for me. By now his friends were almost in hysterics.

"Good evenin', Ma'am. You appear to be alone. I was just wonderin' if maybe you need a ride home? Not safe out there for a pretty woman like you."

"Why, thank you. I appreciate that."

"My name's Satchel." He flashed a big smile.

"Pleased to meet ya, Satchel. I'm Fannie Mae." I picked up my fur-trimmed, black cashmere coat, which I'd draped over the back of a chair. I started to put it on.

"Here, let me help you with that, Ma'am."

Well, at least he has polished manners, I thought. *Maybe he's not so bad after all. I have to admit, he's cute. And he's tall enough.* He pulled his black felt hat off the hat rack, squeezed the front of it to get just the right look, and placed it on his head at a sharp angle. Hookin' his arm under mine, he escorted me to his car, which was parked toward the end of the street near the street lamp.

"You certainly do look beautiful in the moonlight," he observed, and he opened the car door for me, holdin' my hand and helpin' me in. I thanked him. Closin' the door, he hurried to the other side of the car and crawled into the driver's seat.

Smooth. Real smooth talker, I thought. *Good personality. He's sure not lackin' in the confidence department either.*

I'm new in town. Just visitin'. I'm afraid I don't know my way around yet. You'll have to direct me."

"I live just a ways north of here on Corona. I'll show you."

As I gave directions, Satchel reached over and casually put his hand on mine. "Your hands are mighty cold. Looks like you could use a little warmin' up tonight."

"I'm fine." *Bet he's used that line a million times before,* I thought, but I smiled. "Turn right on Williamette, right up ahead, and then it'll be the first left." He let go of my hand long enough to make the two turns, but he grabbed it again once we were on Corona.

"Slow down. It's there on your right, 615 North Corona. The house with the white picket fence."

"Right here?" He pulled over to the curb, and he ducked his head to look out past me. He was obviously surprised as he got his first glimpse of my Victorian mansion, but he concealed it. He simply said, "Nice place."

Before I could thank him, he bounded outta his door and opened mine. Takin' his hat off his head, he made a sweepin' gesture with it and reached for my hand to help me out.

"After you, Ma'am. Let me escort you to your door."

As we walked up the steps, he chattered away nervously.

"You know, you were the prettiest woman in the club tonight. Couldn't keep my eyes off you. None of the other guys could either. Bet they're all jealous I'm the one gettin' to take you home tonight."

A light from the dinin' room filtered through the leaded-glass windows framin' my front door. It cast shadows on the porch as I stood for a moment listenin' to his flood of compliments. *Yep. He's smooth all right,* I thought. *Got a killer smile.*

I unlocked the door. "Thank you very much for bringin' me home. I really appreciate it. I hope you enjoy your visit here. There's a lot to see in Colorado Springs." I opened the door and started to go in.

Without a warnin', he grabbed my hand and pulled me toward him. "Aren't you gonna ask me to come in? The night's still young." His smile had turned to a puzzled frown, but he was still tryin' his best to be charmin'.

"It's late and I have to be up early in the mornin' to go to work."

"But I thought we were gettin' along." His mood was definitely changin'.

"You're a very nice person. You really are. But it's late, and I have to get to bed. Goodnight, Satchel."

It was beginnin' to dawn on him that this was the end of the evenin'. He grabbed my hand again as I started to go back through the door. He looked at me in disbelief.

"Just one minute here. Don't you realize who I am? I'm Satchel Paige!" He continued to pursue an invitation past my front door, but he wasn't makin' any points with me. I figured he'd been focused on winnin' his bet at first, but now it was a matter of pride.

"I assure you, Mister Paige, I know exactly who you are, but like I said it's late and I'm tired, so—"

"I don't think you understand. I've had at least THREE HUNDRED women! Who d'ya think you are?"

I got a big kick outta lookin' him straight in the eye and lettin' him have it.

"Well, I'm Fannie Mae Duncan. That's who I am. And I'm not gonna be number THREE-O-ONE!" With that I closed the door on Mr. Satchel Paige. Momma would've been proud of me.

32. Denver
from the poetry of Lalo Delgado and Corky Gonzales

A big part of Denver's literary heritage lives on in the words of two Chicano poets whose work was deeply informed by their activism in the late 1960s.

Born in Chihuahua Mexico in 1931, Abelardo "Lalo" Delgado grew up in an overcrowded tenement building in El Paso, Texas. At a community center there in 1955, he became an advocate for young Latinos looking for educational and economic opportunities. Despite a largely segregated educational system, he had earned a college degree by the time he left for California in the early 1960s. In California, he worked with Cesar Chavez in support of the farmworkers movement. By the late sixties, he was living in Denver, writing and publishing poetry, and serving in another advocacy position as executive director of the Colorado Migrant Council.

Rudolfo "Corky" Gonzales, born on the east side of Denver in 1929 to a migrant farm worker from Chihuahua and a mother from Colorado, was also determined to get an education. He managed to get through high school with good grades while also working with his father in the sugar beet fields east of Denver. He went on to Denver University where he hoped to get a degree in engineering. When his tuition money ran out, he fell back on other skills and made his living as professional boxer. Later, he opened Corky's Tavern on Walnut Street and 38th Avenue, which may have been Denver's first sports bar. Like Delgado, Gonzales also followed the call into community organizing and activism. In 1967, he became chairman of the Crusade for Justice, a Denver organization that fought for Mexican American rights. In 1968, he continued in that role while also working with Caesar Chavez and Martin Luther King, Jr.. In 1969, he helped organize a walk-out at West High School in Denver, protesting a teacher's use of racist language there. Tensions between police and demonstrators erupted into violence and twenty-five people were jailed, including Gonzales, though he was later acquitted of all charges.

Beginning in the late 1960s, both Delgado and Gonzales were widely read throughout and beyond the Chicano community. The Gonzales poem, "Yo Soy Joaquin," an epic whose narrator leaves his homeland in pursuit of economic opportunity (not unlike his father's journey) went viral by way of alternative newspapers and mimeographed sheets of paper taped to walls and telephone poles. The poem offered a deeper sense of home and identity for alienated Mexican Americans in southern Colorado and the American Southwest (most of which had been part of Mexico prior to the Guadalupe-Hidalgo Treaty of 1848). Here are the concluding lines of that poem:

I have endured in the rugged mountains
    of our country.
I have survived the toils and slavery
    of the fields.
        I have existed
in the barrios of the city,
in the suburbs of bigotry,
in the mines of social snobbery,
in the prisons of dejection,
in the muck of exploitation
and
in the fierce heat of racial hatred.
And now the trumpet sounds,
the music of the people stirs the
        Revolution,
Like a sleeping giant it slowly
rears its head

   to the sound of

tramping feet
clamoring voices
mariachi strains
fiery tequila explosions
the smell of chile verde and
soft brown eyes of expectation for a
better life.

And in all the fertile farmlands,
the barren plains,
the mountain villages,
smoke-smeared cities
We start to MOVE.

La Raza!
Mejicano!
Español!
Latino!
Hispano!
Chicano!
or whatever I call myself,

I look the same
I feel the same
I cry
and
Sing the same

I am the masses of my people and
I refuse to be absorbed.
I am Joaquín
The odds are great
but my spirit is strong

my faith unbreakable
my blood is pure

I am Aztec Prince and Christian Christ

I SHALL ENDURE!
I WILL ENDURE!

"Lalo" *Delgado, who taught at Metro State for seventeen years and served as Denver's poet laureate, found a large and dedicated readership for the books that he began to publish and circulate. "Stupid America," his most famous poem, embodied Delgado's lifelong commitment to justice, opportunity, and the rights of Mexican Americans. Published in 1969, he wrote it after attending an education conference at which white educators blamed Chicanos for their failures in school systems where their needs were not being addressed. As Delgado's friend and fellow educator Estevan Flores put it, "Stupid America," was an "expression from the barrio that captured the emotions of the times."*

stupid america, see that chicano
with a big knife
in his steady hand
he doesn't want to knife you
he wants to sit on a bench
and carve christ figures
but you won't let him.
stupid america, hear that chicano
shouting curses on the street
he is a poet
without paper and pencil
and since he cannot write
he will explode.
stupid america, remember that chicanito
flunking math and english
he is the picasso
of your western states
but he will die
with one thousand masterpieces
hanging only from his mind.

33. Denver
from *The First Third* by Neil Cassady

Neal Cassady was a complicated character—complicated in part because he was so heavily mythologized by the writers with whom he became friends, most notably Jack Kerouac, Allen Ginsberg, and other Beat writers, and later Ken Kesey (and the Merry Pranksters) with whom he became an icon of the psychedelic era.

Born in 1926, Cassady met Ginsberg and Kerouac, by way of a mutual friend, on a trip to New York City in October of 1945. By all accounts, Cassady was energetic and charismatic and made an impression almost immediately on those he met. But he had also grown up without much family support—his mother died when he was ten, and his father, a skid row alcoholic with whom he lived, had little to offer. As a result, Cassady was a survivor, doing whatever it took to get by in a world that had largely abandoned him. That included hustling—he was a regular in Denver pool halls —and stealing cars (as many as 500, he said, by the time he was fifteen). Kerouac would later refer to him as "a holy con man."

Cassady was determined, though, to rise above his boyhood circumstances. He had seen enough of the down-and-outers at the Metropolitan Hotel in Denver, where he lived with his father, to know that he didn't want to end up that way. Born with an active mind and plenty of curiosity, he would later try to learn about writing from his literary friends but, ironically, he may have had more of an impact on their writing lives. Impressed with the ecstatic energy of Cassady's letters, Jack Kerouac adopted a spontaneous, bebop kind of aesthetic that got plenty of attention after On the Road *came out in 1957. Dean Moriarty, the character that he modeled after Cassady in that book, laid the groundwork for his friend's mythic status later in life.*

Writing was especially hard work for Neal Cassady. Inspiration came more readily than the ability to sit still and get words on the page. Nevertheless, he was able to write about his early years in The First Third, *an autobiography published after his death in 1968 by Lawrence Ferlinghetti and City Lights Books, in which he describes his life living*

on the margins long before Denver neighborhoods like Larimer Square
were transformed into the relatively upscale places they are now.
Although the Metropolitan Hotel of his youth is long gone, you can
still find a bar or two in Denver (including My Brother's Bar at 2376
15th Street) where Cassady and his friends hung out. In the following
excerpt from The First Third, *Cassady describes a gritty world at the*
Metro and introduces a memorable roommate.

In peril of collapse it housed about a hundred of Denver's non-transient
bums and still does. On each of the upper floors there were some thirty
odd cubicles whose walls failing by several feet to reach it, made the
ceiling seem incongruously high. These sleeping cells mostly rented for
ten to fifteen cents a night; certain superior ones cost two-bits, and we
had one of these, but only paid a weekly rate of one dollar, because of the
top floor locations since we shared the room with a third person.

This roommate of ours slept on a sort of platform made by a plank
covering a pipe elbow in the building's plumbing. Not just anyone could
sleep there in comfort, for the ledge was only about three feet long, but
he fit in the space snugly enough, because both his legs had been amputated at the thigh many years ago. Appropriately, he was called Shorty
and this fitting of name to fact seemed very funny to me. Every morning
he got up early and with his oversized arms, swung a skinny torso down
those five flights of stairs. I never saw him pause to use the community
washroom on the second floor and presumed the sinks were too high
for him so he made toilet arrangements elsewhere. On the sidewalk he
would get into a dolly-like cart and, using blocks of wood in each hand,
push himself to his begging post. He usually went around the corner on
Larimer Street and stationed himself before the Manhattan Restaurant.
Larimer Street was Denver's main drag in the nineteenth century and the
Manhattan was its best restaurant....

In the nighttime of Metropolitan squalor, we slept side by side, my
Dad and I, in a bed without sheets. There happened to be no clock, so
I relied on Daniel's and Fisher's mammoth tower one to wake me for
school, and it did. Or at least I think this is what woke me, because as
it boomed 7:00 A.M. down to me I always opened my eyes, and from

under the unwashed blanket stuck my alert head into our room's nippy
air. There my father snored, and usually being too drunk to stir, was
oblivious to everything. Turning from the breath's smell out of his
drink-swollen face, I eased my naked self off the creaking cot with shivering quietness. I hurried into some hated remnants of brother Jimmy's
clothes; too-short shoes and knickers which crept above my knees. The
long wool socks I wore failed to effectively close this embarrassing gap.
Most of the time Dad just snored on and on, and since Shorty's shelf was
bare (he sometimes departed while it was still dark outside), I woke to
no commanding voices. Slipping through our door and along a splintered
floor, I passed rooms where other weakened bodies of shattered soul
joined my father in giving noise to a labored sleep. Down worn stairs on
silent feet and a quick step into a sunlit lavatory of activity. Ringing the
enormous room were many nondescript men at their toilet. Most of them
were shaving, some had the "shakes" so that it was quite a job, and, so as
not to cut themselves or face the agony too often, they only shaved when
they were on their way uptown to hustle a dime. Unclean trousers bagged
over run-down shoes. Their heavy coats and frayed shirts hung on hooks
beside them, for when washing they really splashed with janitorial un-
concern. I remember sidestepping these puddles of water as I skipped to
one of the room's large windows and tiptoe-peered through dirty panes
to read the time by guessing at the slant of nearly illegible black hands
against the dingy white glass of the Roman-numeraled clockface atop the
mighty tower of Daniel's and Fisher's department store, Denver's highest
building – it was 7:15. After washing I tripped back upstairs to fetch my
tennis ball and coat and to check Dad for any signs of sobriety or interest
in food, but on most school days he didn't often stir, so I alone I went to
my breakfast.

Again descending the stairs I went through the lobby, empty of loi-
tering men at this hour, and on down several big steps of deeply scooped
stone onto the busy 16th and Market Streets intersection. Big trucks with
chain-drive and hard-rubber tires bounced over Market's slick cobblestone.
Opening for the day's business were the wholesale meat dealers, poultry
houses, fish markets, coffee and spice warehouse and cheese companies—I
was always hungry then—and the employment agencies and restaurants

and bars, and a couple of business concerns I have forgotten, that crowded
into the block of Market between 14th and 18th. On 16th Street, arterial traffic rumbled from an overpass into North Denver—of Denver's half-dozen
ones, only this viaduct had streetcar tracks—a bottleneck of oversized
trams jammed with working people inching toward the Loop, Larimer,
Downtown, and all East Denver clanged past me as I came out of the hotel.
I walked a block up 16th and turned left at the newly opened Dave Cook
sporting goods store on Larimer's corner and went into the building next to
it. This was the Citizen's Mission, run by a Protestant church organization
and strongly backed by a good assemblyman (whose name I've forgotten
although Dad in his daydreams of getting somewhere was always talking
of going to see "So and so, up at the Mission" to get a steady job—now I
remember, Val Higgins!). The Mission gave breakfast and supper to about
two hundred men a day and in return had a well attended bi-weekly church
service, a thing of which its several competitors up and down The Street
could also boast, but I couldn't see why, since they handed out no food. A
couple of years later Father Divine's, up Larimer on 24th in the middle of
the block, began giving meals. They served only lunch, a real tasty one too,
and there was a big whoopdeedo among the boys when this place opened,
for the gap between breakfast and supper at the Mission had been felt by
all of us. But right now we had only the Mission and I was its youngest
member by a good dozen years.

The façade of the Citizen's Mission was of inappropriately gay yellow
stucco. The double center doors entered into an auditorium with massive
wooden pews that could sit a hundred people. Down the aisle was a
raised platform with a front-center box pulpit, also on this stage was an
unmusical piano and a table with a semi-circle of chairs behind it. From
the street there were single doors on each end of the building, the one
on the right led upstairs to the administration offices, but I never used
it and always took the door to the left instead. Getting in an orderly line
of hungry men I moved slowly forward down metal stairs into a warm
kitchen of smells and clatter. Being served cafeteria style, each of us
picked up a tray, spoon, bowl and a cup of tinny material, and we moved
along the wall in a patient wait for our turn before the steam tables. The
first white-aproned woman—all the food handlers were women, smiling

on us and busy with a "cause"—placed two pieces of bread on the tray, the second one ladled a scoopful of oatmeal into our bowls, while the third poured hot coffee. (There was no cream, but plenty of sugar, and one could get a second cup.) We filed to stainless steel benches and sat before long ringing tables of the same material which vibrated so from the impact of our utensils that my sensitive ears filled completely. All around men clustered and we squeezed elbow to elbow for lack of space in the crowded basement room. Sometimes my breakfast companions happened to talk to me, and sometimes they didn't. Either way as I remember it was all the same. Of course I eventually learned that almost all of them were alcoholics, and many of them suffering a great deal from the disease, but there were also several old-age pensioners and other indifferently bunched younger men who were just down on their luck because of the Depression.

On the Mission's left was the Manhattan Restaurant and seated in his cart before its building would be Shorty at work. He sat in the bright morning sun of winter as its cold light came to touch the sidewalk's outer edge, and turning dull eyes on Larimer's crowd he leaned back against the base of a heavily ornate iron drinking fountain the twin faucets of which have long been out of service and whose infant cupids danced in golden contrast over his head. As I passed him on my way toward 17th Street he gave a languid nod which contrasted with the grinning mouth he exhibited in our room's privacy and I realized he put on a different face for the public.

34. Denver
from *On the Road* by Jack Kerouac and
The Ringer by Jenny Shank

In Jack Kerouac's book, On the Road, *Sal Paradise sits in the stands at a ball game under the lights at Sonny Lawson Field in Denver:*

"A great eager crowd roared at every play. The strange young heroes of all kinds, white, colored, Mexican, pure Indian, were on the field. Performing with heart-breaking seriousness. Just sandlot kids in uniform.

Never in my life as an athlete had I ever permitted myself to perform like this in front of families and girl friends and kids of the neighborhood, at night, under lights; always it had been college, big-time sober-faced; no boyish human joy like this."

The enthusiasm that Kerouac recorded in this scene at 23ʳᵈ and Welton (Lawson Field is still there) is replicated today at ball fields all over Denver, like the ones that Jenny Shank describes in her novel, The Ringer. *Denver families love their sports and sports teams, which offer, among other things, the delight of shared stories and the heroes that inhabit them, some of whom, like former Denver Bronco quarterback John Elway, or El Johnway as the little girl in the following excerpt refers to him, become iconic. Sometimes there are rituals that accompany these stories and icons, as in the following description of one Denver sports family.*

Patricia was near the intersection of Federal and Speer, driving toward Ray's baseball game at Ruby Hill, when Mia shouted from the backseat. "Wait! I forgot El Johnway."

"Oh Mia," Lupe said, turning to look at her, "it's just a toy."

Before games, Ray rubbed El Johnway's football-clutching hand over his bat for luck. Mia pointed El Johnway at her brother when he was pitching, as if the action figure emitted game-influencing rays. The longer Ray's winning streak lasted, the more superstitious the kids became. But kids were naturally superstitious. Patricia had started knocking on wood when she was nine after two of her grandparents died in the same year. She feared the bad times that lurked around the corner, so she knocked on wood, hoping the gesture would keep calamity at bay. It hadn't saved Salvador, but the habit remained ingrained. Maybe she could borrow El Johnway for luck tonight—Tío had arranged a phone call with Graciela after the game.

"If we turn around now, we'll be late," Patricia said.

"But Ray will lose if we don't get him," Mia said.

"Isn't El Johnway powerful enough to work his magic from home?"

"Patricia," Lupe said, "don't encourage her superstition."

It was worse than Lupe knew. Ray dressed for games in a particular order: sliding shorts first, then socks, then pitching sleeves. Then he'd eat a snack, always one banana, and two sticks of beef jerky. "Pitchers need potassium and protein," he explained seriously, like a retired ballplayer on a commercial advertising a pain reliever. While he sat at the kitchen counter chewing his banana, he positioned a one-inch photo of Roberto Clemente under his sock next to his skin. Finally, Ray would go back to his room to button up his jersey, pull up his stirrups, and finish with his pants. He always put his baseball cap on with the brim at a slight angle, then swiveled it forward to lock. After that, he wouldn't sit down again until he was in the car on the way to the game, afraid to leave his luck lying somewhere in the house.

"El Johnway isn't superstitious," Mia said. "It'll be your fault if Ray loses."

"Mia, don't talk to me that way." Patricia didn't want Mia to go through life as she had, fearing she could cause bad things to happen if she lapsed in her rituals. So she continued driving toward the field, hoping this would prove to Mia that Ray was in charge of his power.

35. Denver
from *Here is a Land Where Life is Written in Water*
by Thomas Hornsby Ferrill

The murals and poems seen on the first-floor rotunda of Colorado State Capitol Building in Denver came about because of a late night party in June of 1935. As the story is told by Gene Amole, former columnist for the Rocky Mountain News, a group of friends had gathered to celebrate artist Allen True's new studio. One of those in attendance was poet Thomas Hornsby Ferrill. Toward the end of a long night of revelry, Ferrill was holding forth on water as the all-important theme in understanding the West. Most of the other partiers were otherwise distracted, except, that is, for True, who took an interest in the sketches Ferrill made on an old hamburger sack as he spoke. Ferrill suggested that True make some murals for which he would provide accompanying poems. The murals and poems were installed in 1940.

*To support his family, Thomas Hornsby Ferrill wrote public rela-
tions copy for the Great Western Sugar Company. He also wrote for his
wife Helen's weekly newspaper,* The Rocky Mountain Herald, *among
other publications. His peers in the literary community—including poet
Carl Sandburg, who referred to him as the "Poet of the Rockies"—recognized his real gift.* High Passage, *his first collection of poems, won
the prestigious Yale Series of Younger Poets Competition. Later he
became Colorado Poet Laureate, a position he held from 1979-1988.*

*Although he wrote and published many fine volumes of poetry, his
most widely-known words are those that appear on the inside of the
capitol building. Here is the sonnet he wrote for the first panel in that
series of murals and poems.*

Here is a land where life is written in water
The West is where the water was and is
Father and son of old mother and daughter
Following rivers up immensities
Of range and desert thirsting the sundown ever
Crossing a hill to climb a hill still drier
Naming tonight a city by some river
A different name from last night's camping fire.

Look to the green within the mountain cup
Look to the prairie parched for water lack
Look to the Sun that pulls the oceans up
Look to the clouds that give the oceans back
Look to your heart and may your wisdom grow
To power of lightning and to peace of snow.

36. Denver / Aurora
from *The Thunder Tree: Lessons from an Urban Wildland* by Robert Michael Pyle

In his book, The Thunder Tree, *ecologist, author, and poet Robert Michael Pyle describes his boyhood adventures along the High Line Canal, a century old irrigation channel that runs diagonally through Denver and surrounding suburbs. As Pyle points out, his home in Aurora was on the wrong side of Denver to have access to the mountains, so his explorations were focused more on the flat side of town. "From the time I was six," he writes, "this weedy watercourse has been my sanctuary, playground, and sulking walk. It was also my imaginary wilderness, escape hatch, and birthplace as a naturalist. Later the canal served as lovers lane, research site, and holy ground of solace." Ever since the 1970s, when the service road that parallels the canal was opened to the public, thousands of Coloradans have enjoyed the solace of some open space and moving water coursing through the Denver Metro area. Pyle centers this book not so much around his own story, although that certainly provides for some good reading as in the following excerpt, but around the story that the ditch itself has to tell. As he puts it, "My life stories are meant to illuminate the land, not the other way around."*

On this sunny Tuesday in July, we trekked to the canal for perhaps the fiftieth time. We had followed our usual route along the Sand Creek Lateral, the broad side ditch that ran off to the north. Its headgates were closed, so the lateral was dry, but it was lush with growth from the slosh of its full flow against the banks. The morning that had begun so cool and moist was already growing torrid. When we felt the shady breath of the ditch, we sucked it up like the air in the chocolate aisle of Hested's dime store. Turning into it, we walked west along the canal service road, past old farmhouses with rickety barns and bridges and rusting farm implements. No Trespassing signs, posted by landowners and the Water Department, drew us on.

The heat of the day began to build in earnest. Ragweed flagged in the wilting rays, and magpies took to the thickets. We shuffled more slowly, plucking succulent shoots of pigweed and rubbing them until our fingers were green. Our engineer boots were hot and covered with dust. Cumulonimbus climbed the eastern sky. "Think this is far enough!" I asked after a long, treeless stretch.

"I haven't seen the ditchrider," Tom said. "He'd kick us out if he came along, but if we're lucky, he won't." We couldn't see any houses from here, either.

We longed to get off the griddle of the road. Dropping into the shade of a spreading willow, we stripped down to the swimsuits we wore underneath our jeans and slithered into the current. Some fifty miles from its mountain source in the Platte River Canyon, the water was still cool, almost cold.

Denizens of the Great American Desert, we were drawn to water wherever it was to be found. We gravitated to plastic wading pools. We sought out lawn sprinklers, broken hydrants, and warm rainwater running ankle-deep in the concrete gutters of the streets. But the slippery brown flow of the canal was best.

Parents worried about drowning, and rightly so—from time to time some kid would indeed drown somewhere along the canal. They worried about broken glass, and now and then we did bring home a bloody toe. And they warned us of the dangers of polio, supposedly transmitted in dirty water. But that seemed like double jeopardy to us: if we had to have those unpleasant polio shots at school, why should we have to skip the ditch as well? Generations of farm kids used the High Line as their swimming hole, and we did the same.

We hadn't been in the water long before the cottonwood tops began to rustle, announcing the arrival of a summer squall. The morning's easy breeze came up in a wind that sucked the heat out of the day as clouds crowded the blue. Soon raindrops speckled the surface of the ditchwater. Tom and I half hoped for a cool afternoon thunderstorm, but this one was coming a little early. Usually we made it home first, or met the rain on the way.

Lightning scratched the western sky. We were leery of lightning, both in the open and beneath the cottonwoods. A kid we knew claimed he knew someone whose cousin's friend had been struck while caddying.

Everyone knew you weren't supposed to get under a tree, which could act as a lightning rod. And Dad had told us that rainwater could carry the jolt along the earth or into a stream, through what he called ground flash. It seemed nowhere was safe.

Willow leaves blew off the tree as we scrambled wet into our boots and jeans. No longer hot, we were getting damn cold as the ditchwater evaporated off our skin in the wind. By the time we reached the Sand Creek Lateral, cottonwood leaves clattered like rattlesnakes and their boughs creaked close to breaking in the rising gale. This was no ordinary afternoon shower. Then the first hail came.

At first it just stung. Hail wasn't uncommon with our summer thunderstorms. Normally pea-size, it could smart, but it wasn't a big deal. We knew from school that hail occurred when hot air near the ground rose rapidly in powerful updrafts, carrying ice crystals into supercooled vapor in the heights of the towering clouds. Layers of ice formed around the nucleus, making a hailstone that eventually fell to earth. GrandPop had told us of hailstorms that ruined crops on family places further east, but the most we'd ever seen hail do was break off a few flowers. We were still more worried about the lightning. Thunder growled and lightning rent the dark fabric of the cloud bank.

But the thunderclaps and lightning strikes were far apart—we counted "One thousand one, one thousand two, one thousand three"—while the hail was here and now. The stones had grown to the size of marbles and were pounding down like a giant bag of aggies emptied overhead. The hail didn't pass quickly by as it usually did, and it was beginning to hurt. Confused by the rough touch of weather I'd never known before, I fell behind.

"Come on, Bobby! We're almost there."

I could barely hear Tom over the thunder, the wind's wail, and the hail thudding all around us. Hailstones bouncing up met those coming down, creating a percussive curtain that kept us from seeing our feet. But I could see Tom's face, which had gone terribly pale. The wind whipped his cotton shirt, exposing his tanned back already red with welts. Tumbling on the slippery sediment of hailstones, I tried to catch up.

Iceballs pounded down, bruising our elbows, knuckles, knees, and heads. They were bigger than any hail we'd ever seen, bigger than our marbles, and getting bigger. "Tommee," I wailed as a stone the size of a shooter struck me on the collarbone. I squatted beside a locust tree, uselessly: a shattered magpie nest fell from its branches and disintegrated around me, its sticks mixing with the white rubble. Mesmerized by white and out of breath from crying, I felt the blows on my back and watched pellucid eggs of ice roll down toward down toward the ditch.

Tom came back and hauled me to my feet. He said nothing, just clamped his mouth shut with his lips sucked in. I knew that look from Grammy's face when she battled weeds, a turkey on a platter, or shiftless grandson, and I knew it meant business. I stopped crying and let myself be pulled. Dragging me behind him, Tom dove into the ditchbed of the Sand Creek Lateral. Had the headgate been open to the lateral we would have been stuck in the open field. We sought shelter behind a concrete check dam, but it gave no lee. The smells of chopped weeds and rotting leaves filled my nostrils, the pungency of pulverized earth mixed with the wild ozone. Walnut-size hailstones smashed against the dam and ricocheted into our faces. Between sobs I saw that Tom was red all over. His brown hair was plastered over his eyes; he still had his glasses, but he was crying, too.

We tried to run again. Dad sometimes brought ball bearings home for us to play with and now it felt as if we were running on them. I slipped over and over and fell into the mud. Struggling up, I huddled against Tom, hanging on his arm. A great hailstone struck his forehead. He staggered and fell.

When he looked up again, without his glasses, Tom squinted toward a grey-green shape looming in the dull light. "There it is," he cried, but I could barely hear him over the din of the storm. Tom scrambled up the ditchbank and called for me to follow. But the bare slope had turned to mud, and I kept sliding down. The ice bullets drilled the air and drove me back. My boots slipped, my stinging fingers found nothing to grip. I landed in a bed of hail and mud and whimpered, "I can't do it. We're going to die."

Tom's hand, wet and cold, grabbed mine and yanked me up the bank. "No, we're not," he hollered. "Come on, the hollow tree is right up here. See?"

I did see it. I stumbled to the old hollow cottonwood and clutched at its furrowed brown bark, the smooth white edge of its heartwood cleft, glassy wet. Its tattered leaves slapped our faces. We crawled inside the punky charred hollow, and I dropped to my knees, whining and gasping. Tom coughed, choking on ice and dust. He pulled me up, packed me deep into the blackened hold, and fell across me, covering me as best he could. He tried to block the gape with his body, using his battered back like the operculum of a snail. But he was too skinny, and the wind got past him. The storm shifted to the north, blew directly at the hollow, and pummeled us afresh.

Then Tom went heavy and loose against me, and I saw that his forehead was bright blue. I thought he might be dead, after all. A friend of mine, Patrick Ramsey, had died of bone cancer, and in his coffin, he had looked this pale and still. That was the first death I'd ever known, and it left me feeling hollow, scared, and guilty: he was my friend, and I was supposed to deliver his *Weekly Reader*. But near the end, I'd stayed away.

Unable to move under Tom's limp body, I hoped he was only knocked out. We'd often played at knocking each other out with the butts of our cap guns, as our cowboy heroes did in the comics and movies. But here he was out for real and not coming to right away, as the cowboys did. The ice continued to pound the tree and shatter like shrapnel. Broken stones collected at our feet in a cold white crust, like strange snow in midsummer. I felt alone and very cold. Tom moved, then moaned.

Gray rainwater ran down the ditch in a torrent studded by floating hailstones like so many clouded fisheyes. The cornstalks we'd often squatted among, gnawing on stolen ears, lay threshed by the hail. Tom could see little of this without his glasses. Then lightning struck close by, and I was blinded, too. Through the flash behind my eyes I could hear the thunder banging nearer. I no longer worried about lightning. Though I knew this hollow tree had been struck in the past, nothing could get me out of there. My sight returned, but there was only gray. Over the thunder I heard the hail's tattoo on the cottonwood drum, and beneath that my own small voice, pleading for it to end.

Then, after a last punishing volley slipped past Tom's shield to strike me over the kidneys, where a slap hurts most, it did end. The hail faded into the summer storm that spawned it. Wind dropped; the nimbus died.

Soft rain began to fall, the kind we'd expected when the clouds sneaked up on that sultry afternoon. Final thunder thrummed across the eastern plain. The storm passed.

We clung to each other, reluctant to leave the hollow tree in case the hail came back. Slowly, along with the air outside, we were becalmed. Realizing where I was, I felt my old dread of spiders almost as relief. Normally they scared me half to death in such places. Here, scared much closer to death, I'd forgotten the spiders as I embraced the walls of our blessed den. The damp, off-sweet smell of the burned and rotting wood filled my nostrils and left a permanent brand of scent.

After a few more minutes it seemed safe to go. We uncoiled our stiff limbs and scrambled out of the hollow tree, through the skerried waves of toe-chilling nuggets, over to Sixth Avenue. There were no cars in sight. Hail covered the fields, the road, everything, in drifts and sheets, like a winterscape. For a moment it was easy to believe that everyone else was dead and we were the only survivors.

A farmer, out surveying his devastated fields, found us and took us to his home. We recognized the place as the last farm in the neighborhood, kitty-corner from the bulldozed mire of the future shopping center. Tom and I had often slipped across Sixth Avenue to play in DeLaney's barn, keeping an eye out for the farmer, who was sure to chase us off. But today Farmer DeLaney led us into his house, where his wife gave us cocoa and blankets, looked to our knots and welts, and called our mother. I heard her voice, delirious with relief.

Highway 93

Golden to Boulder

37. Golden / Clear Creek Canyon
from *Red Fenwick's West: Yesterday
and Today* by Robert W. "Red" Fenwick

*For almost forty years, Robert W. "Red" Fenwick was a feature writer
and columnist for* The Denver Post. *For much of his career, Fenwick represented the paper throughout its thirteen-state circulation as a reporter,
a columnist—he wrote a column called "Ridin' the Range"—and as a
general emissary. "From Montana to New Mexico, Red Fenwick was the
Post," said a remembrance in the paper shortly after his death in 1973.
His obituary described him as a "friend of children, cowboys, Indians,
rodeo, the US flag, hot-wire linemen, horses, dogs, yucca, and everything
American." He was an old school, roving reporter—found of tobacco and
Old Yellowstone whiskey—who sought out stories in the many nooks and
crannies of the Rocky Mountain region and wrote them down on whatever he had handy. "I covered a whole session of the Colorado legislature
once on a matchbook cover," he once said in an interview.*

*Born in Indiana and raised in Wyoming, he appreciated western sto-
rytellers wherever they were found. Mostly the stories he told were true,
but he also enjoyed a tall tale every now and then. He lets his readers
decide where the facts lie in the following story. Since there are as many
lost gold stories as there are mining regions in the west, maybe they
reflect some truth about the ore-digging experience. Surely the following
tale, since it took place up Clear Creek Canyon near Golden, home of the
Colorado School of Mines Orediggers, was one worth telling.*

The kid named Chester (Friday) Rogers jerked to a stop in half-stride, his
feet paralyzed by fright. A soggy beam of light from his carbide lamp
stabbed the blackness of the old cave and wavered as his hand shook. The
bobbing shadows of dripping stalactites danced crazily on the cavern wall.

What horrified Friday was the thing on the damp floor.

He had penetrated miles deep into the myriad corridors that honey-combed the mountain up Clear Creek Canyon. He had chalked his way in so he could find his way out. Now he wanted to run.

Suddenly, and as unexpectedly as death itself, the beam of light had fallen on the grotesque figure of an ancient and withered man sprawled incongruously on the floor of a subterranean room. Friday wished he hadn't played hooky that particular Friday—a practice which won him the nickname he carried to the grave not so very long ago.

The old man clawed at the beam of light as though it were a living thing. It seared his eyeballs. He squirmed in torture. Then suddenly he broke into a confusing gibberish.

"Don't let anybody get my gold!" he screamed. Then he leaped to his feet and with insane yells raced down one of the black corridors that led from the room.

After a moment, Friday followed—cautiously. His feet again came to a stop, this time at the brink of a bottomless pit that sliced across the floor of the cave. There was only silence below, beyond and all around.

Back in the big cavern Friday took stock of what had happened. In the big room were some scattered cooking utensils and tattered bedding. Apparently the ancient one had lived here many months—if not years.

Friday's light slowly circled the room, came to a halt on a narrow ledge. Back of a protecting rock nestled a row of small bulging sacks.

The boy's fingers groped along the shelf, caught at one of the sacks and pulled it down. It hit the floor with a heavy thud. The string came off and out spilled a king's ransom in gold nuggets.

Friday did a championship sprint toward the mouth of the cave. He stumbled and fell. He floundered into blind turns, lost his way several times but finally gained the shaft opening and half ran, half rolled down the mountainside toward his home in Golden.

Well, nobody believed his story. And Chester Rogers became the butt of many a joke. He returned to the cave eventually with a friend. But nowhere could he find the three corners in the cave where one shaft had led off to the rich cache.

Some folks said Friday just spun the yarn to get drinks at the bar. Some said he had taken one too many drinks and had imagined the whole thing.

But Carl Hall Hungness, who lives at 915 Illinois Street in Golden, recalled the 1890 incident not long ago, and undertook to locate the caves and the "lost cache of the mountain ghost."

He and a friend explored the mountainside and found the cave. For hours they poked through the seemingly endless caverns and passage-ways, but to no avail.

The mysterious caveman and his lost fortune in nuggets had vanished as completely as had Friday Rogers who had crossed the Great Divide, no doubt in continued search of the fabulous find.

But Hungness says any fortune seekers who care to brave a few rat-tlesnakes and fight off swarms of bats, can find adventure—and maybe sudden riches in the old caves now easily accessible by way of the new Clear Creek Canyon road.

The caves are just west of Golden, around the first bend in the high-way, past the first tunnel and just beyond the trickle of water from the mountainside.

Last one in this Sunday just doesn't hanker for hidden treasure.

38. Rocky Flats
from "Rocky Flats: Warring God Charnel Ground"
by Anne Waldman

Just east of Highway 93, in between Golden and Boulder, is the entrance to Rocky Flats, which was a major nuclear weapons production facility for almost forty years beginning in 1951. Workers at this factory complex produced hollow bomb cores out of plutonium and other materials, which were then shipped to a plant in Texas where they were encased in con-ventional explosives. When the plutonium core was detonated, it set off an even bigger explosion, and was therefore referred to as a "trigger." Use of the term "trigger," however, was misleading, since the trigger in this case was also a nuclear weapon capable of mass destruction.

Plutonium 239, a key element in the weapons produced at Rocky Flats, is dangerous in any quantity since it emits radiation. Making weapons was the mission here; environmental concerns regarding plutonium waste were secondary, especially during the plant's early years. Sometimes toxic materials were buried or inappropriately stored on-site. In 1992, several years after a raid by the EPA and the FBI, Rockwell International, the contractor at Rocky Flats, agreed to pay $18.5 million in fines for ten different environmental violations.

Although the production of weapons hasn't been an issue here since 1989 when the plant shut down, concerns over lingering environmental impacts and health hazards remain despite extensive clean-up efforts. Designation of the area as a National Wildlife Refuge does not eliminate those concerns, especially for activists like poet Anne Waldman who was arrested along with Allen Ginsberg, Daniel Ellsberg, and other anti-nuclear protesters at Rocky Flats back in the 1970s.

From the activist's perspective, challenging the corporate and military forces behind the nuclear mission at Rocky Flats was a David vs. Goliath kind of proposition, as Ginsberg expressed in his poem Nagasaki Days: "Cumulous clouds float across blue sky / over the white-walled Rockwell Corporation Factory—/ am I going to stop that?"

If the answer to Ginsberg's question is, "Well, I don't know, but at least I'm gonna try," then the next question is, "what then are you going to do?" If you are a poet/activist, like Anne Waldman or Allen Ginsberg, who believes in the power of language to shape culture and public discourse, you keep writing and speaking out and you encourage others to do the same. As founders of the writing and poetics program at the Naropa Institute (now Naropa University) in Boulder, that's what they did. In the following excerpt from an essay in Disembodied Poetics: Annals of the Jack Kerouac School, *Anne Waldman considers her own role as poet-citizen-activist, and her belief that a school like Naropa can play a part in supporting alternative voices.*

When it looked as if Rocky Flats was set to re-open its plutonium processing operation in Fall of 1991, (although its safety was being fiercely contested at the time, especially after the FBI raid), I attended a town meeting as mother, teacher, poet, citizen. Where I voiced my concerns and quoted from my then-10-year-old son Ambrose's list for ways to guard plutonium, how in fact to *cover it up.* "Get some Indians to come back and make some adobe with ash to cover it up. Let's cover plutonium with all the cigarettes in the world. Let's cover it with linoleum, congoleum. Let's cover plutonium with wood chips that beavers have made." There was something sweet in the boy's innocence, his thinking that there could be a realistic way to bury the monster. I cited cancer statistics, the fact that Boulder has one of the highest incidences of breast cancer in the States, and of prostate cancer in the state of Colorado. I invoked the opinions of reputable surgeons, including my own, who have said the truth about Rocky Flats operations' cancerous effects will emerge a decade from now, too late for the health of many local residents. That there is clear documentation of health risks and cancer statistics from former workers and residents in the area. That there are documentations & photographs of mutated animals born on nearby farms. Sheep with three legs and no hair. Just one example. I said all these things.

I was hissed and booed. The meeting was stacked with workers from the plant itself who made speeches justifying the reopening of the plutonium operations wing as a deterrent to war, as an "operation of peace," as needed more than ever after the war in the Middle East. There were testimonies about the plant providing a decent living for Americans who believed in god and their country. That Rocky Flats was a symbol of American democracy and prowess and dignity. That Rocky Flats had helped America "win the Cold War." My mind was spinning. What could I do as person working with words?

I want to be able to crack the code of language that separates us/me from the warmonger .... I write songs to "call out" the demons. I study lists of tactical weapons. The poems and songs I write live inside images of war and destruction on every level. They attempt to transmute— through language—the warring god realm. They also take me to the town meeting and to the edges of the mandala, which is a ring of fire on the one hand threatening all of space, and on the other burning up false mind views which threaten annihilation of the relative space—world. I conjure the holy fire, the sacred *chandali* in which one throws all past conceptions: god, mother-country, lover, tomahawk cruise missiles, depth/strike bombs. Give up grasping, give up hope, then wake to the dangers to our fleshly bodies and body-planet.... .

Watching and waiting. Articulate the fear, it's a given. It's already happened, Rocky Flats, spurred on by Pentagon directive paranoia....We created this poetics school [at Naropa] as an antidote, an antithesis to the going concerns....In the gap of the flames you might find an empty luminous nuclear-free world, humming with beautiful fierce sounds out of which you take your stand, make your poem.

May all beings enjoy profound, brilliant glory.

39. Eldorado Canyon
from *Everything that Matters: Remembering Rock Climbing* by Pat Ament

In Eldorado Canyon just south of Boulder, some of the finest rock along the Front Range attracts climbers from all over the world. Many of these climbers come to test their skills on various routes and classic climbs that others have established over the years on "Eldo's" towering sandstone walls and cliffs. Others prefer a more informal and out-of-the way experience on any number of boulders in the area where climbers can hone their free-climbing techniques.

In the late 1950s and early 1960s, the first wave of technical climbers began to explore the canyon's possibilities. Artist, musician, and writer Pat Ament was an enthusiastic young climber at that time. Building on skills he had developed as a University of Colorado gymnast, he was known for his climbing prowess. For Royal Robbins, a legendary big wall climber from Yosemite who was visiting the Boulder area, Pat Ament was an enthusiastic and helpful contact who knew all the local climbing routes. In the following excerpt from Everything That Matters, *one of the many books Ament later wrote about climbing (including a biography of Royal Robbins), he describes one of the climbs they did together, a classic route up Eldorado Canyon known as the Yellow Spur. As is often the case for climbers, bonds of friendship*

that develop in the process of climbing are just as important, even more
so in this case, than the ascent itself.

In Eldorado, on the Yellow Spur that visit, he ascended free up vertical
and yellow sandstone, clipped his rope through bent and rusted pitons
still in place from early aid ascents. Those pitons were the pliant,
European kind, a mystery in each we sensed by simply touching it. He
used the rock's small edges for the tips of fingers, pinched a crystal
knob, and set two fingers in a slot. He used a flake, to take him upward.
Suddenly he stopped and looked at me, directly downward underneath
his heels, where I stood belaying. I was on a stance four hundred feet
above the tops of the pines, a wonderful exposure. He inquired as to
where the hard part was. He'd done it, I informed him.

Always will I view the Yellow Spur as where I made an early free
ascent with Royal Robbins up a gorgeous yellow wall of Eldorado rock,
with tints of red and lichen green. It's not nostalgia when I say I'll never
see that yellow rock so rich again, so bright, as when my friend in knee-
length shorts, a T-shirt, white, and wearing Spiders, walked up vertical,
not knowing it was difficult. And how was it that I should be with him,
the soul a host of people thought the world's best?!

A sense that it was right for us to be a friendship went with us that
afternoon, a day so splendid it seemed dedicated absolutely in its bright-
ness to the cause. I stroll through Eldorado any afternoon and look above
to where a straight-up wall of yellow, facing west, is tapered to a pointed
summit at the highest realm of anywhere—at friendship.

Sun will set a million times and send that yellow wall through shades
of orange and purple, dark and gray in morning, windblown, back to red
and yellow in the afternoon. The snow will cover it in winter, blow across
its edges. Long contentions will be born and die away among the jealous
and competitive, but spring and silence on the *Yellow Spur* are beautiful, the
sandstone startled by a downpour. Flakes will drip. A rainbow will be there,
as though it were the Eldorado rock itself. The summer will arrive again,
a raven's plumage lifted by the air, a freight train coming out a mountain
tunnel to the south, an elegance of yellow, Royal freely running up its holds.

40. Boulder
from *Dreams from Bunker Hill* by John Fante

*A writer's sense of vocation sometimes comes in fits and starts, as is
the case for Arturo Bandini, a character in the novels of John Fante.
Bandini, who is widely understood to be Fante's alter ego, is a University
of Colorado dropout drifting from one meaningless job to another when
he visits a library and finds a book that inspires him to become a writer.
Bandini's story echoes the author's real-life experience: Fante dropped
out of CU in 1929 and subsequently moved to California in pursuit of a
writing career.*

    *There, in addition to his later accomplishments as a screenwriter,
Fante wrote a series of novels featuring Arturo Bandini, which came to
be known as the "Bandini quartet." In these books he often revisits the
themes of poverty, Catholicism, and growing up in an Italian American
family, all of which Fante experienced during his formative years in
Denver and Boulder. The following excerpt is taken from the last volume
of the "Bandini quartet," a novel called* Dreams from Bunker Hill, *which
Fante dictated to his wife toward the end of his life, a remarkably productive life by any measure, but especially so given his struggles with diabetes
and related health issues.*

    *Sometimes all it takes is one book to change a life. For Arturo
Bandini (and perhaps John Fante), that book was* Winesburg, Ohio
*by Sherwood Anderson, a group of related short stories about a small
midwestern town and its inhabitants.*

During my second year at the university I fell in love with a girl who
worked in a clothing store. Her name was Agnes, and I wanted to marry
her. She moved to North Platte, Nebraska, for a better job, and I quit
the university to be near her. I hitchhiked from Boulder to North Platte
and arrived dusty and broke and triumphant at the rooming house where
Agnes lived. We sat on the porch swing and she was not glad to see me.

    "I don't want to marry you," she said. "I don't want to see you any-
more. That's why I'm here, so we don't see each other."

    "I'll get a job," I insisted. "We'll have a family."

"Oh for Christ's sake."

"Don't you want a family? Don't you like kids?"

She got quickly to her feet. "Go home, Arturo. Please go home. Don't think about me anymore. Go back to school. Learn something." She was crying.

"I can lay brick," I said, moving to her. She threw her arms around me, and planted a wet kiss on my cheek, then pushed me away.

"Go home, Arturo. Please." She went inside and closed the door.

I walked down to the railroad tracks and swung aboard a freight train bound for Denver. From there I took another freight to Boulder and home. The next day I went to the job where my father was laying brick.

"I want to talk to you," I said. He came down from the scaffold and walked to a pile of lumber.

"What's the matter?" he said.

"I quit school."

"Why?"

"I'm not cut out for it."

His face twisted bitterly. "What are you going to do now?"

"I don't know. I haven't figured it out."

"Jesus, you're crazy."

I became a bum in my home town. I loafed around. I took a job pulling weeds, but it was hard and I quit. Another job, washing window. I barely got through it. I looked all over Boulder for work, but the streets were full of young, unemployed men. The only job in town was delivering newspapers. It paid fifty cents a day. I turned it down. I leaned against walls in the pool halls. I stayed away from home. I was ashamed to eat the food my father and mother provided. I always waited until my father walked out. My mother tried to cheer me. She made me pecan pie and ravioli.

"Don't worry," she said. "You wait and see. Something will happen. It's in my prayers."

I went to the library. I looked at the magazines, at the pictures in them. One day I went to the bookshelves, and pulled out a book. It was *Winesburg, Ohio*. I sat at a long mahogany table and began to read. All at once my world turned over. The sky fell in. The book held me. The tears came. My heart beat fast. I read until my eyes burned. I took the book home. I read another Anderson. I read and I read, and I was heartsick and lonely and in love with a book, many books, until it came naturally, and I sat there with a pencil and a long tablet, and tried to write, until I felt I could not go on because the words would not come as they did in Anderson, they only came like drops of blood from my heart.

41. Boulder / Boulder Creek Canyon
from *Wandering Time: Western Notebooks*
by Luis Alberto Urrea

Boulder is an active urban community adjacent to great swaths of public land. Trails throughout the foothills, canyons, and out toward the plains offer a temporary habitat for hikers, climbers, runners, and cyclists. The place is humming with humans propelling themselves, in one form or another, through the many open spaces and natural areas that surround the city.

While poet and widely acclaimed author Luis Alberto Urrea was going to graduate school at the University of Colorado, he made himself at home on the trail up Boulder Creek Canyon. Saunters up the canyon opened the way into a sense of belonging, even relatedness, with creek, canyon, and the mountains further west. Urrea's book Wandering Time: Western Notebooks, *is a collection of prose and poetry that highlights some of the people and places he came to appreciate while living and traveling in the West. In the following description of Boulder Creek Canyon, he evokes a favorite place that became a welcoming companion.*

Maniac rock climbers across the creek are splayed on the walls like colorful bugs. Magnificence everywhere. The climbers' colors in the fall sun are flavorful against the rock.

Elsewhere in the Boulder Creek News: a tree trunk has made its way down the Front Range, on its journey to the South Platte and the high plains. It has come to rest here, at my own resting place. Stripped of branches and bark, and buffed, planed and sanded by its journey, it's as sleek as a baseball bat. It lies in icy water waiting for the next flood to move it down to the small rapids as the creek turns to cut through Boulder. There, it might make a small dam for a while. It might even freeze in place, ice gluing it to the rocks where eddies are mild enough. Small bass and trout might creep into its shadow and grow dense and slumber through the winter. But spring is surely coming, and when the melt and runoff hit, the whole thing will be resting outside the Boulder library. A new condo for literary fish.

It's funny how a place, in this case a trail, becomes your companion. How spots all along it become familiar, then become friends. As though the footpath were a live thing. From the parking lots in town, to the cliffs at Elephant Rock or Lover's Leap, to the oaks and the pines, the bridges, the small waterfalls. I love them all, and I enjoy sharing them. Everyone who comes here is a generous lover. And the mountain knows it's always our birthday when we come, and it offers us each a brightly wrapped gift. Bright as foil paper. These gifts are personal, and hard to explain.

For example, how would I describe the fluttering dappled surface of this page as I write? If I wanted to tell my distant friends about it, I would have to bring them to this flat rock, on this day, at this time of the afternoon. They probably should be tired. I'd have to open a book to a blank page, wait for a cloud to pass, a beam of autumn sun to slant down through the leaves, and a breeze to set those leaves dancing so their color smears across the sunbeam as their shadows interrupt it. Then I could say: "Behold."

The page itself comes alive. The constant *Sss* of the water sounds like the paper is singing. How can you write that?

42. Boulder / Foothills
from *The Four-Cornered Falcon* by Reg Saner

Living on the edge of Front Range wildlands, not to mention thousands of acres of public open space at the base of the mountains, Boulder residents share their habitat with a variety of four-legged neighbors including black bears, mountain lions, elk, mule deer, and coyotes to name a few. In 2017, the city passed an ordinance that requires trash and curbside compost to be secured in bear proof containers at all times. Certain rules and regulations are necessary for human and non-human residents to co-exist harmoniously. The presence of various four-legged neighbors can be a reminder that community, in an ecological sense, is bigger than its human component.

Reg Saner, long time professor at the University of Colorado and former poet laureate of Boulder, is reminded of that in the following excerpt from his book, The Four-Cornered Falcon. *In the* New Boston Review, *writer and editor Nicholas Bromell describes Saner as "a meditative and philosophical poet concerned with the good old questions— why are we here? where are we going?—and with finding a language for them in the elements, in earth, air, fire, and water." Related queries, which Saner has explored throughout his long writing career, include where and how do we belong? As he suggests in the following piece, one's four-legged neighbors occasionally offer some perspective.*

When I step out our side door, the U.S. Geological Survey tells me that my foot comes down 5,640 feet above sea level. This morning, strolling upslope through grama grass, gumweed, and long-stemmed kobresia on our backyard mesa, toward my personal shelf and lichened slab of sandstone, I need every lug on my bootsoles. The icy uphill trail is newly powdered with six inches of snow, that snow lightly flecked with blood. Some coyote with a cut paw, most likely crystalized by the snow almost instantly, that blood hasn't oxidized to somber red, but it is still a bright scarlet against the white.

"My" shelf? "My" slab? Other mornings, yes; this morning no. What with the ice, I look up only on arrival—where exactly atop my spot lounges a yearling buck, ruminating. I mean literally ruminating, chewing his cud with that sideways grinding of the back molars that reduces silica-laden browse to mush. Enzymed and twice-chewed roughages thus become stuff a mule deer stomach can dissolve.

It's a free greenbelt (gone late-November brown), so how can I complain? But one of my eccentricities is dawn: my Book of Hours, ascent of the heart. By walking a full 120 seconds or so, southwest up the mesa footpath near my door, I can enjoy the panoramic sweep of Colorado's high plain—treeless, unbroken—over which the sun will soon rise, nothing between us. I like that. Enormously. To watch the sun rise that way, out of the sleep of matter, from the sea or up out of the ground, is to stand in the middle of the world.

So I wake, drink *cafelatte* by the quart, read a bit, then go out—often puzzled by the emptiness of our streets, their dark houses; as if each person abed were certain dawn would happen again.

"It always has, hasn't it?" Yes. Which may be why I think of dawns that'll happen without me. I think, too, of blind chance, its accidental filaments fine as root hairs that have grown someone named "me" to be part of dawn's moment. So I've dressed and stepped forth into morning twilight: my "self," a movable circuitry of Here, Now, This ... with those inveterate escapes into Elsewhere that create our true nature.

The view-thief who's taken my place isn't human, probably cares little for panorama, except insofar as openness gives stalking coyotes and mountain lions a tougher assignment. His head wears yearling spikes, two; which will recur, annually augmented till he has the full rack of a mature eight-point buck. Just now, however, his eight-inch antlers look as silly as a boy-man's fuzz moustache.

He heard and saw me coming, but he hasn't budged. Typical. Our Boulder deer have grown so domestic they all but eat the cat food, and this yearling "spike" is a mule deer of true Boulder greenbelt breed. I close to within fifteen feet, then twelve, then less than ten, expecting at every step he'll up and leave. Oh no. He ruminates; he looks me straight in the eye— as if saying, "First come, first served. Take it on up the trail, Buster.

On the trail I take it—another forty feet, and make a stand. While waiting for the sun's glint to break the rim of our vast Colorado plain, I suddenly notice the young buck has a friend. Ten yards south of him, near "my" stunted Ponderosa and some mullein stalks poking up chest high through blue snow, lies a young female, nonchalant as he. Though it irks me a bit not to await dawn from my ritual spot, the usurper is after all a deer. Two deer. Whose lithe and silent kind roved the mesa centuries before Columbus. *I* am grumbling at *them*?

Interstate 25 North (Part 2)
Longmont to Wellington

43. Longmont
from *On the Road* by Jack Kerouac

Driving west into Colorado for the first time, there's nothing quite like seeing the snow-capped Rockies off in the distance: "Wait, are those clouds? If they are, they haven't moved for a while ... Could it be? I think maybe ... Yes they are ... that has to be them ... and aren't they something? ... and don't I want to get there as fast as I can!"

Sal Paradise, Jack Kerouac's narrator in On the Road, *wakes up in a bus station, walks outside and describes his experience: "And there in the blue air, I saw for the first time, far off, the great snowy tops of the Rocky Mountains. I took a deep breath. I had to get to Denver at once."*

Those of us who drive west after that first sighting might be forgiven if we put a little more pedal to the metal. In Kerouac's epic road story, Sal Paradise didn't have that choice; he was hitchhiking, and on top of that he was feeling a little queasy from the altitude, or was it the hangover? Maybe it was both. Still, he didn't waste any time and was out on the highway after a quick breakfast. By the time he got to Longmont, he was beginning to feel human again.

It was beautiful in Longmont. Under a tremendous old tree was a bed of green lawn-grass belonging to a gas station. I asked the attendant if I could sleep there, and he said sure; so I stretched out a wool shirt, laid my face flat on it, with an elbow out, and one eye cocked at the snowy Rockies in the hot sun for just a moment. I fell asleep for two delicious hours, the only discomfort being an occasional Colorado ant. And here I am in Colorado! I kept thinking gleefully. Damn! damn! damn! I'm making it! And after a refreshing sleep filled with cobwebby dreams of my past life in the East I got up, washed in the station men's room, and strode off, fit and slick as a fiddle, and got me a rich thick milkshake at the roadhouse to put some freeze in my hot, tormented stomach.

Incidentally, a very beautiful Colorado gal shook me that cream; she was all smiles too; I was grateful, it made up for last night. I said to myself, Wow! What'll *Denver* be like! I got on that hot road, and off I went in a brand-new car driven by a Denver businessman of about thirty-five. He went seventy. I tingled all over; I counted minutes and subtracted miles. Just ahead, over the rolling wheatfields all golden beneath the distant snows of Estes, I'd be seeing old Denver at last. I pictured myself in a Denver bar that night, with all the gang, and in their eyes I would be strange and ragged and like the Prophet who has walked across the land to bring the dark Word, and the only Word I had was "Wow!" The man and I had a long, warm conversation about our respective schemes in life, and before I knew it we were going over the wholesale fruit markets outside Denver; there were smokestacks, smoke, railyards, red-brick buildings, and the distant downtown graystone buildings, and here I was in Denver. He let me off at Larimer Street. I stumbled along with the most wicked grin of joy in the world, among the old bums and beat cowboys of Larimer Street.

44. Greeley
from *An Overland Journey* by Horace Greeley

"Fly, scatter through the country—go to the Great West," wrote Horace Greeley in 1837. Greeley was the founding publisher and editor of the New York Tribune, *an influential platform from which he preached a gospel of reform. It was a utopian gospel based on agrarian and communitarian ideals, and the West, it seemed to him, offered a geography where those ideals might take root. He was still preaching that message in 1872: "I hold that tens of thousands, who are now barely holding on at the East, might thus place themselves on the high road to competence and ultimate independence in the West."*

Though he may not have been the first person to utter the phrase "Go west, young man," no one popularized the message more than Greeley. Nathan Meeker, one of the reporters on Greeley's Tribune

staff went out west on assignment in the late 1860s and returned with
the idea of starting an agricultural colony—an idea that his boss
wholeheartedly supported. Greeley helped Meeker develop the plan,
backed him financially, and helped him promote the new venture. But
Greeley was only a participant from afar. His travels out west were
mostly limited to the trip he took during the Colorado gold rush in 1859,
an adventure that he wrote about in An Overland Journey. *Here is an*
excerpt from that book which describes his experience of crossing the
Cache La Poudre River, more than a decade before Meeker and his
gang of colonists established the Union Colony, the predecessor of the
community we now know as Greeley, in that same area.

Pushing on steadily over a reasonably level country, though crossed
by many deep and steep-banked dry gullies, and perhaps one petty
living stream, we stood at 5 PM...seventy miles from Denver...on the
south bank of the Cache-la-Poudre...by far the most formidable stream
between the South Platte and the Laramie. Our conductor was as brave
a mountaineer as need be, but he was wary as well, and had seen so
many people drowned in fording such streams, especially the Green
River branch of the Colorado, on which he spent a year or two, that
he chose to feel his way carefully. So he waited and observed for an
hour or more, meantime sending to word to an old French mountaineer
friend from Utah, who has pitched his tent here, that his help was
wanted. There had been a ferry-boat at this crossing till two nights
before, when it went down stream, and had not been since heard of.
A horseman we met some miles below, assured us that there was no
crossing; but this we found a mistake—two men mounted on strong
horses crossing safely before our eyes, and two heavy laden ox wagons
succeeding them in doing the same, save that one of them stuck in the
stream, and the oxen had to be taken off and driven out, being unable to
pull it while...half buried in the swift current. But these crossings were
made from the other side, where the entrance was better and the current
rather favored the passage; the ox-wagons were held to the bottom by
the weight of their loads, while our "ambulance" was light, and likely
to be swept downstream.

At length our French friend appeared, mounted on a powerful horse, with an Indian attendant on another such. He advised us to stay where we were for the night, promising to come along in the morning with a heavy ox team and help us over. As this, however, involved a loss of at least ten miles on our next day's drive, our conductor resolved to make an attempt now. So the Frenchman on his strong horse took one of our lead-mules by the halter and the Indian took the other, and we went in, barely escaping an upset from going down the bank obliquely, and thus throwing one side of our wagon much above the other; but we righted in a moment and went through—the water being at least three feet deep for about a hundred yards, the bottom broken by bowlders, and the current very strong. We camped so soon as fairly over, lit a fire, and having obtained a quarter of an antelope from our French friend, proceeded to prepare [it] and discuss...the relative merits of certain meats, of which I give the substance for the benefit of future travelers through this wild region....

Buffalo I found to be a general favorite, though my own experience of it makes it a tough, dry, wooden fiber, only to be eaten under great provocation. I infer that it is poorer in spring than at other seasons, and that I have not been fortunate in cooks. Bear, I was surprised to learn, is not generally liked by mountaineers—my companions had eaten every species, and were not pleased with any. The black-tailed deer of the mountains is a general favorite; so is the mountain hen or grouse; so is the antelope of course; the elk and mountain sheep less decidedly so. None of our party like horse, or knew any way of cooking it that would make it really palatable, though of course it has to be eaten occasionally, for necessity hath no law—or rather, is its own law. Our conductor had eaten broiled wolf, under compulsion, but could not recommend it; but he certified that a slice of cold boiled dog—well boiled, so as to free it from rankness, and then suffered to cool thoroughly—is tender, sweet and delicate as lamb. I ought to have ascertained the species and age of the dog in whose behalf this testimony was borne—for a young Newfoundland or King Charles might justify the praise, while it would be utterly unwarranted in the case of an old cur or mastiff—but the opportunity was lost, and I can only give the testimony as I received it....

The antelope ham was fresh, fat, and tender; and it must have weighed less by three pounds when that supper was ended....

45. Greeley
James Michener on writing *Centennial*

*In 1936, James Michener accepted a position as director of Social
Studies at the Colorado State College of Education (later to become the
University of Northern Colorado) in Greeley. During his time in that
position, he traveled extensively in the area, often in the company of
his friend Floyd Merrill who was the editor of the* Greeley Tribune. *A
collection of the photos he took on those field trips reveals his interest
in topics like dryland farming and rural life in Colorado, which later
became important elements in his best-selling book* Centennial, *as did
the region's mountains, rivers, and prairies.*

*Even after Michener moved on from Colorado several years later,
his experiences of the place continued to resonate. His first attempt
at a novel set in the West was called "Jefferson," which was also his
fictional name for the state of Colorado. The story, according to his
outline, was meant to evoke the same era, 1936-38, and the same
places he had experienced. Livermore, his fictional setting, was based
on Greeley. Drawing from firsthand knowledge as an educator in the
region, he wanted to tell his story from a schoolteacher's perspective.*

*As it turned out, that first western novel never came to fruition,
at least not in its original form. He only wrote a hundred pages before he abandoned the manuscript and moved on to other projects.
Nevertheless, he still felt a strong connection to northern Colorado,
a connection that eventually led him back to a western story set in
the area—a much bigger story, as it turned out, than the one he had
originally intended.*

Centennial, *which eventually became a bestseller and a television
mini-series, was a massive project, undertaken in part to celebrate the
US Bicentennial. The novel begins with the region's geological origins
and encompasses all the historical eras that follow well into the twentieth century, exploring along the way many of the topics and themes—
the plains, the lives of rural women, dryland farms and those who
worked them—which he had initially considered in "Jefferson." In the*

following quote from his notes on the making of Centennial, *Michener returns to his initial experience living in Greeley where, as he put it, "he grew up spiritually, emotionally, and intellectually."*

In 1972, when I started the actual writing of *Centennial*, I had already lived with the Platte River for thirty-six years, and I wanted all men and women who read my account of its wandering across the plains to become as familiar with it as I was. The mountains had been my associates for three decades, and they would be characters in any story I elected to tell. Especially the prairie, reaching to the horizon in all quarters, had been an object of love, and I intended to write of it in that way. These were the components of a tremendous universe, one that I wanted every reader to share. I wanted the west that I would be writing about to be real, and to achieve this, the reader had to follow the trails I had followed to see the land as I had seen it.

46. Keota
James Michener on Keota

According to John Kings, who wrote about his travels through Colorado with James Michener, the author of Centennial *was especially enamored of three places in this part of the West: Fort Laramie in eastern Wyoming which, as an important trading post, fort, and diplomatic center on the Oregon Trail, and later a faithfully restored historic landmark, offered the writer many insights; Keota, at the time, a mostly abandoned townsite northeast of Greeley that spoke to the dreams and disappointments of those who inhabited the region; and the Satire Lounge in Denver, Michener's favorite haunt for good Mexican food,.*

Keota, due in part to the pathos inherent in the ruins of any prairie town, tugged on Michener's emotions. As a young educator, Michener had come to the Keota school for a classroom visit in the late 1930s. When he came back three decades later to research Centennial, *the school was still standing, but the windows were broken and the students were gone. "Only one thing still functioned," Michener wrote later, and*

that was "the ancient post office .... As I pushed open the creaking door,
the bell jangled, as it had been doing for half a century. A wispy old man
stepped forward to greet us, unusually bright of eye and witty of speech."

That was Clyde Stanley, one of only a few old timers who still
lived in Keota when Michener returned. Once a newspaper owner and
general store proprietor and now the postmaster, Stanley had seen
Keota when agriculture was booming during World War I and he had
seen it through the bust of the Great Depression and the Dust Bowl
years. Michener enjoyed long conversations with Stanley, whose affec-
tion for the town of Keota had not diminished, it seemed, even though
the population had. The author admired Stanley's resilience and good
cheer and created Walter Bellamy, the land commissioner character in
Centennial, with him in mind.

The town of Line Camp in Centennial was largely based on Keota,
which epitomized, for Michener, the ups and downs experienced by
prairie dwellers in the 1920s and 30s. In the following quote, which
appears in a chapter called "November Elegy," he captures the town
well into its demise:

"And worst of all, where were the homes that had been so painstakingly
built, so painfully sustained during the years of drought? They were
gone, vanished down to the building blocks of the cellars. A town which
had a newspaper and a dozen flourishing stores had completely disappeared. Only the mournful ruins of hope remained and over those ruins
flew the hawks of autumn."

47. Wellington
from "Wellington's Trial by Blizzard" by Bill Hosokawa

In 1942, author and journalist Bill Hosokawa was relocated, along with
his family and many other Japanese Americans during the World War
II years, into an internment camp. Shortly after he was released from
the Heart Mountain Relocation Center in Wyoming (where he edited a
camp newspaper), he took a job with the Denver Post, where he worked

as a reporter, columnist, and editor for thirty-eight years. He also published several novels including Nisei: The Quiet Americans, *which describes the experiences of second-generation Japanese Americans.*

On January 2, 1949, one of the worst blizzards of the twentieth cen-tury swept through Wellington, Colorado, which at the time had a pop-ulation of 580 citizens and was the only town on a fifty-six mile stretch of highway between Fort Collins and Cheyenne, Wyoming. Residents of Wellington rallied to rescue stranded motorists up and down the high-way and cared for 125 travelers from fifteen states. Bill Hosokawa later wrote about their efforts in an article for Empire Magazine, *the* Denver Post's *Sunday magazine.*

Within a few minutes nearly a dozen men—heavily clothed, tight-lipped and grim-faced—had slipped into Charlie's place.

One of them was asked what his wife had said about his venturing out.

"She didn't want me to go," he replied. "But I asked what she'd want the boys to do if I was out there on the hill. Then she said: 'You go ahead.' Here I am."

Some days after this episode Charlie Thompson made a remark that explains this rapid, informal mobilization. He said: "There was a job to do, so we went ahead on our own hook and done it." As simple as that.

Dan Gregory's truck led the way. The first few miles were easy. Then the caravan met the full rage of the blizzard screaming unimpeded across the treeless prairie, flinging snow with sandblast force. Headlight beams bounced off this dancing, racing, shrieking wall of wind and snowflakes and diffused quickly into the night's frigid void. At twenty yards the headlights were invisible. The cars crawled forward, the truck in the lead and the sedan clinging desperately to its taillight.

After a while Gregory gave up trying to see through the windshield. He propped his door open, crouched in its shelter on the running board, and steered by looking straight down at the white line along the center of the wind-swept highway. When he lost that line he'd stop and walk around until he located it again.

The first stalled car was a station wagon with a lone woman in it. They picked her up, numb with cold and fear, and put her in the sedan.

A short distance farther on was another car stuck fast in a drift. Working more by feel than sight, Gregory pulled the car free and it was sent on to Wellington with the woman.

Fifteen miles north of Wellington a drift blocked the road completely. It was impossible to tell how long the drift was, or how many cars were in its frozen grip. Head down, gasping for breath, the rescuers tumbled out of their car and into the storm. The feeble glow of flashlights picked out several automobiles up to their hoods in wind-packed snow. There was no hope of digging them free while the wind continued.

But now the rescuers themselves were in trouble. Snow was driving through the radiators of both truck and sedan and melting. Ignition wires became wet, shorted out. Motors coughed, barely limped along on two and three cylinders. They might conk out for good at any moment.

While the drivers nursed their choking motors the others struggled from car to car, hammering on windows and shouting encouragement. To their amazement they found the strandees in good condition—cold, cramped, and hungry, but in no immediate danger.

It was obvious the rescuers could gain nothing by staying at the drift. If they delayed much longer they, too, would be marooned. The three strandees suffering most were helped to the rescue car and the others were left with the promise of aid as soon as possible.

Harmon Wich was still missing. Leo Tolle and his family hadn't been located either. They might be out somewhere in the white wilderness. They might have taken shelter at some isolated ranch house.

But now only the truck was running. Dan Gregory passed a tow chain to the sedan and started slowly back to Wellington with his motor sputtering fitfully under the double load—a weary, half-frozen cavalcade. It was 2 a.m. when they pulled up in front of Charlie's Inn.

Within an hour a second rescue party was on its way up the hill. This time it was better equipped, although many of the men on the first trip went back up again. Al Groth, the feed dealer, brought along his two six-by-six war surplus trucks. The highway department truck headquartered in Wellington, its ignition system protected by hastily improvised inner-tube rubber, was also pressed into service.

Dawn brought no respite for the rescuers. Gusts of wind blew an estimated sixty miles an hour and the snow drifted in as quickly as a shovelful was moved. The wind and flying snow would make eyes water, Bob Eyestone recalled afterward, and in a few moments they would freeze shut. Breathing was an effort. Ice formed in the nostrils and it felt as if a man's lungs would freeze.

It took until noon to reach the end of the drift, which was a quarter mile long. Fifteen cars were stuck in it. One sedan had nine persons, including a six-week-old infant, and a dog in it. Harmon Wich and his son were among those in the drift.

Later one of the rescued said: "I never heard sweeter words than when somebody knocked on the frosted window and said: 'Are you all right? We'll be back for you.' "

As rapidly as possible the stranded cars were emptied, and the occupants, some chattering with cold, were bundled up and sent back to town.

Wellington meanwhile was preparing for trouble. Word gets around rapidly in a small community. An emergency station was set up at the American Legion Hall. Women who only a year earlier had taken a first-aid course manned a receiving depot. The jail was stripped of pads to be used for mattresses. A mattress from the fire station was moved to the hall. Cots were set up. Other women brought in wool blankets and sheets. There had been no word from the second rescue party and the town was prepared for the worst.

The rescued responded quickly to the spirit of Wellington. Those who needed only food and warmth to revive them soon were bustling around helping others. There was always need for another pair of hands to help with the foot-rubbing.

Charlie Thompson says, "There wasn't a home in town that had space that didn't call in and offer a bed."

Mrs. Havens put it another way: "We gave everything we had – time, food, and housing. Whoever had it gave it."

THE FIRST WAVE

For highway travelers headed west, the first wave of the Rocky Mountains may look like distant clouds when it first appears on the horizon. For earlier travelers on the South Platte or Smoky Hill trails laboring west across the Great Plains, snowy peaks under western skies would have been a welcome sight. For those who were already here, these mountains centered the world. Pikes Peak was known as "Tava" or "sun mountain" to the Tabeguache band of the Ute tribe, whose creation story revolved around this prominent landmark. The Arapahoe, who came into this region later on, had a similar reverence for mountains, especially those in the vicinity of what is now Rocky Mountain National Park. They referred to Longs Peak and nearby Mount Meeker as "Nesótaieux" or the two guides. For residents of Colorado's corridor country, mountains define the western horizon. The Front Range begins in the Medicine Bow and Laramie Ranges in Wyoming and runs south to the Pikes Peak massif. Further south, the Wet Mountains, the Spanish Peaks, and the Sangre de Cristos, though they are geologically distinct, continue the north-south wave of mountain terrain that separates the plains from the high country. For travelers and residents alike, mountains, once they are visible, dominate the map.

Highway 160

Walsenburg to La Veta

48. Walsenberg / La Veta
from *Spanish Peaks: Land and Legend*
by Conger Beasley Jr.

The two mountains that we know of as the Spanish Peaks have been land-marks in this region for a long time, as suggested by the following list of spellings, descriptions, and definitions: Wahatoya (Breasts of the World), Huatolla, Huajatolla, Guajatolla, Los Juajatoyas, Wah-to-yah, Las Cumbres Espanolas (the Spanish Peaks), Dos Hermanos (Two Brothers), Twin Peaks, Siamese Peaks, Double Mountain, Dream Mountain, Los Tetones, Mamas del Mundo. As they once were for native hunters as well as immigrants headed west on the Santa Fe Trail, these two mountains are a focal point that orients both locals and travelers.

In his book Spanish Peaks: Land and Legends, *Conger Beasley invites residents of the region to share their impressions of these two mountains: "Scratch a person who's lived awhile around the peaks and you'll uncover stories of strange sightings and curious phenomena: clouds lingering on certain cliffs; lighting striking the same location; wreaths of Saint Elmo's fire curling across the rocks; puzzling air currents that flow when they should ebb; places at the foot of certain buttes infested with rattlesnakes, which some people regard as portals to parallel universes." One longtime resident had this to say: "There's something about these peaks, the two of them standing together, distant and austere. They belong to this world, and they don't. They're aloof and remote, mysterious and strange. They attract all kinds of energy and give back plenty of their own."*

For Beasley, they were hard to resist. Here, he describes a closer encounter.

Later that afternoon I climbed a steep trail leading up to the saddle between the peaks. I was after something, and it wasn't until about an hour later, blowing and puffing, that I realized what it was. I was looking for that midway point between high country and low, between the steepness of the mountains and the gentle, easy glide of the plains. That spot where vertical and horizontal intersect to form an axis that includes the four cardinal directions; a fulcrum of sorts, where I could pause in comfortable repose....

I had the trail to myself, and in slow, plodding steps I mounted higher and higher toward the saddle. The silence was soothing. Yellow leaves from shedding aspens fluttered to the ground. Squirrels dashed across the duff and litter. Piñon jays swooped from tree to tree. At one point I felt a pair of eyes on me, but that may have been my own paranoia. "Who's out there? Who's watching?" Maybe it was a bear checking me out. "Hello, bear. I mean no harm. I'm looking to dance on the head of a pin between mountains and plains."

The steepness of the climb slowed my pace, and two hours into it I realized I was still a long way from the saddle. The light was failing, and I didn't want to be up there in the dark with no food or overnight equipment, so I tore back down the trail, sliding and skating on the loose pebbles and sticks with all the finesse of a trash can rolling down an alley.

"Double mountains aren't that common in the world. At least those rising from a shared foundation. Spanish Peaks ... Janus-faced ... not so much contrasting as complementing the identity of the other. Filling out and augmenting. What if one should take a notion to sail off into space, would the other follow? And what would it look like if it were left alone? We can't conceive of one without the other. Their identities depend upon the presence of the other. In contrast to east peak, west peak looks bigger. In contrast to west peak, east peak is more delicately molded. East peak generates the most legends. West peak attracts more hikers. Their twiceness engenders a cosmos. Together they encompass a world. Singly they replicate little more than their own singularity. In tandem they conflate a universe."

I made these notes in the car after crashing down the Wahatoya
Trail, slipping and falling, sprawling on my side, scraping the heel of
my right hand. Gravity propelling me in a pathetic simulacrum of flight.
Subverting the point of equipoise I had climbed so far to attain.

Highway 69
Walsenburg to Westcliffe

49. Gardner
from *Huerfano* by Roberta Price

In the spirit of Drop City, an experimental art colony founded by some university students near Trinidad in 1965, another alternative community known as Libre took root near Gardner in 1968. As Nelson Holmes writes in the Huerfano World Journal, *the name Libre (Spanish for "free") set the tone for this social experiment. "Those wishing to commit to life at Libre had to make their intentions known to a full council of the residents who would vote on their petition. Each communard would, after approval of their commitment, be responsible for the construction of their own home and the organization of their own lives. In essence Libre was a community of self-sufficient equals engaged in a passionate and altruistic cultivation of both community and the artistic self."*

As Libre was getting established, so too were similar alternative communities in northern New Mexico and southern Colorado. In 1969, Roberta Price, a PhD student at the State University of New York, was awarded a travel grant to come out west and document some of these communities. Unlike other reporters and photographers who only came to Libre for a brief visit, Price stayed on for seven years. In the book Huerfano, *she describes her life there. Here, she tells the story of an awkward situation with some less "experimentally inclined" locals that apparently had a happy, if not giddy, ending.*

I've been craving a donut with my morning coffee. When you get cravings up here, you can't run out to the bakery to satisfy them. Town is forty-two miles away – if you have a working vehicle at your disposal. The only donuts in Walsenburg, anyway, are machine made and slightly stale in their cellophane packaging at Safeway. If your craving doesn't go away, like mine hasn't, you have to make your own donuts. I put the

Joy of Cooking ingredients out on the counter. I've got enough of everything except butter, and I wonder where I'll have to walk to in order to find someone with butter to spare, and then I remember the THC butter in our fridge. If I increase the nutmeg to masks its distinctive, not altogether pleasing flavor, it might work.

It's a crisp, sunny Sunday. The sun still glares strong, but at a lower angle now, hanging in the sky a little less each day, and you can still feel coolness around the edges of the sunlight late into the morning. Working over the warm cookstove with one of the kitchen's double doors open feels just right. I make the donut dough first thing, then let it rise, punch it down, cut out the donuts, and let them rise. Now I'm frying them and placing the plump, golden rings on paper towels all over the counters. David's at the table reading an old *Rolling Stone*. We split a test donut and agree that the extra nutmeg did the trick.

Neither of us hears two riders stop and tie their horses outside. It's unusual that they knock—the door's open and people generally just call out and walk in. I say, "Come on in, the door's open!" over my shoulder without looking up. A moment later, I look up and see the rims of two black cowboy hats poke through the doorway. A pair of skinny young cowboys follow their hat rims inside. They look a lot like the Jehovah's Witnesses who proselytize here every Sunday, though I'm not sure.

"Afternoon, ma'am, we're looking for two strays that we're missing. You seen any?" asks the younger of the two, who wears cheap black-rimmed glasses like Clark Kent's. He's in his twenties, probably—it's always so hard to tell the age of clean-shaven young men with short hair.

This is the first time in six years anyone's come up here looking for cows, and the first time anybody's called me "ma'am." Are there really two lost cows, or are he and his companion just curious? They're surprised to see the rock in the middle of the house and crane their necks. They recover, a little embarrassed, and try to act like they're used to stopping by octagonal houses with five-ton boulders inside. They look around at the plaster cast Tibetan calendar, at the stained glass window of the unicorn turning into a George O'Keefe flower shape by the cookstove. Most of all, they look at the dozens of donuts cooling on the counter. The air's full of freshly grated nutmeg, and crisp, sweet dough smells. They take off their hats.

"Making donuts?" the first one asks.

"Yes." I can't believe he called me ma'am. I'm wearing overalls, my
hair's in braids, and I'm not that much older than they are. "You know, I
haven't seen any strays around here." I say. "Were they pastured nearby?"
I ask, buying time, dealing with a Big Dilemma. It's the Code of the West
to offer coffee, at the very least, to a rider stopping by. We're a lonely,
friendly people. Every driver in the valley waves when he sees anyone
driving toward him on Highway 69, for God's sake. Umpteen dozen
donuts are cooling on my counter, and two cowboys holding their hats
are looking at them and practically drooling. It's a big sin not to offer
them one. These, however, are not your ordinary donuts. You get a good
buzz in ten minutes. I don't approve of slipping hallucinogens in the
party punch ....

David looks up and says, "Howdy, fellas." His southern roots let him
get away with that sort of thing. He looks at the donuts and then at me and
almost imperceptibly raises his eyebrow. I suppress a giggle. I wish I hadn't
eaten the donut half, now that I have to deal with this ethical dilemma.

"They sure look good!" The slightly older cowboy says, ignoring
my inquiry about the strays and David's greeting. On the other hand, I
worry, it's terribly inhospitable not to offer them a donut. They'd be
really offended. I hesitate. On the other hand, if I told them about the
funny shortening, they might make a beeline for the FBI office in Pueblo.
They could be narcs, though I concede that's a little paranoid. Still, if I
don't offer them a donut, I'll have to explain why, and that's not a good
idea regardless of who they are. They stand and shift their weight from
one foot to the other, holding their hats, trying not to stare at the donuts.
I imagine the little lines R. Crumb draws to show an irresistible aroma
rising from the donuts and suppress another giggle.

"I'm Roberta, and that's David," I say, buying time.

"I'm Andy, and this is my brother Phil – Plover," the younger one says.

"Well, Andy and Phil, um, how about some coffee?" I ask. "And a
slice of bread?" They frown a little and look at each other. "Or, say, how
about a donut?" I blurt out.

I nervously sprinkle cinnamon sugar on two donuts and hand them
to the cowboys. Almost anything's better than not being hospitable and

gracious I guess. They gulp their coffee, eat their donuts in three bites, lick their fingers, and look over at the counter again. Another donut is out of the question. The mild buzz from one might possibly go undetected, but upping the donut dosage would be pushing it, and horribly irresponsible.

"More coffee, boys?" I ask. "I've got to get the rest of these donuts packed up for the meeting. I'm worried there aren't enough for everyone, David," I say.

David says, "What mee---" and stops when he sees my look, then adds quickly, "Oh, yeah, *the meeting*!" and laughs. I frown at him.

"Well, we'd better be going," says Phil.

"Thanks for the donuts – they were delicious," Andy says with a broad smile, pushing his Clark Kent glasses up on the bridge of his nose. I walk with them to the door. They get on their horses and ride west down the ridge road toward Turkey Creek.

"They're in for a hell of a ride," David says when I come back in. He picks up his guitar and starts to sing "Happy Trails to You," but it's not what Roy Rogers meant. We never hear whether they found the cows. They didn't come back this way.

When I take Rufus out for a ride two days later, I bump into Johnny Bucci on the middle Gardner road. He's driving his pickup, pulling a trailer with one scrawny cow and a calf in it.

"How's that little mare I gave you?" Johnny asks.

"Fine, she looks good, and her little filly is beautiful!" I answer. I look down at my reins for a minute. "Say, Johnny, did you ever see two young cowboys looking for a stray a few days ago?"

Johnny smiles and say, "Why, yeah, as a matter of fact I did. The two Plover boys. They work some for Bob Hudson these days. Did they come all the way up to your house?" he asks.

"Yeah, they did. When did you see them?" I ask.

"Oh, around sunset, down on Turkey Creek, coupla days ago," Johnny says, rubbing the stubble on his chin.

"Well, uhm, how were they? I mean, how did they ... I mean, how were they?"

"Oh, they were fine, fine," Johnny answers. "They were looking for those strays and having a great ol' time." He grins slyly, adding, "They were a little silly, you know what I mean? I guess I forget what it's like to be young! They're not the type to giggle and all, but, it's funny, they were sitting in their saddles giggling away, looking at the sunset, having a good ol' time!"

"Oh, really? Hmm!" is all I can manage, looking down at my saddle horn. "Well, it was a *good* sunset on Sunday, wasn't it? I gotta get back now, Johnny, nice to see you!" When I turn toward home, Rufus breaks into a trot and tosses his head. He likes the cooler weather. I don't come across any strays as I ride around the mountain in the following weeks, and I never see the Plover boys again.

50. Westcliffe
from *Westcliffe, Colorado: A Short Sketch* by W.O. Mieir

Chamber of Commerce brochures and pamphlets are so predictable in their enthusiasm for local attractions that they rarely rise about the level of puff pieces offering tidbits of useful information. Nothing wrong with that ... they serve their purpose. Tourism, after all, has been an important part of Colorado's economy since early travelers ventured into the area seeking gold. Newspaper editors were often boosters for fledgling mining camps and much of their copy reflected that. Easterners seeking a cure for tuberculosis in Colorado's cool and arid climate came later and resort owners cranked out the copy to attract them. Railroads encouraged tourism and supported the efforts of early travel writers who described the scenery on their railroading adventures.

The Denver and Rio Grande built tracks into this region shortly after a silver boom in 1881. Flash floods along Grape Creek destroyed those tracks shortly thereafter and then again in 1889 after which the line was abandoned. In January of 1898, the Carson-Harper Company, a Denver printer whose cards and artwork were often related to Colorado scenery, published a pamphlet called Westcliffe, Colorado: A Short Sketch of this Most Delightful Resort. *W.O. Mieir, the author, may well have written the text with the hope of attracting tourists or*

perhaps even the railroad, which returned to Westcliffe, via Texas
Creek, in 1901. Whatever his intention, Mieir was not shy when it came
to writing with great passion, some strategic exaggeration, and plenty
of exclamation marks!

Here is to your health! Drink heartily; not of the red, red wine, but of
pure, cool crystal water, bearing not the faintest trace of any mineral;
no carbonate of lime to clog up your system and make you feel old and
rheumatic; no sulphate of magnesia to corrode your stomach; no iron to
lay the foundation of tuberculosis; no compounds of soda to destroy your
liver and kidneys. But drink, drink deep and full of Nature's water from
Nature's still; stilled and condensed in the pure, crisp air of the Sangre
de Cristo Range. 'Tis the Fountain of Youth for which Ponce de Leon
searched in vain, bubbling forth in endless rhythm from the snow-capped
peaks, Old Baldy, Horn's, Humboldt's, Gibb's, Eagle's and scores of
others all vying to reach higher and higher in the clear, blue, germless
sky; water winding its intricate way through canons and gulches, leaping
down precipices of solid granite, sparkling and gurgling in its merry
mission, longing to quench the thirst of sweltering humanity.

God be praised and Science commended for water which yet has to
quench its thirst for mineral! Pure, cold, death-destroying water, un-
tainted with animal and vegetable waste! Water from Nature's great still,
that will, when taken into the system, remove the osseous tendency that
brings on heart-disease, that stops up the capillaries of the skin, making you look old and wrinkled! Water that breaks the bonds of disease,
absorbing its germs and washing them away, leaving the human system
clear, healthy and invigorated with the glow of youth and the inspiration
of juvenility! 'Tis this that makes us wish to live a thousand years, with
Youth eternal!

Such is the water you may drink during your summer outing at
Westcliffe, nestling as she does at the base of the lofty Sangre de Cristo
Range, overlooking an expanse of level valley, twelve miles in width
and fifty miles in length, where lie the finest drives, the Paradise of the
horse-fancier and wheelman. No place in the grand old Rockies offers
a greater variety of opportunities for amusement and sport. The rod

and gun, the wheel, the thoroughbred, all have their patrons and ardent votaries here. The mountain and valley streams abound in trout, while the timber sides of our gorgeous hills and grassy valleys are plentifully supplied with small game.

51. Wet Mountains
from "Snake in the Grass" by Hal Walter

Hal Walter is an author, a burro racer, and journalist who lives at 8800 feet in the Wet Mountains fifteen miles east of Westcliffe. Rattlesnakes are less common at such elevations, though Walter says he runs across them occasionally. He heard from a wildlife biologist that they had been found at even higher elevations on the flanks of Mt. Blanca in the San Luis Valley. In this snake encounter, he approaches his reptilian neighbor with a measure of appreciation and tolerance.

The big snake coiled and commenced to rattle its tail when I was still about ten yards away. It had been sunning in the barrow ditch. When I approached on my morning jog, it had done what all good rattlers do and warned me of its presence.

I made sure where my dog was, then slowly walked up and looked at the buzzworm, coiled and menacing, its body as thick as my wrist, its wedge-shaped head up and alert. My neighbor, I could see from here, was preparing for a horseback ride. I knew that her route would take her past the snake. Figuring I could help prevent a spooked horse and a possible wreck, I jogged home and called to warn her of the snake in the ditch.

"Hal, that snake needs to be killed," she answered quickly. After all, we all have animals—horses, dogs, burros—and that snake is a threat to them. If I wouldn't kill the snake, she'd have to call another neighbor and get him to do it.

The pressure was on.

I hoped the snake would be long gone as I put my shotgun in the truck and drove up to check it out. To my surprise and dismay, the snake had uncoiled and was stretched out magnificently in the ditch. I looked it over, all several feet of it, and decided right then that there was no way I could kill this rattler. I tossed some rocks in its direction, hoping to scare it off, but it didn't even coil.

I got back in the truck and drove up to the neighbor's house. "I cannot in good conscience kill that snake," I told her.

"Oh, Hal, that snake has to go," the neighbor shrieked, shaking her head. "It's going to bite one of our animals."

I told her that if the snake was in my corral or against my house that it would be a different story, but it was just out along the road minding its own business. Besides, the snake had warned me at a good distance. I told her that if that snake doesn't bite one of her animals, the next one will. You can't eradicate them.

I drove off, and when I passed the place in the ditch where the snake had been lying, I noticed that it was now gone.

I recalled running down a trail once and seeing a snake only as my foot came down on its tail. I felt the buzz underfoot. Since I was running, my foot was back in the air by the time the snake rolled over to strike. I received two perfect wounds in the forefoot of my shoe. By the time I had figured out that only my shoe had been poisoned, the rattler was slithering off through the bushes.

An older fellow showed up at my door once and told me that as a boy he had lived in the tiny line shack near my house. Among his other stories, the most captivating was the one he told me about the rattlesnake den he and his father found one autumn in the rock pile behind my place. They stuck a pitchfork inside and the snakes coiled around the tines, forming a ball of buzzworms. It took the strength of both of them to lift it out. They shot many of the snakes with a .22 as they slithered away, but there were still more down the hole. They ended up dowsing the den with gasoline and setting it afire.

It's a strange policy we have here in the West, to kill rattlesnakes on sight, when fewer people die of snakebites than hantavirus, a pestilence spread largely by deer mice, a chief food of rattlesnakes. Yet it doesn't seem the mass-eradication effort has had any long-lasting effect. There's still a good number of snakes around here.

Settlers moving here in earlier days were able to successfully erad- icate some species—most notably grizzly bears and wolves—but rattle- snakes have managed to survive. One can only guess that their mostly nocturnal and elusive nature and the average yearly production of up to twelve snakelets per mama rattler have maintained the population.

Later that day, I drove past the place where the snake had buzzed at me that morning. On the opposite side of the road it lay dead. Someone had come along and done what I wouldn't do. It seemed a shame that the snake had died for no decent reason.

Highway 24

West from Colorado Springs

52. Manitou Springs / Pikes Peak
from *Early Ascents of Pikes Peak* by Woody Smith

Pikes Peak was previously referred to as Tave *(which means Sun Mountain) by the Ute people who lived in this region. The Arapaho knew the mountain as* Heey-otoyoo *(Long Mountain). Lieutenant Zebulon Pike arrived on the scene in 1806 to explore the area, evaluate resources, and locate the headwaters of several rivers, including the Arkansas. On November 26, he and several of his men tried to climb the mountain but had not adequately prepared themselves for such an ascent and turned back, having underestimated time, distance, and the severity of the weather. Dr. Edwin James, who was a member of Major Stephen Long's expedition, made the first recorded ascent of the peak in 1820. Katharine Lee Bates, a Wellesley College professor, made the climb in 1893, and was so taken by the "purple mountain majesties" of Pikes Peak that she composed a poem and later a song she called "America, the Beautiful."*

Another early mountaineer who made it up the mountain was Julia Archibald Holmes who described her ascent in a letter that Woody Smith includes in his book Early Ascents of Pikes Peak. *She and her husband James began their climb from Manitou Springs on August 1, 1858.*

After an early breakfast this morning my husband and I adjusted our packs on our backs, and started for the ascent of Pikes Peak. My own pack weighed 17 pounds, nine of which were bread, the remaining a quilt and clothing. James' pack weighed 35 pounds, and was composed as follows: 10 pounds of bread, one pound hog meat, three fourths pound coffee, one pound sugar, a tin plate, knife and fork, half gallon canteen, half gallon tin pail, and a tin cup, five quilts, clothing, a volume of Emerson's essays and writing materials made up the remainder. We calculate on this amount of food to subsist six days....

The trail was steep and rocky and the creek crossings challenging. After a few miles, they stopped at a spring to fill their canteens and decided to spend the night.

It is now ten o'clock in the evening, and I am reclining before some blazing pine logs beside a torrent in a mountain canyon several hundred feet deep. The straight, slender, tapering pines that stand around so beautiful in their death, smooth, white and sound, have been stripped of the bark by fire, calmly point to a sky more serene, and to stars far brighter than usual. The trees and the sky almost seem to strive together in preserving a deeper silence, but there is music from the foaming stream, sound from a dozen little cascades near and far blend together—a thundering sound, a rushing sound, a rippling sound, and tinkling sounds there are; and a thousand shades of sound to fill up between them.

The burning pine crackles and snaps, showering sparks, cinders and even coals around and all over the sheet I am writing on, as if to mock the tame thoughts they light me to write.

On August 2, 1858, the pair climbed higher, spending the next three nights at another spring about two miles below the summit in a camp she called Snowdell.

Eastward we can look on a landscape of Kansas plains, our view hemmed only by the blue haze of atmosphere, and extending perhaps 200 miles. The beauty of this great picture is beyond my powers of description. Down at the base of the mountain the corral of 15 wagons, and as many tents scattered around it, form a white speck, which we can occasionally distinguish. We think our location grandly romantic.

On August 5, 1858, they left Snowdell for the summit, taking with them nothing "but their writing materials and Emerson." Along the way, the couple paused to roll some rocks into a "yawning abyss."

Starting those stones had been a favorite amusement of those who
ascended before us, and it savored somewhat of the terrible... . After
enjoying this sport a short time we proceeded directly up toward the
summit. Arriving within a few hundred yards of the top, the surface
changed into a huge pile of loose angular stones, so steep we found much
difficulty in clamboring [*sic*] up them. Passing to the right of a drift of
snow some three or four hundred yards long, which sun and wind had
turned into coarse ice, we stood upon a platform of near 100 acres of
feldspathic granite rock and boulders. Occasionally a little cranny among
the rocks might be found in which had collected some coarse soil from
the disintegration of the granite, where in one or two instances we found
a green tuft about the size of a teacup from which sprung dozens of tiny
blue flowers most bewitchingly beautiful. The little ultra-marine colored
leaves of the flower seemed covered with an infinitude of minute sparkling crystals—they seemed children of the sky and snow.

It was cold and rather cloudy, with squalls of snow, consequently
our view was not so extensive as we had anticipated. A portion only of
the whitened backbone ridge of the Rocky Mountains which forms the
boundary line of so many territories could be seen 50 miles to the west.

We were now nearly 14,000 feet above sea level. But we could not
spend long in contemplating the grandeur of the scene for it was exceedingly cold, and leaving our names on our large rock, we commenced
letters to our friends, using a broad flat rock for a writing desk. When
we were ready to return I read aloud the lines of Emerson: *A ruddy drop
of manly blood/ The surging sea outweighs;/ The world uncertain comes
and goes,/ The lover rooted stays.*

I have accomplished the task which I marked out for myself, and
now I feel amply repaid for all my toil and fatigue ... . I would not have
missed this glorious sight for anything at all. In all probability I am the
first woman who has stood upon the summit of this mountain, and gazed
upon this wondrous scene which my eyes now behold ... .

53. Woodland Park
from *Beyond the Aspen Grove* by Ann Zwinger

Naturalist and artist Ann Zwinger, who grew up along the White River near Muncie, Indiana, came to Colorado Springs in 1960 where she began to study western ecology. She had been working on a PhD at Harvard when, as she put it, "she was swept off her feet by a young Air Force pilot." Shortly after they moved to Colorado Springs, Ann and Herman Zwinger bought a mountain property near Woodland Park. Previous studies in ecology, and an ability to render a landscape in words and sketch pad images, prepared Ann Zwinger for the work of getting to know that land. Many hours of recorded observations led to Beyond the Aspen Grove *(1970), the first of many books she would write about the natural world.*

As the title of Zwinger's book suggests, their family refuge was located in an aspen forest. Aspen trees grow well in the higher elevations of Colorado. There are more aspens in thicker concentrations than anywhere else in the US, in part because Colorado offers them plenty of mountain habitat. Not only are their moist green leaves resistant to fire, they thrive in sun-filled areas where wildfires have come and gone. To her study of an aspen grove through the seasons, Anne Zwinger brought the poetic sensibilities of a fine writer and artist and the keen eye of a seasoned naturalist.

I count the spring year well begun when the aspen dangle their three-inch catkins, fuzzy earrings which dust the cabin deck with pollen. The buds spill them out anywhere from late March to the end of April. The catkins appear before the leaves do, open to the pollinating spring breezes. The amount of pollen is prodigious. When I cut a bouquet of spring branches, the table on which they sit is deep in pale sulphur-yellow pollen the next day.

Our log notes the appearance of the first leaves between May 14 and May 20, the third week in May consistent over the years. The leaves are a pale lucid green, circles cut out of green tissue paper and overlaid in shifting patterns. Now is the time to hang out the hammock and feel, in the chill warmth, intimations of summer. A week ago the light was too

bright for reading comfortably in the grove; now the leaves make kalei-
doscopic shadows on the book page ... .

The day before summer is also the time for the most brightly colored
of all western birds, the western tanager ... . The male has an enamel-red
head, black back, and brilliant yellow breast. The female is pale—dappled,
cool, yellow green—colored to blend into the foliage where she nests.

At midday the male comes and alights on the aspen trunk nearest the
deck, about head height, and lunches with us, looking like a refugee from
a tropical rain forest, brilliant and handsome and a little out of place. We
eat lunch with a sandwich in one hand and binoculars in the other ... .

The children weave in and out of the day on their own errands. It
is as if the adults watch from the wrong end of a telescope trained on a
section of stage landscape. Periodically figures come into view, a frieze
of youngness running across the set, first from one wing of aspen, then
the other of pine, diagonally upstage or down, sometimes stage front,
sometimes behind a scrim of aspen leaves, sometimes swiftly, sometimes
in a pavane. They belong to the land ... not to their parents. They are
small sprites of the substance of leaf and shadow, interweaving with
the patterns of flickering sunlight. The figures seem to pause briefly,
then rearrange—moments of stop-motion alternating with moments of
movement ... .

Fall comes at its own pace in this grove. Protected by surrounding ridges,
these trees may not turn until the first week in October. All in a few days
they become fired with a blazing light, a torch holding back the winter
frosts. On a Thursday they are still green; on a Sunday, they are golden.
The leaves range from citron to copper, saffron to gilt, glowing with
light. They shower down with each gust of coming winter, buttering the
still-blooming lupine, catching the purple asters and the last black-eyed
Susans. The mahogany-red rose bushes snag them. The juniper waylays
them in needled branches, holding them upright in a card file of autumn.

The Danaän shower of gold enriches the ground. The sweet musty
smell of fall inches thick under the hammock. It is a fragrance of aspen
dust and honey and sunshine. The air is golden, as rich and sweet and

heavy as an old Chateau d'Yquem. The trunks, reflecting the light and
the fallen leaves, are gilded. The silence is soft and warm and full,
between intermittent rustlings of gold-tissue paper wrapping up the glow
of summer. Now, if ever, the sounds that hold human flesh within cir-
cumscribed familiarities dissolve in the permeating golden light. Nothing
exists except motes of aspen dust glinting in a shaft of sunlight....

In the winter the aspen woodland is a thousand eyes. When the wind
blows, the trees of the grove rock in unison, keening over lost summers.
Empty black branches, formed like clutching hands, scratch at the sky.
The boles are pallid in the white winter sunlight, gleaming like bleached
bones, on a shade darker than the shadowed snow at their bases. At the
foot of each trunk is a tiny crescent of open ground, facing the sun. The
warmth reflected by the light-colored trunks warms the snow and opens
the turf to foraging by the deer mice who live in the community.

     A deer mouse hunts at night and his tracks through the aspen grove
form cat's cradles from one tree to the next. The amount of tracking
shows this to be a busy grove. Perhaps it is still warm enough In
December to find bark beetles or a few late sluggardly insects. The
seedhead of a black-eyed Susan lies shredded. And then the neat precise
tracks lead to a sprig of wild timothy. Here the dried stem is bent down
by two tiny forefeet—the seeds nibbled, and chaff spilled on the new
snow. And then tiny paired footprints hop on, incessantly searching for
food to keep body heat up in the below-zero nights to come....

     When the January snow showers come, all outlines are obscured by
white filaments. I see the aspen grove amorphous and remote, framed in
the paned windows of the cabin. It is like being on the inside of a cocoon
looking out. The cabin is steely cold before the stoves are lighted.

     But even in the middle of winter the top branches of the aspens are
studded with the buds of spring to come. The smaller leaf and larger
flower buds are covered with a tiny resinous reddish-brown scale like a
beetle's back that protects the bud from cold and desiccation, from the
destructive rapid freezing and thawing of frigid nights and hot winter
sun. The bud scales protect more against drying than the cold, for the
cold is necessary for deciduous trees to stimulate renewed growth in

spring. The aspen must be below 40 degrees for several months in order
to open leaf and flower in spring.

Even on the darkest winter day the buds on the leafless branches give
a faith in spring to come, an assurance we sometimes are much in need
of when night closes in at four o'clock and the streams are totally covered
with snow and even the birds seem to be stilled by the breathless cold.
The land seems unnaturally quiet, as if someone had just said "Shhhhhh"
and in the sudden hush you can hear your heart beat.

54. Divide / Cripple Creek-Victor
from *Good Evening Everybody* by Lowell Thomas

*In 1890, after Bob Womack discovered a rich vein of gold in the rolling
hills west of Pikes Peak, thousands of hopeful newcomers flooded into
the region for what became the last and biggest gold boom in Colorado.
In 1900, when eight-year-old Lowell Thomas came to town with his
family, Cripple Creek and Victor were still thriving. "In those early
years," Thomas wrote, "when mine operators were interested only in
high grade ore, the rock of lesser value was crushed and some of it
became a part of our roads and city streets. All our streets were, quite
literally, paved with gold."*

In Good Evening Everybody, *part one of his two-volume autobiography, world traveler, broadcaster, and author Thomas, describes
his childhood home in the mining town of Victor, Colorado: "Our first
home was a three-room house in Victor, the city on the slope of Battle
Mountain where most of the richest mines were .... We played marbles
with steel ball bearings picked up around mine-shaft houses .... We
threw rocks at every target because rocks were everywhere." The backyard mineshaft he dug out with his cousin resembled the ones they had
explored up on the mountain and had "a gallows frame on top and a
double-deck cage to hoist the rock .... Our mine," Thomas wrote, "had
everything but the gold."*

*Like other Colorado towns populated during an epidemic of gold
fever, there were "more saloons and gambling halls than stores, with a*

red-light district—a tenderloin—only a few blocks away." As Thomas wrote many years later, the combination of a "no-questions asked frontier town and the chance to strike it rich, lured a gaudy cross section of humanity .... On the heels of this freewheeling crowd came some freewheeling, soul-saving luminaries," one of whom was temperance crusader Carrie Nation, whose visit to Cripple Creek was brief, but memorable nonetheless.

The newspapers called her the Kansas Tornado, and with good reason. A skyrocketing, hatchet-swinging temperance agitator, Carry Nation had ten years of well-publicized saloon-busting behind her when she swept into Cripple Creek vowing to "smash all the beer joints and dives from Poverty Gulch to the Last Chance saloon in Victor." So awesome was her reputation that every saloonkeeper on Bennett Avenue boarded up his place and hunkered down to wait for the storm to pass. That is, everyone but Johnny Nolan. Johnny, the proprietor of the velvet-draped Manitou, the lushest drinking and gambling establishment in the district, bravely announced as how he was not about to be buffaloed by Carry Nation. In fact, he invited her to the Manitou "to preach some to the fellows. Haven't I always been on good terms with the lads in the Salvation Army?"

All of which didn't help him ward off disaster. She started off with a sermon at Army Hall. "I knew I was needed here, for," said Carry, "this foul cesspool is the most lawless and wicked spot in the country." Then, followed by the Salvation Army band and a crowd drawn by the suspense in the air and maybe the smell of blood, she marched down to preach at Johnny Nolan's—six feet of scowling sobriety, cape flowing behind and altogether a most imposing figure of a woman.

But there was to be no more preaching that night, just action. For the first thing that caught the fearsome Madams Nation's eye as she stepped into Johnny's place was his pride and joy, a life-size painting above the bar called *Venus Emerging from the Sea*, Venus being amply proportioned and alluringly garbed in the altogether.

"Hang some blankets on that trollop!" Carry Nation commanded in a voice that could be heard out on Bennett Avenue.

"We got no blankets," said genial Johnny. "What kind of a place do you think this is?" Then he went after her, as she suddenly began tearing down his red velvet draperies.

"Take your foul hand off me!" she boomed, elbowing poor Johnny belt-high and sending him sprawling. Whereupon she pulled the famous hatchet out from under her cape and set about hacking away the offending picture with her well-known Carry Nation fury, stopping only often enough to sweep every bottle of whiskey in reach to the floor.

Until that moment, the clientele had been transfixed by the fireworks. But now, with bottles rolling all over the place, they scrambled to rescue what they could. The Salvation Army fled. Soon the Manitou looked as though it had been hit by a cyclone and left with some casualties, Johnny Nolan on the bottom. By the time the police arrived, Carry was so caught up in her hatchetry they had to put handcuffs on her before they could lead her off to jail.

There she would have spent the night—as well as the next thirty days, for she didn't have the fifty dollars to cover her fine—had it not been for the intervention of big-hearted Johnny Nolan. Slightly dazed and still bemoaning the loss of his beloved *Venus*, he appeared before the district judge and offered to pay Carry's fine if only she'd, for God's sake, take the midnight train to Denver. And so the story had a happy ending—and Johnny even managed to get the Manitou open for business the following day. In honor of the genial saloonkeeper, although Cripple Creek today is a shadow of its former self, there is still a Johnny Nolan saloon on Bennett Avenue.

55. Florissant
from *Saved in Time*
by Estella B. Leopold and Herbert W. Meyer

In the following passages from Saved in Time: The Fight to Establish Florissant Fossil Beds National Monument, *National Park Service paleontologist Herbert W. Meyer explains how these fossil beds came to be and paleobotanist Estella B. Leopold recalls the fight to create this national monument.*

The story of Florissant's famous fossils begins 34 million years ago in a dense forest along an ancient stream valley in the Rocky Mountains. Leaves freshly fallen from trees were carried gently in autumn winds, while insects buzzed with life in the forest. From time to time, ash and other debris from nearby volcanoes inundated the basin, burying plants, insects, and other animals .... Through a unique set of circumstances, these organisms became inscribed in the annals of time, preserving an ancient world in stone.

The fossil beds entomb the remnants of an ancient ecosystem and encompass a great diversity of organisms ranging from tiny one-celled creatures to enormous trees and even mammals. But, scientific investigations at Florissant have uncovered much more than the identities of individual species. We now know a great deal about the life and times of this fleeting Florissant interval 34 to 35 million years ago. This was at the very end of the Eocene epoch. The Eocene was a prolonged warm period that lasted about 20 million years and was typified in the Rocky Mountains by warm temperate to subtropical climates. It was a period of great biotic diversity during which trees grew near the poles and the whole Earth was warm. When the worldwide climate cooled rather suddenly soon after Lake Florissant's existence, the region's flora scattered and a few species became extinct. The sharp cooling introduced a period called "Ice House Earth" in the early Oligocene about 32 to 33 million years ago, which eventually led to the Ice Ages beginning about 2.5 million years ago.

Before the major changes of Ice House Earth, Florissant was the last outpost in the Rocky Mountain region for a few subtropical plant species. In the long history of Earth, the Florissant ecosystem was one of a kind. In the modern world, there is no place else like it.

Having done extensive fieldwork in Colorado with the U.S. Geological Survey and as a professor at the University of Washington, Estella B. Leopold recognized the Florissant fossil beds as an invaluable page of earth history. Like her father, the great ecologist and author Aldo Leopold, she believed in the ethical care of our lands and ecosystems. In 1964, as part of a broader conservation effort that included legal

efforts to block development in the Florissant Valley, she began leading
field trips to acquaint a wider public with the extraordinary national
treasures found there. Victor Yannacone, one of the environmental
lawyers who took up the cause, summed up the conservation position:
"using the Florissant fossils for real estate development is like using
the Rosetta Stone for grinding corn." In this passage, Estella Leopold
describes the battle for conservationists.

By the mid-1960s, this remarkable formation of nature in the Florissant
Valley ... was at risk. A growing population had made central Colorado
an increasingly desirable place to live and real estate interests saw
a chance to cash in on homeowner desires. When the Park Service
announced in 1964 that the area would be proposed as a national monument—a status that would protect the land from development—the risk
to Florissant ironically accelerated, as real estate developers quickly
attempted to buy up the increasingly desirable land from local ranchers.
A-frame housing was sprouting up, and developers were buying up land
along the margins of the proposed monument. The logic of the developers
was simple: the more of the core area they were able to start bulldozing
and building on, the less attractive would be the idea of a national monument there, and should a monument be declared, the surrounding land
was likely to increase in value ... .

At first, saving the Florissant fossil beds and their unique and irre-
placeable plant and insect fossils was a priority for only a few stalwart
and determined Coloradoans and their supporters. These supporters
included not only Colorado conservationists but also scientists who
recognized the extraordinary importance of the Florissant fossils, and
perhaps surprisingly, some of the local ranchers whose land included the
spectacular fossil Sequoia stumps ... .

The efforts to save Florissant and preserve it for future generations
were essentially twofold in nature: first building the citizens' movement
and education campaign designed to put pressure on Congress to grant
monument status to Florissant without delay; and second, introduction of
legal moves to block further real estate development in the area.... When
the citizens' group took real estate developers to court, they sought a

restraining order to keep the bulldozers from rolling over the fossil beds to dig roads for housing developments.

The fact that the citizens' groups were ultimately successful in their efforts set an example for how the citizenry could fight against property rights that would demean and disturb special lands .... By making Florissant a national monument in 1969, the United States guaranteed protection to an important natural place ... a quiet place where we can stand in the graveyard of a great fallen community—the Florissant ecosystem of the Eocene ... and where we can feel the pulse of the restless Earth.

Interstate 70
Denver Foothills to Loveland Pass

56. Idledale
from *Dwellings* by Linda Hogan

*In her poems, essays, and novels, Linda Hogan draws from her
Chickasaw heritage and an indigenous perspective that regards all
of creation as sacred. She writes, as she explains in the preface to
her book* Dwellings: A Spiritual History of the Living World, *"out
of respect for the natural world, recognizing that humankind is not
separate from nature. Some of this work connects the small world
of humans with the larger universe, containing us in the same way
that native ceremonies do, showing us both our place and a way of
seeing." In the following incident from* Dwellings, *which took place in a
mountain canyon west of Denver where she lived while teaching at the
University of Colorado, Linda Hogan honors that "way of seeing."*

For years I prayed for an eagle feather. I wanted one from a bird still
living. A killed eagle would offer me none of what I hoped for. A bird
killed in the name of human power is in truth a loss of power from the
world, not an addition to it.

My first eagle feather, one light and innocent, was given to me by
a traditional healer I'd gone to see when I was sick. He told me a story
about feathers. When he was a child his home had burned down. All that
survived the fire were eagle feathers. They remained in the smoking ruins of their home, floating on top of black ash and water. The feather he
gave me was one of those. I still keep it safe in a cedar box in my home.

Where I live is in a mountain canyon. It is not unusual to see golden
eagles in the canyon, far above us. One morning, after all my years of
praying for a feather, I dreamed I was inside a temple. It was a holy place.
Other people were there, looking at the ornately decorated walls, the
icons of gold, the dried and revered bodies of saints, but my attention

was turned toward the ceiling. It was pink and domed, engraved with gold designs of leaves and branches. "Look up," I said to the others. "Look up." Still dreaming, I spoke these words out loud, and the sound of my own voice woke me. Waking, I obeyed my own words and looked up, seeing out the open window of my room. Just as I did, a large golden eagle flew toward the window, so close that I could see its dark eyes looking in at me for a moment before it lifted, caught a current of air, and flew over the roof of the house. I jumped up and ran barefoot outside to see where it was going.

If I told you the eagle was not in sight, and that there was a feather in the road when I reached it, you would probably not believe me. I, too, have seen how long it takes a feather to land, carried as they are by unseen currents of air. Once I waited for a hawk feather to fall. I covered distance, looking up, to follow it, but it never set down. It merely drifted until it was no longer in sight. But on the day of my dream, a feather was there. On the ground had fallen the gift of an eagle, soft white with a darker, rounded tip.

I know there is a physics to this, a natural law about lightness and air. This event rubs the wrong way against logic. How do I explain the feather, the bird at my window, my own voice waking me, as if another person lived in me, wiser and more alert? I can only think there is another force at work, deeper than physics and what we know of wind, something that comes from a world where lightning and thunder, sun and rain clouds live. Nor can I say why it is so many of us have forgotten the mystery of nature and spirit, while for tens of thousands of years such things have happened and been spoken by our elders and our ancestors ... .

There is something alive in a feather. The power of it is perhaps in its dream of sky, currents of air, and the silence of its creation. It knows the insides of clouds. It carries our needs and desires, the stories of our brokenness. It rises and falls down elemental space, one part of the elaborate world of life where fish swim against gravity, where eels turn silver as moon to breed.

How did the feather arrive at the edge of the dirt road where I live? How did it fall across and through currents of air? How did the feathers survive fire? This I will never know. Nor will I know what voice spoke through my sleep. I only know that there are simple powers, strange and real.

57. Georgetown
from *My Rocky Mountain Valley* by James Grafton Rogers

*James Grafton Rogers served as dean of the law school at the
University of Colorado and Assistant Secretary of State under
President Herbert Hoover. He was the first President of the Colorado
Mountain Club and an avid student of the natural and human history of
his home state. As the mayor of Georgetown, he initiated and supported
historical preservation projects. He also wrote a book called* My Rocky
Mountain Valley, *which gathers his daily observations on mountain
life in the upper Clear Creek Valley. Below its origins near Loveland
Pass, Clear Creek runs through a wide glacial valley to Idaho Springs,
then veers east from I-70 and rushes down a narrow and rocky canyon
to Golden. In the following excerpt—his entry for May 27th—Rogers
follows the creek as it flows through time.*

I spilled sawdust in Clear Creek today by accident while picnicking at the
pioneer tunnel halfway up Loveland Pass. A handful of sawdust fell from
an old can found in a cabin at the portal. (Sawdust was kept to start fires
in mountain cabins.) The sawdust spread in the torrent and began its long
journey to the Gulf of Mexico.

It was natural to think about its travels, past Georgetown in a day,
past Idaho Springs in another perhaps, and Golden the next. Then into the
South Platte near Denver, on past to Omaha to the Missouri; to Kansas
City; to St. Louis, to Memphis and New Orleans. Unless the particles
stranded or were worn out in the abrasion, they faced one of the longest
water journeys in the world. I wonder if the Nile or Amazon could provide
a pilgrimage much longer. Surely with all the long bend to the north ahead
of these little chips, no other fragments floating on the Mississippi water
can travel much farther than do these as they swim from the headwaters of
the South Platte River at Loveland Pass to the Gulf of Mexico.

In 1800 those chips would not have passed a white man short of the
Missouri River or, let us say, for a thousand miles. Later in 1840 they
might have passed two log cabins before they reached the Platte, one near
the forks at Empire, one on the plains at the mouth of Clear Creek. Both

were hunting camps of Louis Vasquez. In 1850 the two cabins were ruins and the chips would have reached Nebraska and the Oregon Trail before encountering a European. In the fall of 1858 one settlement existed on Clear Creek, a sprinkle of fifty cabins on the plains just outside the mountains. The village was called Arapahoe. This was a placer gold camp which lasted only a few months. There was no trace of it five years later nor is any trace there now but a bronze historical tablet.

In July 1859, less than a year later, all this vacancy and desolation was gone. The chips would have passed bearded prospectors panning the gravel along almost every mile of stream to the plains. At Georgetown there were only explorers that year, but at the site of Idaho Spring thousands of men were shoveling and washing sand at Jackson Diggings, Spanish Bar and Grassy Flats. Even wagons could be seen as far upstream as Spanish Bar. From that date on to the present the valley was taken over by Americans. A chip set afloat in 1877 would have seen railroad engines, little puffing narrow gauge steam locomotives belching sparks all along the canyon. Now these in turn are gone. The sawdust will travel all its miles and months to the sea in the faint odor of gasoline and diesel oil fumes, not the smell of horse sweat, nor even coal smoke and cinders.

The water pours down merrily as it always did from the snow drifts in the spruce woods. Nothing very permanent has happened, nothing moved far. The same birds, most of the same animals go to and fro as they did in the wilderness. Most even of the flowers are the same as they were. What has changed? In a century, if the white man perished, few traces of him would remain—only some broken pavement, stone walls, some heaps of crushed rock and gravel. His presence in the mountains has been brief. The water would soon erase his works if once he left.

58. Graymont / Bakerville
from *Halfway to Heaven* by Mark Obmascik

Denver journalist Mark Obmascik has written about a wide range of topics, including the Columbine High School Massacre for which his team of Denver Post *reporters won a Pulitzer Prize. He has also written several books on outdoor pursuits. One of them,* The Big Year, *a book about some obsessive birdwatchers, was later made into a movie with Jack Black, Owen Wilson, and Steve Martin. The other book,* Halfway to Heaven, *describes his quest to climb all of the mountains in Colorado whose summits are higher than fourteen thousand feet (commonly referred to as "fourteeners").*

His publisher introduces Halfway to Heaven *in this way: "Fat, forty-four, father of three sons, and facing a vasectomy, Mark Obmascik would never have guessed that his next move would be up a 14,000-foot mountain. But when his twelve-year-old son gets bitten by the climbing bug at summer camp, Obmascik can't resist the opportunity for some high-altitude father-son bonding." In the following excerpt, he describes their attempted ascent of Grays Peak, which begins several miles south of this exit.*

The trail begins at 11,280 feet, and somebody has filled my lungs with sand. You OK, Dad? I'm not OK, but I'm not quitting either. My twelve-year-old is smoking me up the trail. Dad, you OK? I open my mouth to talk, but what comes out in a sound described by my son as a goose that swallowed a bugle. He laughs. I do too. Enough father-son communication for now ....

At 12,000 feet, the first yellow rays of dawn spill over the trail, and the view reminds me why I'm trying this. It's spectacular: a massive wall on our left, a talus peak on our right, and a breathtaking rock amphitheater dead ahead. Above it all stand our intended targets – the summits of Grays Peak and Torrey Peak, which stretch about three-quarters of a mile apart, linked by a high saddle that dips 550 feet in the middle. We're planning to stand atop both before most people back home in Denver are cemented to their work desks for the day.

Now the trail really goes up. We take twenty steps, rest, and push twenty more. There's a jackhammer pounding my eardrums, which alarms me at first, until I'm able to cite it as evidence to my son that I truly do have a heart ....

Unfortunately, when I glance up, I realize he's in no shape for surprises. On the trail ahead his feet are wobbling like he's in his fifteenth round with Muhammad Ali. I remember that malady, which comes when you're dizzy from altitude or worn out from climbing. Either way, it's not a good sign.

We rest and … I tell him … that Grays Peak is the tallest point on the Continental Divide in North America.

Tallest point? That pegs the testosterone meter for Cass. We trudge higher.

At 13,500 feet, we had scaled the equivalent of one-and-a-half Sears Towers, and the burden shows. He takes five steps, rests, and then wobbles five more…We rest. Then we progress a few hundred more feet before his boots go goofy again….

My son looks at me with an idea: Dad, how about if you carry my backpack? No big deal, I tell him, and stuff his daypack into my larger sack. He stands to take another step and nearly somersaults backward. No more happy feet—just wacky feet.

How close are we? He asks. Doesn't matter, I tell him. The mountain will always be here. We can try again another day.

I hold his arm and we turn tail in retreat. Cass gains strength with every step down, and we're soon low enough for him to walk by himself. I tell him how proud I am of him. It takes a lot more maturity to turn around on a peak than to press ahead and put yourself in danger.

Yada, yada, yada, he says, and then yaks it up for the next hour hiking back down. He's blabbering on about school, friends, summer camp, girls, cell phones—the full cornucopia of preteen stuff—without any encouragement from me. I chalk it up to altitude drunkenness, but I'm not complaining. It's fun to be buddies again.

59. Loveland Pass
from *Long Haul* by Finn Murphy

Since 1980, Finn Murphy has been a long-haul trucker who specializes in moving people and their belongings across the country. Moving van drivers are known in the trucking trade as "bedbuggers," and their rigs, which in Murphy's case is a fifty-three-foot eighteen-wheeler, are

referred to as "roach coaches." In his book, Long Haul: A Trucker's
Tale of Life on the Road, *Murphy offers up some of the highlights from
his many miles of travels—more than a million so far—on a wide range
of American roads.*

*It is hard to imagine a trucking route more challenging than US 6
over Loveland Pass in the middle of a nasty storm. With the exception
of trucks hauling hazardous waste that are prohibited from traveling
through the Eisenhower Tunnel or those that just can't fit because they
are taller than thirteen feet and eleven inches, most truck drivers choose
the less challenging I-70 route. But sometimes, when the traffic gets bad
enough, as it does in the following story from* Long Haul, *a trucker will
take his chances on the old route over the Continental Divide.*

Loveland Pass, Colorado, on Route 6 summits at 11,991 feet. That's
where I'm headed, having decided to skip the congestion at the
Eisenhower Tunnel. Going up a steep grade is never as bad as going
down, though negotiating thirty-five tons of tractor-trailer around the
hairpin turns is a bit of a challenge. I have to use both lanes to keep
my 53-foot trailer clear of the ditches on the right side and hope nobody
coming down is sending a text or sightseeing.

At the top of the pass, high up in my Freightliner Columbia tractor
pulling a spanking new, fully loaded custom moving van, I reckon I can
say I'm at an even 12,000 feet. When I look down, the world disappears
into a miasma of fog and wind and snow, even though it's July. The road
signs are clear enough, though – the first one says RUNAWAY TRUCK
RAMP 1.5 MILES. Next one: SPEED LIMIT 35 MPH FOR VEHICLES
WITH GROSS WEIGHT OVER 26,000 LBS. Next one: ARE YOUR
BRAKES COOL AND ADJUSTED? Next one: ALL COMMERCIAL
VEHICLES ARE REQUIRED TO CARRY CHAINS SEPTEMBER 1 –
MAY 31. I run through the checklist in my mind. Let's see: 1.5 miles to
the runaway ramp is too far to do me any good if the worst happens, and
35 miles per hour sounds really fast. My brakes are cool, but adjusted? I
hope so, but no mechanic signs off on brake adjustments in these liti-
gious days. Chains? I have chains in my equipment compartment, required or not, but they won't save my life sitting where they are. Besides,

I figure the bad weather will last for only the first thousand feet. The practical aspects of putting on chains in a snowstorm, with no pullover spot, in pitch dark, at 12,000 feet, in a gale, and wearing only a T-shirt, is a prospect Dante never considered enumerating in his circles of hell. The other option is to keep rolling—maybe I'll be crushed by my truck at the bottom of a scree field, maybe I won't. I roll.

I can feel the sweat running down my arms, can feel my hands shaking, can taste the bile rising in my throat from the greasy burger I ate at the Idaho Springs Carl's Jr. (It was the only place with truck parking.) I've got 8.6 miles of 6.7 percent downhill grade ahead of me that has taken more trucks and lives than I care to think about. The road surface is a mix of rain, slush, and (probably) ice. I'm one blown air hose away from oblivion, but I'm not ready to peg out in a ball of flame or take out a family in a four-wheeler coming to the Rocky Mountains to see the sights.

I downshift my thirteen-speed transmission to fifth gear, slow to 23 mph, and set my Jake brake to all eight cylinders. A Jake brake is an air-compression inhibitor that turns my engine into the primary braking system. It sounds like a machine gun beneath my feet as it works to keep 70,000 pounds of steel and rubber under control. I watch the tachometer, which tells me my engine speed, and when it redlines at 2,200 rpm I'm at 28 mph. I brush the brakes to bring her back down to 23. If it's going to happen, it's going to happen now. My tender touch might cause the heavy trailer to slide away and I'll be able to read the logo in reverse legend from my mirrors. It's called a jackknife. Once it starts, you can't stop it. In a jackknife the trailer comes all the way around, takes both lanes, and crushes against the cab until the whole thing comes to a crashing stop at the bottom of the abyss or against the granite side of the Rockies.

It doesn't happen this time, but the weather's getting worse. I hit 28 again, caress the brake back down to 23, and start the sequence again. Fondle the brake, watch the mirrors, feel the machine, check the tach, listen to Jake, and watch the air pressure. The air gauge read 120 psi at the summit; now it reads 80. At 60 an alarm will go off, and at 40 the brakes will automatically lock or just give up. Never mind that now, just don't go past 28 and keep coaxing her back down to 23. I'll do this twenty or thirty times over the next half hour, never knowing if the trailer will hit a bit of ice, the air compressor will give up, the Jake will disengage, or someone will slam on the brakes in front of me. My CB radio is on (I usually turn it off on mountain passes), and I can hear the commentary from the big-truck drivers behind me.

"Yo, Joyce Van Lines, first time in the mountains? Get the fuck off the road! I can't make any money at fifteen miles an hour!"

"Yo, Joyce, you from Connecticut? Is that in the Yewnited States? Pull into the fuckin' runaway ramp, asshole, and let some men drive."

"Yo, Joyce, I can smell the mess in your pants from inside my cab."

I've heard this patter many times on big-mountain roads. I'm not entirely impervious to the contempt of the freighthauling cowboys.

Toward the bottom, on the straightaway, they all pass me. There's a Groendyke pulling gasoline, a tandem FedEx Ground, and a single Walmart. They're all doing about 50 and sound their air horns as they pass, no doubt flipping me the bird. I'm guessing at that because I'm looking at the road. I'll see them all later, when they'll be completely blind to the irony that we're all here at the same time drinking the same coffee.

Highway 34

Loveland to Rocky Mountain National Park

60. Lyons
from *Dumb Luck and the Kindness of Strangers*
by John Gierach

*John Gierach has been fishing the foothills of northern Colorado's
Rockies for a long time, most of his life in fact. For many years, he lived
on the St. Vrain River in Lyons, but more recently he moved further north
into Larimer County. He may live in a different house now, but the small
streams, high lakes and headwaters west of Lyons are still his "home
water." Having fished this watershed for a half century or so, he knows
it well, because the details of a good riparian habitat and its seasons
are not lost on an experienced fisherman. Those details, and the stories
he tells about flyfishing in Colorado and elsewhere, have delighted his
readers in magazine columns and in numerous books for many years.
Although he has fished all over the world, he is still devoted to the water
he knows best, a connection he explores in this excerpt from his book,*
Dumb Luck and the Kindness of Strangers.

I live in the foothills of the northern Colorado Rockies with dozens of
trout streams within day trip range, so it's easy for me to recommend
fishing close to home. The advantages are obvious. You can play hooky
to go fishing at a moment's notice; it only takes one trip to pack your
minimal gear (you know how little you need because you need so little);
you know right where you want to go and have plenty of backups in
case someone has high-graded your spot; and a rained out day isn't a
deal breaker—you just go home and come back when the creek clears.
Eventually fishing becomes such a normal part of daily life that you can
stop for a half gallon of milk on the way home ....

A good-size trout in any of these creeks will be around 10 inches
long, with plenty smaller and a few larger. A 12- or 14- incher is a real

nice fish and in the forty-plus years I've fished here I've landed a handful
in the neighborhood of 16 inches, including one lovely cutthroat that
almost brought me to tears and probably would have if there hadn't been
a witness present. And more recently there was an 18-inch brown trout
that made me *glad* I had a witness along to measure the fish and back up
the story. But even then we got looks from friends that suggested they
thought we'd shared a recently legalized doobie and gotten hysterical
about a 14-incher. I was insulted at first, but then decided that if anyone
chose not to believe in the hidden pool where the big trout lives, it was
okay with me ... .

When I'm fishing alone I'll occasionally just walk the creek waiting
for some sign or start casting and figuring I'll know it when I see it.
Sometimes it's as obvious as a sputtering hatch and a pool of rising trout.
Other times it's something peripheral, like a patch of ripe raspberries or
a few doorknob-size boletus mushrooms so small and fresh they're not
yet wormy, that makes me stop. (I carry brown paper bags in my daypack
for these finds, although often I'll just graze on these berries on-site.)
On rare days it's something as vague as a quality of the light or a certain
stillness in the air that seems to make the water vibrate with possibility,
but I think that's less mystical than it sounds. It's just that some of the
things you know about your home water operate beneath the level of full
consciousness and only reveal themselves disguised as intuition.

Sometimes I even have dreams about these creeks. In one that woke
me up bolt upright before dawn I hook a fish so big that when I tighten
the line and the fish begins to struggle I realize the bed of the stream I'm
standing on is actually the fish's back. I look down to see the fist-size
cobbles turned to black spots on a bronze background, which make this
a brown trout the size of a school bus. That's it; there's no plot, no story
line, just that one image that leaves me awake and blinking. Sometimes I
have dreams so inexplicable that I assume they were meant for somebody
else and leaked into my head by accident, but that one—whatever it
means—is mine alone.

I do love to catch trout—it becomes a hard habit to break—but more
often now I find myself going out close to home not to clean up on fish,
but just to prove to myself that they're still there. So far they always have

been…in fact, these creeks near home have held up better over more than half my lifetime than almost anything else I can think of… .

I only have one friend that I've known for as long as I've fished my home water. We don't see that much of each other anymore, but when we do get together—usually to go fishing—we pick up right in the middle of a half-century-long conversation that will end only with one of our funerals. I've fished a lot of places and met a lot of people, but there are only a handful of streams that I know inside out and an equally small number of people whom I consider to be close friends. But a few of each is enough when you're loyal as a dog to all of them.

61. Estes Park
Steven King and The Stanley Hotel

At the beginning of his book, The Shining, *Steven King includes this disclaimer: "Some of the most beautiful resort hotels in the world are located in Colorado, but the hotel in these pages is based on none of them. The Overlook and the people associated with it exist wholly within the author's imagination." It may be true that the Overlook Hotel, as King describes it in* The Shining, *is largely imagined, but it is also true that the story initially came to him during a brief stay at The Stanley Hotel in the fall of 1974.*

Perched on the edge of a mountain in Estes Park, The Stanley Hotel has been an important part of the landscape here since it opened in July of 1909. Freelan Oscar Stanley, who had originally come west for the restorative qualities of the dry mountain air, built The Stanley Hotel after recovering from tuberculosis. With a fleet of Stanley Steamers—the steam-powered vehicle that he had invented with his brother—he transported well-heeled visitors to his hotel and helped establish Estes Park as a tourist destination.

By the time Steven King arrived in the fall of 1974, the hotel was an Estes Park institution. It was the last week of the season for The Stanley, so hotel employees were making preparations to close up for the winter. Having seen a sign that said, "Road may be closed after

November 1," King was already intrigued with the notion of an isolated winter setting. At the hotel, when he inquired about a room, he was told that he would need to pay cash, which he did, since the last of the credit card receipts had already been sent to Denver. King and his wife Tabitha settled into Room 217, a room number, as it turned out, that would reappear in his novel.

A strong autumn wind buffeted the hotel that night, adding to the high lonesome atmosphere that stirred the author's imagination. King and his wife were the only diners in the restaurant. Orchestral music piped into the dining room drifted down long corridors, emptied of all the other guests who had been staying there. In George Beahm's book, Stephen King: America's Favorite Boogie Man, *King recalls a dream he had later that night: "I dreamed of my three-year-old son running through the corridors, looking back over his shoulder, eyes wide, screaming. He was being chased by a fire-hose. I woke up with a tremendous jerk, sweating all over, within an inch of falling out of bed. I got up, lit a cigarette, sat in a chair looking out the window at the Rockies, and by the time the cigarette was done, I had the bones of* The Shining *firmly set in my mind."*

In The Shining, *Jack Torrance, a down-on-his-luck writer takes a winter caretaking job and arrives with his family at an old hotel called The Overlook (which bears some resemblance to The Stanley) near a small mountain town (not unlike Estes Park). His young son Danny almost immediately takes to exploring the hotel's nooks and crannies. Because "something bad" once happened in Room 217, he has been warned to stay away. That, of course, attracts his morbid curiosity. "It was a dreadful kind of curiosity," King writes, "the kind that makes you peek through your fingers during the scariest parts of a scary movie. What was beyond that door would be no movie."*

Being the master of suspense that he is, King builds the tension as the boy stands outside of the locked room with pass key in hand. Will he or won't he open the door? For a while, Danny can't make up his mind. What is it about room 217, anyway? At this point in the story, Danny decides not to unlock the door, so the question persists, as it does to this day, for visitors to The Stanley Hotel where Room 217 is the most requested accommodation.

62. Rocky Mountain National Park / Many Parks Curve
from *A Lady's Life in the Rocky Mountains* by Isabella Bird

*Longs Peak, standing at 14,259 feet above sea level, is visible from many
locations in Rocky Mountain National Park, including Many Parks
Curve on Trail Ridge Road. The mountain has been an important landmark for native and Anglo people. The Arapaho referred to Long's Peak
and nearby Mount Meeker as Nesótaieux, "the two guides." John Wesley
Powell's surveying party recorded the first Anglo-American ascent of
Long's Peak on August 23, 1868. By the time Isabella Bird decided to
try and make the ascent in the fall of 1873, several other women had
summited successfully, among them Addie Alexander in 1871 and Anna
Dickinson several weeks before Bird's arrival in Estes Park.*

*By her own admission, Isabella Bird, a proper and diminutive
English woman who had recently turned forty, was not well-suited for
mountaineering: "You know I have no head or ankles, and never ought
to dream of mountaineering," she wrote in a letter to her sister. "Had I
known that the ascent was a real mountaineering feat I should not have
felt the slightest ambition to perform it." Whatever she lacked in terms of
climbing ability, she largely made up for with passion and determination
and with her decision to hire the right guide (though her first impression
of "Mountain Jim" Nugent was hardly reassuring):*

"Jim" was a shocking figure; he had on an old pair of high boots, with
a baggy pair of old trousers made of deer hide, held on by an old scarf
tucked into them; a leather shirt, with three or four ragged unbuttoned
waistcoats over it; an old smashed wideawake, from under which his
tawny, neglected ringlets hung; and with his one eye, his one long spur,
his knife in his belt, his revolver in his waistcoat pocket, his saddle
covered with an old beaver skin, from which the paws hung down; his
camping blankets behind him, his rifle laid across the saddle in front of
him, and his axe, canteen, and other gear hanging to the horn, he was as
awful-looking a ruffian as one could see.

Not only was "Mountain Jim" Nugent a seasoned veteran when it came to mountain travel, he also turned out to be a patient and courteous guide without whom Isabella Bird would have never reached the summit. At times, she wrote, Jim dragged her up the mountain "like a bale of goods, by sheer force of muscle." In the process of their mutual ascent of Longs Peak, they developed a strong bond of friendship, unlikely though it may have seemed upon their first meeting. In the following excerpt from her book, A Lady's Life in the Rocky Mountains, *Isabella Bird describes the experience.*

At the "Notch" the real business of the ascent began. Two thousand feet of solid rock towered above us, four thousand feet of broken rock shelved precipitously below; smooth granite ribs, with barely foothold, stood out here and there; melted snow refrozen several times, presented a more serious obstacle; many of the rocks were loose, and tumbled down when touched. To me it was a time of extreme terror. I was roped to "Jim," but it was of no use; my feet were paralyzed and slipped on the bare rock, and he said it was useless to try to go that way, and we retraced our steps. I wanted to return to the "Notch," knowing that my incompetence would detain the party, and one of the young men said almost plainly that a woman was a dangerous encumbrance, but the trapper replied shortly that if it were not to take a lady up he would not go up at all. He went on the explore and reported that further progress on the correct line of ascent was blocked by ice; and then for two hours we descended, lowering ourselves by our hands from rock to rock along a boulder-strewn sweep of 4,000 feet, patched with ice and snow, and perilous from rolling stones. My fatigue, giddiness, and pain from bruised ankles, and arms half pulled out of their sockets, were so great that I should never have gone halfway had not "Jim", *nolens volens,* dragged me along with a patience and skill, and withal a determination that I should ascend the Peak, which never failed. After descending about 2,000 feet to avoid the ice, we got into a deep ravine with inaccessible sides, partly filled with ice and snow and partly with large and small fragments of rock, which were constantly giving away, rendering the footing very insecure. That part to me was two hours of painful and unwilling submission to the inevitable; of trembling, slipping, straining, of smooth ice appearing when it was least expected, and of weak entreaties to be left behind while the others went on. "Jim" always said that there was no danger, that there was only a short bad bit ahead, and that I should go up even if he carried me!

Slipping, faltering, gasping from the exhausting toil of the rarefied air, with throbbing hearts and panting lungs we reached the top of the gorge and squeezed ourselves between two gigantic fragments of rock by a passage called the "Dog's Lift," when I climbed on the shoulders of one man and then was hauled up. This introduced by an abrupt turn round the south-west angle of the Peak to a narrow shelf of considerable length, rugged, uneven and so overhung by the cliff in some places that it is necessary to crouch to pass at all. Above, the Peak looks nearly vertical for 400 feet; and below, the most tremendous precipice I have ever seen descends in one unbroken fall. This is usually considered the most dangerous part of the ascent, but it does not seem so to me, for such foothold as there is is secure, and one fancies that it is possible to hold on with the hands. But there, and on the final, and, to my thinking, the worst part of the climb, one slip, and a breathing, thinking, human being would lie 3,000 feet below, a shapeless, bloody heap! "Ring" refused to traverse the Ledge, and remained at the "Lift" howling piteously.

As we crept from the ledge round a horn of rock I beheld what made me perfectly sick and dizzy to look at—the terminal Peak itself—a smooth, cracked face or wall of pink granite, as nearly perpendicular as anything could well be up which it was possible to climb, well deserving the name of the "American Matterhorn."

Scaling, not climbing, is the correct term for this last ascent. It took one hour to accomplish 500 feet, pausing for breath every minute or two. The only foothold was in narrow cracks on minute projections on the granite. To get a toe in these cracks, or here and there on a scarcely obvious projection, while crawling on hands and knees all the while tortured with thirst and gasping and struggling for breath, this was the climb; but at last the Peak was won. A grand, well-defined mountain top it is a nearly level acre of boulders, with precipitous sides around, the one we came up being the only accessible one....

From the summit were seen in unrivalled combination all the views
which had rejoiced our eyes during the ascent. It was something at last
to stand upon the storm rent crown of this lonely sentinel of the Rocky
Range, one of the mightiest of the vertebrae of the backbone of the North
American continent, and to see the waters start for both oceans ... .

We placed our names, with the date of ascent, in a cut within a crev-
ice, and descended to the Ledge, sitting on the smooth granite, getting
our feet into cracks and against projections, and letting ourselves down
by our hands, "Jim" going before me, so that I might steady my feet
against his powerful shoulders ... . I had various falls, and once hung by
my frock, which caught on a rock, and "Jim" severed it with his hunting
knife ... . We were driven lower down the mountains than he had intended by impassable tracts of ice, and the ascent was tremendous. For the
last 200 feet the boulders were of enormous size, and the steepness fearful. Sometimes I drew myself up on hand and knees, sometimes crawled;
sometimes "Jim" pulled me up by my arms or a lariat, and sometimes I
stood on his shoulder, or he made steps for me of his feet and hands, but
at six we stood on the "Notch" in the splendor of the sinking sun, all
color deepening, all peaks glorifying, all shadows purpling, all peril past.

63. Rocky Mountain National Park / near Alpine Visitor Center
from *Even Mountains Vanish* by SueEllen Campbell

For the attentive visitor, there is much to learn in Rocky Mountain
National Park. Although the grandeur of mountains like Longs Peak
and the overwhelming presence of their geological story may be front
and center, some of the less obvious life forms in the park, like a little
flower known as the alpine forget-me-not, are no less remarkable and
may also have a few things to teach us, as naturalist and author SueEllen
Campbell suggests in this excerpt from her book, Even Mountains Vanish.

You might say that forget-me-nots huddle against the ground with their arms wrapped tightly around themselves for warmth. The one I studied with my magnifying glass – "my" flower – clung close to the earth, as I did, safe within a boundary layer of still air that sheltered it from the wind and would keep daytime summer temperatures some twenty degrees warmer than just a few inches higher up. It grew densely, too, the outer parts sheltering the inner, each leaf, like my own layers of clothing, making a shield for the next. A central cluster less than two inches across, a handful of satellites linked by stems that had taken root themselves, maybe four inches at its widest point: even a plant this small might have been decades old – speedy growth compared to lichens, but still slow by human measures. Its frequent neighbor dwarf clover, I read in one book, grows no more than four leaves each summer yet still qualifies as an "aggressive invader of bare ground."

I could see no green on my flower's stems or leaves, just a thick sweater of wavy white hairs, silver in the scudding sunlight. These filaments would trap heat and moisture, deflect wind, and block ultraviolet rays. Though the average annual precipitation is twenty-five inches, most of it falls as snow, and where the wind blows hardest, the ground stays mostly dry. Thus many flowering plants on the tundra are furry, though not often quite as furry as this one was, while many others have fleshy, waxy leaves, two means to the same end, protection against environmental bad news.

Forget-me-nots favor one of the toughest and driest micro-habitats, the very rocky meadows call fellfields. Except for a lichen or two that floats free of any attachment, plants here must be well anchored by roots either wide or deep. In the Alpine Visitor Center just up the road from Poetry Curve, I'd gazed into a glass case at another diminutive flower whose taproot was six feet long, and everywhere under the surface of the tundra, everywhere beneath my stretched-out body, grew complex mazes of roots, space to store carbohydrates over the winter to power the next year's flowering and growth. Like virtually all its neighbors, my forget-me-not was a perennial, able to pace its activities to last over several seasons. Even more efficiently than most, it would have formed leaves, shoots, and buds late the summer before then kept them alive over the winter, for a head start on this summer's flowers.

And such flowers! Under conditions this harsh one might expect a sturdy sort of blossom, something with muscle and sinew, a floral workhorse. But these forget-me-not blossoms were delicate and tiny, maybe a quarter inch across, fully open. They had five rounded petals, and at the center, marked by a fine circle of bright yellow, a deep black funnel collected warmth for the stamens and pistils, tiny parts I couldn't find even with my magnifying glass. I knew these blossoms were as small as their lowland cousins, but as they always do, they seemed larger and more emphatic, partly because the scale here was entirely different, foreground reduced and background expanded, but mainly because they were so saturated with pigment. Lowland blossoms, in comparison, might have been soaked in bleach. It was hard to believe anything could be so blue – not far from the cobalt of old glass Noxema jars, but velvety and incandescent like the sky on those winter evenings when the air turns purple and the atmosphere seems the size of the universe. This plant looked like the night sky in reverse: a shining silver ground with a random scattering of brilliant blue flames.

Sometime later, in a lighthearted moment, I thought about what these plants might have said to me about survival. Suppose the lichens were to whisper in my left ear and the forget-me-nots in my right. *Be patient,* they would surely counsel in unison. *Move slowly and keep a low profile. Find a space you don't have to fight for. Think ahead, conserve your resources.* In my left ear: *Accept that the same thin skin that admits nourishment also makes you vulnerable. Remember that strength depends on cooperation. Share pieces of yourself with the world.* In my right: *Knit yourself a warm sweater, a safe, calm space just your size. Put down deep roots. Be passionate. Make beauty. Bloom like mad.* And together again: *Gather your energy from the ground, the snow, the sun.*

64. Rocky Mountain National Park / Colorado River Trailhead
from *The Spell of the Rockies* by Enos Mills

Born in Kansas in 1870, Enos Mills came west to the Rockies at the age of 14, hoping for better health and some adventure, both of which he found in the Estes Park area. At 15, he made his first ascent of Longs Peak, a summit he would visit another forty times on his own and 300 more times while working as a mountain guide. Additional travels led him to Montana and on to to the West Coast, where a chance meeting with John Muir reaffirmed his dedication to writing and conservation. He returned to Estes Park where he devoted the rest of his life to the conservation cause, most notably as one of the primary advocates for the place that became known as Rocky Mountain National Park on January 26, 1915.

Mills traveled all over these mountains, as a guide and mountaineer and as a state snow observer measuring snow depths to predict the spring and summer runoff. For many years, he brought along a remark- uble collie and mountain dog name Scotch with whom he once traveled on a winter exploration near the headwaters of the Grand River (which we now call the Colorado). Mills had been on snowshoes for a week exploring the headwaters region. Sleeping beside a fire under the protection of an overhanging cliff at 10,000 feet, he and Scotch had been comfortable enough. That all changed the day they were caught in a mountain blizzard. In the following excerpt from his book, The Spell of the Rockies, *he tells the rest of that story.*

We went forward in the flying snow. I could scarcely see, but felt that I could keep the way on the broken ridge between the numerous rents and cañons. On snowy, icy ledges the wind took reckless liberties. I wanted to stop but dared not, for the cold was intense enough to freeze one in a few minutes.

Fearing that a snow-whirl might separate us, I fastened one end of my light, strong rope to Scotch's collar and the other end to my belt. This proved to be fortunate for both, for while we were crossing an icy, though moderate, slope, a gust of wind swept me off my feet and started us sliding. It was not steep, but was so slippery I could not stop, nor see where the slope ended, and I grabbed in vain at the few icy projections. Scotch also lost his footing and was sliding and rolling about, and the wind was hurrying us along, when I threw myself flat and dug at the ice with fingers and toes. In the midst of my unsuccessful efforts we were brought to a sudden stop by the rope between us catching over a small rock-point that was thrust up through the ice. Around this in every direction was smooth, sloping ice; this, with the high wind, made me wonder for a moment how we were to get safely off the slope. The belt axe proved the means, for with it I reached out as far as I could and chopped a hole in the ice, while with the other hand I clung to the rock-point. Then, returning the axe to my belt, I caught hold in the chopped place and pulled myself forward, repeating this until on safe footing.

In oncoming darkness and whirling snow I had safely rounded the ends of two gorges and was hurrying forward over a comparatively level stretch, with the wind at my back boosting along. Scotch was running by my side and evidently was trusting me to guard against all dangers. This I tried to do. Suddenly, however, there came a fierce dash of wind and whirl of snow that hid everything. Instantly I flung myself flat, trying to stop quickly. Just as I did this I caught the strange, weird sound made by high wind as it sweeps across a cañon, and at once realized that we were close to a storm-hidden gorge. I stopped against a rock, while Scotch slid in and was hauled back with the rope.

The gorge had been encountered between two out-thrusting side gorges, and between these in the darkness I had a cold time feeling my way out. At last I came to a cairn of stones which I recognized. The way had been missed by only a few yards, but this miss had been nearly fatal.

Not daring to hurry in the darkness in order to get warm, I was becoming colder every moment. I still had a stiff climb between me and the summit, with timber-line three rough miles beyond. To attempt to make it would probably result in freezing or tumbling into a gorge. At last I realized that I must stop and spend the night in a snow-drift. Quickly kicking and trampling a trench in a loose drift, I placed my elk-skin sleeping-bag therein, thrust Scotch into the bag, and then squeezed into it myself.

I was almost congealed with cold. My first thought after warming up was to wonder why I had not earlier remembered the bag. Two in a bag would guarantee warmth, and with warmth a snow-drift on the crest of the continent would not be a bad place in which to lodge for the night.

The sounds of wind and snow beating upon the bag grew fainter and fainter as we were drifted and piled over with the latter. At the same time our temperature rose, and before long it was necessary to open the flap of the bag slightly for ventilation. At last the sounds of the storm could barely be heard. Was the storm quieting down, or was its roar muffled and lost in the deepening cover of snow, was the unimportant question occupying my thoughts when I fell asleep.

Scotch awakened me in trying to get out of the bag. It was morning. Out we crawled, and, standing with only my head above the drift, I found the air still and saw a snowy mountain world all serene in the morning sun. I hastily adjusted sleeping-bag and snowshoes, and we set off for the final climb to the summit.

The final one hundred feet or so rose steep, jagged, and ice-covered before me. There was nothing to lay hold of; every point of vantage was plated and coated with non-prehensible ice. There appeared only one way to surmount this icy barrier and that was to chop toe and hand holes from the bottom to the top of this icy wall, which in places was close to vertical. Such a climb would not be especially difficult or dangerous for me, but could Scotch do it? He could hardly know how to place his feet in the holes or on the steps properly; nor could he realize that a slip or a misstep would mean a slide and a roll to death.

Leaving sleeping-bag and snowshoes with Scotch, I grasped my axe and chopped my way to the top and then went down and carried bag and snowshoes up. Returning for Scotch, I started him climbing just ahead of me, so that I could boost and encourage him. We had gained only a few feet when it became plain that sooner or later he would slip and bring disaster to both. We stopped and descended to the bottom for a new start.

Though the wind was again blowing a gale, I determined to carry him. His weight was forty pounds, and he would make a top-heavy load and give the wind a good chance to upset my balance and tip me off the wall. But, as there appeared no other way, I threw him over my shoulder and started up.

Many times Scotch and I had been in ticklish places together, and more than once I had pulled him up rocky cliffs on which he could not find footing. Several times I had carried him over gulches on fallen logs that were too slippery for him. He was so trusting and so trained that he relaxed and never moved while in my arms or on my shoulder.

Arriving at the place least steep, I stopped to transfer Scotch from one shoulder to the other. The wind was at its worst; its direction frequently changed and it alternately calmed and then came on like an explosion. For several seconds it had been roaring down the slope; bracing myself to withstand its force from this direction, I was about moving Scotch, when it suddenly shifted to one side and came with the force of a breaker. It threw me off my balance and tumbled me heavily against the icy slope.

Though my head struck solidly, Scotch came down beneath me and took most of the shock. Instantly we glanced off and began to slide swiftly. Fortunately I managed to get two fingers into one of the chopped holes and held fast. I clung to Scotch with one arm; we came to a stop, both saved. Scotch gave a yelp of pain when he fell beneath me, but he did not move. Had he made a jump or attempted to help himself, it is likely that both of us would have gone to the bottom of the slope.

Gripping Scotch with one hand and clinging to the icy hold with the other, I shuffled about until I got my feet into two holes in the icy wall. Standing in these and leaning against the ice, with the wind butting and dashing, I attempted the ticklish task of lifting Scotch again to my shoulder—and succeeded. A minute later we paused to breathe on the summit's icy ridge, between two oceans and amid seas of snowy peaks.

Highway 14
Fort Collins through Poudre Canyon

65. Laporte
from "The Door Beyond" by Laura Pritchett

Laura Pritchett, who grew up on a small ranch northwest of Fort Collins in Laporte, remembers her childhood this way: There was "a whole gaggle of us, including raccoons and rabbits and goats and pigs. Newborn calves in our kitchen in the middle of the night, their soft hooves sliding across linoleum as they tried to nurse from Coke bottles filled with milk. Peacocks wandering into the kitchen, cats giving birth into our shoes in our closet, frozen dead animals in the freezer."

In a prolific writing career that includes many novels and essay collections, Laura Pritchett tells stories that are rooted in Colorado. Though she considered moving elsewhere at one time, the gravity of her home place has been so strong that she eventually chose to settle only a few miles down the road from the ranch where she grew up. Here, in an essay called "The Door Beyond," she describes her home place then and now.

La porte. The words are French for "the door" or "the gate," and LaPorte, Colorado, is the portal I went out of and then went right back into, as if caught up in a circular revolving door. I grew up on a small ranch there, moved away, returned, moved around the area a bit, thought of leaving for New York or some place with a literary center, and then did the opposite by buying a home and an acre of land surrounded by many other acres of land at the base of the foothills, at that very door. There was enough literary-ness right there, I decided, with books all around me and artists of all types, including experts in the art of living life, everywhere. Like a dog circling around before resting, I finally flopped down with a happy sigh. With that purchase a year ago, and the renovations since, I shut the metaphorical door for good, because I knew then, and know now, this area is where I wanted to live and belong.

LaPorte got its name from French trappers, who prized this valley because it rested near an entryway into the Rocky Mountains—an entryway carved by a river named Cache la Poudre, which means "hide the powder." In one story, a caravan of trappers and travelers were attacked, and they needed to bury their powder. In another, the travelers simply needed to lighten the load. In either case, legend has it, they buried their extra guns and gunpowder somewhere around here, and locals have been looking for that cache ever since.

And where the river tumbles out of the mountains, slows its pace, spreads out—there is LaPorte. The word encompasses a gateway to the mountainous region north of the South Platte River that extends from the Plains to the Continental Divide. But for most, the word LaPorte means a cluster of stores before you head up into the mountains. To the left, drivers will see the Swing Station and post office, and then a hardware store, vet clinic, and small grocery store; to the right is a gas station, a pie shop. They'll see snow-covered fields in winter, hay balers putzing down swaths of cut grass in late summer. They'll see a farmhouse with a silo, misty air puffing from horses' nostrils, tall grass dipping in the wind.

In some sense this town is smaller now than it was in the 1860s, when there were four saloons, a brewery, a butcher shop, a shoe shop, two blacksmith shops, a store, and a hotel. The town housed trappers, traders, Natives, the military, an Overland Stage station, the county courthouse. LaPorte was the biggest settlement north of Denver.

Now there's a smattering of stores and still a lot of traffic along the main road, Overland Trail. Only now LaPorte's not a gathering place; it's not even a real town—rather, it's an unincorporated entity, a community under county jurisdiction, a place in limbo, a secret place that is home to people who like it that way.

My family's ranch is still there, and like all ranch families we call the pastures by name: Big North, Seep Field, Big South, Pond Pasture, The Hill, Back Valley. The place is cut in half by an abandoned railroad track, paralleled by a rutted dirt road with a snake of grass in the middle. On one side the ranch is bordered by the Cache la Poudre River, on the other by an old pioneer cemetery. It is a stretch of grasslands resting just below the first foothills of the Rocky Mountains.

The pastures all have their lures. Pond Pasture has ponds for ice skating in the winter and swimming in the summer. Big South houses a bunch of gnarled trees, each with twisted trunks forming caves and niches for hiding. The Hill has an old mysterious stone something to explore—a game run, the experts say. My favorite place, though, is at the western edge of the property. If I walk down the abandoned railroad track past the fields, past the irrigation ditches, past the bridge, there is an area where rock was blasted to make a passageway for the railroad tracks. Here the ranch is most wild. It is home to black bears, bobcats, raccoons, snakes. I have to press aside bushes and duck under branches, and when I emerge I am covered in seeds and wisps of plant life and whispers from the past.

Surprisingly little has changed in LaPorte since I was a girl. There used to be a dirt lot that housed a flea market on Saturdays. The general store, built in the 1860s, has been torn down. Some big houses got built in the foothills. There are fewer pickup trucks and more Subarus. There are more bicycles than horses on the road, though you still see the latter, too.

This place is an ecotone in both ecology and in humanity, and I've come to believe that LaPortians have a secret pride that their town attracts and holds more than its fair share of the quirky. There are survivalists, hippies, beekeepers, people on the very far religious right and the very liberal left, lots of people with their own gardens, lots of people who work with their hands, and people who love LaPorte.

The ranch, too, is very much the same. The river course has changed a bit, as it should, and water levels are significantly lower year-round, now that water is diverted upstream. The cattle are gone, and the developers call more frequently. There are still the same cycles of work—haying, irrigating, harvesting apples, mending fences. And other cycles, too: My son worked at Overland Foods in high school, just as I did. When old enough to do so, both my children got tattoos—my son the coordinates of this place etched in his skin, my daughter an outline of the mountains as seen from the first ridge. I write book after book set in the area. Without speaking of it, we have all etched this exact place—this door—into and around our lives.

La porte. The door to the mountains. Here's what I hope: that some future person will walk through town and feel a little in love. She might circle around and come to rest. She might wonder about who came before and who loved it, too. She will see that when the sun sets, the water in the river sparkles, the grass takes on a reddish hue, a blue heron flies to an outcrop of rock. And she will hear a phone ring, a child yell, the grumble of traffic on Overland Trail, a route that carried so many other travelers, and she'll be aware of this place as a door into the beyond.

66. Bellvue
from "Sailing Through the Night" by John Calderazzo

Those who make their home along the edge of the Front Range know mountains as the dominant feature of the western horizon. Their days are measured by the sun as it rises over the plains, trails across the sky, and disappears behind the first wave of peaks that shape the eastern edge of the Rockies. Not only does the Front Range alter one's experience of space, it also transforms the weather. Wave disturbances that occur when air is forced to flow over these mountains often result in formidable downdrafts along the eastern slope. Chinook winds occur in winter when these downdrafts are accompanied by unseasonably warm temperatures. Cold fronts traveling across the Front Range can also instigate down-drafts which are called bora winds. Long-time residents of Front Range communities like Bellvue, where writer, poet, and former Colorado State University professor John Calderazzo lives, find ways to adapt them-selves to the presence of wind—generating energy, for example—but the wind isn't always pleasant, and can even be a hazard. Fortunately, as Calderazzo points out, other elements of mountain life along the Front Range can offer compensation, even healing.

For more than twenty years I've been thinking about a few seconds of film. In a newsreel taken in Asia during the Vietnam War, a saf-fron-robed monk sitting in the lotus position allows himself to be doused with gasoline. Suddenly he explodes into fire. Yet somehow he continues to sit without moving or crying out, continues to meditate even as the terrible flames shoot up the side of his face. Finally, he crumples to the side, a human torch illuminating the unreal horror and waste of war ... .

Often these days I lie awake at night and listen to the wind sweeping out of the mountains and over my comfortable Colorado home,
wind that roars like fire, and I wonder what brought that man to make
that decision. A mother's son full of bravery and fear and desire—had
he lost hope in a world full of war? Or was he mostly affirming life,
believing that his final act would inspire other acts to stop violence?
Or was he gripped by something beyond my understanding, an emotion
or a way of thinking like an invisible color on the spectrum of human
experience, a band of light shimmering that I still haven't learned how
to see?

Or maybe it's not the monk I'm haunted by. Maybe it's me, my confu-
sion about how to handle the seemingly endless bad news of the world. I
have come to probably the halfway point in my life, a life blessed mainly
with privilege and good fortune, yet more and more often I worry about
how I'll get through the rest of it without giving in to cynicism or self-in-
dulgence or despair ... .

For three nights now, winds have boomed like surf against the bedroom
wall. They rattle the double storm windows next to my head. Fifty miles
an hour, sixty, seventy—they plunge from the high country into our
valley. No matter how many pillows I burrow under, I can hear our big
cottonwoods creaking and cracking.

I'm desperate for sleep, desperate not to wake SueEllen. Last night,
after hours of being elbowed and kicked, she pulled me close and whispered, "Those elk we saw last week in the meadow—remember? How
still they sat in the sun, and wildflowers everywhere, Queen Anne's Lace,
Indian paintbrush, mountain bluebell ... ."

SueEllen's night mantras: meditations on loveliness, haiku just for
me. Often they help. But not last night. Or tonight—the gusts roar in
from some far corner of the universe, and our big blue spruce shudders
and lashes the window behind my head. It's a tree the previous owners
planted after the neighbor's picnic table came flying through the glass.

I close my eyes and try to think of good things—marriage and job,
deep friendships, our small cheerful nieces—but suddenly I'm staring at

the ceiling, then out through the backyard window and up into the blades
of our windmill. On calm nights the windmill stands against the stars
like a giant silver daisy shining in moonlight. But tonight the blades are
flying. They're a propeller, a murderous flower whirring, whirring.

A squall starting up in my skull, prying loose nightmares, clots of
thought: Amazon rainforests bulledozed into dust, a midnight phone
call—aren't they always at midnight?—saying a friend has died in
a car wreck, a monk sitting in robes of fire. This is the time of night
when anything can come sailing through the window, when one thought
multiplies to infinity. This is the time of night when tumors grow.

"Oh, John... " sighs SueEllen, twisting away to salvage what she can
of her sleep. So I throw an arm over her and watch elk drift through green
mountains, feel my cross-country skis glide over diamond fields of snow.

67. Colorado-Wyoming Border
from *The Meadow* by James Galvin

*If you decide to drive north on Highway 287, you will eventually come
to the Colorado-Wyoming border. Such borders may be arbitrary in
their origins, but as states develop their own cultural identities, they
often take on new meaning. For example, the two universities at either
end of this stretch of road—the University of Wyoming in Laramie
and Colorado State University in Fort Collins—refer to their football
rivalry (which goes back to 1899) as the Border War. As each team has
a mascot—UW Cowboys and CSU Rams—so too, each state chooses
to emphasize certain aspects of its geography and culture. Wyoming
billboards describe a place that is "Forever West." Colorado license
plates are green and mountainous. Different places, different myths,
and sometimes you can almost feel the shift as you cross the state line.*

*But both states lay claim to writer and poet James Galvin, whose
family's ranch straddled the border and who wrote about the land and
its inhabitants in a book called* The Meadow. *Galvin's book focuses on
a 350-acre hay meadow though the eyes of several generations of caretakers, including members of his own family, who struggled to make a*

life and a living there. In this portrait of Lyle Van Waring, he describes
an aging rancher whose intimacy with the meadow and its other resi-
dents reflects many years of hard work and quiet observation.

The way people watch television while they eat—looking up to the
TV and down to take a bite and back up—that's how Lyle watches the
meadow out the south window while he eats his breakfast. He's hooked
on the plot, doesn't want to miss anything. He looks out over the rim of
his cup as he sips.

The meadow is under two feet of snow, which looks gray but not
dirty in this light. Leafless willow branches make an orange streak down
the middle. Each year the snow tries to memorize, blindly, the landscape,
as if it were the landscape that was going to melt in spring.

The wind has cleared a couple of the knobs above the meadow, and
the silver-gray sage throbs out. Above that stands the front line of timber,
where the trees begin, or end, depending, still dead black though the sky
has brightened behind it, a willing blue. Nothing is moving across the
meadow this morning.

Yesterday sixteen elk streaked across the hillside above the meadow.
Lyle could easily imagine what they had done to the fence where it runs
under deep drifts on the east side. They walked through it, not even feeling
the barbs through the winter coats. They dragged broken wire through
the woods, strewing it like tinsel. He'd find the pieces in the spring like
tendrils of steel briar growing along the ground. It doesn't make him angry
anymore, as it did in the early years. He figures the elk have been crossing
that section of timber to forage on the north side of Bull Mountain for a
lot longer than there has been anyone here to build fence and get pissed
off every time the elk tear it up. Now he splices the fence with baling wire,
which is lighter, so it will break easier and always in the same place and
not get dragged so much or pull out posts.

The first light hits the meadow and the kitchen window, and it's like
Christmas lights going on. The trees go from black to loden green. The
snow turns a mild electric blue and sparks.

A white crown sparrow lights on a small juniper branch that bends
down and springs back up. Lyle says, "What kept you?" The sparrow

hops onto the windowsill as a chickadee lights and begins bouncing up and down on the juniper branch just left by the other. "And you, you cheerful little sonofabitch, you don't waste no time either, do you?"

Lyle slowly straightens his stiff joints as he gets out of the chair and shuffles (his shoes are still untied) over to the wood stove. He picks up the plate with the extra pancake, carries it back to the table, and sits down. He cranks the window open about an inch—not enough for the birds to come in and kill themselves trying to get out—pinches off some warm pancake and crumbles it on the outside sill. "Little beggars."

When the day's first visitors have finished their crumbs and flown, Lyle picks up a two-month-old newspaper Ed Wilkes brought and begins to read, but he is soon interrupted by a tiny beak tapping on the glass. This one is a junco, and then the chickadee is back, bouncing from branch to branch chirping. Lyle gives them some crumbs. Addressing the chickadee, "I don't know what you're so goddamn happy about all the time."

There's a racket of chirps and squawks by the front door. Lyle unbends out of the chair again, takes another pinch of flapjack to the door, and steps outside on the stoop. The screeching squawk is a Stellar's jay, who flees the wire he's perched on as soon as the door opens. He's had enough stones and snowballs pitched at him to know. To the little row of sparrows that has returned to the perch Lyle says, "That hatchet-head won't bother you now." All at once they fly down and light on his uplifted palm. They peck off pieces of cake and flee back to the wire like greedy children waiting another turn. When the pancake is gone Lyle goes back inside to wash the dishes.

Once, coming back from town, I saw Lyle's truck parked at the Wooden Shoe. I stopped to say hello. Lyle was building a new garden fence, and as I approached, he held up his hand, a signal not to come closer. Then he leaned his shovel against the post he was setting and walked slowly across the garden to where a barn swallow was perched on a rail. Lyle took off his glove, and with the back of his huge index finger, touched the swallow gently under its throat, then ran his finger down once, gently, over its breast. Then he put his glove back on and walked away, and bird took to the air again.

Lyle said, "Up close them swallows are the funniest damned things you ever saw. They fly like angels and then up close they look like little clowns. The damnedest thing."

68. Poudre Canyon
from *Hunting for Hope* by Scott Russell Sanders

*Even if you are driving up Poudre Canyon in the middle of winter,
massive boulders choking off parts of the river's channel can evoke
images of the whitewater turbulence you might witness here during the
peak of the summer run-off. It's humbling even to imagine the kind of
power inherent in a river moving down such a steep gradient in this
narrow canyon, let alone experience the Poudre's whitewater firsthand,
an encounter that Scott Russell Sanders describes in his book* Hunting
for Hope: A Father's Journey.

*The father and son river trip he describes comes in the context of
a challenging time in their relationship. They embark on their western
adventures at a time when Scott Sanders realizes that his despair over
the corruption, environmental degradation, and violence he sees in
the world has cast a shadow over his son Jesse's experience, and Jesse
isn't too happy about that. But in their brief time rafting the Poudre,
Sanders, the author of many books and formerly a distinguished professor at the University of Indiana, recalls a few moments when the
physical demands of an adrenalin-infused introduction to big water
paddling, and the sheer vitality of the river itself, lift him and his son,
at least momentarily, beyond the obstacles that have hindered their
relationship and into the presence of joy.*

We clambered into the raft—Jesse and I up front, the veteran guide and
the other trainee in the middle, Harry in the stern. Each one of us hooked
one foot under a loop sewn into the rubbery floor, jammed the other foot
under a thwart. Before we hit the first rapids, Harry made us practice
synchronizing our strokes as he hollered, "Back paddle! Forward paddle!
Stop! Left turn! Right turn!" The only other command, he explained, was
"Jump!" Hearing that, the paddlers on the side away from some looming
boulder or snag were to heave themselves *toward* the obstruction, in
order to keep the raft from flipping.

"I know it sounds crazy," said Harry. "But it works. And remember: from now on, if you hear fear in my voice, it's real."

Fear was all I felt over the next few minutes, a bit for myself and a
lot for Jesse, as we struck white water and the raft began to buck. Waves
slammed against the bow, spray flew, stone whizzed by. A bridge swelled
ahead of us, water boiling under the low arches, and Harry shouted,
"Duck!" then steered us between the lethal pilings and out the other side
into more rapids, where he yelled, "Left turn! Dig hard! Harder!"

He kept barking orders, and soon I was too busy padding to feel anything except my own muscles pulling against the great writhing muscle
of the river. I breathed in as much water as air. The raft spun and dipped
and leapt with ungainly grace, sliding through narrow flumes, gliding
over rocks, kissing cliffs and bouncing away, yielding to the grip of the
current and springing free. Gradually I sank into my body.

The land blurred past. Sandstone bluffs rose steeply along one shore,
then the other, then both—hundreds of feet of rock pinching the sky high
above into a ribbon of blue. Here and there a terrace opened, revealing a
scatter of junipers and scrub cedars, yet before I could spy what else might
be growing there it jerked away out of sight. I could tell only that this was
dry country, harsh and spare, with dirt the color of scrap iron and gouged
by erosion. Every time I tried to fix on a detail, on bird or flower or stone,
a shout from Harry yanked me back to the swing of the paddle.

The point of our bucking ride, I realized, was not to *see* the canyon
but to survive it. The river was our bronco, our bull, and the land through
which it flowed was no more present to us than the rodeo's dusty arena
to a whirling cowboy. Haste hid the country, dissolved the landscape, as
surely as anger or despair ever did.

"Forward paddle!" Harry shouted. "Give me all you've got! We're
coming to the Widow-Maker! Let's hope we come out alive!"

The flooded Poudre, surging through its crooked canyon, was a
string of emergencies, each one christened with an ominous name. In
a lull between rapids I glanced over at Jesse, and he was beaming. His
helmet seemed to strain from the expansive pressure of his smile. I
laughed aloud to see him. When he was little I could summon that look
of unmixed delight into his face merely by coming home, opening my
arms, and calling, "Where's my boy?" In his teenage years, the look had
become rare, and it hardly ever had anything to do with me.

"Jump!" Harry shouted.

Before I could react, Jesse lunged at me and landed heavily, and the raft bulged over a boulder, nearly tipping, then righted itself and plunged on downstream.

"Good job!" Harry crowed. "That was a close one."

Jesse scrambled back to his post. "You okay?" he asked.

"Sure," I answered. "How about you?"

"Great," he said. "Fantastic."

For the remaining two hours of our romp down the Poudre I kept stealing glances at Jesse, who paddled as though his life truly depended on how hard he pulled. His face shone with joy, and my own joy was kindled from seeing it.

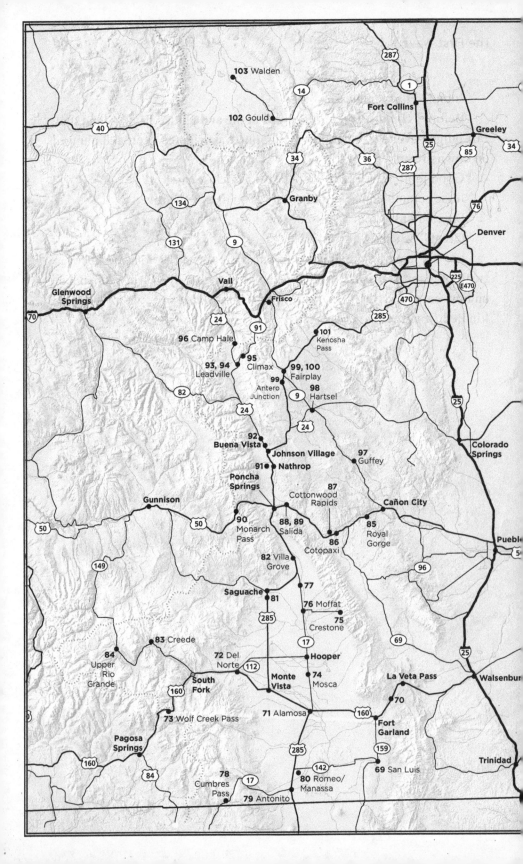

THE HIGH PARKS AND VALLEYS

On paper, the north-south line of the Continental Divide, as Colorado historian David Lavender once wrote, looks like an abused crankshaft. It maintains a north-south axis overall, but along the way it zigs, zags, and bends, first toward the headwaters of the Colorado on the western side of Rocky National Park, and later into the heart of the Weminuche Wilderness. Its final segment in the state follows the relatively straightforward South San Juans into northern New Mexico.

Where the Divide runs, rivers begin. On the eastern slope, the biggest of those (from south to north) are the Rio Grande, the Arkansas, the South Platte, and the North Platte. Each of those rivers gathers water from the eastern side of the Divide and flows through a valley or park on its way to the lower elevations. Park, in this case, refers to a wide expanse of open grassland surrounded by forests and mountains. Three parks and a valley correspond with these rivers: they are the San Luis Valley (once referred to as San Luis Park), the Upper Arkansas Valley (which lacks the expanse of the three parks, but butts up against the Divide and collects the headwaters of a major river), South Park, and North Park. The high-country grasslands found in these areas offer good winter habitat for elk and other wildlife species. In the 1830s, trappers were especially fond of South Park because of the large buffalo herds it supported. North Park has been referred to as "the bullpen" because of its abundant game animals.

These high grasslands have also fed lots of livestock. The ranching tradition continues in these parks and valleys, as does farming, especially in the San Luis Valley. The surrounding mountains have shaped the regional economy as well, first because of gold and silver

*found near towns like Fairplay, Leadville, and Creede, and more
recently because of the recreational opportunities they offer.*

*Early on, these high parks and valleys were mostly seasonal
hunting grounds. Winter camps were often made in the lower elevations.
In South Park, for example, the Tabeguache Ute—the "People of
Sun Mountain" who wintered at the base of Pikes Peak—spent their
summers along the flanks of the Mosquito Range, an area that offered
good hunting as well as a plentiful supply of chert for making weapons.
The Ute presence lingers along the western edge of the Arkansas Valley
where mountains like Antero, Shavano, Ouray, and Chipeta were
named after prominent Ute leaders.*

SAN LUIS VALLEY

Highway 159

New Mexico to Highway 160

69. San Luis
from "Little Bethlehem" by Fred Baca

*The community of San Luis has deep roots. It is the oldest continually
inhabited town in Colorado. After gaining its independence from Spain
in 1821, the Mexican government issued five large land grants to
encourage settlement of this region. One of them, the Sangre de Cristo
Land Grant, covered much of what we know today as Costilla County.
Hispanic settlers in this area took possession of the land grant in 1851
and so began the agricultural community of San Luis.*

*It is also a community of deep faith. The Shrine of the Stations of
the Cross, built by the Sangre de Cristo Parish, is located on the top
of a mesa—La Mesa de la Piedad y de la Misericordia (the hill of piety
and mercy)—in the middle of San Luis. Local sculptor Huberto Maestas
designed and produced the bronze statues that depict the stations of
the cross—the final hours of Jesus's life before his crucifixion—on the
mile-long trail that winds up the side of mesa. Both the shrine and the
stations of the cross were offered as gestures of faith. In this excerpt
from an essay called "Little Bethlehem," Fred Baca considers the
meaning of the shrine in the context of the community that created it.*

White rocks are arranged on the brown hill to proclaim SAN LUIS
OLDEST TOWN IN COLORADO. The fog enshrouds most of the boast
except for COLO. The second vowel looks like a *D*. It is winter, and yes,
the valley is typically cold this morning. I have come from the other side
of the Sangre de Cristos. I have awakened at the coldest hour to bear
witness to the work of my cousins. In their certitude, the *gente* of the

valley have placed stations of the cross on this new Calvary. I am not on a pilgrimage. I am not a believer, though I think I believe in their belief. A church outside makes sense to me. It makes so much sense, the way the forest makes sense.

I have chosen this frosted morning because I wish to experience the stations viscerally. The cold always makes me withdraw a bit, like a turtle tucking its head. A narrower perspective might let me see more. I know enough to know what I don't know. My questions are the obvious ones. What compels the construction of such an extensive iconography in a place regarded as the poorest as well as the oldest in Colorado? I want to look at it as an act of art, but I already know that it is more than that. A certain integrity compels us to art. That kind of compulsion is here, but it goes beyond my understanding of simple integrity. In art we are the intended audience. This open church doesn't seem intended for people. It is situated for God to see.

The ascent begins across a bridge. It is a sweeping climb. Obscured along the trail are squat pinon trees rimed with icy vapor. Revealed through the diaphanous drapery of fog, they are a fantastic, spectral display. It is a silent morning. If the roosters are crowing, their alarm can't cut the frost that creates a dreamlike transition, helping my scattered mind ponder the racial memories of those who made the path.

Adapted to the shift in time, I encounter the first station. Jesus is accused. The bronze figures are smaller than human. They, too, are the color of the rock. The statues appear less to have been placed there than to have been lifted from the ground during some past eruption, a natural manifestation of the land. Like the boulders on any mountainside moving imperceptibly in time, these figures are in motion. They are dynamic on a universal scale.

Jesus! What a Jesus! Like none I have seen, and yet like all I have seen, but didn't recognize. It is not a Jesus of European origin, nor even of Jerusalem. This Jesus has thick lips, large hands, worn feet, and a stout and hearty stature. I know his deep eyes are the eyes of my grandfathers. Like they, he, too, is a *Pentitente*. A Brother of Light. *Verdad*. This Jesus is the Jesus they know, the Savior they have imitated for centuries in this land.

But it is His hands that are most informative. This Jesus is the image of the people as they find themselves on the land. His hands are disproportionate, larger than His face. The people have isolated the hands. The hands represent what they value most about themselves. Their concept of struggle with the land. They accept their fate in their hands. They touch the soil and reap its benefits. Of course that would be how they see their God.

Our nameless grandmothers were the daughters of the Ancient Ones. The stations of this cross tell their story, how they were blended in the harshness of the inevitable. The Spanish, the first immigrants, were forced to accept what the natives already knew about the land. They had come here to claim it, but it claimed them. They came to understand that they couldn't own the land; they were part of it. They adjusted their Christianity to reflect that irresistible reality. For 300 years, the *mestizos*, whose children came to this valley, practiced the religion that they found necessary to survive this place.

The posture of every figure in the procession reveals a truth. Each character in the drama—Jesus struggling, the women lamenting, disciples assisting—is in ascension amidst turmoil. The world around them is in a gradual state of erosion, but the people are undefeated. The mortal anguish depicted is accepted as the condition imposed on them for the blessing of their existence. We are all born to this terminal illness we call life. The people of the valley understand the struggle should be about the challenges of life, not the inevitability of death. The statues climb the mountain, knowing that the struggle is the meaning.

Highway 160
La Veta Pass to Wolf Creek Pass

70. La Veta Pass to Fort Garland
from *Tramp Across the Continent* by Charles Lummis

*In 1884, Charles Fletcher Lummis, a journalist working in Cincinnati,
Ohio, accepted a job offer from the* Los Angeles Times *and set out for
the West Coast on foot. During this 3500-mile trek, Lummis filed weekly dispatches to the* Times, *which he described as the "wayside notes"
of a happy vagabond, "written in hurried moments by the coal-oil
lamps of country hotels, the tallow dips of section-house or ranch, the
smoky pine-knots of the cowboy's or hunter's cabin, the crackling fogon
of a Mexican adobe, or the snapping greasewood of my lonely campfire
upon the plains." Shortly after the conclusion of his one hundred and
forty-three day "tramp across the continent," Lummis settled in as
city editor of the* Los Angeles Times, *where he would continue to work
until he suffered a mild stroke in 1887. After a period of recovery in
New Mexico, Lummis went on to write extensively about the American
Southwest as editor of a West Coast magazine called* The Land of
Sunshine *(and later* Out West*).*

In Tramp Across the Continent, *the book he wrote about his
cross-country journey, Lummis filed reports from the San Luis Valley
and other Colorado places. After spending the night at a prospector's
cabin near La Veta Pass, Lummis entered the Valley in the company
of Shadow, his canine companion, and a "sturdy hunter" named
Washburn who was "clad in fringed buckskin from head to foot."*

In front was the lovely San Luis Valley ... and at our right the stupendous
bulk of Sierra Blanca, tallest and noblest of all Colorado's congress
of Titans. As for Shadow, he seemed to feel the exhilaration, too, and
kept us in a roar with frantic but unavailing pursuit of his first jackrabbits. The weather turned ugly, and a spiteful sleet pelted our faces; but

Washburn's modest reminiscences made the way short. Almost before we knew it, we had passed deserted Fort Garland and came in sight of an ancient adobe hut on the banks of Trincheras Creek. Here we met the trapper's brother, a sawed-off Hercules not over five feet in height, but enormously powerful in chest and shoulders. He was sauntering easily along with the king of all antelopes upon his shoulders, as though its one hundred and fifty pounds had been a pillow. We went into camp together, and ate and smoked and talked far into the night, and then rolled off to sleep under the heavy wagon sheet. Around the walls hung queer, round, shield-like affairs, looking worthless enough, but each standing for eight or nine dollars even in that market—for they were all prime beaver-skins. The animal has to be skinned so as to make the pelt circular, in order to preserve its full value; and these furry disks, some three feet in diameter, are bound to willow hoops to dry. In those days the creek all along those meadows was full of quiet ponds and substantial dams built by these wonderful four-footed engineers. They can generally fell a tree, a foot through, as exactly to the desired line as could any old lumberman, but should the tree chance to fall wrong, they leave it and attack another. I have known no pleasanter days than the many spent in spying upon the work of a beaver colony as the voiceless artisans dam running streams, cut the green clubs for their winter food, or mud-plaster the roofs of their conical lodges with their trowel tails.

71. Alamosa
from "Esperanza" by Kathy Park

For the last thirty years, writer and artist Kathy Park has lived in the San Luis Valley—painting, carving in stone and wood, teaching at Adams State University, and spending as much time as possible with her horse Esperanza. While moving into a new home on the eastern edge of Alamosa, she watched the way her horse settled into a pasture that was already inhabited by a motley community of equines who had a well-established set of habits and customs. After a rocky entry into this new herd, Esperanza established herself, but only after observing

from the periphery, which can also be a useful strategy for humans
adjusting to a new community.

In our new place east of Alamosa, we've inherited a herd of seven: two
bays, three paints and two red mules. Well, not really inherited. We're
honoring a previous agreement our sellers made with a man from La Jara
who boards his herd in our sixteen-acre field until the grass is gone or the
water tank freezes. It hasn't been cold enough yet to freeze the tank, but
the grass is very thin, and some of the herd are starting to look it. When
they see me come to bring Esperanza in for the night and give her hay, they
stand at the fence, nickering low in their throats. I can hear their request
quite clearly, and I'm tempted, but I'm also reluctant to start throwing them
hay too. They're not mine, and the man will be coming for them next week.

The two black and white paints look the worst. Narrow-chested, long-
legged and long-hooved, they are ribby and gaunt along their backbones
and haunches. Maybe they're older horses and their teeth are worn down.
The mane on one of them is dreadlocked with an old braid that was
never combed out, now riddled with stems, stickers and seeds. They're
sweet and docile to be around, or maybe they're just beaten down. Until
Esperanza arrived, they occupied the lowest rung of the pecking order.

Next up from the bottom are the two red mules, a John and a Molly,
meaning one is male and the other female, although neither will ever be
fertile as is true of most mules. They're round bellied and healthy, easy
keepers, and they both love their long ears to be scratched. They're very
gentle around us, but woe be to any intruder in the field. Yesterday I saw
them chase two dogs out of the field that were drinking water from the
spill puddles around the horse tank. They worked as a team, herding the
dogs at a gallop until both dogs scrambled under the barbed wire, tails
tucked, running for home.

When I first set Esperanza loose in the field—her head held high
and tail straight up, pronging in a proud extended trot—she ran straight
into a rude awakening. The mules took one look at her and pinned their
ears back. Teeth bared, they harried her most of the day, chasing her all
over the field with all but one paint in hot pursuit. I watched and worried.
Should I intervene? Save her from getting hurt? Keep her locked in her

corral? But then I noticed that she learned, albeit reluctantly, to keep her distance from the herd, as if there were an invisible perimeter which she dared not penetrate lest the two enforcers push her back outside. A tough lesson for my alpha mare—and not without suffering a few scrapes and bite marks—to realize she's not automatically queen of the herd, but instead an outcast, lower even than the two gaunt paints. Maybe, out on the periphery, she can learn to trade some of her high-headed exuberance for some caution and humility.

Then comes the big white paint, probably an Appaloosa mix by the look of his eyes and roan blotches and spots. A VERY easy keeper, this gentleman is actually fat. When he stands near the two gaunt paints, I can definitely see the advantages of being higher up on the pecking order: first dibs at food. I haven't made friends with this horse that much. He lets me approach him, but he's not very personable, and there's something dull around him, uninspiring because he is un-aspiring. I'd like to see him enjoy himself for once in the field, but mostly he's all about eating and preserving his place in the order. And being mean to Esperanza.

Highest on the pecking order are the two bays. They're both stout, long-backed quarter horses with small chiseled heads and huge rumps, indistinguishable except that the mare has a faint crescent moon on her forehead and a couple white socks. At first I thought the bay gelding was in charge. No other horse dares to enter his space without his consent. He doesn't need to harry or chase anyone like the mules and the white paint do; all he does is flick an ear back and narrow his eyes, and every horse instantly back pedals to give him space. Except that yesterday, after we had unloaded and stacked the second half of our hay bales for the winter and Henry had raked up the loose hay and thrown it over the fence, I noticed the bay gelding yielding to the bay mare, granting her first dibs at a small pile of hay. She didn't do anything but move to the hay pile—no ear flick or lowered head or withering look. Nothing at all, and still he yielded. She must be the herd's leader.

I marvel at the power she wields without any threat or use of force. Power simply through her presence and clear intention. I wonder if she was ever the new kid on the block, eager but inexperienced. Hers is the kind of status Esperanza would like to enjoy, but hasn't yet earned. Hers is the kind of status I wouldn't mind having myself.

72. Del Norte
from "Fremont's Fourth Expedition" by Micah McGehee

Northwest of Del Norte are the La Garita Mountains. There, in the winter of 1848-49, Colonel John Charles Fremont's ill-fated fourth expedition, the purpose of which was to seek out a transcontinental railroad route, met up with the perfect storm of rugged mountain terrain and unforgiving winter weather.

In her book The San Luis Valley: Land of the Six-Armed Cross, *Colorado historian and long-time Del Norte resident Virginia McConnell Simmons describes their retreat from these mountains: "Finally on December 22, Fremont admitted defeat and turned the expedition back .... On December 24, they had to dig through six feet of snow with dinner plates .... On December 27, conditions had become so desperate that a party of four set out for help .... The [other] men broke up into three groups, called messes, each of which was to scavenge its own food supplies."*

Micah McGehee, a member of one of those "messes," described the days that followed in an article which first appeared in the May 1910 issue of a magazine called Outdoor Life. *Shortly after the gloomy campfire scene he describes at the end of this excerpt, a rescue party arrived and they escaped the grisly alternative that lay before them.*

Day after day we stayed there but no game came near. Occasionally we could hear the distant, dismal howl of a wolf as if weary with waiting for its work .... We found a handful or two of rosebuds along the river which we divided and ate, and Dr. Kern found a few small bugs upon the water where the ice was broken and ate them. We had already devoured our moccasin shoes, and a small sack made of smoked lodge skin. We dug in the ground with our knives for roots, but it was useless labor.

We became weaker daily, and to walk thirty steps once a day after
some dried cottonwood sticks to keep our fire fatigued us greatly. Our
strength was rapidly failing. Andrews died in the course of the night
as he lay by our side after lingering for several days and, the next day,
Rohrer was nearly gone, talking wildly, a fearful expression of despair
resting upon his countenance. The mention of his family at home had
served to rouse him and keep him going longer than his strength would
otherwise have borne him up; but now it was too late; his case was over.
Taking from Andrews' pocket a small gilt-embossed Bible, carefully
preserved ... we laid his body to one side and covered it with a blanket;
then we sat down, waiting until Rohrer should die, intending (as soon
as the breath left his body), to commence another move down the river,
continuing by slow degrees until our powers should entirely fall.

As we sat waiting, ------------ came over to the fire where Taplin, I,
and Stepperfeldt were sitting and, in a sad tone, said: "Men, I have come
to make a proposition. I don't know how you will take it. It is a horrid
one. We are starving. In two or three days more, except something is
done, we will all be dead. Here lies a mass of useless flesh, from which
the life has departed, which, as soon as we leave, will be the prey of
wild beasts. There is enough to keep us all alive .... Now I propose, that,
instead of leaving it to become food for wolves, we make use of it to save
human life. It is horrid, I know, but I will undertake to do the butchering,
as you may call it, and you need have nothing to do with that part; you
need not even see it done. Do you agree to my proposition?"

All sat in silence, then several of us objected, and I spoke up and
said: "... I fully appreciate our situation, but I think that by making up
our minds to it and remaining quiet, we can hold out three days longer,
by which time, after finding that we cannot possibly bear up longer, there
will then be time to think of adopting such a horrible alternative.'

We remained around the fire, stirring it as little as possible and
firing signal guns at frequent intervals during the day. Rohrer died. Two
days passed and no relief came. Several times we imagined we heard
an answer to our signal and would rise up to listen, but being as often
disappointed, we had ceased to notice.

73. Wolf Creek Pass
from *Instant Karma* by Wayne Sheldrake

*In 1938, shortly after construction of the road that crosses the
Continental Divide between the towns of South Fork and Pagosa Springs,
a skiing entrepreneur named Kelly Boyce installed a rope tow on the
north side of Wolf Creek Pass, which he ran off the engine of an old
Chevy truck. He charged skiers a dollar to ride the lift up toward the
Divide. Shortly thereafter, the US Forest Service contracted with the
Civilian Conservation Corps to build a warming hut at the base of the
ski hill. In 1955, the ski operation crossed over to the other side of the
highway where it is currently located and where it benefits from heavy
winter storms which bring an average of 450 inches of snow per year.*

*Wayne Sheldrake came to the mountain as a young ski instructor. Over
the years, he continued his exploration of the mountain in almost every
imaginable condition, but nothing pleased him more than a big storm. The
bigger, the better. One day, as he tells it, he was laying low in the lodge
after a late night, when some skiing buddies came in out of an epic storm
and told him that there was so much snow on The Face, one of steepest
runs at Wolf Creek, that it was nearly impossible to ski. Sheldrake took
that as an invitation to find out for himself. He reported on the adventure
in his book* Instant Karma: The Heart and Soul of a Ski Bum.

I waddled to the overlook of The Face. The closer I got to it, the deeper
the snow. Far down in the whiteness, I heard the diesel growl of the
Thiekol. There was nothing but bottomless, heavy snow between me and
the road it was packing ... .

I'd seen people on The Face sucked down until snow stacked up
chest-high, like white mud. Straight back down the lift line would be the
best route. It was steep, maybe 40 degrees for the first two hundred feet.
I'd need all the momentum I could get to clear a knoll about half way
down. If I bogged down there, I'd be digging. What if the snow fractured
and slid? Who would know I was there?

I aimed for the steep flank under the chairlift. The skis—208 cen-
timeter racing skis—picked up speed, but they didn't float. They sank.

I was in snow up to my knees. Then the skis dove and I dropped in up
to my neck. I felt like an undertow was taking me down. The only way
to resist the suction was to dive face-first into the whiteness. I held my
breath. Snow splashed on my goggles and poured down the back of my
parka. I felt like I had stepped off a high dive and now, under the surface,
my feet dangled weightlessly into cold depths. I was sure the whole hillside had broken away and taken me with it. Avalanche. But almost as I
determined my oblivion, I felt lift, suspension. I felt the snow holding me
as it moved. The drifting sensation was vaguely aerodynamic. I fought
to stay upright, my arms swimming forward. I dropped the handles on
my poles and grabbed at the snow. I stretched my legs, reaching for the
bottom, for anything stable. If I squirmed hard enough, the flow seemed
to match the yaw and pitch of my descent. Snow wrapped around my
chest, wrapped my thighs as I surged along. My head went under.

...Was it possible to drown right side up? It was quiet. I was oddly
aware of the snow's hiss as it moved up the front of my coat and cascaded
over my shoulders. Swarms of feathery snow mashed against the lens of
my goggles and peeled away from the plastic. Visibility: one inch.

The skis came alive with their own pendulous consciousness. This
happens sometimes. You feel like the skis know more than you do, as
if they're possessed of their own tactile sentience, infused with their
own sixth sense. You let them go and follow. I felt them veer enough
to mimic the incline of the slope. I stretched to get my neck above the
surface. I was suffocating. Although moving seemed imperative and
the snow moved faster and faster, the speed frightened me. First of all, I
was blinded by pure whiteness. Second of all, I don't usually ski straight
down steep runs. It had to be an avalanche ... .

It was like falling into a dark elevator shaft and wondering what floor
the elevator was on. The snow maintained its speed. I found equilibrium
in it, somewhat like a sky-diver guiding himself in a defined channel
of air. It sloshed urgently, like water through a down spout. It plunged,
pushed me, and I plunged with it.

But then, it suddenly slowed; it stalled. For a moment it felt thicker
and deeper. It swirled, as if I'd dropped into a tight, soupy eddy. I swam
to keep from being twisted around. Inexplicably, lower layers released

as the rest of the snow gained momentum again, taking me with it. The
snow stalled and started, stalled and started, which scared me as much
as the falling. I felt if I stopped, I would be hopelessly stuck, buried, my
whereabouts unknown .... Amidst the panic, I had one flashing comfort.
The pulsation of the movement—like a slow heart—convinced me that,
at least, I was not in an avalanche ....

   I felt the slope get flatter. My goggles and then my whole head
emerged from the surface like a periscope .... My lungs raled for air, as
if I had just swum the length of a swimming pool underwater. I choked.
My eyes watered. I looked back up the hill. I saw the luminous blizzard,
shadowy lift towers, and empty chairs passing each other in the white
smear. The fury of the wind filled my ears straight through my hat. It
seemed like an hour ago I had been on top of the mountain looking down
and hoping.

   Instantly, I knew I was going back up.

Highway 17
Alamosa to Highway 285

74. Mosca
from "Hurriedly" by Trudi Kretsinger

As Mosca farmer and rancher Trudi Kretsinger says, any experience of landscape depends on the eye (and attitude) of the beholder. Some landscapes demand more of the beholder—time and patience, for example. The San Luis Valley, she suggests, is one such place. Over time one realizes that any visit to a place like Great Sand Dunes National Park, given changes in light, and weather, and in the shifting sands themselves, is entirely unique.

We have such a short growing season here in the San Luis Valley; in order to get a crop, we have to move fast, fast all summer. One afternoon a couple of summers ago, I was rushing home from checking the cattle we were pasturing at the Medano Ranch and feeling grouchy for being in a hurry. So I stopped at The Pit Stop in Mosca for gasoline and an ice cream bar to see if I could get myself to calm down. A fancy new van pulled up at the gas pump, and an elderly man and his middle-aged daughter emerged. They left two kids in backseat who were ogling my ice cream. The woman went inside and the man circled the vehicle a couple of times, very fast, as if he were running a race. I thought I was in a hurry until I met these people. The man stopped where I stood and said, "Say, you know how to open the damned gas tanks on these things? We borrowed this car from my son and we can't figure it out."

The man jangled change in the pockets of his Bermuda shorts while he waited for my answer. I was driving a 1978 Ford pickup. We had just replaced the rolled-up sock that had served as a gas cap for some months. "I don't know that much about new cars, but my mother has one and hers has a little button inside next to the... "

"It's next to the trunk-release knob," the woman exclaimed as she came out of the store. "I'll get it, Dad." And she quickly got to the business of filling the tank. The kids were climbing out of the car. Their mother forced them back in with the whip of her voice. "Get back in the car! We don't have time for you to get out!"

The man turned back to me, still fiddling with coins in his pockets. "Say," he said. "What is it with these Dunes?"

"What do you mean?"

He ran a hand over his head. "We went down to that turn off that says, 'Great Sand Dunes,' but we didn't see anything. How long does it take?"

"I guess it takes about fifteen minutes to get there. Maybe twenty."

"No, I mean how long does it take to see them? We don't have much time."

I was taken back. "It could take years to see them, I suppose." I pointed east to the Sangre de Cristo Mountains. "You see those mountains over there?" The man nodded quickly. "You see those flesh-colored mounds that it looks like the mountains are standing on?" Another nod. "Those are the Dunes. They go on and on. And they're changing all the time. Every minute, every puff of wind, they're changing."

"Well, what's there to *do* over there?"

I chomped the last of my ice cream bar and tossed the paper in the trash. "You know, if you're in a hurry, you might ought to drive up to the shopping mall in Pueblo or the amusement park in Denver. I mean, the Dunes are really something you really can't see in a hurry. You have to kind of experience them."

"Are they worth it?"

No one had ever asked me this before. "Yeah," I said, headed to the cab of my truck. I was through talking to him.

"Leave that woman alone!" the woman shrieked at her father. She was cleaning the windshield. The children were bouncing in the backseat.

"But she's a local," he said. "She'll *know*!"

I suppose he assumed I was a local because most people traveling cross-country would not do so in boots covered in mud and fresh cow manure. I explained that while I live here I wasn't truly a local. To be *from* here, you have to have lived here before you were even born.

"But you've been to the Sand Dunes, right?"

I nodded.

"So what do you like?"

I was still aiming to get in my truck and drive away from these people, beginning to believe they didn't deserve to go to the Dunes. But I couldn't resist his question. "First of all let me just say that you're a lot like a lot of people I see coming in here from other places. The San Luis Valley is different. It's a subtle, soft-spoken place. Things don't just knock you on your butt like they do in other places. Most of the things that are wonderful about here aren't real predictable either. Like you'll be driving to town and, lo and behold, your neighbor has chosen just that moment to move his sheep down the road and all you can do is sit there, and take in the wonderful sea of wool, and afterward squish dingle berries with your tires. I mean, that's not something you can exactly plan. But it's real pleasurable unless you're in a hurry.

"Or the light, that's a big thing around here. You just look out across the floor of the valley toward the mountains and, depending on how the sun hits the clouds, you'll see the most incredible spectrum of color. And then, the clouds shift or the sun tilts funny and the whole scene changes. Again, it's not exactly something you can hurry up and see. Or know when it's gonna happen."

"What about the Dunes, though?" The man seemed be defying his own impatience, hanging around to hear the answer to his question. "What's there to see at the Dunes?"

"Dad! Let's go!" the woman hissed from the driver's side door. He made a gesture in her direction that looked like a man swatting a fly.

"Shush up!" he said without looking at her. Then, to me, he spun his hand in the air, over and over, meaning to keep talking to finish what I was saying. Quickly. Quickly.

"What I like to do is climb up on the Dunes a ways when there's a full moon, and watch it rise over the mountains and spill all over the valley. That's enough to make a person faint." The man looked at me blankly.

I continued. "Do you like to see naked women? If you go right at sunset and you climb up a ways and the sun catches the dunes just right, they look like row after row of brown-skinned women lying on their sides, hip after hip after hip. It's just beautiful."

The woman yelled one more time. She started her van. The man told his daughter to shut up, turned, and said thank you very much to me. I got in my truck and pulled away, leaving them to a heated discussion about the meaning of life and time and travel. I never knew which way they went. They helped me to go home the back way, the slow and dusty way, the way you have to squint against the afternoon sun.

75. Crestone
from *Heading Home* by Peter Anderson

Depending on who you ask, you may hear Crestone described as a hippy town, a destination for spiritual seekers, or a haven for end-of-the-road mountain eccentrics. It is a place that people love to label, but it's also a place that is almost impossible to categorize because it is so eclectic and because there is no other place quite like it.

Crestone was originally established to support gold and silver mining operations on the western flank of the Sangre de Cristo Range. Later, locals were employed on a huge ranch, which had once been a Spanish land grant. After the ranch changed hands in the early 1970s, it was subdivided and developed for a new generation of residents. One of the developers, a Canadian financier named Maurice Strong, moved here with his wife Hannah Marstrand Strong who embraced a different vision for this out-of-the-way community. With the idea of creating a meeting place for the world's great spiritual traditions, the Strongs created the Manitou Foundation, which awarded nine land grants to various religious organizations including a Catholic Carmelite Monastery, several Buddhist centers, and a Hindu ashram.

Large swaths of public land which surround Crestone guarantee measures of space and silence that appeal not only to religious communities, but also to those seeking a simpler and more contemplative way of life. It is that contemplative ethos that underlies the attraction this place has had not only for religious communities, but also for artists, back-to-the landers, seekers of one kind or another, and retirees.

In an essay called "Vulture Gulch," which appeared in a collection called Heading Home: Field Notes, *my three year-old daughter evoked that quality of this place as well as I ever will.*

Around our house, piñon and juniper elders offer us a little shelter from the wind that often blows in hard from the southwest. Nearby, a little to the south, a line of aspens that follows Crestone Creek down the mountain offers yet another windbreak and harbors warblers and western tanagers during the warmer months, as well as a colony of turkey vultures. In the mornings the vultures leave their nearby roost, drifting down along the line of aspens then cottonwoods that follow the mountain drainages onto the valley floor, scanning county roads with eye and nose for the latest roadkill. In the evenings, we watch them come home to their perch on the flanks of the Sangres, circling by overhead and spiraling down to their roost in the aspens along Crestone Creek. The arroyo they often seem to follow to and from their roost runs by our house. We call it Vulture Gulch.

One day, I enticed my three-year-old daughter into her travelling pack and carried her down the road for a visit with vultures. It was early enough in the morning that few of them had left. As we followed the trail along the creek into a little clearing we saw them overhead, at least twenty vultures, several of them facing toward the sun, their wings outspread and gathering sunlight.

"Don't disturb them, Papa," Rosalea said after a minute or two looking up at them in that clearing. We kept walking. Down the trail, several vultures flew overhead.

"Where do you think they're going?" I asked Rosalea.

"They're going to school church," she said.

"Where's that?" I wondered.

"It's way out there," she said, pointing out over the valley. "And it's where your dreams go when you close your eyes."

76. Moffat
from "Antelope and Jackrabbit" by Peggy Godfrey

*Peggy Godfrey, who has been ranching in the high desert next to the
Sangre de Cristos for almost fifty years, describes herself as a "free
range poet." Her experiences working outdoors often provide the raw
material for her poems and stories. As she puts it, "Composting disas-
ters into poems and stories is my version of value-added agriculture."
Here is an essay from a collection of her poems and essays called*
Stretch Marks.

What a welcome sight—the deep green cumulus alfalfa, fragrant vio-
let-tinged crowns of blossoms. Un-irrigated fields, an old alfalfa stand
filled in with brome and wheat grasses, across the county road from my
house grew lush this year after three well-spaced June rain showers. Last
year's drought scarcely provided cover for the persistent gopher diggings!

My hay-mowing equipment broke down on a Tuesday midway
through this fifteen-acre project. Each day's delay pushed against my
hopes to finish up. Wednesday I watched a lone antelope grazing between windrows just south of the uncut area. A timid species, she was
closer to my house than I'd ever seen antelope venture. I wondered if
she had given birth already. Wildlife often separate themselves from a
herd for birthing, as do cattle and sheep. On Wednesday evening she
was visible from both the road and my house, lying down among the tall
alfalfa clumps—an unusual "here I am" announcement.

Thursday morning I raked hay on the east side of the deep trench
that runs north and south through the forty acres. I'd cut a double swath
around two of the west pieces on the same day I'd cut the east side, so I
brought the rake around. Up from her hiding place fifty or sixty yards
away from me sprang an antelope and close on her heels was her jack
rabbit-sized baby. She cut a path to the little two-track road, through the
gate headed south. If the little guy hadn't been leaping and bounding
as antelope do, I'd have never been able to see him. She would pause to
let her wee one catch up, then off again she'd go. When there was more
than a quarter mile between us, they stopped for a breather. Suddenly

I realized that had the haybine belt not broken, I'd have cut down her birthing sanctuary, perhaps worse.

It is an awesome experience to realize that with the evidence at hand, I was retroactively glad for the inconvenience of the breakdown. The whole of life is so much more than I can know or imagine. It's humbling and thrilling to receive these intimate glimpses into the mystery.

77. Between Moffat and Highway 285
from *Life with Pickle* by John Mattingly

The demographic composition of Saguache County includes cattle ranchers, alfalfa farmers, and more recently cannabis growers whose greenhouses are scattered all over the valley floor; it includes migrant farm workers in Center as well as county and federal government workers in the town of Saguache; Catholics worship at a historic church in La Garita, while Buddhists practice in a recently constructed retreat center in Crestone. For a relatively isolated rural area, Saguache County has a surprisingly diverse population.

John Mattingly, a long-time farmer who lives a few miles north of Moffat, also cultivates words as a contributor and columnist for several magazines including Colorado Central *and* The Fence Post. *His wry and witty observations of rural life in Colorado are gathered in several works of fiction and nonfiction. In* Life with Pickle, *his short stories feature a fictional character who has worked on farms and ranches not unlike those that Mattingly has known over the course of his lengthy career as "an ag guy." In the following tale, Pickle encounters the "yin and the yang" of Saguache County.*

Every Fourth of July, the community gathered for a barbecue and craft fair. Pickle always attended. He visited with neighbors he hadn't seen for months, and the food was great.

The local wild game processor, Jim Doogan, donated an elk every year and cooked it in various ways and dimensions over an applewood flame. Ernie Binton had a brother on the East Slope who grew sweet

corn; Ernie always donated a pickup load to the cause. He cooked the
ears in full husk over charcoal, then peeled them back and dipped the hot
ears in a tub of homemade Guernsey cream butter. For dessert there were
at least two dozen different kinds of pies.

Kids ran around playing games, laughing, or occasionally screaming
with either fear or delight. A band of local cowboys known as "Ed McNutt
and the Backups" crooned a country carol from a slabwood stage backed
with velvet rugs bearing images of palm trees and tropical sunsets.

Pickle was on his fourth go-around through the food line, talking
with Darrell Bee about a fellow from Texas who'd just bought the Falling
Feather Ranch and paid too much. "Ain't no way he'll ever pay for it
with cows," said Darrell, for about the tenth time. Darrell was also the
low man on the totem pole at the ranch where he worked. He and Pickle
shook their heads in bewildered disgust.

Pickle happened to look through a gap in the crowd toward the
craft fair, where he noticed a woman sitting cross-legged on the ground.
Directly behind her hung a blanket sporting a decorative circular design.

Darrell noticed Pickle's stare and said, "She's one of the new
Pilgrims." Pilgrims were people who recently had moved to the ranch
country, charmed by the solitude and low rents. "She's some kinda doctor.
Go on over and see her, Pickle. She'll fix you right up."

Pickle ate another round of elk and corn before screwing up the
courage to drift by the strange lady. He studied the sign: BRAIN
BALANCING and AURA ADJUSTMENTS. Pickle looked at the woman
for a moment and she held him with her gaze. "Look at me for just a little
longer," she said.

Pickle obeyed, mostly because he couldn't see any immediate alternative. The woman stared at him so hard he was afraid she might bore a
hole through his head with her eye waves.

"Your brain is very unbalanced," she said, finally.

"I wouldn't know about that," said Pickle, though he was somewhat
concerned.

"By the way, my name is CC Sensuay." She extended her hand and
Pickle shook it. "Are you aware that you have a left brain and a right
brain?"

"No I wasn't," said Pickle. "I always thought I had just the one brain, and sometimes, some of the people I work for doubt that I've even got that."

CC didn't smile. "Are you right-handed?"

"Yes ma'am."

"What is your name?"

"Pickle."

CC didn't flinch or make any sort of snide allusion, which impressed him considerably. "Your left brain, Pickle, is your rational side; your right brain is your intuitive side. To actualize in harmony, you must balance the two sides." Again, she wrapped him with her gaze. "My sense of it is that you are a very powerful person, but you are not in balance, so you are not in command. I feel a steep shift away from your rational side, but instead of elevating your gestaltic, or intuitive powers, it is literally weighing them down. Would you like a treatment?"

"No." Pickle envisioned sharp things, such as pitch forks, poking into his brain.

"It won't hurt," said CC. "I work strictly with the energy fields around the brain, so, except for the initial relaxation and orientation, you won't feel anything."

"If a person's brain *was* unbalanced, how would they know it?"

"They usually don't know it, and that's just the sad reality of it. But after an adjustment, many people experience more energy and power."

"Where do you live?" asked Pickle. He was interested in energy and power, but reluctant to turn his brain over to a foreigner.

"I rented the cabin on the Slash J Ranch," said CC.

"So you know Billy Jay?"

"My father knows Billy from hunting, which isn't exactly the preferred connection ... for me." For a moment, the veneer of CC's therapeutic mysticism fell down and Pickle felt more comfortable. "But the cabin has an energy that I like, Pickle. I can feel the homesteaders who built it and lived there. I feel their hardships. Have you ever had an experience like that?"

"Might of," said Pickle.

"Well, let's not get distracted. We were about to start a balancing treatment." She pushed back the decorative blanket that hung from the tree branch behind them, revealing a mattress covered with a bright pink sheet. "Recline here, with your head pointing this way." She pointed to the uphill end of the mattress. Pickle hesitated, noting that several local ranch hands were observing him with transparent amusement. He paced away from the mattress, circled around and dropped the decorative blanket to obscure their view before reclining on the pink sheet.

CC massaged Pickle's neck and head and he became relaxed, then sleepy, and finally he drifted into a dreamy condition where he felt himself pull away from the earth, his arms hanging down below him. He felt CC applying pressure alternately to the right and left side of his head, and even though he heard chuckles from the likes of Darrell Bee, he found himself enjoying the treatment. Long before he wanted it to stop, he heard CC's voice coming to him as if she were at the end of a long tunnel. "OK, Pickle, you can slowly come back to the present, conscious state. Don't get up until you are ready. For the next three days, I want you to drink lots of water and do not consume any dairy products. You will notice a gradual shifting within your power center. If you feel unbalanced, don't hesitate to call me."

Next morning at the shop as the men were all standing around getting ready to work, Pickle learned that news of his treatment had reached Larry D. "Hoo-wee, Mr. Pickle got his brain balanced." He leaned over and looked at Pickle sideways.

Normally, Pickle received Larry D.'s remarks as the acknowledged inferior, but this morning he didn't feel particularly inferior. "I'd say you should get your brain balanced too, Larry D., but there's a minimum size requirement."

All the men were so stunned by the command of Pickle's retort that the remarks suddenly turned on Larry D.

Highway 285
Cumbres Pass to Poncha Pass

78. Cumbres Pass
from "Meditación en Dos Ojos:
Garcia Lake at Cumbres Pass" by Reyes Garcia

*When Reyes Garcia came home after serving in Viet Nam, he returned to
his family's ranch on the Conejos River near Antonito. Connecting with
home territory was good medicine. It was that desire for connection that
led him up to the lake near Cumbres Pass that bears his family name.
The story, as he heard it from his elders, was that the lake was deeded to
his grandmother, Teodora Epsinosa de Garcia, hence the name, Garcia
Lake. The lake is formed from two underground rivers, which surface in
the form of two springs. "Dos Ojos," Garcia writes, "can mean two eyes
as well as two springs ...just as the two springs pool together in one body
of water [the lake], our own eyes sight together to form an image of the
world in depth." Working with that image, Garcia came to think of the
lake as a place to invite a deeper vision of the world.*

*Seeking that kind of vision has been part of Garcia's vocation for
a long time. Garcia has offered classes in philosophy, religion, environmental studies, indigenous studies, southwest studies, and writing
at Fort Lewis College, Adams State University, and Colorado College.
The following passage reflects all those interests and describes an
experience at Garcia Lake that forever changed his vision of the world.
"My mother always used to say that Cumbres lake was bottomless,"
he writes. "Gradually, I have come to believe that the world itself is
bottomless, unfathomable, infinitely deep."*

The waters of the springs called me, and I went and camped among the
Engelmann spruce. An epiphany came to me that began in the evening
after much thunder and lightning, while I was sitting in my army poncho,
watching raindrops splash on the glass-smooth surface of the lake. In

slow motion on the water, they made indentations innumerable in number and variety. The grace and beauty of their dance and song existed beyond words. Each splash and dimple contributed to a rain of roundnesses of infinite perfection that seemed to go on for an eternity, as if a switch for continuous repeat had been flipped. I seemed to enter a mythic time and space within the rain on the lake.

In this strange mood, after the sun had gone down, I lay face up, army bag and poncho under me on the grassy shore, looking up into clear night sky. I began to feel an uncanny fear of the vastness of the starry night. Fear became horror when suddenly, with my whole body, I sensed that I was looking *down* into the cosmos, beyond the Milky Way and down into the abyss. My heart was pounding as hard as it had during mortar attacks in Vietnam. I spread my arms wide and clutched the grass, holding on to the earth. I did not want to fall into the night. I was hanging by grass from the bottom of the earth, the endless darkness burning with terrifying nuclear power, pulling me into itself.

Just as suddenly, and with an absolute lucidity, I remembered exactly where I was. I could hear the two springs easing into the lake, the tinkling of their pure water. "I am in the heart of my homeland," I whispered to myself, and let go of the grass. I said aloud to the night sky, "*Llévame si te gustaría!* Take me if you want!" My total fear became total trust.

I fell asleep smiling and woke up smiling. Memory of that night still brings on an unassailable confidence, not in myself per se but in this marvelous planet, spinning on its axis and orbiting the sun in a cosmos so big, so complete in itself, so full of mystery that, at such times, surrender is the only sane response.

79. Antonito
from *Letters from the Headwaters* by Aaron Abeyta

Antonito began as a sheep herding camp known as San Antonio Junction, referring to its proximity to the Conejos and San Antonio Rivers. When the Denver & Rio Grande Railroad built its line south from Alamosa, the town was renamed Antonito and became an

*important town on the railroad line. By the time it was incorporated in
1889, Aaron Abeyta's family was already deeply rooted in the region.*

*Abeyta makes his home in Antonito, where he has served his commu-
nity as mayor, high school football coach, and the co-founder, with his
wife Michelle, of a community school. Students with roots in Antonito
and other valley towns found him to be an ally and a powerful mentor
in the classes he taught at Adams State University in Alamosa. But his
roots are wider and deeper than any one community, encompassing the
San Juan Mountains where his family ran sheep in the summer months,
as well as the high valley pastures where they tended to their animals in
the colder months. Similarly, his vocation is wider and deeper than any
one job. In his role as a poet and storyteller, Abeyta speaks out for the
region that is his homeland and for the people who live there. His work
encompasses a wide swath of geography and history, as in the following
excerpt from a letter included in his book,* Letters from the Headwaters.

Dear George,

… Some part of me feels like all you have to do is press play and
I will begin again in some innate migration to the llanos, mountains, churches and rivers that form my home. I suppose it is no
accident that I chose the word migration. My people came to my
valley home and lands of New Mexico over 400 years ago and
have been stealing or stolen from ever since … .

I tell my students that we are by nature a migratory people.
Our own migration is like Orion's, the constellation just now
back in our night, and his winter journey through the sky. He
begins himself, tilted to the east, lying on his side, and moves
slowly upright in the southern sky before falling again on his side
in the west. And then there is my own abuelito who personified
this for me, who fell into his western sky on February 15th at 1:35
pm. By now you must be wondering what my many loose con-
nections, stars, migration, religion, family are trying to do here.
Ultimately, they must be together and will be my place.

To me the idea of a place, a sense of place is somewhere we come back to at all costs and at all hours of the day or night. I often think of the monarch butterflies and their yearly migration to the south where they will finally rest in the Mexican pines ... . I mention the butterflies because they remind me of my town and how many of us return despite the poverty, and like the monarchs fewer and fewer make the journey with each passing generation. My town is still poor, though every year the river canyon west of my home is gobbled up by homes made of beautiful scraps. The lumber which goes into the homes is standard grade, the same stuff that clogs canyons and shorelines everywhere so that some-one can have a view. The scraps, those are measured in terms. For the most part these transplants buy only the necessities from my town, gas and fishing licenses. We see very little of the wealth that grows three stories high on a ridge where pine and aspen used to mingle. We are a beautiful people that too many think of as scrap ... .

One last thing amigo—earlier, I mentioned my abuelito and his passing. His star is somewhere beyond the San Juan's grasp, fading slowly from this hemisphere and brilliantly into another. I mention him because I miss him and because I believed, and to a certain extent still do, that he is permanently a part of this place, my home ... . I never got to say goodbye to him, though I was at his bedside on that February afternoon when it seemed even the sheep in the field below his home stopped moving. The only thing in the air was his last breath and the mumbled prayers of some-one speaking too fast in Spanish.

So you see, George, there is no sense to goodbyes because our human mind will not let go what it knows will return. I see my abuelito at the table playing solitaire, chopping wood, driving off to the sheep camp or simply standing there broad shouldered. This too, memory, is our place, and this round home we call earth, she disappears from herself and from us at times but returns in whatever positions are native to her and our memory. These canyons that wrinkle her and the butterflies that fan her and rest in her hair keep coming, migrating toward us and through us or perhaps it is the other way around. We cannot say goodbye to our places, no matter how they change, we must always return to them. George, we make each place our own by the things we return to it, living or remembered.

80. Romeo / Manassa
from *Alex and the Hobo*
by Jose Inez Taylor and James M. Taggart

The following story is excerpted from Alex and the Hobo, *a work of fiction told from a nine-year-old boy's point of view. The author, José Inez "Joe" Taylor, based the story on his own coming-of-age experiences here in the San Luis Valley during the early 1940s. Most of the book, which includes ethnographic analysis from James Taggart, is set in Antonito, but the following story takes place on the edge of the San Luis Hills, an uplifted fault block of older volcanic rocks out in the middle of the valley east of Romeo and Manassa.*

Highway 142, which heads east from Highway 285 at Romeo, is part of Los Caminos Antiguos Scenic Byway, a route that is rich in history and legend as the name (which means ancient roads) suggests. The road crosses the Rio Grande and passes through the San Luis Hills, which are weathered and rounded except for some interesting volcanic intrusions and remnants like the rocks described by the old rancher in the following story. As the story suggests, a numinous, even supernatural sense of the valley's high desert landscape, is often associated with the deeply rooted religious heritage of the San Luis Valley.

The day was perfect for the five-mile drive to the ranch. The sun was shining brightly, the fields were green, and the trees and willows lining the lane were alive with their new leaves. They drove down a road that rambled between two rivers, the Conejos to the north and the San Antón to the south. The two rivers meet each other several miles to the east and then emptied into the Rio Grande, flowing south to New Mexico and into

Texas. Red-winged blackbirds chirped their cheerful tunes in a cattail swamp. Alex's father pulled in at the ranch, and the Sánchez family met them with a warm and friendly greeting. Alex's mother, his sisters, and his younger brother were invited into the house. Alex went in the truck with his father and Mr. Sánchez to the corral to fetch the ewe. He spotted an old man sitting under a big shade tree. He thought of his grandfather as he walked over to the old man.

"Good morning," Alex greeted him.

"The same to you, young man. And who might you be?"

"I'm Alex, Señor. And you, what's your name?"

The old man acted friendly, Alex thought, so he felt comfortable talking.

"I like your ranch. Were you born here?" Alex asked.

"Yes, I was, and so was my father."

"There in that house?"

"No, son. Over there, next to those hills," said the old man, pointing to a barren rise on the east.

Alex spotted a rock formation that looked like some prehistoric animal looming at the foot of the hills. It reminded him of something he had seen in a schoolbook.

"Have you ever been to those rocks over there?" Alex asked as he pointed in the direction of what looked like an ancient creature.

"Yes, and did you know those rocks are strange? They hold a mystery. The Indians considered them sacred."

"Are they sacred and that other word you said: myster... ?"

"Mystery."

"Is it a mystery, Señor?"

"I'm not sure. Maybe not to everybody, but to me they are. Maybe not sacred, but strange in a way."

Alex looked at him, confused, not sure of what he meant, but the old man had a serious look on his face, as if recalling something that had happened in his past. He waited for the old man to continue.

"I was there several times, but not alone. Then one time I had to go by myself. I was only a boy. Not much older than you are now."

"Was it scary for you?"

"Not at first, but then it was late in the day. We had a flock of sheep grazing over there, and I had to go herd them home. Well, the sun was down, and it was close to dark. I remember it was during Lent. Matter of fact, it was Wednesday of Holy Week. I got to the flock about a half-mile from there. That's when it happened."

Alex stood in silence, wide-eyed, waiting for the man to continue.

"There behind me, but to my right, I saw this big ball of fire rolling over the prairie. I stood and watched it as it rolled right into those rocks. For a while, flames shot up into the sky and they lit up the whole prairie."

"Wow! I bet you were scared!?"

"*Jito*, I was scared, all right. I've never been as scared as I was then. I even cried from fear."

"Holy Moley. What did you do then?!"

"I left the sheep, ran for home, and told my father."

Alex wondered what he would have done in the same situation.

"What did he say? Did he believe you?"

"No, he didn't that night. He thought I was making it up just to get out of herding the sheep. He got mad at me and made me go with him and bring them home."

"Was that the only time you saw them?"

"No, *jito*. We saw them the next night. Both my father and I did." The old man nodded his head. "He believed me then, and every year since I've seen them during Lent and Holy Week. Every year I sit and look for them and I see them. This last Holy Week I saw them again.

Alex had not known about the lights by the rocks because he was new to this part of the valley. Legend had it that these lights or balls of fire appeared often. Many a traveler going through had seen them, cowboys and shepherds among them, but few came right out and spoke to just anyone about what they had seen.

"Does anyone ever go over there?"

"Oh, yes. Some do, but I've never gone near them again. Not right up to them, like some have."

"But why do they go there if they're mysterious?"

"Well, son, some say there's a treasure buried there and they go looking for it."

"Have they found it?"

"No, *jito*. Not that I know of, but they did find treasure in these parts. That I'm sure of."

"Are you the only one in your family who has seen these balls of fire, Senor?"

"No. My mother, my son, and his wife have, and many of our neighbors have too. But only during Lent and mostly in Holy Week."

"That's scary. I'd like to see them someday."

"As I live and breathe, you will."

81. Saguache
from *The Last Ranch* by Sam Bingham

Highway 285 between Monte Vista and Saguache runs long, straight and flat across the western edge of the San Luis Valley. Locals call it "the gunbarrel." As you travel north toward Saguache, you see fewer center pivot sprinklers irrigating fields of barley and potatoes and more grasslands devoted to grazing livestock. In The Last Ranch: A Colorado Community and the Coming Desert, *Sam Bingham describes the challenges of ranching in this high desert environment. Eight inches of rain fall on this valley in an average year, but as Bingham says, "no gambler would bet on the average."*

When William Eugene Whitten bought his land here in 1898, "the grass grew belly high in the foothills, springs were abundant, [and] chico brush held less dominion over the plain." All the Whittens succeeding him have run their sheep and cattle on land that produces less forage than it did when it was first settled. In describing the efforts of the Whittens who are trying to sustain a family tradition, Bingham offers readers a few "snapshots" of ranching life (circa mid-1990s) in this high desert valley.

The graying fence rails in the Whitten's corral, according to Donnie, were cut by his grandfather around 1900. That in itself is another symptom of desert life. The record stays. Nothing rots. The fence rails will last forever. So will the ruins of the homesteader's cabins, abandoned by the dozens during the Depression. So will the sky-raking skeletons of willow that homesteaders transplanted for shade and that, like their transplanted planters, grew more ambitiously than the alkali soil could support and died at the height of their grandeur. Except, being willows, they never quite died, so green shoots still sprout here and there on the huge bleached trunks....

Nothing in the atmosphere at 52495 County Road T on the threshold of an uncharted adventure into spring gives much excuse for brooding, however. The three children, Sarah, six, Clint, eight, and Nathan, ten, having been released from homework by Karen, are kicking soccer balls and chasing loose chickens around outbuildings and relics of a century of survival that still quake with life. There are hutches of rabbits of various kinds, and pens of Spanish and Nubian goats, and a horse and motor-cycle for riding the range. There are stock trailers and broken harrows, and a maybe workable horse-drawn potato planter, and a hierarchy of old trucks to serve as organ donors for one another, and a boxcar from the days when the San Luis Valley Central still made a profit shipping livestock from Moffat to the main line of the Denver and Rio Grande Western at Alamosa.

A shed, where a lot of Whittens were born when it used to be Grandad Whitten's cabin, still stands near a towering willow, and nearby rests the wagon that hauled from the mountains the immortal aspen poles to build it. And in the double-wide mobile home that has taken over from the old cabin there is a party line and the number of the prayer circle from the Methodist Church, and an IBM computer with the latest accounting software, and enough cow and sheep in the freezer for unlim-ited hospitality.

82. Villa Grove
from *The Life of an Ordinary Woman* by Anne Ellis

Just north of Villa Grove is the turn off to the remnant of a once bus-tling mining camp called Bonanza. Bonanza was the childhood home as

*well as the burial place of Anne Ellis. Ellis's accounts of her life as a
child and later a mother in Bonanza are especially valuable given the
dominance of older male voices in the literature of Colorado's early
mining communities.*

As Elliot West points out in the foreword to Anne Ellis's classic, The
Life of an Ordinary Woman, *her story included a series of tragedies:
"her father deserts her family, her exhausted mother dies (on Christmas
day) when Anne is sixteen, and her stepfather disappears soon afterwards. Her first husband dies in a mining accident, her second of
appendicitis, and a daughter of diphtheria."*

*And yet, Anne Ellis, describes herself as "the happiest person I
have ever met." She brings an indomitable spirit into all of her life circumstances. In the following tale, she describes a childhood expedition
to gather raspberries accompanied by her younger brother, Ed, and an
unreliable burro packer and family friend named "Picnic Jim."*

Picnic unpacked our things at a miner's tent, where we were planning to
make our camp. Just now our things are thrown on the ground under a
tree—no time to waste on camps, we want to pick berries …. Here Picnic
left us, telling us to pick away, and he would come for us in the evening.
We started, working hard and fast, never looking up, and when we do,
all the trees look the same and the trail has vanished, but we don't care,
berries are what we want. At last the pails are full and mashed down till
the juice rises to the top; now we know we are tired and hungry and want
Picnic to come. We try to find the trail, but are confused in that forest of
dead timber; then we know we are lost …. Ed starts to cry, he is so little
and tired, and I want to, but know it won't do.

Then dark comes, and we are at an old tunnel, the timbers partly
caving in, but anything is better than those naked trees on every side.
Here we set the berries inside, and while doing this I find part of an old
mattress left there. This I pull out and go on exploring, peeking in every
corner, and am rewarded by finding part of a box of matches behind the
lagging. These were lit carefully, part of the stuffing from the mattress
was used, and how wonderful when it blazed up! I drew myself up and
told Ed, 'No fear of lions now, they're skeered of fire.'

… After a long time, I think I hear a new call—my heart is beating so I can hardly listen. Then again, and yes, it is a call. I jump up and answer, and soon hear someone running and jumping through the slide rock and fallen timber. It is Picnic, who, after leaving us, had a chance to pack berries back to town. He took the job, went over, got drunk, and forgot about us … .

Someone in the course of the day asked him, "How are you serving the Lord, nowadays, Picnic?" … At the mention of this he remembered and was sobered at once, got his patient old jack, which probably had not been fed or watered all day, [and] made it 'get a move on … . When he heard my first answer, he only ran harder, coming up to me with a bound. 'Are you all right? What a brave kid!'

Later on in life, she brings a different sort of resilience into an incident involving her husband's overindulgence at a downtown celebration.

When I look from the window and see Herbert in the midst of the bunch, the silk hat on one side of his head, I can hardly believe it. A weakness comes in my knees and stomach, but I go quietly about my work. Neighbors come to see how I am taking it, but I talk on every subject except drunk men and high hats. When evening comes, so does Herbert. I have a good supper waiting; he comes in daringly, still hatted, and looks at me as much to say, "Yes, I am drunk, and what are you going to do about it?" Just what I had been wondering myself. I say and do none of the things I had intended to say and do, only, "Come on to your supper before it is cold." When he is eating, I walk to the bed where the high hat is resting, pick it up in my hands, carry it to the kitchen table, ram the butcher knife into it, then hack it up, lift a stove lid and cram it into the stove. He opens his eyes rather wide, but never says one word and neither do I.

Highway 149
South Fork to Slumgullion Pass

83. Creede
The poetry of Cy Warman and an early dispatch from
Creede in the *New York Times*

*Cy Warman saw Colorado from the engineer's perch in a locomotive and he
witnessed it as newspaper editor during the boom years of the mining camp
that became Creede. He was known for a while as the "Poet of the Rockies."
After retiring from the railroad to Creede in 1891, he started the* Creede Daily
Chronicle. *While serving as editor of that paper, he wrote about all the prospectors who flocked into the hustle and bustle of this fledgling mining community.*

Creede

Here's a land where all are equal—
Of high or lowly birth—
A land where men make millions,
Dug from the dreary earth.
Here the meek and mild-eyed burro
On mineral mountains feed—
It's day all day, in the day-time,
And there is no night in Creede.

The cliffs are solid silver,
With wond'rous wealth untold;
And the beds of running rivers
Are lined with glittering gold.
While the world is filled with sorrow,
And hearts must break and bleed—
It's day all day in the day-time,
And there is no night in Creede.

During its early years, there was no night in Creede in part because of
the electric lights that lined the street. Only a few other mining commu-
nities had such a luxury at that time. But it was the full-on excitement, if
not hysteria, of the mining boom in 1892, as described in the following
article (no byline—author unknown) from the New York Times *on*
February 26th of that year, that really kept the place running around the
clock. If there was a sense in which "all were equal," as in the idealized
mining frontier of the poem where anyone might strike it rich, Warman
also knew that those who came to town with some cash in hand were "a
little more equal" than others. As the New York Times *report suggests,*
there was some tension brewing between "the squatters" who had phys-
ically assumed ownership of their properties and the investors who were
pouring into town to secure title to the same.

The sale of the school lands which adjoins the town site of Creede, and
which the State began selling at auction today created intense excitement,
owing to the uncertainty of the State or anybody being able to give a
clear title to these lands. Affairs have assumed a threatening phase, although no bloodshed has occurred. Squatters have built upon these lands
and declare they will not be beaten out of their claims by speculators, a
great many of whom are in town. It is between these two parties that
trouble, if any occurs, will be had.

That part of the town which slept during the night was awakened early this morning by an explosion on the face of the hill north of Jimtown.
A squatter had erected a frame building. The original settler, who had
left when he indicated what he intended to build, came along with a large
quantity of giant powder. The squatter's establishment was scattered all
over the face of the mountain.

People are flocking in from all quarters. Trains are loaded, and the
trails are covered with humanity on its way to the new camp. The few
streets that are laid out are so crowded that travel is next to impossible.
The saloons and gambling dens are filled to the doors. They have been
in this condition continuously since yesterday morning. In the lodging
houses and what are known as hotels there is not room for one third of all
the people. The railroad company kept all the sleeping cars that arrived

yesterday on the track and allowed them to be used by the excursionists at night. About 2000 people remained all night in the saloons.

Creede all last night resembled a town under siege. Men kept blasting the rocks for locations in the side of the mountain. All night long the crack of revolvers could be heard. Every man who had a weapon seemed to be bent on using it. Sometimes he pierced the ceiling of a saloon or gambling den or knocked the light out, but more frequently he went to the door and pierced the atmosphere.

The firing of the revolvers seems to have been a preconcerted arrangement of the men who were opposed to the land sale. The harmless shooting was intended for the new arrivals who were suspected of being anxious to speculate on realty. Of course the miners and the better element of the town had nothing to do with this peculiar attempt at persuasion or warning. They took no part in the effort to force a demonstrative boycott on outsiders, but still the tactics had their effect and they certainly did not add to the speculative value of the land.

… It is expected that when purchasers go to take possession there will be exciting times for Creede.

84. Upper Rio Grande
from *Deep Creek* by Pam Houston

"When you give yourself wholly to a piece of ground, its goodness enters your bloodstream like an infusion," writes Pam Houston in her book Deep Creek. *"You will never be alone in the same way again, and never quite dislocated. Your heart will grow down into and back out of that ground like a tree."*

What does it mean to give oneself to a piece of ground? In Deep Creek: Finding Hope in the High Country, *Pam Houston describes what it has meant for her. Her relationship with a 120-acre ranch southwest of Creede began in 1993. She was thirty-three years old and her first book of fiction,* Cowboys Are My Weakness, *had just come out. She had all of her life belongings packed up in a Toyota Corolla, she was on the lookout for a place to call home, and she had just fallen in love with a ranch that she couldn't*

*afford. But she took the proceeds from her book and offered to make a 5%
down payment anyway. When the owner unexpectedly agreed to take a
chance on her, she faced the huge challenge of paying off the balance. With
a lot of hustle, a willingness to travel almost anywhere to further her writing and teaching career, and a faculty position later on at the University of
California (Davis), Houston proved up on her part of the deal.*

    But that's only the beginning of the story she tells in Deep Creek. *Her
story is also about healing from the trauma of her own family history
and dealing with the grief she feels as she grapples with planetary
degradation and suffering. For that, the ranch becomes her refuge. It is
about learning this place and maintaining a connection with it even when
her career takes her elsewhere. And it is about her devotion to the ranch
and the animals that live there and finding in return the kind of solace, if
not hope, that has otherwise eluded her.*

… Top off the horse water, top off the sheep water, double-check the
heaters in the troughs. Listen to the reassuring thump of cold boot soles
on frozen ground, the contented burps and purrs of the chickens as they
peck around after their organic scratch grains, the otherworldly whoosh
of wing beats overhead—the bald eagle who winters upriver, back after
his one-year hiatus. This is how the ranch heals me with its dailiness, its
necessary rituals not one iota different than a prayer.

    The forecast is calling for wind and possibly snow tonight but right
now it is perfectly still and almost 20 degrees, too warm for my heavy
barn coat. The creek at this time of year, with all of the freezing and
unfreezing, is an ice sculpture, the willows lining it with pencil drawings,
the mountaintop beyond it already feet deep in snow.

    Olivia, still a pup, is charging and leaping to see above what's left
of the tall grass while William patrols the perimeter. From here I can
see Middle Creek Road, Lime Creek Road, as well as the state highway
across the river, and though this represents some fairly large percentage
of all the roads in Mineral County, for the hour we'll be walking, not one
car will go by.

    Out here, on this acreage, I've learned not only to hear my own voice,
but to recognize what makes my heart leap up and then go toward it: the

snowshoe hare—halfway through his biannual color change—William
scares up along the back fence, his big white feet flashing as his still tawny body gains distance. A coyote, sitting, dignified and still as a church,
two hundred yards across the pasture, watching us make our way to the
wetland, and then the flash, when William sees him, and he sees William
see him, his total evaporation into thin air, like a ghost dog come from
some other plane of being.

These are the things that have always healed me; it just took me
half a lifetime to really trust them, to understand how infallible they
are. Moving through space, preferably outdoor space, preferably outdoor
space that maintains some semblance of nature, if not *this* nature, some
other nature. When I'm happy it's a carnival out here and when I am
sad it is almost too beautiful to bear—but not quite. It is definitely too
beautiful to contemplate leaving. I climb the hill where John Robert
Pinckley—the first man to build a cabin on this land—and his children,
Bob and Ada, are buried, and I know well that when I claimed these 120
acres they also claimed me. We are each other's mutual saviors.

Sitting at the Pinckleys' gravesite, William pressed up against one
thigh and Olivia on the other, looking across the river at Bristol Head all
aglow in the low winter light, I am certain the world is not out to hurt but
to heal me, and I'll hold on to it with both hands for as long as I am able.

Highway 50

Royal Gorge to Monarch Pass

85. Royal Gorge / Parkdale
from "River Driver" by Hank Myers

*Thousands of whitewater boaters float the Arkansas River every
summer. After a rollicking hundred-mile stretch of whitewater, which
begins up near the tiny town of Granite, the river enters the Royal
Gorge. It wasn't until 1949 that two Swiss boaters—Robert Ris and Max
Romer—successfully navigated (and portaged in places) the rapids that
are found there. The next party to make it through the Gorge—Tyson
Dines of Littleton, John Sibley of Philadelphia, and Raymond Zuberi of
France—paddled an "eight man life raft."* The Rocky Mountain News
*reported that they were "swept down the eleven miles from the west
entrance ... to the east entrance near Canon City in slightly under three
hours .... They navigated the whole distance except for one point where
they had to lower the raft by ropes over a fifteen foot waterfall. Veteran
rivermen of Canon City applauded the feat as remarkable, even though
the low water aided the group by slowing the swift currents."*

*One of the earliest attempts to navigate the river through the Gorge
took place in the spring of 1873, when two young men set out from
Parkdale in a small wooden boat. An account of their misadventures
appeared in the* Denver Times *on March 3, 1902. "I was a river driver
once," said Hank Myers. "It is about thirty years ago that I served my
apprenticeship to the trade and I concluded after that one season I was
not big enough to follow the business."*

*In 1872, the Atchison, Topeka, and Santa Fe Railroad was buying
railroad ties from woodcutters up in California Gulch (near Leadville).
They contracted with a man named C.M. Scribner to float the ties*

down the Arkansas River. As many as 75,000 ties were taken downriver toward Pueblo. When Scribner and his men came onto the Royal Gorge, they sent the ties down, hoping that they would turn up at the lower end of the canyon. Hank Myers continues:

The contractors found that they put in far more lumber than showed up at the mouth of the canyon. The next spring they offered one dollar apiece for ties lodged in the canyon which could be delivered to Canon City. This was big money and it took me and another greenhorn about two minutes to make up our minds that we could make fortunes and have some fun at the same time. The other fellow, Todd was his name, was as ignorant as I was about river driving. Nevertheless, we got ourselves a camp outfit and boat and took them to the head of the canyon.

The way the water rushed into that hole in the rock would have scared out anyone who had sense enough, but with the dauntless bravery born of ignorance, we never hesitated ... . We pulled away from the shore and the boat went faster and faster, with Todd at the oars. I was about to tell him to go easy when with a swish we shot into that hole in the mountain. Whether that boat went sideways or upside down I never could tell and I modestly refrained from asking Todd, for when I next saw him, he was sitting on a rock letting the water drain from his clothes and whiskers. He was so tearing mad that one could get little satisfaction from him anyhow.

By the time we got our sense collected and began to size up the situation, the boat and what of its contents would float must have been near the outlet of the canyon. We were in a pretty bad fix. There was no possibility of getting back up the canyon for the water completely filled the gorge.

It was cold down there and the roar of the water made anything but music to our ears. Our provisions were gone, the only thing being saved from the river a small coil of rope. This turned out to be our salvation. We got together some timber and made a raft, and had enough rope left for a tail to hold it by.

There was nothing we could do except go on down the stream and watch for a place to climb out, and failing that, go clear through ... . The sun never shone in there and we never knew but the next hundred feet would bring us to a waterfall where our raft would go to pieces and we would be done for. Besides, we were weak with hunger.

It was on the fifth day of our incarceration, we were about played out and were talking seriously about giving up the job, when we discovered a narrow washout that appeared to reach the top. We started up it thinking it might end as many others did in a sheer wall of rock. As we toiled up and the cut widened, hope gave us new strength, but when we reached the top we were completely exhausted and hungry .... We threw ourselves down on the ground and slept soundly.

When we awoke somewhat refreshed, we knew the country and found that we had only two miles to walk to a cabin where we could get something to eat. We had traveled ten miles in that canyon and for years after, the roar of a mountain torrent sent cold shivers through me.

86. Cotopaxi
from *Nothing Here But Stones* by Nancy Oswald

In 1880, Emmanuel Saltiel, a Portuguese Jew who owned a silver mine in this area, founded the Cotopaxi Town Company. In an effort to increase the population of potential laborers for his mine, Saltiel approached an organization called the Hebrew Immigration Aid Society (HIAS), which was set up to help relocate persecuted Jews fleeing Russia. Promising "rich and productive farmland" for these refugees, Saltiel managed to convince this organization to send a group of immigrants to his fledgling community. In May of 1882, sixty-three hopeful immigrants arrived in Cotopaxi. Unfortunately, both the farmland—most of which was located on rocky hillsides—and the housing— small cabins, many of them without doors or windows—fell short of what had been promised. Later, the immigrants would garner support from Denver's Jewish community as well as the Denver Post *which ran an investigative report on their plight. Hearing what had happened, the HIAS sent along $2000 in relief, but the initial settlement period was still one of great disappointment and hardship.*

Nancy Oswald, an author, speaker, and retired elementary school teacher living in Salida, writes historical fiction for middle grade and young adult readers. In her book, Nothing Here But Stones, *Oswald offers a fictionalized version of this story from the perspective of an eleven-year-old girl named Emma. In this scene, Emma witnesses her father trying to find a way through their desperate situation.*

A large round stone lay only a few feet away. I rolled it over below the window and stepped up on it. Now I could see clearly into the room, to the far side where four men sat at a small table. The fourth man was Mr. Reis ... the man from the hotel ... the man who left our houses unfinished.

Mr. Black cleared his throat and opened a tall flat book, and Papa took some papers from his pocket and unfolded them on the table. That is when a fear began to creep inside me, thinking about that morning when I found Papa at our table, sound asleep, with his head resting on our Bible.

One arm was draped over a pile of papers, and his hand curled around his pen. When I tried to wake him, I could see rows of numbers on the papers ... the same papers he had now.

"In a few weeks," Papa said, "our crops will be harvested, and we will have enough to pay our debt."

The rock wobbled beneath me, and I lost my balance, tipping sideways. I pulled myself up just as Benjamin had finished translating this for him.

Mr. Black shook his head gravely, staring at his black ledger. "It is almost August. The harvest will not be until September," he said. "I have already given you more credit than I should."

Papa tapped his foot against the table leg. After a long silence, the fourth man, Mr. Reis spoke. "I'm in need of workers in my mines. With jobs, you can extend your credit."

"For what pay?" Papa asked.

"One dollar and fifty cents a day. If your people will work at night, I can pay more."

Papa shook his head. "And who will harvest our crops if we are all working in your mine?"

The rock rolled again. This time it bumped the side of building, making a loud clonking sound. I ducked my head and held my breath, hoping no one had noticed.

"It is not our problem how you harvest your crops," Mr. Reis said stonily. "Your credit has run out."

Slowly, I inched up again and peeked over the sill. Papa fingered the breast pocket of his coat and pulled out a piece of velvet tied with string. When he unwrapped it, I could see the glow of Mama's wedding ring. I let out a little gasp and tipped sideways again, grabbing the sill to keep from falling. I pulled myself up in time to hear Papa say, "I can offer this as a guarantee" –he paused– "until our harvest is in."

I clung to the sill, digging in with my fingernails, afraid to watch and afraid to look away. Mr. Black took the ring from Papa and held it up in the light from the opposite window. Little sunbeams danced through it. He spoke in English to Mr. Reis, who did not look happy with what Mr. Black said. Next, Mr. Black spoke to Papa. "If you cannot pay your bill, I will have to keep the ring."

Papa nodded.

"Mr. Reis can guarantee you a wage. Are you sure?"

"We have come here to farm," Papa said firmly.

Mr. Black rewrapped Mama's ring in the cloth and took it to his cash register. Papa turned away, and for a moment I thought he was looking at me, but he was staring at the grooves in Mr. Black's floor so that he would not have to watch Mama's ring disappear.

87. Cottonwood Rapids
from "The Bull of Whitewater Rapids" by S.C. Dubick

A Time Magazine *article (July 6, 1953) had this to say about the FIBARK (which stands for First in Boating on the Arkansas) downriver boat race: "The first riverboat race on the Arkansas, in 1949, ran nearly 60 miles, from Salida, down between the quarter mile-high walls of the awesome Royal Gorge, and out again. Only a daring Swiss pair finished; most others dropped out short of the gorge, where capsized boatmen, flanked by*

*sheer rock palisades, have little choice but to sink or be swept, dead or
alive, through the canyon." By 1953, the race course had been shortened
(finishing in Cotopaxi). "Though safer," the article said, "the present
course is still a grim ordeal by white water, spiced by three major rapids
threatening upsets and death to even the best boatmen."*

*Of those three rapids, Cottonwood proved to be the biggest challenge
for many of the racers, as suggested by this report in the* Mountain Mail,
*Salida's newspaper: "the boaters were mighty skilled at handling their
craft, but they all got dunked in treacherous Cottonwood Rapids." The
following account, written by S.C. Dubick in the May 1973 issue of* Saga
Magazine, *describes his preparation for the race. Part of that involved
a high water run though Cottonwood in a two-man canoe with paddling
partner Fritz Nenninger.*

That day, we were successful down every inch of the course—except for
Cottonwood Rapids. I chickened out and forced a portage. Fritz con-
sented, on one condition: We would conquer Cottonwood the following
morning.

The night seemed too short and the next day we didn't talk much
during the ride up to Cottonwood. Once we saw that the water was still
higher, not another word was uttered. My fingers were slippery with
sweat, and the canoe slid from my hands as we pulled it off the car.
Sweat showered down my wetsuit … .

We pushed out into the current and it was impossible to get a firm,
comfortable grip on the paddle. Ahead, the brown river was glass smooth,
but it suddenly dropped out of sight. We hugged the boulders along the
left bank. The sound of a wind seemed to rise from beyond the lip.

The canoe glided. Its hull bulged against my toes as it absorbed a
few long, smooth swells. The river banks moved by a little faster. A tiny
wave splashed across the bow from the left. Beyond the lip, the white
water grew with each paddle stroke.

Suddenly as if in a whirling amusement ride gone berserk, the canoe
dropped over the precipice of racing water. That ended our only chance
to escape, and our fear was swallowed into the roaring mouth of the river.
A mountainous wave exploded over the deck and the boat twisted and

squeaked in pain as it sucked in water. I lunged over the bow, stabbed the blade deep in and drew the leaping boat into the dime-sized spot where we could get through. Fritz fought the stern away from the standing wave that howled on our right. The knife-sharp rocks whooshed like a hurricane wind as we gushed past. An eddy threatened to catch and splinter us against the wall. I thrust the bow away and towards the worst of the brawling turbulence. The river erupted into a thunderous stampede as we battled to stay in our channel. Luck held. Suddenly, the rumbling died and the river was as quiet as a spring-time pond. Conquered! We laughed, and it was the kind of laugh you let loose when you fall out of an airplane and your parachute doesn't open until you're 100 feet above the ground.

88. Salida
from *Deep in the Heart of the Rockies* by Ed Quillen

On the way to becoming a regular columnist for the Denver Post, *Ed Quillen honed his thoughtful and often amusing perspective while covering the mountain town beat in various rural newspapers and in* Colorado Central, *a regional magazine that he and his wife Martha founded and published in Salida. Quillen (1950-2012) was often described as a libertarian populist, which is another way of saying that his perspective on the world was hard to categorize. He valued the gritty, down-to-earth, aspects of mountain town life and regretted the "dismal effects" of rural gentrification "such as ferns and smoke free environments in what had once been comfortable saloons, hardware stores turning into boutiques, workers priced out of housing, etc." He had a few tongue-in-cheek public policy suggestions to preserve "traditional" mountain towns such as "destructive covenants." If upscale folks could put restrictive covenants in their deeds to enhance property values "by forbidding wind chimes, artificial flowers, porch swings, children, etc., the same legal technique could also keep property values low, so that people could afford to live near their work. Members of a neighborhood association could adjust their deeds to require that all yards contain a clothesline, woodpile, four mongrels, two porch appliances and a minimum of three unlicensed vehicles." As the following excerpt from his book* Deep in the Heart of the Rockies *suggests, Ed Quillen preferred those places that were still a little quirky and rough around the edges.*

Salida has been "discovered" quite often in recent years .... It makes various lists, "Great Outdoor Towns" or "Wonderful Art Towns" and the like. Since I'm not in the business of touting real-estate here, it would suit me fine if Salida were neglected, since the process is so destructive.

First the place gets discovered by a writer or two, who extol its down-home authentic nature, uncorrupted by industrial tourism and ensuing hordes. That leads to more publicity and more tourists, which attracts the attention of chains and franchises. The ma-and-pa cafes and motels get replaced by national brands. Whatever unaffected charm the place had is gone, but by then the writers have discovered a new place to trash by putting it on a list.

Of course, I'm a writer, too, and I like money as much as the next guy. So I've been tempted to produce a list of "The Best Rural Towns to Live In," based on these criteria:

Average nap time of a dog lying in the middle of Main Street.

The probability that the bartender is the only person in the saloon with a steady job.

No home mail delivery. People have to go to the post office every day to get their mail, which means they can keep up on local gossip and thus feel involved in the community.

Size of the police department. Ideally, there isn't one, and sheriff's office is at least twenty-five miles away, although there's a resident deputy known for his low-key and friendly ways.

Number of resident eccentrics to point out to visitors—people like "the town drunk," "the village idiot," "the guy with all the junk in his yard," and "the cat lady"—a widow in an old frame house with at least twenty felines wandering in and out. Every settlement has these, but in the towns that make the list, everybody knows who they are.

Certainly there are many other factors—a high average age of the town's pickups, an abundance of cranks and troublemakers, a wide variety of housing that ranges from teepees and trailers to an old mansion or two—and this information would have to be gathered and collated. That sounds like too much work, so the good towns are probably safe from me.

89. Salida / Hutchison Ranch
from *Under the Angel of Shavano*
by Wendell F. Hutchinson and George C. Everett

Veterinarian, historian, and author Wendell Hutchinson had deep roots in the Upper Arkansas Valley, as did rancher George C. Everett, a long-time member of the Chaffee County Pioneer and Historical Society and co-author of their book Under the Angel of Shavano. *The Hutchison Family ranch, which is located two miles west of Salida, was established by Joseph Sykes Hutchinson and Annabel McPherson in 1868. Six generations later, the Hutchinson Family is still raising cattle on the same land. Visitors can find out about this area's ranching heritage at the Hutchison Ranch Learning Center. The following account in* Under the Angel of Shavano *describes the work of moving cattle as practiced throughout this valley a few generations after the first ranchers settled here.*

There was no set rule as to how and when cattle would be put on the trail. The best results were obtained by moving at daylight in the cool of the morning. As the sun came up cattle might graze or drink when suitable watering places could be found. They would rest through the heat of the day, then be put on the move for a while in the evening. A rider or scout would have the trail selected and camp sites picked out and then work to make the destination to the best advantage of the cattle. The cowhand's job was to follow instructions from the trail boss and as there were no hotels or established camp sites the cowboys took things as they came— rain, cold wind, and dust. The first trail herds had only pack outfits or some had two wheeled carts pulled by oxen. By the time the last Eddy Brothers trail herd pulled into the Upper Arkansas Valley more modern methods were established. Two wagons were used; one was the mess wagon with groceries, cooking supplies, dishes, and a sheet iron stove and the other was the bed wagon. The weight was kept to a minimum and no excess baggage in either cook or bed wagon was taken. Usually the grub was plain but substantial.

Driving a trail here was a 24 hour a day business and, as mentioned before, the stampede was always a great danger on the trail. Two or more men, as the captain decided was necessary, were on guard with the herd and cavvey; others were sleeping or resting until it was their turn to relieve the first guard.

Frequently a herd contained a dozen or so old, wild steers which had developed the stampeding habit. They were continuously on the lookout for some excuse to run and if no excuse presented itself they created one. At any moment they were ready to take off, spooking the balance of the herd. Usually the chronic troublemakers knew each other and would hang around close together. A herd of stampeding steers lost weight and the trail boss made an effort to dispose of the mischief makers when he had an opportunity. Sometimes they simply shot the outlaw animals.

There also was a problem of slow travelers, referred to as "drags". These were a nuisance as they were just lazy and did not make much headway on the trail and these, too, were disposed of if the boss found a market at any price. The majority of the herd was manageable and could be driven and controlled if the cowboys used a reasonable amount of judgment.

A water barrel was carried on the wagon for drinking and cooking purposes. Fuel was another matter; sometimes wood or brush was available, also cow chips were used which made a good hot fire in dry weather though when damp did not burn so readily. Under these conditions it also gave out a smudge odor which did not smell exactly like roses. After a midday rest, the herd would be put in motion once more. When they arrived at the bed ground which had been previously selected, the herd was stopped and was allowed to graze and be watered if water was available.

This also required judgement and skill and a thorough knowledge of bovine mentality. Experience hands could do a nice job of watering and bedding them down. The bedded herd must have ample room but be compact, not overcrowded. Watering a large thirsty herd was no amateur's job. Men on the night herd usually worked in pairs from two to four hours. They were mounted on their quietest and best horses as they sung and hummed a little (hardly classed as songs) but the noise and attempts to sing certainly were western American. These nightly song birds were not out there vocalizing for their own appreciation; they were actually singing to soothe and reassure those old mosshorn "brush poppers" that all was well.

At break of day they once more regained their feet and commenced their grazing and drifting to Poncha Pass. A cowboy usually had one personal horse, and equipment including his saddle, rope, chaps, spurs and a slicker. Such personal things as he desired, and whatever was not in use, were nearby in the grub or bed wagon. Rawhide was used for many purposes and to make or repair equipment. The Texas boys felt that if anything could not be fixed with rawhide it was not worth fixing. Many early Coloradoans used bailing wire for the same purpose.

90. Monarch Pass
from "The Ghost Highway of the Rockies" by Frank Gimlett

Frank Gimlett, also known as "The Hermit of Arbor Villa," became for many years a roadside attraction at the top of Monarch Pass. Gimlett, who owned property between Maysville and Garfield (now Monarch), had worked as a mine superintendent in the area for a few years beginning in 1900. Although he then moved to Salida where he worked for the Salida Wood and Lumber Company for many years, he celebrated his brush with the early mining era and promoted himself as a living relic of that time period. He began writing and publishing pamphlets about the "gold and silver west" which he sold, in full and photogenic prospecting apparel, to tourists on Monarch Pass.

Gimlett was good at generating publicity. In 1939, for example, he tried to claim rent money from an irrigation company down valley whose water, he said, came down from his five mining claims near the Continental Divide. Around the same time, he petitioned President Franklin Delano Roosevelt, without success, to change the name of nearby Mt. Aetna to Mt. Ginger Rogers, in honor of his favorite Hollywood star. In 1938, when the highway department chose to reroute Highway 50 along the northern edge of Garfield (now the town of Monarch), Gimlett claimed that the highway department had run its new route through a cemetery full of miners and other early residents (including, perhaps, some of their treasures). Gimlett never shied away from the kind of drama and hyperbole that characterizes this excerpt from book number six of his series, in which he refers to Highway 50 as "The Ghost Highway of the Rockies."

Yes, all too soon the highway vandals and ghouliteers will lay waste the city square and five miles of graveyards on National Highway 50, and according to present plans, will unearth the bones and spirits of these old pioneers, the trail blazers and builders of the gold and silver west .... .

Once again I walk through the Junction City graveyard where the spirits of Jim Baker, Two Gun Spike Murphy, Two Fingered Mike and One Eye (Patch Eye) Pedro, and Wyoming Kate await in great suspense to see if their bones too are to be scattered along the highway grade, and great would be the surprise if the engineer of that mechanical ogre (the power shovel) should uncover a few petrified bodies ... whose spirits unleashed will bring them many sleepless nights .... .

Behold by the glare of the bright head lights, the shovel man sees atop the loaded truck a grinning skeleton, staring toward him through eyeless sockets, from a skull still covered with long sandy hair now waving in the breeze .... . A feeling of guilt and remorse overcomes the man, and still imbued with a spark of respect he lays aside the desecrated bones, several skulls with bullet holes still in evidence, ... but the damage has been done, and atonement comes too late. The wreckers and devastators have made the debacle complete. If these devastators would have been more human, more careful and subtle in their methods, perhaps some of their wives and sweethearts might even now be wearing many of Wyoming Kate's sixteen thousand dollars worth of diamond ornaments that adorned the skeleton of this dazzling personality of the good old days.

Highway 285
Poncha Springs to Johnson Village

91. Nathrop
from "Mountain Mama Tales" by Kizzen Laki

In the early 1970s, a new magazine called Mother Earth News *encouraged a keep-it-simple and do-it-yourself rural lifestyle, a folk singer named John Denver had a big hit with a song called "Rocky Mountain High," and a wave of young migrants who had grown up in urban and suburban regions of the country sought out a new home in the mountains of Colorado. It was the first decade since the inception of the US census that rural growth exceeded that of urban areas and the population of young people in Colorado Mountain towns like Salida and Buena Vista reflected that.*

Kizzen Laki, a veteran newspaper editor now living in Crestone, Colorado, was one of a group of young back-to-the-landers who settled into a group of cabins, once part of a Presbyterian church camp, several miles west of here in Chalk Creek Canyon. They hauled their own water, cooked with wood, and took whatever odd jobs they could find to support their young families. "We were young and hardy and poor and the winter of 1978/79 just about did us in."

By the first week of December that winter, central Colorado got a heavy deep snowfall—a couple of feet in places—and then the wind started to blow. The front page of the December 6, 1978 Mountain Mail *newspaper in Salida featured a report from the National Weather Service: "The storm which dumped 16 inches of snow in Salida last night is expected to continue into tomorrow ... expect six to ten-foot drifts and possibly another foot of snow before this is over with ... By 8 am Villa Grove reported six to eight foot drifts and a foot of new snow... Buena Vista had better than a foot. Temperatures are predicted in the 5 to 15 degree range. Poncha, Monarch, and Wolf Creek passes were closed, roads were treacherous, mail was not being delivered, schools*

*were closed." That was just the beginning of the storm that lasted for
weeks. In one of the "Mountain Mama Tales" that she writes for the
Crestone Eagle, Kizzen Laki recalls an epic trip to Salida and back.*

The cabins in Chalk Creek were about 8 miles west of Nathrop and
Highway 285. Both roads drifted shut. The plows came and opened them
up. They drifted shut. The county brought snowplows with blowers to
Rodeo Road and cut a track with 10ft high walls of snow—that still drifted shut. Our trips to Buena Vista became infrequent, then stopped. The
road up from Nathrop became a snowfield blown smooth—fence posts
giving the only indication that there was a road there somewhere.

   We were all holed up in the cabins. Excited, at first, by nature's
power. But, as the wind whipped snow up to the eaves, and drifts buried
vehicles it got to be scary and very hard as we attempted to haul water
from the well house to our homes and livestock.

   In those days most of us worked construction, odd jobs and the summer tourist trades. By November we were mostly out of work and getting
food stamps to feed our families. If you've ever tried to feed your family
on food stamps, you know it's hard to make them last a month —even
when you are making everything from scratch.

   By the end of November we were all pretty much out of anything
other than rice and oatmeal and looking forward to picking up our food
stamps in Salida the first week of December. But we couldn't get there.
As the storm worsened county offices closed, including the food stamp
office. Finally, the wind won the battle with the snowplows and the main
highway from Buena Vista to Salida was essentially closed for four days.
Nothing was moving from Leadville to Alamosa.

   We were glued to the radio as we became more isolated, waiting for a
break in the weather. Finally it came. The roads were opened, but it was
recommended you have 4-wheel drive or chains. I had neither, but what
I did have was a trusty and gutsy 1961 Volkswagen Bug painted like a
ladybug with a huge luggage rack strapped to the top—and I was hungry
and game and a little crazy with cabin fever.

   The cabins were 1/4 mile off the paved road, and our access road was
deep with snow. A neighbor with 4-wheel drive pulled my Bug to the

main road, where I was able to drive to a point appx. 300 ft. above the cabins. Carol and I, with the husbands cutting trail though thigh-deep snow, pushed and pulled 6 months pregnant Sandy up the hill to the road.

We finally made it out of the camp and slowly drove across icy roads to Salida to join the line of those who had now been out of food stamps for almost 2-weeks.

I urged my friends to shop quickly and I cautioned them to go easy on groceries, but we were all out of everything. We filled the back of the Ladybug, strapped boxes to the oversize luggage rack on top, put pregnant Sandy in the middle of the back seat and jammed in the remaining sacks of groceries around her. We couldn't have squeezed in another potato.

As we left Salida the sun was starting to go down, temps were plummeting and the wind was picking up. Snow was again blowing across the highway and there was hardly any traffic. The farther north we drove the worse it got. We considered turning around, but we had nowhere to stay in Salida and $400 worth of groceries freezing on the roof. We had blankets across our laps in the chilly unheated VW and the landscape was grim.

When we came to turn west at Nathrop on County Road 162 we were facing an arctic landscape. The road ahead was covered with blowing snow. My headlights picked up some good truck tracks across the fresh snow. "Should we go on? Only eight miles."

Eight miles in a howling freezing wind. Eight miles of almost no visibility. Eight miles of no heater, and no one who would travel that road after us that night.

"Sure."

Crazy, dangerous, foolish. We could have died.

A mile in I realized we were in big trouble. We lost sight of the road completely and could only judge where we were by the fence posts to either side. Just aim for the middle. The truck tracks would disappear, resurrecting as cuts in the finger drifts now growing across the road grabbing at our wheels. I drove the VW in second gear revved up high. Keeping my speed up as we plunged into each drift trying to keep our momentum up to break free on the drifts. "Come on baby, you can do it!"

I called to my ladybug. While Carol, my co-pilot, continually and wearily scraped my frosted breath off the *inside* of the windshield with a tuna can as I peered out trying desperately to see.

There was no way or place to turn around. If we had stopped, we would have been hopelessly stuck. There was no home to walk to for miles and with a windchill way down below freezing we wouldn't have made it. We were cold already. Nobody knew where we were, and we would have frozen to death in the Volkswagen. We knew this. We didn't talk. We prayed. White knuckled, me driving, we plunged on.

Angels, Gods, and Guides look after brave fools and women bringing home the groceries, at least in this case they did. We came down the hill from the plateau into the quiet of the canyon. We could see stars overhead. As we approached our access road I debated whether or not to attempt it—but the thought of hauling all our bags and boxes down the hillside was more than we could bear.

I was in the zone now—and Carol and Sandy said go for it! As I dropped down off the pavement into the tracks we had made in the morning I saw that the men had shoveled out a 1/4 mile of tire tracks. My wheels grabbed the tracks, snow from the center flew up in a spray in my headlights and on my hood like sparklers as I plowed on down the road to the cabins. Home. We made it.

Knees still shaking, we dug a half-frozen Sandy out of the back—happy to be alive. The men ferried the boxes and bags of groceries to the proper cabins amazed that we made it through. Carol, Sandy and I thawed ourselves and cooked wonderfully warm suppers for our families.

I really loved that Ladybug.

Highway 24
Buena Vista to Minturn

92. Buena Vista
from *Rocky Mountain Letters* by William H. Brewer

Two members of an 1869 geological survey are responsible for the ivy league names that identify some of the fourteen-thousand-foot mountains in the Collegiate Peaks Wilderness west of Buena Vista and the Upper Arkansas River Valley. Botanist William H. Brewer (Yale) and geologist Josiah D. Whitney (Harvard) were gathering information on the mountain regions of Central Colorado in the summer of 1869, during which time they were afforded some fine views of the mountains they named after their respective alma maters. In addition to his work as a botanist (in the field and as the first chair of Yale's Sheffield School of Science), Brewer wrote colorful letters to his wife and other family members during his travels on various surveys in California, Colorado, Greenland, and Alaska. In one of his Rocky Mountain letters, which were gathered and published by James D. Houston in 1992, Brewer describes his attempted ascent of a high peak west of Buena Vista.

Lying to the west of the Arkansas River is a great wilderness of mountains, a terra incognito so far as maps and geographies are concerned, although perhaps fully penetrated by prospectors and half-civilized adventurers.... How we yearned to know something of them!

... Monday (August 16th), I started out on my horse alone to look up the way. Here let me say that my Black proves to be a most magnificent mountain horse. I like him better than any other I ever rode on such work. For six miles from camp I had already looked up the way—first across the monotonous plain for an hour, then fording the swift Cottonwood Creek, then up a moraine to the base of a great ridge or spur running down from some side peaks in front of the main peak. Up this I struck, sometimes cutting my way with my heavy knife through thickets of poplar, then up a grassy slope, now among fallen timber, then among loose rocks, then along the rocky crest of the ridge—but ever *up, up, up*— the ridge rising for three or four miles at the rate of perhaps a thousand feet per mile. I picked out a way, one you would surely say no horse could travel, sometimes leading him, sometimes riding, now dismounting and trying other ways to see which was the better. Once, I missed my bowie-knife, and it cost me over an hour's hard work, up and down the steep ridge, to find it—but find it I must and find it I did—then on again. In this way I worked my way up to the top of that ridge, then along crests over 13,000 feet high, where doubtless neither horse nor white man had ever been before—now along trails worn by mountain sheep (the chamois of the Rocky Mountains), then along the crest towards the peak. I was looking for two things—first, a way up practicable for pack mules, next, a place to camp nearer the last peak to be ascended. I found both; in fact, two camping places, one rather too far off, the other much nearer and much more difficult to reach. I did not attempt to reach it that day, as I must return. From the summit I had grand views of a rougher mountain mass just south, all furrowed into cañons steeper and grander than anything I had before seen here in the Rocky Mountains—peak beyond peak, valley beyond valley, unnamed and unknown. It was a hard, solitary day's work, and I got back after a twelve hours' ride.

So much of this. The sun set some time ago, and we have a most gorgeous coloring of clouds over the pretty landscape. In the meantime, it is getting too dark and too cold to write anymore. But what a gorgeous sky we are having!

93. Leadville
from *Olden Times in Colorado* by Carlyle Channing Davis

Several days after Carlyle Channing Davis arrived in Leadville one January night back in 1879, he and two business partners put out the first edition of the Leadville Daily Chronicle. *Their timing couldn't have been better. In the midst of Leadville's second and biggest gold and silver boom, five hundred copies of the paper's first edition sold*

out quickly. A year later, riding the wave of Leadville's burgeoning
population, the Chronicle *had a paid circulation of seven thousand*
readers. As indicated in Davis's initial observations of downtown
Leadville after hours, there was plenty to report on.

The scene unfolded was unlike anything I ever before had seen or
conjured in my imagination. The main thoroughfare was pretty closely
and compactly lined with houses on either side for a distance of two
miles, following the contour of the gulch, all of log or rough-hewn slab
construction, only a few of them two stories in height. Every other door
seemed to open upon a saloon, dance hall or gambling den. There were
no street lights, but the thousands of coal oil lamps indoors cast fitful
flashes of baneful light across the way.

The board walks on either side were filled to the center with a constantly moving mass of humanity from every quarter of the globe and
from every walk in life. The stalwart teamster jostled the banker from
Chicago; the deep-lunged miner, fresh from underground workings,
divided the walk with debonair salesmen from Boston; the gambler and
bunco-steerer walked arm-in-arm with his freshest victim picked up in
the hotel lobby. Apparently every nationality was represented in that
throng of fortune seekers, their garb and carriage and address aiding in
the classification.

At that hour, long past midnight, few could have had any mission
other than sight-seeing, hence the mass was constantly being augmented
or diminished by the crowds pouring in and out of the scores of resorts
with which the thoroughfare was lined. Had one the least cause for haste,
he was compelled to seek the roadway, not so densely thronged with the
curious, excited, impetuous sight-seers. Belated Concord coaches hauled
by six-horse teams, huge freight vans, lumbering prairie schooners and
all manner of wheeled vehicles toiling up and down the street, separated
from the board walk by parallel lines of snow piled in the gutters to a
height of three or four feet.

The buzz of conversation, the resounding snap of drivers' whips,
the crunching of steel-shod wheels in the icy thoroughfare and the
frequent profane shouts to weary horses and mules, that mingled with

the questionable musical sounds from the orchestras within, filled the air
with a compound of sounds scarcely soothing in its effects upon unac-
customed ears. Taking in the spectacle, I joined the throng, passing from
door to door and witnessing scenes that almost beggar description.

Chief among the places visited was Pap Wyman's combination con-
cert and dance hall with every game of chance known to the fraternity in
full blast—faro, keno, roulette, stud poker, pinochle and whatnot. On the
face of a monster clock behind a bar scintillating with a wealth of crystal
was painted the significant invitation to guests, "Please Do Not Swear,"
while upon a slanting shelf on the counter, facing the motley throng,
was a large Bible, whose well-thumbed leaves gave strong indication
that it had been frequently consulted. An orchestra of many pieces was
grinding out popular music for the dancing that never lagged, and which
kept up until the dawn of day drove the weary participants to wretched
sleeping quarters, the heavens only knew where.

Here, perhaps, were a score of girls and women of the underworld,
of varying ages and types of attractiveness, attired in more or less
picturesque and fantastic garb, some wearing little surplus apparel of any
description, dancing with bearded bullwhackers, uncouth delvers in the
mines with soil-besmeared attire to mark their vocation; with the dapper
clerk out for a night's lark—with anybody and everybody disposed to
clasp their soiled waists, whirl them through the mazes of a two-step
or a polka, and then accompany them to the bar, the only compensation
exacted by the house, but quite ample, since each number consumed but a
few moments of time and the drink at the close was as inevitable as fate.

94. Leadville
from *A Victorian Gentlewoman in the Far West*
by Mary Hallock Foote

*Trained as an artist, Mary Hallock was an accomplished illustrator for
many New York publications before she married a young mining engineer named Arthur De Wint Foote with whom she traveled through the
gold and silver West. Fascinated with the rough and tumble world she*

encountered in towns like Deadwood and Leadville (where she lived during the early 1880's), she captured the atmosphere of the mining frontier in her illustrations and in the dispatches she sent to popular eastern magazines like The Century.

Mary Hallock Foote's artwork and writing, which included several novels based on her mining town experiences, earned her a reputation as a keen observer of life on "the frontier." But it was a considerable archive of her personal letters that caught the attention of historian and author Wallace Stegner several decades after her death in 1938. He based Angle of Repose, *his Pulitzer prize winning novel, on her life as described in those letters. Although Stegner had secured permission from her descendants to base a fictional story on her correspondence, some critics maintain that he borrowed too heavily and even reproduced some of her original descriptions without attribution. But he also celebrated her remarkable life story, albeit in a fictionalized way, and brought her work back into the awareness of many western literature aficionados.*

Mary Hallock Foote's voice, as represented by this excerpt from her book A Victorian Gentlewoman in the Far West, *embodied a journalist's eye for detail as well as the aesthetic sensibilities of a seasoned artist.*

The Leadville scene, when it wasn't snowing or sleeting or preparing to do both, was dominated by a sky of so dark and pure and haughty a blue that "firmament" was the only name for it. Beneath that floor of heaven sat those Mighty Ones in a great convocation, those summits which turn the waters of the continent east and west.

A.'s first location for our cabin was jumped by a professional in that line of business who stood him off the ground with a shotgun. A. laughed at him and went back to the real-estate office where the lots were for sale and chose another and, as it turned out, a better one. The land had not been paid for—even if it had, I trust he would not have wasted blood on a Leadville cabin site .... But there seems to have been this one jumper and he pursued his avocation too long. One evening, in the face of one of those great, silencing sunsets, as we watched it from our cabin porch – down in the town where lights pricked through the twilight, this man, and a holdup thief whom the town was equally tired of, were at that moment being lynched by hanging in front of the prison door. A. knew it as he stood there beside me, but he did not speak of it—he never spoke of it till years after. He saw no reason why a woman who had no business down there should break into that life which twilight covered, or question what was going on in those houses whose lights from our distance looked not unworthy neighbors of the stars. If I had any philanthropic or social duties in Leadville that summer, I have to confess that I wasn't even conscious of them. I went on with my little job—those engravers' blocks to cover with drawings—and my husband went on with his. For company he brought to the cabin such men as he saw fit, measured by his own standards, together with those between whom and ourselves there had been links in the past. And in that odd little room, in a place which, the year before, had been nowhere, we had guests who would have been distinguished anywhere—this being one of the well-known compensations which offset the perpetual changes and general unrest of the life of an engineer in the field.

Our cabin was built of round logs at a dollar apiece, and they were not very long logs either. It was all in one room, lined with building paper which had an oak-grained side and a reverse of dark brown; one width of the brown we used as a wainscot, and the walls were covered with the oak side put on like wallpaper, and where the edge joined, pine strips painted black were nailed over them with an effect of paneling. The open-beamed ceiling to the ridge pole was papered between the unbarked log rafters, like the walls. So our color scheme matched the woods and on this quiet background we added pinks and blues and greens by pinning up the Geological Survey maps of the Fortieth Parallel. When the geologists came out and were our guests, they stared around and laughed to see this frivolous use of their brains and research .... James Hague insisted that geology had never been turned to better account! They mocked each other gaily of the impertinence which they considered peculiarly feminine (it was in fact my own idea) to stick up Old Silurian and the Tertiary deposits for the sake of their pretty colors!

95. Leadville / Climax Molybdenum Mine
from *The Making of a Hardrock Miner*
by Stephen M. Voynick

*The Climax Molybdenum Mine has been a presence in the high country
near Leadville (and an important source of employment) since it started
shipping ore in 1917. At one time it produced more molybdenum—a
silver metal used in strengthening steel—than any other mine in the
world. As the market for this metal has fluctuated, so too has its output
and work force. After a long period of dormancy, it reopened in 2012
with a workforce of 400 employees.*

*Prior to landing a job at the Climax Molybdenum Mine in 1970,
Colorado author Stephen Voynick had only a limited understanding of
underground mining which he summed up as follows: "I considered it
to be a dangerous occupation pursued by strange men in remote places, something beyond the realm of conventional experience. My total
concept may have been involved in a single photograph of a man in a
hard hat with a miner's lamp, coveralls, and a safety belt. That man,
impersonal, yet congenial if he could have talked, was operating a rock
drill in a nameless underground cavern. Accompanying the photograph
was a dry text which further insured his anonymity by telling only cold
statistics of the mineral industry."*

*After a series of odd jobs which he took to finance various travels
and adventures, Voynick found himself thumbing through the classi-
fieds of the Sunday* Denver Post *looking for a job with a decent and
reliable paycheck. The ad that caught his attention pictured a miner
with hardhat and lamp. The caption read, "Shine A Little Light Into
Your Future," and beneath that "Hiring Immediately; No Experience
Necessary." Shortly thereafter, he found himself, "wearing the hard
hat and lamp of a hardrock miner and riding a cage into the dark cold
depths of a Colorado mountain." He chronicles his experiences in a
book called,* The Making of a Hardrock Miner. *Here, he describes his
first few days on the job under the tutelage of a veteran miner named
Jim Wizen.*

"Anybody here done any minin'?"

A nasal twang from the back said something about helping his old man dig a seam of coal out of the side of somebody's hill.

"I mean real minin'. Underground."

Silence.

"That's what I thought." With the point effectively made as to who would talk and who would listen, the bright blue eyes that peered from the forest of wrinkles lost some of their formality and the voice softened a bit. "Then everything I'm going to say to you will be new, so listen up. If you got questions, ask 'em."

Chairs creaked as bodies shifted and got comfortable.

"First thing, remember, nobody led you men up here by the hand. You're here because you think you can make more money here than you can anyplace else. Anybody come for a different reason?"

No comment from the lovers and parole jumpers.

"Good. Then we got no liars here."

That brought a subdued chuckle and broke the ice. This wasn't the first welcome speech the old man had given.

"Men, underground minin' is a little different than anything else you ever seen. Believe me. I've been here twenty-seven years and I seen a lot of men come and go. Some didn't last their first shift, others are foremen now. It's all what you make of it. If you come here to play around and have a good time, you're gonna get hurt and hurt bad. Maybe killed. Worse yet, you might get somebody else hurt, a good man maybe. There's a thousand ways to get hurt down there and you gotta be watchin' for every one of 'em all the time. Forget where you are for one minute, one second, and they'll be haulin' your ass out of there in a basket."

The faces of the twenty-seven "miners helpers," not one of whom had ever set foot underground, could have been cast in stone. Not a single expression revealed even a hint of doubt, of concern, of the soul searching that begins with the realization that this job might not be exactly what they had in mind.

... We put on the boots, hard hats, strapped the lamp batteries onto our belts, clipped the lamps to the hard hats, hung respirators around our necks, put on the glasses, and followed Wizen out to the Storke Level portal. A large network of railway tracks became reduced to a single track at the concrete entranceway. The portal itself was covered by a metal snow roof to keep the tracks and switches clear of the snow, which, at this elevation, could fall at any month of the year. After a final head count, Wizen led us through the portal into the adit, the long entrance tunnel leading to the interior mine level. Nineteen Miner's Helpers followed, tripping and stumbling, cursing, trying to adjust lamp beams under ill-fitting hard hats. Two miners, waiting for a lift on an inbound train, gave Wizen a wave for recognition, glanced back at his trailing carnival troupe, looked at each other and shook their heads.

When we had gotten about two hundred yards into the adit, Wizen called us together. "Okay, now listen," his voice echoed off the rock walls. "This track we're standing on is the only one in or out of the Storke Level, so every single train uses it. One-switch is still another half mile further, so we get a lot of traffic here. Bet we got a siren warning system that'll tell you just what the traffic is doing, so all you got to do is listen to find out what's happnin'. One blast means a train is comin' out, and two means you got one inbound. When you hear either, start looking for a place off in the rib, one of them manholes. That's what they were made for and they're the safest place to wait out a passing train."

As if on cue, a long, single, haunting wail of the siren echoed down the adit and Wizen herded us into a manhole. A light appeared in the distant gloom and a deep, growing rumble preceded the approach of the muck train. A thirty-ton motor, a heavy, brutal, filthy looking beast, bathed in the alternate flashes of blue and white light from the arcing trolley runner overhead, lumbered by with the oddly human and vulnerable face of the motorman peering from a grimy window. Loaded muck cars, twenty of them, rumbled by lurching precariously from side to side. I thought of the guy with the crushed chest.

When the adit was quiet again, Wizen said, "The only other signal is a steady wail. That means all traffic has to clear the adit because they're haulin' out an injured man."

Now there were only twelve Miner's Helpers. The remainder of the week was spent divided between underground familiarization and classroom lectures in which safety was nearly the sole topic. There were

literally hundreds of safety regulations that applied to underground mining and Wizen dutifully tried to explain each. This was more an exercise
in rhetoric than anything else, for the language of mines and miners is
unique unto itself and, for the uninitiated, is very confusing. Accurate
descriptions of underground operations and working mines are, for that
reason, rarely conveyed to persons who have not themselves worked underground. The miners' vocabulary has been almost singularly responsible for
isolating their profession from the more common and widely understood
currents of labor experience. Listening to Wizen read, translating as best
he could the long list of regulations, served only to create a general awareness of the myriad of ways to get hurt or killed underground. Full appreciation and respect for the hazards of underground mining, I would learn, are
things which develop only with time and experience.

During the brief forays underground, the basic elements of the new
language came into use. What had always been a tunnel was now a drift,
the sides, or walls, of those drifts were ribs, and the overhead was the
back. "Going underground," for the class of neophyte miners, meant little
more than that; walking along haulage drifts, keep clear of passing trains,
and, occasionally, clearing out a few railway switches with mucksticks,
the miners' term for the lowly shovel.

Wizen delivered many underground lectures, the longest and most
detailed of which dealt with the phenomenon of falling rock, pointing out
repeatedly that this was the single largest cause of underground injury.
Walking slowly along the dark drifts, he studied the rock over our heads,
pointing out certain features he deemed worthy of our attention.

"Now see that slab there?" he asked, casting the beam of his cap
lamp over a suspiciously protruding rock about the size of a garbage can.
"She's cracked clear 'round. You can see it. Wouldn't take much to bring
'er out of there. Slab that big could kill a man if it hits 'im right."

The offending killer slab, now bathed in the weaving lights of a
dozen cap lamps, became the object of close collective scrutiny.

"How often them stones fall off the ceiling?"

Wizen smiled wanly and paused a second before answering. "You
mean, how often do them slabs come out of the back?" The old man had
the patience of Job.

Another pause while his student contemplated the semantic correction. "Yeah."

"Now that's something that's up to you. Up to each one of you. The very first thing you'll do when you get to your working places at the start of every shift is bar that loose crap down. You got scaling bars all over this mine and you're expected to use 'em. Anything you bring down can't fall on you later, right?"

A chorus of umms. With all heads turned upwards in awe, there was enough light on that rock to make it grow.

Producing a scaling bar, an eight-foot-long steel bar with a flat angled tip, Wizen ordered, "Okay, now everybody get out of the way, get back where you can watch this."

Gingerly poking the celebrated hanging rock which, by now, seemed to have grown in size, Wizen inched closer, probing for leverage. Getting a bite with the bar, he pressed downward and the rock moved a few inches with a heavy, groaning sound. The old man, who doubtlessly had barred down thousands of these things in his long career underground, moved still closer to get a better bite and execute the *coup de grâce*. When the bar had barely touched the ruck, it groaned again and fell out with astounding speed, smashing into the ground about two feet in front of Wizen's toes with a sickening thud. Not quite expecting it, Wizen lurched backwards, catching his feet on the rail and falling on his back with a second mighty thud. Had he stood his ground, it would have been a truly magnificent performance.

But such glory was not to be. For a long minute, the old man lay in the drift, his agony and embarrassment spotlighted by the frozen beams of a dozen lamp caps. When it had been ascertained that it was his pride that absorbed most of the impact, he wearily shrugged off the offers of assistance and climbed slowly to his feet in the awkward silence.

Wizen looked calmly and thoughtfully at the rock that had fought him to a draw and, with a wry grin, quietly mumbled a phrase I would hear again. "Gettin' too old for this shit."

96. Camp Hale
from *Climb to Conquer* by Peter Shelton

*In 1942, the US Army built a high-altitude training camp, at an elevation
of 9,500 feet, in between the towns of Leadville and Redcliffe. Camp
Hale, which was located near Pando Station on the route of the Denver
and Rio Grande Railroad, housed as many as 15,000 soldiers. Little
remains of their barracks, which were built in straight lines across these
alpine meadows. Soldiers stationed here learned how to ski at nearby
Cooper Hill (now Ski Cooper). They were also trained in mountaineering, cold weather survival, and the use of weapons and ordinance.*

In his book Climb to Conquer, *adventure writer Peter Shelton tells
the story of the army's Tenth Mountain Division, from its inception in
Vermont, through the early training years at Camp Hale, and on to the
Apennine Mountains in Italy, where an elite group of the army's mountaineering troops scaled an "unclimbable" cliff, stunned the soldiers
stationed there, and began to move the German army out of northern
Italy. Several Hollywood movies filmed at Camp Hale—*Mountain
Fighters *in 1943, and* I Love a Soldier *in 1944—also touched on that
story and helped to attract additional recruits. In this excerpt, Shelton
emphasizes the challenges that faced trainees at Camp Hale, especially
those recruits who were newcomers to the mountain environment.*

In the end, although numbers are not precise, of the fourteen thousand
soldiers who constituted the 10th Mountain Division at full strength, about
half were volunteers who came through the National Ski Patrol System.
The remainder were supplied by the Army through transfers from flatland
divisions, primarily the 30th, 31st, and 33rd Divisions from Louisiana and
Tennessee. Most of the NSPS volunteers, whether they were skiers or not,
came in with at least some outdoor experience. They'd supplied the three
letters of recommendation. They were keen and physically fit, and they had
an affinity for the mountains, or thought they might. And they generally
took to the mountaineering ethos created by the 87th, with its singing and
camaraderie and willingness—joy even—for strenuous work in the high
country. These men adored Camp Hale and took to the training with gusto.

Many of the transfers had a much harder time of it in Colorado, which for them became Camp Hell. They hadn't asked to be there, and they hated every part of it. They hated the snow, the skiing, the cold. The air at 9,200 feet didn't supply nearly enough oxygen for men used to the altitude in Memphis. And to make matters worse, the air in the valley floor was frequently polluted with smoke from the camp's five hundred coal stoves and the Denver & Rio Grande locomotives chugging over the Divide three times a day. In fact, the air was so bad during high-pressure inversions, it sickened scores of men, and not just the Southerners. Many a committed mountaineer also developed what was called the "Pando hack."

Unlike other camps, Hale was largely cut off from the rest of the world. Even if you could wrangle a pass, Denver was a nine-hour train ride away. By car the trip took half that, but almost no one had a car. The nearest town was Leadville, a once grand silver camp fallen on hard times. But Leadville was off-limits to the troops, because, in this busted, Depression-era mine town, one ancient profession continued to flourish. Nowhere to go, nothing to do. USO troupes feared the altitude and shunned the place, and the service clubs offered nothing stronger than 3.2 beer.

Worst of all for the flatlanders was the prospect of strapping long, recalcitrant, slippery wooden boards to their feet. Skiing was a mystery designed to humiliate and embarrass. Warm-country soldiers took to calling their skis torture boards—"toe-chah boahds." One sergeant became so enraged after a day of floundering in deep snow, he chopped his skis into tiny pieces and fed them into a fire. When Robert Woody arrived at Camp Hale, a ski trooper at last in April 1944, the first man he ran into at his barracks was an unhappy noncom with a distinctive drawl. "Where are the skis?" Woody asked with innocent enthusiasm. "So, ye want to ski?" his bunkmate asked, spitting tobacco. "Well, I hope ye bust your ass."

Many of these men asked for and received transfers out of the 10th. But there was a common wisecrack among those who stayed and learned to survive the mountains. They said: "Anyone who transfers to combat from the mountain troops is yellow!"

SOUTH PARK

Highway 9

Parkdale to Hartsel

97. Guffey
from *Between Urban and Wild* by Andrea Jones

After many years of living along the Front Range, Andrea and Doug Jones chose to relocate from Four Mile Canyon west of Boulder to Cap Rock Ridge near Guffey on the southern edge of South Park. These are two very different edges: while Four Mile is on the edge of the urban-suburban corridor that characterizes much of the Front Range, Cap Rock Ridge is an edge between small town rural life and a more spacious life outside of that small town. In the latter situation, Andrea and Doug had enough ground to pasture a couple of horses.

As a writer and naturalist and a keen observer of her lifelong habitat in Colorado, Andrea Jones writes about the experience of making a new home on the southern edge of South Park. In her book, Between Urban and Wild, *she considers the following question: What does it mean to inhabit this ground as opposed to holding legal title to it? Paying attention, for one thing. One way to do that, she suggests, is by observing her animals. How do her horses, Blue and Moondo, respond to this place? As she trails them through the pasture, their preferences reveal the nuances of terrain, vegetation, and micro-climate. They also invite her reflections on the experience of companionship and death from a horse's perspective.*

The bowl's slope captured the morning rays, and the boys soon picked out favorite spots for napping; trailing them there, I learned that these were places where the wind eddied to calm. With his shambling gait, Blue was not fond of the rockier areas around the perimeter of the bowl and spent most of his time low in the basin where the footing was more even and most of the grass was fine-textured blue grama. Moondo seemed to enjoy variety in his grazing, giving a clump of mountain muhly a flat-top trim with a single bite and then seasoning the mouthful with a frond of yarrow. When he came across them, he devoured dandelions, showing a taste for bitter greens. If the grass was going to seed, he twirled the heads together with his upper lip and yanked them out, leaving the leafy blades for another day. He was fond of the fuzzy white flowers of Platte thistles, plants so spiniferous that I don't dare touch them without gloves on. After carefully nipping a bulbous blossom off, he would take his time rolling the morsel around in his mouth to position it for chewing with a minimum of poking.

Watching the horses was easier than watching wild animals, who tend to flee when they detect my presence. I could ogle the horses as long as I wished, without trying to be sneaky and without relying on the house as a wildlife blind. I also had the luxury of knowing I was seeing the same individuals on a regular basis. With a few exceptions—the raven with the crippled foot, the doe with a long split cleaving her left ear—wild animals are anonymous, indistinguishable from one another. I can say that Moondo and Blue had preferences and personality traits because I knew I was seeing the same animals from day to day and month to month ... .

A year and a half after we brought the horses to their new home, it came clear that it was time to let Blue go. He fell one day while I was out of town, and it took both Doug and a veterinarian to get the old horse back on his feet. By the time I got home a few days later, Blue had already fallen again at least once; Doug was able to get him up, but his stability was gone. His hindquarters would teeter farther and farther over until he had to throw his week hind leg out to catch himself, winding up faced ninety degrees from where he'd been. This curlicue locomotion was treacherous and tiring. He could no longer stand with one hind leg cocked in a resting posture, and he had become afraid to lie down, knowing he might not be able to get up again.

He was clearly exhausted, and we began making arrangements to have him put down. Given the choice, I wanted Blue to die in circumstances of relative peace, before he got hurt in a fall, at a time when both

Doug and I could be present, in a place where it would be easy to deal with his remains.

I solicited advice from a couple of veterinarians on what to do with Moondo when we had Blue euthanized. The old-school guy told me I should give Moondo a sedative and isolate him from the event. Our new vet, the young woman who had come out to help Doug the first time Blue fell, advised us to not let him observe the euthanasia but to allow him to see and sniff the body afterward. When she arrived on the appointed day, I put Moondo's halter on him and took him for a walk down the driveway while Doug held Blue. We hadn't gone far before the vet drove past us on her way out. She gave a short wave, but didn't stop.

I turned Moondo around and we headed back to the barn. Once we topped the slight rise at the end of the driveway, I could see Blue, lying on his side in the parking area in front of the barn. When Moondo noticed him, his ears pricked up and he stared intently and began testing the air with deep breaths. By the time we were a hundred yards away, he was rigid, head high and nostrils wide in the familiar posture telegraphing that something was terribly wrong and that we should get out of here *now*. He slowed, snorting and staring, then stopped a few yards away from the body, refusing to move closer. Holding the end of the lead rope, I walked to Blue's head and bent down to pat him one last time.

The moment I touched Blue's unresponsive forehead, Moondo's head dropped and his body sagged, the alarm draining out of him. I don't know how horses process the concept of death, but I no longer have any doubt that they do. Moondo understood Blue was dead. He stepped forward and sniffed the old horse's nose, and stood for a few minutes, head down. When he listlessly picked at a patch of nearby grass, I guessed that he had investigated enough and turned him loose in the barn pasture. Instead of heading toward the gate leading to his favorite field, Moondo stood quietly near the barn, looking at Blue's body.

Moondo and Blue had not exactly been best friends, but they had been their own little herd, and I braced myself for the separation anxiety I expected once Blue was hauled away. Instead of pacing and running around the pasture whinnying, however, Moondo persisted with the stoic demeanor he'd shown after he had determined that Blue was dead. He called out a couple of times when I took him on trail rides over the next few weeks, but those vocalizations had an aspect of a query rather than desperation or distress. He seemed to understand that Blue was gone and not merely displaced.

None of which is to say that the event didn't affect him. He was depressed, refusing to come in from the big pasture for grains several nights. He began napping with his nose nearly touching a boulder that jutted from the ground out in the basin, an eminence we dubbed Companion Rock. His beloved field seemed to offer solace during his period of mourning. We made a point of visiting him several times a day, and he expressed his appreciation by grooming our necks and shoulder with his lips as we patted him.

98. Hartsel
from "The Incompleat Angler" by John J. Lipsey

In 1925, in preparation for his first fishing adventure into South Park, John Lipsey checked out a book called The Art of Dry Fly Fishing for Trout *from the Colorado Springs Public Library and practiced casting techniques in his back yard. His fishing companion offered further instruction before they left town later that summer for a weekend fishing the South Platte. They stayed at the Hartsel Hotel, which was popular with weekenders from Colorado Springs and apparently served up a good steak—"trout fishermen prefer a good steak," Lipsey wrote, "(even more so after returning empty handed from a full day on the river)." In a pamphlet called "The Incompleat Angler," which he wrote for friends and family, Lipsey describes the art of fly fishing from a beginner's perspective, and does so, as this excerpt suggests, with plenty of humility and good cheer.*

About a half-mile west of town, my friend unloaded me and my equipment, pointed out two or three places where there were always plenty of fish, left me, and went off further to attend to his own fishing.

I assembled my beautiful gear and went to the lower end of the reach to which he had assigned me. My casts, I thought, were perfect—though my leader would make a splash. Standing sometimes on the dirt bank, but usually on the shingle or on boulders in the stream, I whipped thoroughly that fork of the South Platte. I recognized from the book's descriptions and pictures the proper places to drop the fly, and I worked the holes, and particularly just below the riffles. I moved slowly up along the serpentine course of the narrow river for about a mile. I got a few strikes, but the fish easily disengaged themselves.

Once, standing wet-footed on a boulder in mid-stream, I saw just below me a rainbow feeding. I grasped the leader and dangled the fly directly in front of the trout's nose. He went on eating something he pre-ferred more. I moved the fly until it tickled his nose, but he just nudged the fly away and continued to eat in the same spot. Evidently he was not in the mood for that kind of fly. I tied two other and different flies on the leader to determine what the fish did want. No better luck.

But I did find some of my equipment useful. The sun went behind a cloud, and the deer-flies came out in swarms. They bit, if the fish did not. I donned gloves and my fly-helmet. What a wonderful thing it was to be a fisherman who knew how to take care of himself! Shortly after twelve I arrived at a bridge near the end of my beat, and my friend came driving down from somewhere upstream where he had fished with no net result. We sat in the warm shade of the car and ate the lunch the hotel had provided for us.

A small boy rode up on a bicycle and asked if we wanted to buy some minnows. I said no. Being a true fly-fisherman, I scorned the suggestions that I use an ignoble lure. But my friend said: "Don't be stubborn. Never argue with fish. Give them what they want. If they want minnows, give them minnows." The minnows were packed in salt in Prince Albert tobac-co cans, pocket size, easily concealed about the person. He bought one can for me and one for himself, and cautioned me to say nothing of this trans-action to the other fishermen. He showed me how to impale a minnow on the fly-hook. It was not like putting the minnow on an ordinary bare hook. You could always say, if you should take a fish, "I got him on a Royal Coachman." I agreed, because I wanted to kill at least one fish.

We fished the balance of that hot and weary day. I caught nothing. Neither did he.

When the sun slipped behind Buffalo Peaks, we returned to the hotel, washed, and sat on the front porch to watch the other fishermen come in, dragging their feet in their heavy boots or flopping along with the tops of their waders drooping disreputably. Some had no fish; most had one or two. Leon Snyder, the hardest-working fisherman in the Rocky Mountains, had most: three medium-sized rainbows. Because only a few of us had had much luck, we could all agree amiably that fishing was poor. Somebody opened a bottle of foul-smelling mountain lightning. So, by the time they washed, and dinner was ready, they all seemed to think this was a very fine world indeed and the finest part of it was South Park.

Highway 285

Trout Creek Pass to Kenosha Pass

99. Highway 285
Between Antero Junction and Fairplay
from *Spring's Edge* by Laurie Wagner Buyer

Author and poet Laurie Jameson (Laurie Wagner Buyer when she wrote her book Spring's Edge *from which the following account is excerpted), spent many years working on remote ranches in the Rocky Mountain region, including the DM Ranch located just west of Highway 285 on County Road 22 to Weston Pass.* Spring's Edge: A Ranch Wife's Chronicles *is her account of life on the DM with her former husband, rancher Mick Buyer, whose family had deep roots here in South Park. There is no end to the work involved in maintaining this ranching operation. And calving time, coming as it does as winter heads into spring (which is really just a wetter version of winter at this elevation) is one of the most stressful and demanding seasons for any rancher. In this description, she describes the chores that come with the season as well as some of the quieter moments in between that help to keep her going.*

Friday March 4th
The illuminated dial reads 3:44 a.m. when I push the turn-off bar on the clock. The furnace clicks on. When I venture off the porch the air is still, soft, cool as silk, but not cold. Without the wind's pervasive bold voice, I hear the river running, a long-missed melody of rushing trills, crescendos, and decrescendos as water cascades over and under ice, around snow drifted bends.

The new ma hovers over her black calf that lies in a heap, legs askew, evidence that he has tried to stand. He hasn't made much progress, since he is only about ten feet from where we left him when we pulled him from his mother. He has not been licked clean. Birth mucus has hardened on his hide like shellac. One piece of the womb sack, plastered along his back, gleams white and transparent as a wedding veil. When I approach, ma "mmhhhs" at the calf. At least she knows he's hers. Because he lies in a damp, squishy spot soaked with birth fluids, I drag him forward by a front leg onto drier ground where there is old hay and good footing. With a concentrated heave on my part, I get the heavy bugger to stand, splay-legged and quivering, alert and anxious. I steady him while he takes a few wobbly steps; then I back off. Ma comes over curious: "mmhhh." To calm her, I throw a jag of hay at her feet and she grabs a mouthful, chewing voraciously. Slowly, I reach for the iodine on a high shelf and crouch aiming carefully, to spray the calf's damp, dangling umbilical. He flinches at the caustic sting of the disinfectant and staggers under his mother's neck, then turns toward her flank. If he will suck while the heifer stands and eats, he will have a grand start on the first day of his life.

Many ranchers disapprove the notion of leaving the heifer and her calf alone to work out the complicated details of their bonding. Some would wash and dry the calf, get it up, confine the heifer, and make the calf suck, fiddling and fooling around, anxious and worried that the calf would die. Mick, raised in an outdated but still commonsense-oriented school of thought, believes that nature is the best teacher. He learned his skills from following his grandfather and his father, and I have learned through following him through fifteen calving seasons ... .

Returning to the house to light the morning fires, I see a bright bold cluster of streaming stars, a comet, on the northeastern horizon. Old timers felt that comets were an omen, a foretelling of things to come. I stand and study the stars, searching for answers, any answers, but there is only an eternal stillness that leaves me feeling alone, without guidance or direction.

In the darkness surrounding the house, I sense movement, then see Mick's darker shadowy shape in the porch doorway, waiting for me ... . I take a step toward him. Then another. It isn't much of a map to follow, but for today, anyway, I know where I am going. There's breakfast to cook and cows to feed. There's a man, with a heart as big as all the heavens, who needs my helping hand.

100. Fairplay
from *Angle of Repose* by Wallace Stegner

*Angle of Repose, Wallace Stegner's Pulitzer Prize winning novel, takes
place in the mining West as seen through the eyes of Susan Ward, a
promising writer from the New York literary world, and her husband
Oliver, a mining engineer who is hired on to various mining, hydrolo-
gy, and construction projects. Stegner based their story on the letters
of writer and illustrator Mary Hallock Foote, who lived in western
communities like Deadwood and Leadville with her engineer husband
Arthur De Mint Foote. Shortly after their arrival in the hardscrabble
town of Fairplay, Susan's introduction to the Mountain West includes a
night spent in a marginal (at least by contemporary standards) boarding house, followed by a harrowing journey over 13,185 foot Mosquito
Pass, via horse-drawn wagon, to Leadville. Needless to say, Susan's
initial impressions of the mining frontier were anything but reassuring.
Mary Hallock Foote may have had her own trepidations about a new
life in the West as well, but she also approached her circumstance
as an adventure and an artistic opportunity. (For more on Foote and
Stegner's use of her letters in the story he tells in* Angle of Repose, *see
the "Leadville" entries).*

A Night in Fairplay:
They reached the corner, turned left, found the boardinghouse. A man
sitting in his undershirt, drinking coffee, said yes, they had a bed. It
wasn't much for the lady—just curtained off. Oliver looked at her once
and took it. The undershirted man picked up his lamp and led them up
bare stairs and along a hall whose blue muslin walls waved and crawled
with the wind of their movement, to a door that had no key. After she
was inside, and sinking down on the bed, Susan saw that the room had
no walls, either—only that same blue muslin, called Osnaburg, nailed
to a frame that went no more than six feet above the floor. Under the one
broad roof every eight-by-ten cubicle in the place shook to the same cold
drafts, and glared the same sick blue in the lantern's light. She could hear
the sounds of sleeping all around. It was so cold she could see her breath.

Oliver knelt at the bedside and took her in his arm. His lips were on her cold face. "I'm sorry," he whispered, echoing the clerk. "I'm sorry I'm sorry I'm sorry."

"It's all right. I think I could sleep anywhere."

"I wish we were already home."

"So do I."

"In this place we can't even talk."

It seemed to her that she heard every noise from midnight until near morning—dogs, drunken men in the street, footsteps that came down the hall and, it seemed, stopped before her door, so that she lay listening fearfully for a long time.

Then someone in the next cubicle sat up, yawning and squeaking the bed. He lighted a lamp whose glow shone blue through the cloth wall and threw huge windmill shadows among the rafters. She heard him stamp into his boots. The light rose and moved and receded down the hall. Outside, a rooster crowed some way off, and right underneath her someone split kindling with a quick thunk, thunk, thunk. Exhausted, frazzled, wide awake, she turned in the bed, fighting for cover, and found that Oliver's eyes were open. He always woke that way, as quietly as if he had been lying there waiting.

"Can't we get up?" she whispered.

The Road Up Mosquito Pass toward Leadville:
The thin air smelled of stone and snow, the sun came through it and lay warm on her hands and face without warming the air itself. Up, up, up. There was no top to this pass. Oliver said it crested at more than thirteen thousand feet. They were long past all trees, even runted ones. The peaks were close around them, the distance heaved with stony ridges, needles, pyramids in whose shadowed cirques the snow curved smoothly. The horses stopped, pumping for air, and as they rested she saw below a slumping snowbank the shine of beginning melt, and in the very edge between thaw and freeze a clump of cream-colored flowers.

"I'd like to walk a little. Could I?"

"You won't want to walk far. We're around twelve thousand right now."

"Just a little way. I can keep up with you."

It felt good to use her legs, but she had no wind at all. With a handful of the little alpine flowers in her hand and the whole broken world under her eyes, she puffed on after the democrat, and was glad when it stopped and waited. But when she caught up, Oliver was standing out in front looking closely at the bay horse. The moment she saw the closed expression of his face she knew something was wrong. She looked at the horse, spraddle-legged, dull-eyed, with pumping ribs and flaring nostrils, and heard the breath rattle in his throat.

"All right," Oliver said after a few minutes. "No more, now. You'll be sick yourself." He helped her up in the seat. He was panting; even in the reminding wind his face had the shine of sweat. They hung, fighting for oxygen, on a steep narrow ledge below the place where the road finally curved around out of sight. The shelf had been literally blasted out of the mountain with black powder. Beyond the curve of the road there was nothing in sight. They must be near the summit, or at it. Snow sagged against the inward cliff and around the big blocks of broken stone. The outside dropped away so steep and far she didn't dare look.

"How much farther?" she said. "Can he make it, do you think?"

"It's going to be all right. Just up this last pitch and then it's down. We could take him out and let the black pull it."

He blew out his breath, with a down-mouthed, acknowledging look of relief. Then she saw his eyes change. "Wait. Listen."

He cocked his head with his hand raised, for only a second, long enough for her to hear something, she couldn't tell what—perhaps only the empty roaring of the sky. He dropped his hand, threw a look right, then left. The buggy sagged and rolled a half wheel backward as he leaped onto the step. At that instant appeared around the upper bend a pair of trotting horses, then another pair, the another, then the rocking cradle of the stage. She saw sparks clash from rock under the tires. To her horrified eyes it seemed a runaway, out of control.

Oliver's whip cracked on the rump of the black horse, then the bay, the black again. Susan grabbed for the dash. They jerked wildly in toward the cliff, among the blocks of stone. And there was not room, she knew it with a certainty that froze her mind.

The sick horse, on the inside, floundered among the rocks and deep snow. Oliver lashed, lashed, lashed it—oh, how could he? She screamed and grabbed for his whip arm; he shook her off without even looking at her. The left wheels reared up, climbed, crashed down, climbed again; the buggy titled so steeply that she hung on in frantic fear of sliding straight off under the hoofs and wheels. Oliver's hand shot out and grabbed her. She screamed again, the air was full of a rumble, a close, tense, voiceless rush, and the stage passed her so close that if she had her arm extended it might have been torn off. Glaring up into the dangerous shadow as it thundered by, she saw a lean, hook-nosed face, a figure with feet braced against the dash, lines that hummed stiff as metal. And she saw the stage driver's queer, small, gritted smile.

Still hanging onto her arm, but leaning far inward toward the cliff like a sailor high-siding a blow, Oliver guided the buggy up over a last rock to a bumpy landing in the road. The air still reeked with the hot smell of horse and the spark odor of iron tires on stone. The noise of the stage diminished behind and below them. They turned to watch it go.

"God Almighty," Oliver said, and slid back into the seat beside her. "You all right?"

"I think so."

"Too close."

She was staring in pain at the sick horse. It tottered on its legs—she could see the deep trembling that ran from pastern to knee. Its nose went clear to the ground, it shuddered and began to sink. Instantly Oliver lashed it harshly with the whip, lashed its mate, leaped to the ground and kept on lashing. The horse tottered, strained, was dragged forward, the buggy crawled painfully upward. Susan sat white and trembling, hating his cruelty, hating the pain and exhaustion of the sick beast, hating the heartless mountains, the brutal West.

101. Kenosha Pass / Platte Canyon
Spirit that Form'd This Scene by Walt Whitman

In October of 1879, poet Walt Whitman boarded a westbound train out of Denver. The Denver, South Park and Pacific route entered the mountains

*by way of Platte Canyon, following the North Fork of the South Platte
River up to the spine of the Front Range. The tracks, which were still under construction in South Park, ran only as far as 10,000-foot Kenosha
Pass. Because the sixty-year-old poet had some health concerns, he was
reluctant to embark on a horse-drawn journey over 13,185 foot Mosquito
Pass to Leadville. Although he had previously thought he might like to
visit Leadville, Kenosha Pass was as far as he got—far enough, as it
turned out, to inspire some poetic reflections.*

*The ride up the canyon made a big impression, which he recorded
in a letter. "I have found the law of my own poems amid all this grim yet
joyous elemental abandon—this plentitude of material, entire absence
of art, untrammel'd play of primitive Nature—the chasm, the gorge, the
crystal mountain stream ... the fantastic forms, bathed in transparent
browns, faint reds and grays, towering sometimes a thousand, sometimes
two or three thousand feet high—at their tops now and then huge masses
pois'd, and mixing with the clouds, with only their outlines, hazed in the
misty lilac, visible."*

*From the summit at Kenosha he witnessed the "paradisiac loveliness"
of South Park, surrounded by mountain peaks "in every variety of perspective, every hue of vista, [which] fringe the view." Further reflection
on the spiritual dimension of his travels into the high country resulted in
the following poem.*

Spirit that Form'd This Scene
Written in Platte Cañon, Colorado

Spirit that form'd this scene,
These tumbled rock-piles grim and red,
These reckless heaven-ambitious peaks,
These gorges, turbulent-clear streams, this naked freshness,

These formless wild arrays, for reasons of their own;
I know thee, savage spirit—we have communed together,
Mine too such wild arrays, for reasons of their own;
Was't charged against my chants they had forgotten art?

To fuse within themselves its rules precise and delicatesse?
The lyrist's measur'd beat, the wrought-out temple's grace—
column and polish'd arch forgot?
But thou that revelest here—spirit that form'd this scene,
They have remember'd thee.

NORTH PARK

Highway 14

Gould to Walden

102. Gould
from *Timber Times and Tales* by Earlene Belew Bradley

In the early twentieth century, Gould was primarily a logging town. In April of 1939, Alba and Ona Belew and their five children arrived in Gould after a long trip from the Ozarks in a 1933 Chevrolet. They were packed "like sardines in a can" recalls Earlene Belew Bradley, whose father moved his family here for health reasons and for the prevailing wages which were better here than they were for timber workers back in Missouri. "Although snow still covered much of the ground," Earlene writes, "ankle-deep mud ran the gamut of the narrow, north-south access roads to the slab-sided cabins—one of which we would soon call home." Those slab-sided cabins, built by the Michigan River Timber Company to house their loggers, are gone, but the remains of the old Penfold Store, where the Belew family and other locals could purchase some basic supplies, can still be seen.

In her book, Timber Times and Tales: An Early History of Gould, Colorado, *Earlene Belew Bradley gathers stories from the heyday of the Michigan River Timber Company when as many as 300 people—many of them loggers and their families—lived here. In the following story, her brother Don Belew remembers a night on the town.*

To a ten-year old kid out for a little excitement with a small, rowdy group of buddies, Halloween night had a feel of mysterious expectation. It was the last year of the tumultuous 1940s in the small mountain timber camp of Gould, Colorado.

As the rakish old moon reflected off the pine shrouded slopes of Owl Mountain, a wisp of ice crystals sliced off the freshly fallen layer of snow and blew across the meadow between the rows of slab-sided shacks. Long shadows of gently swaying aspens on the adjacent hillside spiked the imagination, as ghosts and goblins dressed in heinous homemade apparel darted among the rustic homes, dimly lit with kerosene lamps or gas lanterns.

From across camp, an occasional muffled bang of wood crashing onto the soft snow gave testimony that yet another outhouse had fallen down the hillside. The older boys were again enjoying their favorite Halloween sport and were even more gleeful if they were lucky enough to catch a forlorn soul within one of the flimsy, slab-sided privies as they swayed it in the breeze. It was certain they gave no thought to the torturous setup job they were creating for their dads the next morning before they headed to their grueling day's work up on the mountain.

Methodically, we made our way up and down each of the three long rows of houses, careful to visit each dwelling and either get our just treat or thoroughly rub a broken bar of soap across the windows of those unfortunates who were not home, did not have a light on, or failed to provide us with our rightful "goodies."

As we neared the old Penfold Store, rumor was out among the soliciting contingents that a special treat awaited those brave enough to make their way behind the old store and knock on the door of the old gentleman who lived in one of the small cabins. One question kept penetrating the chilly night air: "Have you been to Cecil's yet?"

Two distinct memories linger clearly through these many years since that Halloween night. First was the large brown paper grocery sack filled with a curious mixture of crunched cookies, popcorn, caramel-coated popcorn balls broken into small pieces, peanuts with cracked shells, and various other goodies that weren't all that appetizing when viewed in one big heap. Occasionally, a sucker, or small Baby Ruth, or Butterfingers, in their original wrapping, could be salvaged from the mess.

Next, I remember the man named Cecil Morrow—a bearded, robust logger. With his large stomach, bushy hair, and rumpled beard, Cecil was a formidable figure to approach on Halloween night. But if the rumors were true, it would be worth the risk.

We edged slowly past the spooky old Penfold Store that had seen better days by the late 1940s, although a portion of the building was still in use as a cookhouse.

By the time we arrived at Cecil's door, we were mesmerized with anticipation.

"Knock! Knock! Knock!" on the rough-hewn wooden door. Slowly, footsteps—"Thump! Thump! Thump!"—crossed the loose floor planks of the cabin.

Suddenly, the door swung wide open and there was Cecil.

"Handout?" the largest, bravest kid managed to say in a shaky voice.

"Trick or Treat?" the smallest kid, in back of the others, meekly suggested.

Cecil grinned broadly as he reached inside the pocket of his ragged bib overalls and pulled out a dirty tobacco pouch. Digging into it with his forefinger, he pulled out the treasures we were seeking—each of us received a whole dime.

A successful night was assured. Any other bounty collected on that Halloween night would be purely incidental. We would go home happy!

103. Walden
from *The View from the Folding Chairs* by Michala Miller

Michala Miller, born in 1933, came of age in North Park during World War II. "While all community functions took a back seat to the war effort," she writes, "there were traditions that continued such as the summer parade and rodeo." A small-town parade may not seem like a big deal to urban dwellers whose lives are inundated with various distractions and entertainments, but for a young person who only came to town once in a while, it was momentous, especially when you and the rest of the Camp Fire Girls had taken on the project of decorating a float. In her book, The View from the Folding Chairs, *Miller describes North Park during the 1930s and 40s, recalling events like the summer parade in Walden.*

We used balling wire to attach the boughs along the sides of a flatbed truck and wired the trees to the back of the cab. In this woodland scene we all sat cross-legged around a pretend fire in the center of the bed. The rear of our float was adorned with a homemade banner made of butcher paper. Tacked between the brake lights it stated our name, which was something like Chicaboo, plus in smaller letters, "Camp Fire Girls."

The business part of town was about two blocks long, but the parade route started at the community church, and by the time we had gone down the main street and doubled back we'd cover at least eight blocks.

First marched the flag bearers, followed by the rodeo queen and her lady-in-waiting riding palomino horses. Next came the band, which consisted of a handful of high school musicians riding in the back of a pickup, and behind them the floats. The parade was composed of three so-called floats: a woman's organization, a load of logs headed for the sawmill, and we "Camp Firers." The remainder of the parade was made up of horses and riders. Even some very small children rode with a parent holding a lead rope. Lots of horses, usually four or six abreast, passed in review, many of which would make a second appearance that afternoon at the rodeo. Without the four-legged animals, it wouldn't have been much of a parade.

Three men were picked at random to be the float judges, and that year my father was picked. He used the term "railroaded into it," but since no one objected to his obvious conflict of interest, he had the job. The judges stood in front of the bar about halfway down the block and across from the drug store. They faced west so that the morning sun was not in their eyes while they judged, or maybe that was just where the three of them met.

Mine was the first float, right behind the musical pickup, and we got lots of applause. Next was the load of logs with the driver waving and honking his horn and, finally the third bunch, the "women's group," who tried to sing as they passed in review. They were also on a flatbed truck sitting on folding chairs and wearing old-fashioned dresses. One woman worked a butter churn, shoving the plunger up and down, while another sat at an old treadle sewing machine. Their theme must have been pioneer women, but the judges weren't too impressed for we got first prize

and five dollars for our coffer. Second prize caused a problem when one
of the judges voted for the load of logs.

"The women will be mad as hell if we put the load of logs ahead of
them," argued the other two.

Wisdom prevailed with three dollars and second prize going to the
pioneer float, and a buck for third prize landing in the pocket of the
driver of the load of logs. Several ranchers along the sidewalk commented on the good looking horseflesh parading by, but horses didn't compete
for the money.

All too soon the parade was over. Everyone stood around for at least
an hour to visit. Visiting time was almost as scarce as gasoline and
parades. I may have helped remove the boughs from the flatbed but, more
likely, I was doing my share of the talking. A free day in town with lots
of folks to share it was rare.

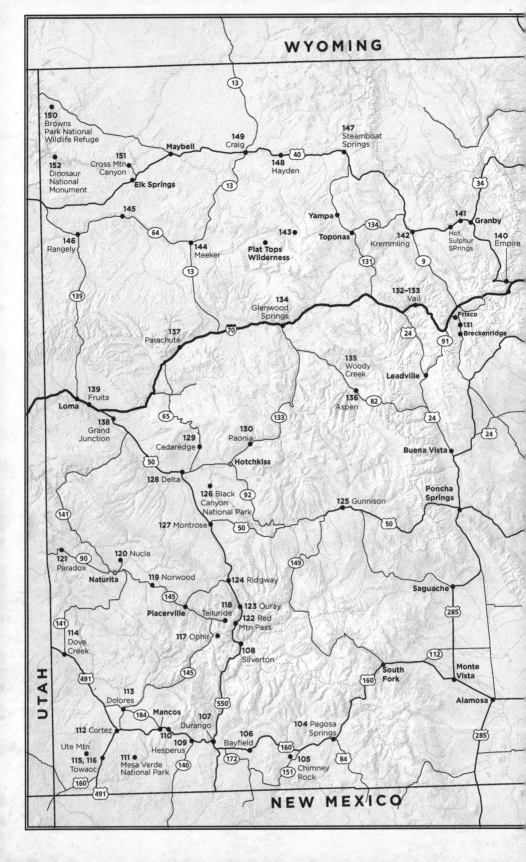

WESTERN SLOPE

The Western Slope encompasses the entirety of Colorado west of the
Continental Divide—a region where mountain ranges like the Elks and
the San Juans trail off into vast sheets of uplifted sedimentary formations—sandstones, siltstones, and shales—which the Colorado River
and its tributaries have eroded into a jumble of ridges, mesas, and
canyons. Resistant layers of rock cap the great mesas of the western
slope—ranging in elevation from Mesa Verde (7,500 feet) in the south
to the Flat Tops (11,000 feet) in the north; in between is Grand Mesa
which separates the Colorado River from the Gunnison, one of its major
tributaries. All of the Western Slope rivers, which collect about seventy
percent of the state's water, eventually flow into the Colorado, though
some like the Green, the Dolores, and the San Juan wait until they cross
over into Utah to do so. Although the Colorado takes center stage in the
riparian story that shapes so much of the Western Slope, its tributaries
play important roles in delineating these three sub-regions.

Central: The Colorado and the Gunnison
The Colorado River gathers itself in the headwaters country on the western edge of Rocky Mountain National Park, rolls through the wide mountain valleys of Middle Park, and tumbles through deeper canyons further
west on its way to meet up with the Gunnison River in Grand Junction. The
main human thoroughfares (I-70 and US 50) in the west central part of the
state follow these rivers and the valleys they have shaped.

South: The San Juan Basin
Although the San Juan Mountains contribute snowmelt to the Gunnison
by way of rivers like the Cimarron and the Uncompahgre, they also offer
their waters to the Piedra, Pine, Animas, La Plata, and Mancos, all of

which flow south into the San Juan. The San Juan Basin of southwestern Colorado has a distinct native heritage both because of the remnants of ancestral Puebloan culture found at places like Mesa Verde, as well as the remaining homelands of the Ute People whose reservations run along the southern border of the state. Portions of Highway 160, the busiest east-west thoroughfare in the Basin, follow the route taken by earlier travelers though the region including the Utes, Navajos, and various Spanish explorers.

North: Yampa, White and Green Rivers
Desert Shrub woodlands—which consist of sagebrush highlands as well piñon-juniper forests—are especially prevalent in the western portions of the northern tier. Highway 40, a major east-west route throughout the state, follows the Yampa River which gathers water from the Continental Divide east of Steamboat Springs as well as the Flat Top region further south. The Flat Top region also contributes to the headwaters of the White River. Both the Yampa and the White Rivers run a relatively straight-ahead east-west course toward the Green River, which ultimately delivers their waters to the Colorado.

Earlier Inhabitants of the Western Slope
Traces of early agricultural lifestyles have been uncovered by archaeologists, especially in the southern area where the ancestral Puebloans were most prevalent, but also up north in the Fremont culture sites around Dinosaur National Monument. Hunting and gathering cultures may have been less susceptible to changing environmental conditions like drought over the long haul. Nomadic sites found on the Western Slope date back 13,000 years. The Utes, who brought their mountain way of life from ancestral lands in the Great Basin, were well established here until white settlement encroached on their hunting grounds in the mid-1800s. Ute words like Uncompahgre, Tavaputs, *and* Yampa *(a word that identified a useful root plant), still identify some of the major geographical features of the western slope.*

Highway 160

Pagosa Springs to Bayfield

104. Pagosa Springs
from *Ghost Grizzlies* by David Petersen

*The South San Juan Wilderness, which skirts the Continental Divide east
of Pagosa Springs, is as wild as any mountain region in the state. As early as 1952, most authorities believed that the last of Colorado's grizzlies
had been extirpated from the area. Then, in 1979, a hunting guide from
the San Luis Valley named Ed Wiseman claimed he had been attacked
and severely mauled by a 400-pound grizzly, which he subsequently
stabbed with an arrow. At least part of Wiseman's story was true (he had
the battle scars and the grizzly carcass to prove it). But what about the
rest of the story? Did he initially provoke the bear with a rifle shot? Did
he really end up killing it with an arrow?*

*Author and avid hunter David Petersen was skeptical at first, as were
many others who had heard Wiseman's story. Later, while researching
and writing his book* Ghost Grizzlies: Does the Great Bear Still Haunt
Colorado?, *Petersen accompanied Wiseman to the scene of the encounter near the headwaters of the Navajo River in the heart of the South
San Juan wilderness. He listened to Wiseman's account while carefully
recording the details of the scene and followed up this meeting with a
thorough examination of the hide and skeleton at the Denver Museum of
Natural History where it is stored. Ultimately, Petersen determined that
the physical evidence supported Wiseman's story, which he had been
more inclined to believe after spending time with the man. In this excerpt
from* Ghost Grizzlies, *he recalls their trip into the South San Juans.*

On his feet, Ed walks with a decided limp—a nagging reminder of his wrestling match with a grizzly. In the space of a little over a minute, Wiseman's right leg from ankle to knee was literally pulverized. The left leg, right hand, and both arms were injured, and his right shoulder was bitten completely through. Seventy-seven is the number of scars he wears today … .

As Ed leads through the trees, I ask if it feels at all strange to return to this place where he was almost killed in a manner most bloody and anachronistic by a beast that was not supposed even to exist. "Only the first time," he says. "It was nine months before I'd mended enough to get back up here, and I happened to be alone. I wasn't really scared, but I was definitely apprehensive; I kept looking behind me to make sure there wasn't something there … ."

My guide stops and points, then strides up to a misshapen fir, its waist-thick trunk growing almost parallel to the ground for a length of a man, then bending upright to its proper orientation, like the neck of a giant swan.

"This is it," he says. "Right here. This bent tree makes it easy to find. I was hunting along this game trail," he points, "standing right in front of this bent tree. The bear came charging out from over by the cliffs. It saw me and swerved in my direction. Next thing I know, the two of us are tumbling over a log. Right where you're standing is where the fight took place."

… It doesn't take long to circumambulate the scene of the action: a tiny glen at the heart of a stringer of mature scaly-barked Engelmann spruce and blistery gray subalpine fir. The trees here, one and all, are too fat to shinny up, even had there been time to try, which Ed has made clear there wasn't … .

Ed calls on a metaphor to describe his hit or miss memories of the attack and subsequent events. "In normal circumstances," he explains, "the mind works like a movie camera, recording a constant flow of events—unlike a still camera, which can only record one frame at a time and misses a lot of action between. During the attack, my mind switched to the still-camera mode, leaving me with some very sharp snapshots, but lots of blank frames in between.

"My first memory is seeing the bear running toward me from about thirty yards, and realizing it was charging. I hollered No! No! ... I was carrying my bow in my right hand, and I thrust it out in front of me like a shield. The bear never broke its run, never got up off all fours, and in a flash it was on me, slapping the bow out of my hand.... I wound up on the ground with my head facing away from the bear's. It had my lower leg in its mouth, shaking me like a puppy would a rag. I distinctly remember feeling the skin of my leg get real tight, then hearing the flesh rip as it gave way, but I don't recall any pain.... Then I spotted one of the arrows that had been knocked out of my bow quiver laying there on the ground real close, the broadhead pointing toward the bear. It's hard to stay still for long with a grizzly gnawing on you, and the way things were going, I was afraid that if I kept playing dead much longer, I'd be dead. So I reached out and grabbed the arrow with my left hand, rolled over on my back, and stabbed upward.

" ... I can't recall actually stabbing the bear a second time—the motion itself—but I remember fixing to.... Within seconds, though, she dropped the leg and stood over me, blood spurting from the wound in her neck and onto my chest.... My next memory is of the bear walking away." Ed points to the broken log. "She just walked over there and laid down, turned her head to the left, put her left front paw on the log and rested her chin on the paw. I've seen bears die, and I knew she was gone."

105. Chimney Rock National Monument
from *House of Rain* by Craig Childs

In the eleventh century, on an exposed ridge adjacent to the rock towers that we know as Chimney Rock National Monument, the ancestral Puebloan people built a great house capable of sheltering as many as 360 residents. At that time, these people also inhabited nearby river valleys, a far more hospitable habitat than a rocky outcrop at an elevation of 7000 feet. Why then had they gone to the trouble of building up on this ridge? What was the attraction to this place? As near as we can tell from the vantage point of the present, the answer had to do with the sky.

*The ancestral Puebloans understood their position in time and space
by way of the night sky. Careful observation of the stars and planets
helped them to anticipate the turning of the seasons, something that
would have been important in a culture dependent on hunting, gathering,
and agriculture. Chimney Rock, as it turns out, is an important reference
point as the moon travels across the sky during the lunar standstill
cycle. For example, every 18.6 years, the moon reaches its northernmost
position. As the sun sets on winter solstice, the full moon rises, perfectly
framed by the twin towers of Chimney Rock. For the astronomers of the
ancient Puebloan culture, this was a significant, predictable, and powerful moment, as were other appearances of the moon from this "lunar
observatory" during summer solstice and the equinoxes.*

In his book House of Rain, *author and adventurer Craig Childs ex-
plores ancestral Puebloan territory throughout the American Southwest.
Here he takes his readers up the ridge at Chimney Rock on a cold
December evening.*

When the sun had nearly completed its circle on this short winter day
and began riding low in the southwest, other people showed up. This was
not a summer tourist crowd, but a group of twenty or so researchers in
various scientific disciplines. Forest Service workers walked ahead of
them, chipping ice off the trail and salting the rock steps as if casting
rose petals for arriving pilgrims. An elderly ethnohistory professor came
behind them stamping her cane. Two astrophysicists, both somewhat
elderly, followed her, tottering along the trail to reach the great house.
Behind them came other researchers, archaeologists.

A tall man name Ron Sutcliffe had made all the delicate calculations,
determining when and where the moon would rise. He had come for
months of moonrises, waiting like a silent monk at three in the morning,
noon, sunrise; checking and refining his computations in preparation
for tonight's event—the first night in almost eighteen years that the full
moon would appear between the towers ... .

As I watched Sutcliffe pace the deck, I imagined a person of much
the same station a thousand years ago, also nervous as everyone lined
up—macaw feathers blooming from their hair, turquoise and shells

adorning their bodies. Among the crowd, there may have been some well-dressed and fierce-looking people who had come all the way from southern Mexico and could not be disappointed. There must have been such a person as Sutcliffe, a moon watcher who made the final call and said that after almost two decades, the moon would rise at this moment and could be seen only if everyone stood in this particular place ....

This was not an entirely scientific undertaking. We had all come merely to see what could be seen, to place ourselves at what may once have been a sacred crossing of time and place. Twenty warmly dressed people huddled behind the field of cameras. They were silent, focusing all their attention on a single point, a dark space in the distance.

"First light," Sutcliffe said. "There, first light."

He was pointing at a faint glow pinched between the two towers—not the bare moon itself, but almost .... Voices stirred. One of the astrophysicists commented that this must have been a powerful event to witness long ago. Wistfully, he said it was too bad no one worshipped this particular moonrise anymore. I wondered, does he not see this cluster of cameras we have set up? Does he not notice that twenty of us have crowded together in a windy December chill atop this ridge just to watch a single moonrise? In my mind this was an unquestionable form of worship, but I did not say anything. It was not my place, and I did not want to miss the first fleck of light.

Sutcliffe said that it was best to remain quiet for the duration.

He asked for the time.

Someone said 5:29. He said nothing else.

Into the breach of the towers an eggshell light broke the sky. The moon rose, exactly when and where Sutcliffe had said it would, piercing the space between the towers.

Once the moon was free in the sky, the talking resumed, laughter near the fire lookout. Forest Service docents announced it was time to leave; everyone must have a flashlight; please walk very carefully .... People began moving around the great house toward the narrow trail below ....

Below us a procession of lights moved into the darkness—people strung out for a quarter mile, each flashlight illuminating a circle of ground along the switchback trail. Their lights stretched into a singular column of lanterns swaying along the lower ridge. Strung all together, the people looked like worshippers, with their small white globes dangling in the blackness. As I watched them descend, I thought they looked as if they were stepping off into space, their lights trailing over the open vault of the land.

106. Bayfield
from *When the Legends Die* by Hal Borland

Author and journalist Hal Borland wrote for the Denver Post, *several Philadelphia papers, and eventually the* New York Times *where he held various positions for the better part of his career (1937-1978). He also wrote several novels that were set in his home state, one of which—*When the Legends Die—*was later made into a feature film. In this novel, Borland tells the story of Thomas Black Bull, whose parents raise him in the traditional mountain ways of their Ute ancestors, until a family tragedy forces him to attend a school on the nearby reservation. This episode, which takes place during a trip to a Bayfield trading post with Albert Left Hand, his sheep-ranching boss, demonstrates his skill as a horseman, which will eventually lead to a career on the professional rodeo circuit.*

Drowsy Bayfield had its Saturday afternoon crowd. A dozen saddle horses were hitched at the long rack in front of the general store, and wagon teams and a few saddle horses were in the cottonwood grove at the end of the street. The two saloons spilled loud talk and laughter onto the board sidewalk. Cowhands loafed in doorways and at the edge of the walk. They glanced up as Albert Left Hand drove up the dusty street and stopped his team in front of the big store. Thomas sat in the wagon, holding the reins, while Albert went in and talked with the trader. He made his deal then came out and ordered, "Go around back and unload."

Thomas drove the team up to the corner and around and back down the alley to an open shed where Albert Left Hand was waiting. Thomas unloaded the stinking pelts and piled them as Albert Left Hand directed. Then Albert Left Hand gave him a nickel. "For the pop," he said. He took charge of the team and Thomas went back the way he had come, to the main street.

He didn't know where to get the pop. Looking, he came to the saddlery shop. In the window was the most beautiful saddle he had ever seen, ornately tooled and polished till it shone. He stared at it, admiring with all his heart. Then he saw the bridle hanging from the saddle horn. It was a black and white horsehair bridle with long round-braided reins. He recognized the bridle. It was a bridle he had made, with a pattern he had thought up. It had a price tag. Five dollars. He gasped. Five dollars! He hadn't got anything for it because it was work assigned to do, schoolwork, and when it was sold to a trader the money went to pay for his keep.

He stared at the bridle and the price tag, and his eyes returned to the saddle. There was no price tag on the saddle. It cost too much to say, he decided. But if the bridle was worth five dollars, and if he could make bridles and sell them, then some day he could buy that saddle. He didn't have a pony for the saddle, but some day he could buy a pony too.

He was still there in front of the window, staring at the saddle, when two cowhands came out of the nearest saloon. They talked loud and laughed. They saw the boy and the tall, slim one jabbed a thumb into Thomas's ribs and demanded, "What's your name?"

Thomas stepped back and tried to hurry away, but the cowhand caught his arm. "I asked what's your name?"

"Thomas."

"All right, Tom. Want to earn a quarter?" He winked at his dark-haired companion.

Thomas didn't answer.

"Know how to ride a horse?" the cowhand asked. "Sure you do. All Indian kids do." He drew a quarter from his pocket. "Look, Tom. You go get my horse and ride it back here and I'll give you this quarter."

Tom stared at the quarter. He had never owned a quarter. This man was offering him a quarter just to ride a horse. He looked at the cowhand again, wide-eyed, and started to leave.

The cowhand caught his arm again. "Just a minute! Get the right horse or you don't get the quarter. The black gelding with a one-ear bridle and a red and white saddle blanket. He's hitched right down there in the cottonwoods."

Again Thomas started to leave, and again the cowhand caught his arm. "Ride him. Don't try to lead him. Understand? He don't lead very well." His companion laughed.

Free at last, Thomas hurried down the street. He found the horse, hitched by a neck rope. It was so skittish he had to drive it around the tree until the rope was wound tight. Then he snubbed the reins to the saddle horn, untied the rope, got his foot in the stirrup. The horse danced away, but he swung into the saddle as it began buck-jumping. With the reins snubbed it couldn't get its head down, but it buck-jumped in a circle among the trees before he knew he could ride it, knew he had its rhythm and his own balance. Then he gave it a little slack in the reins and it bucked viciously a time or two before he got it headed up the street. Still holding its head high with the snubbed reins, he rode it to the waiting cowhands. He got off and handed the reins to the one who had sent him on the errand.

The cowhand growled, "You snubbed the reins. You didn't let him buck."

His companion laughed. "He brought the horse, didn't he? He rode him. Pay up, Slim. And let's see *you* ride him."

Slim gave the quarter to Tom. A little knot of men had gathered and someone asked what was going on. The short dark-haired cowboy grinned. "Slim sent the kid to bring his horse. Now Slim's going to ride him. Unless he's afraid to."

Slim laughed. "I can ride anything with hair and four legs."

"Well, prove it, man. Get in the saddle and prove it."

Slim shortened the reins in his left hand, caught the saddle horn and reached for the near stirrup. The horse shied, tossed its head, got slack in the reins. Slim swung into the saddle, but before he hit the seat the horse ducked its head and began to buck. Slim couldn't find the other stirrup. He didn't have a chance. Three jumps and he was loose. The fourth jump sent him sprawling.

Someone caught the horse and brought it back. Slim got to his feet, cursing, dusted himself and picked up his hat. He limped back to the sidewalk. His companion, laughing, asked, "Want another try, or shall I put the boy on again?"

"Go to hell!"

Highway 550

Durango to Silverton

107. Durango
from *A Land Alone: Colorado's Western Slope*
by Duane Vandenbusche and Duane Smith

In the early days of many Colorado mining towns, newspapers promoted the resources around their communities, hoping to attract the business interests to bolster their fledgling economies. Southwestern Colorado, said the Durango Record, "was a land not only flowing with milk and honey, but seamed with silver and gold and floored with gold." So wrote Caroline Romney, the paper's publisher and editor, who had come to Durango from Leadville. It was unusual to find a woman running a newspaper back in the 1880's. According to Colorado historians Duane Smith and Duane Vandenbusche, co-authors of A Land Alone: Colorado's Western Slope, *"the combative personal journalism of her generation did not faze Caroline Romney; she proved more than a match for her male contemporaries." The following passage from their profile of Romney portrays a woman who worked hard to find and sustain a niche on the edge of Colorado's mining frontier.*

From Leadville she had come through winter snows, freighting her Gordon hand press by wagon, because no railroad train would reach Durango for another seven months. To the astonishment of her freighters she withstood the trip, established an office in a tent, and raced to publish the first daily paper, a race she won. Forty years old and a widow, the New York-born woman made her mark on Durango in the months ahead—gathering news, writing editorials, managing the paper, selling advertisements; nothing daunted her.

Caroline Romney was a hustler in the competitive newspaper world. She had to be in Durango, where two other weeklies and four dailies competed for readers in a town of only 3500. Issue after issue defended

Durango's interests and approved or reproached actions and people, all the while recording local events....She championed her town when it went through a lawless period in March and April, 1881, and took out after one of the offending parties, the locally based Stockton gang. Their threats did not intimidate her; some members of the gang planned to "tree" the editor, until they discovered "he" was a woman.

She exhibited her editorial vehemence in the cause of women's rights. "Prove your fitness for men's pursuits, by doing successfully what men did," she advised. On February 19, 1881, editor Romney wrote: " The best way for women to pursue, in business enterprises at least, is not to wait for men to accord them their rights, but to go ahead and take them. Such women have so much practical work to do, that, as a rule, they haven't much time to talk about women's rights. They do what is better—they act them."

108. Silverton
from "Across the Great Divide" by Stephen J. Meyers

Nestled as it is in a high mountain valley between mountain passes where winter storms and avalanches periodically seal off the only highway in and out of town, Silverton is not an easy place to live—never has been. If you want evidence of that, visit the Mining Heritage Museum in town where the challenges faced by early miners and other pioneers are well documented and on display. Silverton locals have a visceral understanding of the resilience it takes to live here year-round.

Stephen J. Meyers, who lives near Durango now (but previously lived in Silverton for many years) knows about that firsthand. For most of his life, he has been living in the Upper San Juan Watershed. He raised his family here, has written a half dozen books on the region, and has been fishing the waters of the Animas and San Juan rivers for decades. Still, he is not, nor will he ever be, a local, at least not by the standards held by lifelong residents like the proud citizen of Silverton he describes in the following essay.

It was called "Across the Great Divide," a big oral history project. You
know, oral history—eager young PhD anthropologenic-ethnographog-
rapher-historiologists sticking microphones in the faces of wrinkled
old folks, encouraging them to talk about the place the way it was back
when. The honored wrinkled, scared to death, begin slowly. *Should I talk
now? Is this thing on? Now? I remember the first car that drove into town
over Stony; well, they drove it once it got here, but they hauled it over
the pass with horses! How am I doing?* You're doing fine. But this was
not to be a one-on-one. A public event was planned. A panel of locals
picked, an evening circled and the honored wrinkled named: a butcher, a
market owner, a retired miner with rocks in the box, a boarding house
owner, and a housewife. They had between them some four-hundred long
winters and fleeting summers in the mining town that wouldn't quit. (It
finally did quit two decades later, but that's another story.) Fancy pants
posters were posted, announcements announced, and everyone who was
anyone planned to attend.

The library board, proud sponsor of the event, were patting themselves so hard half of them developed badly bruised backs. Then the
trouble started. In the best prose he could muster (and it was damn good
prose if you ask me—angry recluses in those days wrote more like Tom
Jefferson than Ted Kuczynski), the miner intoned, he accused, he stated
with indignity *The housewife is not real! No! She is an imposter!* Yes,
she'd lived on Reese Street for over sixty years. Yep, she went to the
brick school and the wooden schoolhouse before it, raised two San Juan
girls, daughters that had been well fathered by the man whose father's
father sat on a hillside nearly a hundred years before and said to his partner, "Let's look for gold over on the sunny side." But, no, she's not a local.
She is an immigrant, an interloper, an indecent pretender who'd come
from somewhere else. A foreigner, and she's conveniently neglected to
tell the august library board that she came over the pass from Stony, just
like that car, hauled by horses when she was six! Technically, if you want
to get picky, she isn't even a Western Sloper; being born as she was in
the headwaters of the Rio Grande on the other side of The Divide over in
Creede! *I respectfully submit,* the miner wrote, *that she be immediately
removed from this worthy panel of true locals.*

Reading the letter, and knowing my own Yankee roots, I began to feel very much like a brookie in cutthroat country. The foreigner from Creede, the sweet soft-spoken mother, quietly arranged to be out of town that night. The librarian read the letter she'd sent the board declining to attend. It was written with an elegant hand and even more elegant prose, describing her childhood of wood smoke and snow, gray-brown muddy springs, green golden summers with blue iris popping up in the yard, autumns of flaming aspen, red-meated trout taken from the Highland Marys, and waiting every night for her husband to come home from the Sunnyside, praying he would not be buried beneath a slab, fall into a bottomless ore pass, die in a blast, or succumb to bad air in the old workings. And yes, she admitted, with great remorse and knowing well the accepted rules, that she was not a local. So when you ask me, "Steve, are you local?" I'm afraid I have to say after only forty-eight years in the San Juans, a short stint in the mines, a wife dying in the shadow of Kendall Mountain, a son born and raised under the protection of a Grand Turk and a Sultan, I'm not a local. But I'm beginning to learn the rules, and I am rather fond of the place.

Highway 160

Durango to Towaoc

109. Hesperus
from *Education of a Wandering Man* by Louis L'Amour

Louis L'Amour wrote Westerns mostly—stories and novels that evoked a mythic West full of good guys, outlaws, and a frontier sensibility valuing self-reliance and perseverance. He was a stickler for accuracy, especially in describing specific places he knew from his extensive travels. As a young man and an itinerant laborer, he was introduced to this area when he came to help a friend develop a mining claim near Durango. After establishing himself as a writer many years later, he returned periodically, usually in the month of August, to hunker down in Room 222 at the Strater Hotel in Durango, where he soaked up the Old West ambience of the place, worked on his books during the morning hours, and spent his afternoons exploring the Four Corners region. That room has since been designated a National Literary Landmark, honoring his prolific literary career. (At the time of his death in 1988, almost all of his books—eighty-nine novels, fourteen short-story collections, and two full-length works of nonfiction—were still in print.)

L'Amour sold many millions of books. Quite a few of his titles were made into television shows and movies. His great success enabled him to buy an 1800-acre ranch west of Hesperus. Here the East Fork of Cherry Creek flows down from the La Platas, through a narrow valley where the ranch house and other assorted buildings are shaded by ponderosa pines, and out into the hay meadows below a prominent sandstone landmark known as Maggie Rock. Sedimentary rock layers predominate as mountains rolling off to the west give way to the canyon country geography of Mesa Verde National Park, just to the south of which is Ute Mountain Tribal Park. In his memoir, The Education of a Wandering Man, *L'Amour describes a trip to the Ute Mountain Tribal Park, where a memorable night camping amidst the dwellings and*

ceremonial chambers which the ancestral Pueblo people abandoned
in the thirteenth century piqued his imagination and perhaps informed
parts of The Haunted Mesa *(1987), his last published book.*

Accompanied by three archaeologists and a Ute Indian, my family and
I spent a night in a cliff dwelling on the Ute Reservation. The archaeologists arranged the affair and we drove out in four-wheel-drive vehicles
to arrive just before sundown. The cliff dwelling was in a deep canyon
filled with trees, some of which had been lighting-struck. It was in a remote area and we climbed down into the canyon to find our places. There
had been no cleanup there. The place was as time left it: a few scattered
human bones, some tiny corncobs, a few shards of broken pottery.

Kathy and I chose a *kiva* (ceremonial center) in which to spread our
sleeping bags, and shortly after we arrived, there was a thunderstorm.

Nature seemed to have deliberately planned our entertainment, for
there was rolling thunder, unusually loud because of the narrow canyon,
and many flashes of brilliant lightening, but only a few scattered drops of
rain fell. Nature put on a grand show for upward of an hour. Then the sky
cleared, the moon came out, and we had a truly magnificent night.

Art Cuthair, the Ute who was with us, may well have been the first
Indian to spend a night in a cliff dwelling since the Anasazi abandoned
them. Many Indians are uncomfortable at disturbing the spirits of the
former inhabitants. (Art has been involved in stabilizing some ruins and
in laying out trails for the guided tours the Utes give for visitors wishing
to see the dwellings as they were found.)

We settled in for the night, each in his or her own way. I was determined to remain awake and enjoy every moment of the experience to the
utmost.

Often we heard eerie sounds, whisperings and movements. The
wind? The leaves? Small animals or birds? Or something else?
Something from the past, perhaps, something from the forgotten years?

The moon was bright, and soon coyotes were singing their plaintive
songs. Other Indians had stopped by to see us but would not stay the
night. They went to sleep out of the canyon, away from the cliff houses.

Some of us slept; some remained awake with me. None of us talked.

It was a time for listening. Once, faint and far-off, there seemed to be the sound of a flute or some wind instrument.

It is sometimes said that few archaeologists have ever spent a night in a cliff dwelling, and that no archaeologist has spent two nights. However, I regretted the coming of day, although ready enough for breakfast.

110. Mancos Hill
from "The Hush" by Grace Katherine Anderson

US Highway 160 follows part of the historic Ute Trail from the Animas River to the Mancos River, skirting the southwestern base of the La Plata Mountains. Many dirt roads and pathways also follow Ute trails into the mountains to ancestral hunting grounds. Grace Ott Anderson, who grew up on the southern edge of the La Platas, has written about her home mountain range for various newspapers and magazines. Here, she recalls a family outing on a snowy November morning, the first day of hunting season.

We would gather in the basement, eyes downward, shouldering jackets, red vests, canvas packs, then our rifles, feeling through the darkness. The darkness was living, and we moved through it like water, cultivating silence within the darkness, building the silence by listening, waiting, expecting the next pulse, the next inhale, the next wave of twilight. We moved as parts of a whole, filing out of the basement, down the gravel driveway, into the carryall, loading into the vehicle, wincing to muffle the clank of metal buckles on metal interior, heavy wooden stocks on rubber gun racks, thick boots, and bulky jackets, taking our seats, breathing. Doors closed by pulling, not slamming, a quick, yank, then the neat click of striker on plate. We'd muffle the sound of the engine turning over with our collective silence, willing the headlights to show only the road and not to be noticed by anyone or any creature, save the rocks and ruts that snaked beyond Caviness Mountain to Eberling's Camp where we'd park.

We'd file out of the truck, shoulder our packs and begin dropping into East Mancos Canyon. Holding our rifles on the downslope side, we'd fan,

stalking slowly along game trails, over blow-down timber, through thick
brush, the hazard of new snow on fallen aspen leaves, always the prospect
of slipping, falling, sliding down to the river. We'd reach for the invisible,
intangible cord that might lead us to the elk herd, or maybe to a couple of
bulls, all that we'd need to fill the freezer for the advancing winter. Soggy
twigs would break underfoot and we'd use the weight of the silence and the
pre-dawn darkness to smother the snaps and pops. We'd contour around
the precipitous ridges of the Twin Canyons then we'd gather on the edge of
the spruce-fir forest and gaze toward steep, grassy Townsend Basin. Hearts
pounding, breath pluming, our minds a single will, within the silence
within the darkness. We'd wait while the starlight guttered, blackness
brightening into blue-black revealing pewter blue clouds, leaden with snow.
We'd huddle, some standing, some leaning, some seated on downed timber.
When one of us would speak, it'd sound below a whisper and we'd lean in,
holding our breath. We'd lower our hooded heads and half-close our eyes
half knowing what the speaker would say.

In the breath of a breeze swirling toward us, our dad stands, cradling
his rifle, muzzle pointing downward, leading the rest of the way toward
the benches, along the ridges, round the alpine forested wall that spills
us into the Basin. Will the herd, or just a couple of bulls, step into the
snowy globe of rock and slope and sky?

The silence is dark, heavy, yet lithe, and we move evenly together.
Now the silence thickens. Light simmers over the peaks and spills into
the Basin. The silence contracts and tightens like a taut bow, the moment
before release.

111. Mancos / Mesa Verde
from *The Professor's House* by Willa Cather

On December 1888, Richard Wetherill and his brother-in-law Charlie
Mason were riding along the Mancos River searching for missing cattle,
when they took a turn to the west and rode a gently sloping canyon
up toward the rim of Mesa Verde. Thick stands of piñons and junipers
made their search difficult, but as they topped out on the mesa, they

rode into a clearing which afforded them a view across the canyon.
What they saw there, Mason would say later on, was "the grandest
view of all among the ancient ruins of the Southwest." We know that
ruin today as Cliff Palace, one of the most impressive structures left
behind by the ancestral Puebloan people.

Their "discovery" got the attention of novelist Willa Cather who
visited Mesa Verde in 1915. "One must always think with envy of the
entrada of Richard Wetherill the first white man who discovered the
ruins," she wrote. Wetherill and Mason may not have been the very
first non-native people to find these ruins—at least there are those
who have disputed that claim—but they were surely among the earliest,
and their story was especially compelling to Cather. In 1909, she had
written a story called "The Enchanted Bluff" about some Nebraska
boys getting ready to explore a nearby mesa once inhabited by Indians.
The Wetherill-Mason account offered her a historical framework for
taking that theme even further, which she eventually did in her novel,
The Professor's House.

Like Wetherill and Mason, Tom Outland, the protagonist of her
novel, rides out to the rim of a canyon on a snowy winter day and
witnesses a largely forgotten world. While Cather's version of the story
changes various details for dramatic effect, her description of this
remarkable place, as well as her take on a humble cowboy's reaction to
it, still ring true.

When I had gone up this canyon for a mile or so, I came upon another,
opening out to the north—a box canyon, very different in character. No
gentle slope there. The walls were perpendicular, where they weren't
actually overhanging, and they were anywhere from eight hundred to a
thousand feet high, as we afterward found by measurement. The floor of
it was a mass of huge boulders, great pieces of rock that had fallen from
above ages back, and had been worn round and smooth as pebbles by the
long action of water. Many of them were as big as haystacks, yet they lay
piled on one another like a load of gravel. There was no footing for my
horse among those smooth stones, so I hobbled him and went on alone

a little way, just to see what it was like. My eyes were steadily on the ground—a slip of the foot there might cripple one.

It was such rough scrambling that I was soon in a warm sweat under my damp clothes. In stopping to take a breath, I happened to glance up at the canyon wall. I wish I could tell you what I saw there, just *as* I saw it, on that first morning, through a veil of lightly falling snow. Far up above me, a thousand feet or so, set in a great cavern in the face of the cliff, I saw a little city of stone, asleep. It was still as sculpture – and something like that. It all hung together, seemed to have a kind of composition: pale little houses of stone nestling close to one another, perched on top of each other, with flat roofs, narrow windows, straight walls, and in the middle of the group, a round tower.

It was beautifully proportioned, that tower, swelling out to a larger girth a little above the base, then growing slender again. There was something symmetrical and powerful about the swell of the masonry. The tower was the fine thing that held all the jumble of houses together and made them mean something. It was red in colour, even on that grey day. In sunlight it was the colour of winter oak-leaves. A fringe of cedars grew along the edge of the cavern, like a garden. They were the only living things. Such silence and stillness and repose—immortal repose. That village sat looking down into the canyon with the emptiness of eternity.

The falling snow-flakes, sprinkling the pinons, gave it a special kind of solemnity. I can't describe it. It was more like sculpture than anything else. I knew at once that I had come upon the city of some extinct civilization, hidden away in this inaccessible mesa for centuries, preserved in the dry air and almost perpetual sunlight like a fly in amber, guarded by the cliffs and the river and the desert.

As I stood looking up at it, I wondered whether I ought ... not to go back across the river and keep that secret as the mesa had kept it. When I at last turned away, I saw still another canyon branching out of this one, and in its wall still another group of buildings. The notion struck me like a rifle ball that this mesa had once been like a bee-hive; it was full of little cliff-hung villages, it had been the home of a powerful tribe, a particular civilization.

112. Cortez
from *The Sorrow of Archaeology* by Russell Martin

You can't go home again. This old sentiment, also the title of a Thomas Wolfe novel, reminds us that nothing stays the same. We can never return to a place as we remember it in the distant past. Sometimes the physical place has changed; it no longer resembles home as we once knew it. Sometimes the change is more subjective; we have changed over time and no longer relate to family, neighbors, and place in quite the same way.

In Russell Martin's novel, The Sorrow of Archaeology, *Sarah Macleish returns to her childhood home in Montezuma County, the southwestern corner of Colorado, after having gone off to medical school and established a practice in Boulder. Certain qualities of her homeland, though almost timeless in some respects, strike her as fresh and new: "When we rounded the curve on Mancos Hill on a warm and welcoming evening in early May—snow still capping the peaks of the La Platas and cottonwoods leafing beside the little river a mile off to the west—I was shocked to discover that I was excited somehow. The profoundly familiar valley tilted up in the northern and western distances and the Abajos and San Juans seemed to float far beyond; Ute Mountain heaved up out of the earth as it always had, and the mesa still sealed off the south, but something discernible had changed. Something in the rich aroma of springtime—or perhaps in the soft light that languished till dusk—was arresting and appealing and unlike everything that I was sure I knew and understood about the place."*

As her story unfolds, Macleish reflects on how her home as changed. She also realizes that moving back home, despite all the changes, wasn't as much of a challenge as she had anticipated. "It seems to me now," she says, "that when people say you can't go home again, what they're correct about is only that you can't reconstruct a time." As she points out in the following passage, Montezuma County isn't the place she left behind, though not everything has changed. Having come home after establishing herself elsewhere, Macleish engages a once familiar place with a fresh perspective.

Cortez late in the 1980s turned out to be a surprisingly different place from what it had been in the middle 1960s. The suspicious and paralyzing fear of a world in which change was becoming the only constant seemed almost to have vanished by the time I returned. Satellite dishes now appeared to be planted atop every farmhouse, and working-class men looked like the hippies who had seemed so terribly subversive two decades before. Although attitudes toward Utes and Navajos still seemed mired in stereotype too often, I actually sensed a nascent appreciation for the fact that this was a place in which faces were several hues.

Three decades after the oil boom of the early 1950s, parts of Montezuma County still looked as though a Korean War battle or two had been fought on American soil, and any sort of land-use planning was still plainly and simply a Communist plot; the mannequins in the windows of The Toggery still looked like they belonged to an era epitomized by Desi's exasperation with Lucy, and poverty still seemed to leave too many lives forlorn.

Unlike my patients in Boulder, who often wanted an hour-long explanation of even the simplest disease's pathology, and who too often wanted to debate whether the drug I'd just prescribed was the next worst thing to thalidomide, patients in Cortez tended not to question my diagnoses or plans for therapy. "Well, you're the doctor," they'd say, as if the MD were proof that I could work any number of miracles, and I soon learned that a patient sent away without some sort of prescription was a patient who'd be certain I'd stolen his money. Yet I liked most of the people in my hometown who came to me for care. I liked the wry old geezer farmers who swore they'd never been sick a day in their lives, unless you counted that time when a combine took two of their fingers; I liked the prim and matronly ladies, some petite and fragile, others substantial and portly, who would wear their best dresses just to sit in our waiting room, and who seemed nothing short of astonished that a sweet girl like me had managed the mysteries of medical school; I liked the teenagers who proudly announced that they were getting out of this shit-town, and that before they stopped anywhere along the way, they were going to see the ocean.

Most of all, I think, I was attracted to the young mothers, a few of whom had high-schoolers of their own already, women who knew

before their fortieth birthdays that life wasn't going to keep the promises
they once were sure it had made. Too often they were women for whom
child-rearing had seemed all-consuming at one time, everything they
could ask for, but who now sensed—some of them still with toddlers in
tow—that their kids would force their way free in seemingly no time at all,
leaving them with half a lifetime yet to live and little enthusiasm for what
those years would hold. They were women with husbands who would get
drunk and want to make love with them on Saturday nights, but who would
spend the rest of the week in a strange and private isolation that refused to
be broken down, the wives wishing in the end that someday the men just
wouldn't come home.

As I treated these contemporaries of mine for migraines or irritable
bowel syndrome, for insomnia or duodenal ulcers or any one of a dozen
other disorders whose primary cause likely was chronic stress, I sometimes
wanted to say, *Hey, go away: Go home and pack a bag and leave a note on
the kitchen table saying you don't know if you'll ever be back.* I wanted to
tell them to start new lives surrounded by different scenery, but somehow I
never did, in part because I knew I'd be afraid to start again myself.

113. Dolores
from "The Trailers of Montezuma County" by David Feela

*Montezuma County, which includes the towns of Mancos, Cortez,
Towaoc, and Dolores covers 2000 square miles in the southwestern
corner of Colorado, encompassing an area rich with archaeological
sites. The area's native heritage, which is highly visible in Mesa Verde
National Park, Canyon of the Ancients National Monument, the Ute
Mountain Tribal Park, and the Anasazi Heritage Center, draws visitors
from all over the world. But as Dolores resident David Feela suggests
in his book* How Delicate These Arches, *many of these visitors move
from one well-known archaeological landmark to the next without taking in the nuances of contemporary local culture. In "The Trailers of
Montezuma County," one of the essays included in the book, he offers a
light-hearted appreciation of a modern-day sheltering strategy.*

It's like a soap-opera romance, this ongoing affection of mine for the old style single or double-wide mobile homes, more commonly known as trailers.

To me their appeal is strongest when I'm driving a gravel county road, and out in a field I see one, perched like an alien spacecraft on a few open acres. Or, I'm turning into the shaded niches of a well-worn trailer park, and it's there, like a time machine, made of corrugated tin and glass. Sometimes it's been repainted, and never the bland manufacturer's color from 30 years ago, but a fresh swath of purple, or yellow, or even turquoise or pink.

I should know: I've been parked since 1986 in a 1972 double-wide. I don't know if it was new when it arrived on the property. It has no wheels, but when I have to climb into the crawl space beneath the mobile home, I can see where wheels would have been mounted. There's not much security down there, knowing that tornados have a sweet tooth for mobile homes. They twist trailers and then spit them out again, but it's still a strange thought: A home could roll in like a tumbleweed and then roll back out again.

My unit is also old enough to probably be illegal, manufactured during the era of pressed board flooring and thin galvanized metal roofing. I've done the mobile home roofover (similar to a middle-aged male combover) and I flush my toilet with caution, realizing that a flood could turn my flooring into waffle wood. Luckily, I live in a generous county that essentially believes, if you can drag it here, we can put up with it, which is why the hardier of these trailers should be preserved, designated as historic local treasures, of no lesser magnitude than those infamous bridges from that county in the Midwest.

The mobile home's survival offers us a reminder of a time when a family's housing ambitions were scaled back to, say, reality. No median sales price hovering around $200,000. No floor space with enough square footage to hold a line dance for a football team. Mobile homes are proof that people could actually live with less, and I did. I do now, and its constraint makes certain I continue to do so.

Many others are still living that way, which is why I always slow down to admire these domestic time capsules. The vintage trailer is a covered bridge of sorts, spanning two banks: One side rooted with working people who could at one time own their own homes, and on the

other side the current real estate market, where a lifetime of slowly di-
minishing mortgage debt is the glimmer at the end of the tunnel. I know
some people consider yesterday's trailers trash when compared to today's
modular, custom, set-on-a-slab, instant triple-wide castles. It is fair to say
that a trailer does not have the investment potential of a ranchette with
a massively imposing entrance gate. Maybe so, but I'd rather spend my
days renovating the past than making payments on someone else's future.

I'll admit that much of a trailer's styling, especially during the '60s
and '70s, was a little too boxy, but it's tough to argue with a classic
advertising slogan, home is where you park it. For me, the idea of being
self-contained has never lost its appeal.

Housing needs are basic for all people, but available housing has
taken a nasty turn away from anything approaching basic. In a nearby
town, for example, 15 homeowners in the Riverview Trailer Park were
evicted to make way for a 39-unit condominium development, some units
starting at a lofty $250,000. Such practices happen all across the West
each time an economic boom in real estate sends trailer homeowners
scurrying for cover. For our own protection as locals, before the next
real estate bubble pops, we'd better all be wearing condos, the only safe
housing available.

Where's a romantically inclined professional photographer when you
need one? Maybe a lanky Clint Eastwood type, someone with an eye
to show us the implicit beauty in an antiquated hallway without wheels.
And even if the trailers look a little shabby by current standards, they
embody a fiscal fantasy we're in danger of forgetting. They stand for
autonomy, at least as long as they're allowed to stand.

114. Dove Creek
from *Unforgettable Characters of Western Colorado*
by Al Look

In his book Unforgettable Characters of Western Colorado, *author
Al Look refers to Daniel Brown Hunter as "the sage of the sagebrush." Like a lot of small-town newspaper editors in the early days
of Colorado—he homesteaded near Dove Creek in 1918—he was a
one-man chamber of commerce. As Look put it, "Editor Hunter never
quit boosting the 'worthless expanse of inedible sage' after he and
Mrs. Hunter homesteaded broke and unknown in the Duck's Nest area
west of crossroads Dove Creek. When he died nearly forty years later,
Hunter was called Mr. Dove Creek. He was a member of a score of
civic, state, and national organizations. From his one-man wordmill he
could look out upon schools, paved highways, churches, electric power
lines and bean elevators, which he had helped create with his magic
vocabulary." Hunter was a prolific and entertaining wordslinger who
never "used one word when ten words would do."*

Dan Hunter showed me his garden with rows fifty feet long. He had
planted everything in the seed catalogue "to see if it would do good out
here." In the virgin soil corn was long, pumpkins huge and cabbages as
big as buckets. Hunter picked up the stem of a skinny plant and looked at
it. "This is supposed to be dill, but it doesn't seem to be putting on any
pickles." It was many weeks later that we both learned that dill does not
grow pickles. Twenty years later, this is how he described his garden:

Golden pumpkins smiling in the sunshine, eggplants tinted by the
Iris-hued colors of an evening's rainbow, melons sparkling with
honeydews from heaven, potatoes whose eyes wet with the onion-
tears that were shed as they witnessed the roasting-ear shoots pierce
the heart of the blood red beet, carrots rooting the earth as they
undermined squash vines whose withering leaf brushed aside the
volunteer okra stalk struggling to bloom from the nectar deposited
by a golden-winged honey bee as it winged its flight to steal a chalice

from the nectar'd pinto beans, cabbage whose heads were covered with silken threads from growing corn, rosy cheeked tomatoes bearded with waving whiskered wheat gayly smiled upon the lovely melon blushing beneath its shaded vine; all reminded us that this Dove Creek country is a frontiersman's paradise and Edenic garden where every household may live and prosper beneath his own vine and fig tree.

115. Towaoc
from "Whispers from the Past"
by Regina Lopez-Whiteskunk

Various bands of Ute peoples have been present in the Four Corners region for a very long time. One of those bands, the Weenuche ("long time ago people"), were also referred to as the Weminuche. They were hunting and gathering people, who followed deer and elk into the mountains during the warmer months and into the lower river valleys during the winter. In their travels through the region, they gathered a wide assortment of roots, berries, and other useful herbs and plants.

In 1868, as white settlers began to filter into the region, The Utes agreed to a treaty limiting their territory to the western third of Colorado. In 1873, because of encroaching prospectors and miners, the US government reneged on that treaty and the Utes were limited to lands south of the San Juan Mountains. Remnants of those lands are located near Ignacio (the Southern Ute Reservation) and Towaoc (the Ute Mountain Ute reservation). Remnants of the original reservation are located near Ignacio (home of the Southern Ute Reservation) and Towaoc (home of the Ute Mountain Ute Reservation).

Regina Lopez-Whiteskunk, mother, grandmother and member of the Weminuche Band of the Ute Mountain Ute Tribe, was born in Towaoc and raised in the Four Corners Region. She has been advocating for land, air, water and animals since she was young, and has traveled extensively through the country sharing the Ute culture through song, dance, words, and lectures. She was also co-chair of an intertribal coalition supporting the establishment of Bears Ears National Monument.

In an essay that appears in Jonathan Bailey's book, Rock Art: A Vision of a Vanishing Landscape, *she writes about the bond she feels with her ancestral homelands.*

In the beginning, the movement of our people was, and still is, sovereign. Our existence as Native American people is tied to the land. We feel the earth beneath our feet, we utilize the water and land in many different ways; it nurtures our spirits, our souls, our lives, our existence.

Our lives are prayer, beginning with our birth. When our grandparents welcomed us into this world, our lives, our walk—our prayer—started. We are who we are because of our ancestors—because of *their* prayers, because of what the land provided for them then and for us today and what it will provide tomorrow. The hills, the rocks, the twisting of the rivers, the breeze from the gentle winds know no boundaries. State, county, and reservation lines mean nothing to the landscape, which tells stories of the people and days gone by. Our movement and the landscape are bound together. Prayers are walked, lived, and answered. Our elders have told us where to collect the herbs and of places we can go to draw strength, where we can go to feel the earth beneath our feet. Mother Earth knows our footsteps, for I have danced, run, and walked, treading my path ever so respectfully.

I hike into the canyons to see the rocks and the stories from long ago. I stop and feel saddened when I see bullet holes, words scratched in places that show disrespect for the story, the story that tells me of the trails and water ways of the surrounding landscapes. I go into these spaces to listen to the trees sing to me and ease my restlessness, to seek a sense of healing from within.

The earth is my connection to the knowledge of the land and the stories that are whispered in the gentle winds. I have prepared for ceremony in prayer, I have taken off my shoes, I have walked barefoot, connecting with our Mother Earth, seeking knowledge, strength, and grace. She feels and knows my steps, for I have tread on her before, in prayer. I kneel down beneath a large cedar tree, allowing for the hundred years of wisdom to be communicated in a way no one will ever understand.

I visit sacred places and spaces to celebrate the symbols carved on the canyon walls. I celebrate by announcing my presence with prayers, dances, and songs. "Hear my voice and acknowledge my actions and movement," I ask. As I move softly, I acknowledge the ancient movements of the ancestors who once roamed the landscape and left their stories etched into the walls and upon the land. The stories on the canyon walls are a gift shared with people, no matter the language we each speak. In protecting the landscape, especially the rock art, there are many conversations to be had. The threats are numerous, but hope remains in our hearts of understanding from all colors and places.

Our parents and elders always taught us that, when out on the land, be mindful of those who once came through before us. In another time, the area was their home, pharmacy, and hunting site. They taught us that, in their time and space, the old ones return—be respectful. We are the caretakers, we leave what is out there, and we keep the space sacred. It is our responsibility to keep the footsteps and movement of the past sacred, for that was our beginning. Oh grandpa, my heart sings a song as I honor the ancestors resting in peace out on this land. We honor and celebrate the care, reverence, respect, and the opportunity to be a voice for the sacred time, space, and places out on the land. The canyon walls are our guide and recorded knowledge. I pray it will remain for seven generations and beyond. Hear my words, join my song, dance my dance, and celebrate the prayers of our elders.

116. Towaoc / Ute Mountain
from *West of the Divide* by Jim Carrier

Known traditionally as Wisuv Karuv ("mountain with yucca"), the mountain west of Towaoc, commonly referred to as Ute Mountain, is a prominent landmark in the Four Corners regions. It is also a significant cultural space for the inhabitants of the Ute Mountain Ute Reservation. Every spring, Ute Mountain people gather on the mountain west of Towaoc for the Bear Dance, the oldest Ute dance, and one that originated with the tribe, which celebrates the coming of the season. During the summer, families and friends also gather here to support participants in the Sun Dance, a strenuous and spiritually demanding ceremony practiced in native communities throughout the US and Canada. In a book called West of the Divide: Voices from a Ranch and a Reservation, *journalist Jim Carrier, who traveled the West as a correspondent for the* Denver Post, *offers the following portrait of Sun Dance chief Terry Knight, his family, and this important annual event on the mountain.*

The lightning arced across Ute Mountain and caught the dancers in the dark. It froze them as a strobe would, in painted moments of ancient ones. Then it rained. In the glow of a campfire their bodies glistened yellow and red. But they kept moving in their sun dance quest, no doubt aware of a great power.

"We always get rain," said Terry Knight, the sun dance chief. "It's a sign, a blessing." For more than 100 years the Ute Mountain Utes have held their dance, seeking such signs from their god. They fast, they dance, they meditate in a search for power, for themselves and their people. "You dance to show the Creator you are alive and well and making tracks," Terry said. "Good tracks on mother earth."

The Sun Dance is held each July in a high mountain meadow dotted with evergreens. The mountain is both sentinel and namesake for the reservation and its people. The Ute word for the peak means "mountain with yucca." White men call it the Sleeping Ute. It is the last spur of the Rockies in Colorado's southwestern corner. The reservation that surrounds it is the last vestige of what once was the Ute mountain kingdom.

The Sun Dance is held near the Ute's big heart, facing east to catch the sunrise. "East is the direction of life," said Terry. "We believe we came from the sun." He stood at the back of a high, round corral made of logs and cottonwood branches, open to the east. On either side of him were fifteen men, young dancers in the midst of a fast. They were bare-chested except for ochre painted on. They wore long skirts of beautiful colors. They held eagle plumes in their hands.

Before them, in the center of the corral, stood the sun dance pole, a cut cottonwood shaped like a huge upright slingshot with willows laid across the crotch. The pole, said Terry, represented the entity, the channel to the Creator.

Night and day, for four days, the dancers charged the pole and
retreated, back and forth in a personal gait. There were shuffles, hops, a
prancing kick. While they blew whistles made from eagle bones, their
bare feet marked a twenty-five-foot path in the dirt. "Making tracks with
your feet, making tracks with thoughts and sacrificial manner," said
Terry. "You're presenting yourself to the Creator by dancing to and from
the sacred tree."

It was mesmerizing to watch. The word primitive came to mind. But
that carried an erroneous sense of backwardness. This was no folk dance
or costumed recreation of an old art form, a pictograph sprung to life.
The dance was beautiful and complex, transcendent of one-dimensional
stereotypes, so often made of Native Americans: the warrior war-whoop-
ing, a weaver on her knees, a chief in his bonnet saying "How." The Sun
Dance is living history, a living faith, one tied to the very identity of
those dancing and watching. To dance is to *be* Indian....

Terry and his family have deep roots and abiding love for the Ute
Mountain Ute Reservation. They are, as Terry put it, "typical in the old
way." They have seen a bit of the world but choose reservation life.

Their patriarch is Charles Knight, eighty, a livestock producer and
an elder in every sense of the word. His hard work—and spirituality—
passed to his children. His ex-wife, Kate, who is also eighty, brought
discipline to the household. Her children still call here "the General."
She's the one who insisted they go to school every day....

The Knights live where they always have, on a dry 595,000-acre reserve.
It is Four-Corners country, flat and forever, broken only by mesas on the east
and dry washes. The Mancos Riverbed cuts through but rarely runs with
water. Except for 325 people who live in White Mesa, Utah, northwest of Ute
Mountain, nearly all of the 1,675 tribal members live in Towaoc. , , ,

The family was there to support Terry, but the ceremony was as much
for them—families, tribal members, the congregation—as it was for the
dancers. "It's like when I go to church. I get the same feeling," said Judy,
who brought fresh willow sprigs from a nearby spring to hand to the
dancers during a break. The dancers, who ate or drank nothing, touched
the cool greens to their bodies. Then Judy joined her sisters near the
drum to wave willow branches and sing.

While Terry danced, brother Carl drummed and piled wood for the fire. Carl helped build the dance corral, and like all the Knights speaks easily of spiritual matters. They were raised outdoors, hauled in wagons and made part of ceremonies like the Sun Dance from an early age. "I never let go of things I grew up with," said Carl. "When I drive along and see a flower, I ask where did it come from? Who put it there? There's a long story to that."

As the sun dance day turned to night, and day again, the crowd at the corral grew. They lined up around the circle and crowded the opening to the east. Judy carried more willows. Her son was dancing, too. Charles walked slowly to the pole and spoke to the dancers in Ute, urging them on.

From his side of the pole Terry stood with an eagle wing and prayed for people who came forward. A man in a wheelchair, a child. His own mother, Kate, a small frail woman suffering from a gall bladder ailment. Terry dusted her with dirt and fanned the wing over her. "I admitted doses of good blessings," he said later. "From grandfather the Creator, the four directions, and dust from mother earth, the substance we are created of."

The Sun Dance ended with a special ceremony in which the exhausted, dehydrated dancers drank a clay-and-water mixture. Outside the arbor, gifts of cash and linens were given to visitors by the sun dancers' families. Then they held a feast.

Books have been written about the Indian Sun Dance, the tenor being that it brings power to the disenfranchised and redemption to the troubled. I asked Terry about the benefits.

"Weight loss," he said with a quick grin. Then he answered: "Spiritual rejuvenation, self-satisfaction. A general overall good feeling. As soon as it's over, you're looking forward to next year."

WESTERN SLOPE CENTRAL: COLORADO AND GUNNISON RIVERS

Highway 145 / 90

Lizard Head Pass to Paradox

117. Ophir
from *Fool's Gold* by Rob Schultheis

Author and journalist Rob Schultheis, who covered wars in Iraq and Afghanistan, has also written several books about Colorado and the West. He knows about mountain living, having spent most of his life in the Telluride area. Mountain town dwellers in the San Juan Mountains and elsewhere in the high country of Colorado live close to the weather, all kinds of weather, which requires planning, preparation, and the right equipment and gear. Still, in an unpredictable environment where the mountains generate their own weather, the elements bat last. But that is all part of living life outdoors as much as possible, which is why many high-country residents choose to live here, as Schultheis suggests in this excerpt from his book Fool's Gold.

By nine-thirty it's time to hit the high country. If anything, the skies are darker, more menacing, the clouds denser. But if we don't go now, we're not going at all. Driving south across Turkey Creek Mesa we get a fine view of impending storm. The Wilsons have wrapped themselves in a dark gray blanket of Garbo-like disdain. Shrouds of evanescent mist, what the Navajos call Female Rain, hang in the skies off toward Utah. More gloomious masses of black wrath jostle for position off toward the east and southeast, grumbling and muttering.

And it's beautiful. The forests have never looked so green, the meadows so dense, the wildflowers so brilliant with waterlogged colors.

It's a darkness that shines, for those of us crazy enough to be out in it. We happy few, we may get struck by lightning, or catch pneumonia, but it's worth it.

We settle for a ramble up above Ophir, up Waterfall Canyon. We park the car by Paul Machado's house and clamber down the slope to the stream. Cross over a slippery log and start up the narrow track through the steep forest. The woods are going crazy this year with mushrooms, lichens, cloud ears and mosses, threads and bulbs, chessmen, miniature terrestrial coral gardens, lewd tuberosities that look like items from a Pleasure Chest catalog, scalloped whoziwhatsies like the clouds in a Tibetan thangka, as the great silvery Internet of mycelium that underlays the forest floor fires off everything in its arsenal.

We pick about a pound and a half of boletes on our way up, to accompany a couple of steaks we have stashed away at home. This summer we've been eating wild mushrooms breakfast, lunch, and dinner, mostly chanterelles but sometimes boletes.

Whoah! There, growing out of a midden of gray gravel, is a big old *Amanita muscaria*, like an upside-down, red, 100-watt lightbulb freckled with white, perfect for that pagan Christmas tree. Eat it and you'll have visions, and maybe die in agony in the process. Better find yourself some sheep droppings or cowpies with Rocky Mountain varieties of *Psilocybe cubensis* sprouting from their tops. One of the local witch doctors filled her hat with them over by Norwood last week and handed them out in the saloons.

The forest smells a hundred thousand years old, timeless. Ah, the treasures of the Ice Age Aftermath we were lucky enough to be born into! Not to mention our luck at living in such a rare mountain niche, a cleft of snowmelt and beaver-created oasis in these desert ranges.

A whizzbang of lightning up toward Lizard Head, a sharp crack of thunder ... paradise, indeed. Stiff Patterson has red columbines growing out of his front walk right in downtown Telluride, through the cracks in the concrete. Up Eider Creek, you can smell the licorice, pine-tar funk of elk where their migration routes cross the trail.

Last week we just managed to reach the summit of Ajax Peak and start down before a lightning storm bombarded the high screefields.

Today we're down low enough to avoid lightning, but the weather still nails us. First the forest begins to roar all around us. Then the rain hits, in a solid mass. We're wearing "waterproof" clothing, Gore-Tex in Nancy's case, some oilskin-nylon blend in mine, but we may as well be buck naked. Within five minutes we're soaked. And cold: each drop of this mountain rain contains a grain of ice, a diamond. Put it under the microscope, and it's easy to imagine you'd see one of those wintry scenes in a plastic ball: tiny people, dancing in a forest white with hoar.

By the time we make it back down to our car, our skin is gray with mild hypothermia. The clouds have devoured the mountainsides overlooking Ophir; the roof of the sky has fallen in. As we drive home, rocks are plummeting down onto the highway, loosened by the deluge.

Just before it sets the sun emerges. It keeps raining, raining fire, and a rainbow appears over the Telluride Valley. Another rainbow appears inside it. Then another. Then a fourth. People come out into Main Street from the bars, shops, and offices, whooping and hollering. The mountains appear through the clouds, shimmering with fresh snow on their tops. They are lit with an ethereal red glow ..., then it all goes dark. It keeps raining all night long.

...This is why we live here. The golden steam rising from mushrooms in the pan, the cold rain shattering on the roof, a soft roar like the sea.

118. Telluride
from *Tomboy Bride* by Harriet Fish Backus

Even today, the road to the Tomboy Mine, several thousand feet above Telluride, is not for the faint of heart. Narrow switchbacks. Rocky cliffs. Thousand-foot drop-offs. It is a formidable jeep trail under the best of conditions. Now imagine that same road in winter. Below-freezing temperatures. Thick layers of snow and ice. Two old horses pulling a sleigh up the same treacherous road. This is how Harriet "Hattie" Fish Backus and her husband George rode up the mountain above Telluride in the late 1890s. Their destination? A two-room shack in a high altitude (11,800 feet) mining camp where George had hired on as an assayer and Hattie was expected to manage their household. For a former schoolteacher from San Francisco, the task of sustaining oneself under these conditions might have been challenge enough. But as the following account from her book Tomboy Bride *suggests, this was only the beginning of a demanding and adventurous life on the high side of the mining frontier.*

Shortly after that Christmas day I had a new adventure. Johnny Midwinter, the foreman, suggested that he and George take me into the mine. George thought I would enjoy it.

Johnny met us at the entrance. Outfitted in a miner's long rubber coat and sou'wester I entered the tunnel where Johnny fastened a miner's candlestick in the loop on my hat and with a dramatic gesture of his pudgy hand, lighted the candle.

Possibly, because I had made the effort to send help to the roustabout which prevented an accident, Johnny decided my interest in the mine warranted a wider understanding of its ramifications. After we walked some distance along the main tunnel he turned to me with a smile and said, "We'll start up this ladder in what we call 'a vertical raise.' Just climb slowly behind me and George will follow you. When we get up to the stope, take the candle out of your hat and carry it straight up and as far from your face as you can."

What did he mean by a *stope* and would I recognize it when I reached it?

Step by step, clinging to the rungs, we climbed straight up the three by four opening in the rock. As water dripped from above and hit my hat and face, the candle sputtered. I stepped carefully for fear of tripping on my skirt. With the strange feeling of carrying a candle on my head I stared steadily at the ladder. The flickering light shone dimly on the walls caging us in, three sides of solid rock and the fourth made of timbers for the ore chute alongside. Each rung was a little harder for me to reach and cling to. By the time fifty rungs were beneath us I began to waver, then I hesitated, but remembering that George was close below and might be thrown off balance, I plunged on. After one hundred feet of this fearsome climb we reached the top of the ladder where the rock closed in over our heads.

Even today, many years later, the memory of that moment hits hard at the pit of my stomach!

Broken ore almost completely filled the cross shaft, leaving only a crooked passage to crawl through, two feet wide, three feet high. Faintness and vertigo swept through me. But not for anything would I let George or Johnny know how desperately fear gripped me. I could hardly breathe. There must have been oxygen but I couldn't pull any of it into my lungs. To cover the sick feeling of panic I made the excuse, which was real enough, that I needed to catch my breath after the exhausting climb. Unable, in that flat space, to sit up I lay flat on my stomach, resting, doubting that I could go on.

Through the pounding of my heart I could hear myself saying, "Hattie, you must go on. You are the wife of a miner. Keep going and get it over!" But my head was swimming and my stomach churning. I lay there until terror subsided somewhat, then told Johnny I was ready.

Holding the candle safely before me I inched along, face down, clawing at the rocks with my one free hand, dragging my legs forward, my long skirts hampering every move. Only occasionally could I catch the gleam of Johnny's candle ahead. Unable to look back I could hear George calling a word of encouragement as he followed.

But what if the rock overhead should cave in? The thought was torture. I struggled to wipe it from my mind. In the darkness, broken only by a flicker of the nearby candle, I twisted, turned, writhed like a snake, stopped many times to rest and capture a mite of courage.

It was one hundred and fifty feet of pure hell!! Yet I lived through it. We had crossed the awful stope and there remained the descent, straight down another hundred-foot ladder in a well, scarcely four feet square, cut in solid rock. It seemed easy. I had room to breathe. With each rung lower there was more space above my head. The tunnel at last! I hurried toward the streak of daylight at its mouth, and the great outdoors. Heaven!

119. Norwood
from "Almost Animal" by Amy Irvine

Being a 6th generation Utahn didn't mean that Amy Irvine would feel welcome in her home state—at least not while she was working as a public lands advocate and living in the rural communities of southeastern Utah. Many residents of towns like Monticello and Blanding are fiercely proud of their pioneer ancestors and their remarkable desert crossing to more hospitable lands on the southeastern edge of Mormon territory. As a result, they have a proprietary sense of privilege when it comes to land use decisions in the region. It didn't matter that Irvine also had deep Mormon roots. As an activist associated with the Southern Utah Wilderness Alliance, she was not, nor would she ever be, fully accepted in a county renowned for its antagonism to environmental concerns.

So she began to look elsewhere for a place where she could begin her new life as a mother. She and her partner at the time found some land on a mesa just over the state line in western Colorado. It wasn't easy to leave the canyon country of southeastern Utah, with which she felt such a deep bond. At least, looking west, she could still see her homeland. And the opportunities to experience a wide and wild edge of the world were plentiful. The tale that follows took place while she was exploring some territory west of Norwood.

On a dirt road beneath a sun scuttled high in the rafters of desert sky, a mountain lion sits dead center. The horse and I are headed straight for him. I say *him* because it's a hulk of a cat—not the first I've seen but the biggest. My mount should be panicked and dancing sideways, yet there's no balk in his step. Which makes no sense. I'm new to horses and cattle drives but even I know that lions put horses in a panic. My mount though, a dirty white Arabian I've only just met, seems game for a head-on collision.

The horse's name is Micah. Or Mica. I didn't ask which. It depends on the spelling, but he's either a minor prophet or glittering mineral. I'm betting on the former because he's not so shiny. He also knew before I did about the problem up ahead. I'd seen the animal stroll lithely out of

the brush and onto the crest of the hill but dismissed him as a large dog—
the kind that patrols most of the mesa's ranches. I missed him because I'd
been fretting about the baby at home—the one I haven't been apart from
in nine months save for a quick nap or shower.

The horse had nickered in low octaves, trying to get me to wise up.
In my defense, the hundred head of cows hadn't seen the lion either—
they too, were focused on their babies. I let a few pairs slip past me and
this riles Micah. He snorts, tosses his head. The first flies of summer peel
off his mane into air already hot and dusty despite a cold, wet spring.
That's the American Southwest for you—three feet of snow one week
and bone-dry dirt the next—even at 8,000 feet of elevation and climbing.
Had I not looked up then, had I blinked, I would have missed that the
tail of the ranch dog didn't wag. It twitched. I would have missed how
the horse's ash-gray ears pricked, how his eyes hardened into ironwood
orbs. Which brings us back to the moment at hand, when Micah, without
consulting, puts his head down and trots forward with the resolve of a
war horse, the heft of hurricanes. I know he will leave me on the good
hard ground if I don't get up to speed and fast.

I snap to. Kick Micah forward with a sureness that is feigned but it
works and then we're moving not as two creatures but one. Loose gravel
pops like hot coals under his hooves as we leave the herd behind. The
flank riders shout at us to hold back but we are going, going, and all
things tame and known fade in our wake as we pass through the outer
banks of some other realm, both rough-hewn and uncharted. Here, Micah
is a different horse. Here, I am another kind of woman. I imagine myself
as one of those ancient women horse warriors of Siberia, who hunted and
battled from the saddle, their legs bowed like ships' hulls when they died.
Some were mothers. Some were wives. But all of them rode, all the time.

With citrine eyes the big tom glares, then stands and fakes a yawn—
the way house cats do, to hide their delight when you walk through
the door at day's end. He pretends to stretch but he's balled up at the
haunches—ready to pounce or run. The horse and I call his bluff—I can't
believe I'm in on this. Not just in, but *all* in.

The lion squints, like he's sizing us up, and then he turns, springs,
soars. All four velvet paws have left the ground, he's no longer a cat but a

fantastic griffin. Into the scrub oak and pinion he goes, the residue of his body a beige-black smear that lingers like smoke, like magic.

I halt Micah, whose respect I may have just earned; quite willingly he turns the one-eighty I've asked for. Now we're gazing at the oncoming herd and the civilized world at the bottom of the hill—with its neatly furrowed fields and straight-shot ditches, the barbed-wire borders of pastures, the buck and rail of barnyards and paddocks. And the town of Norwood—its main drag lined with hanging baskets of petunias, the fairgrounds, tiny post office and clinic.

But it's what's beyond the mesa's rim that makes my heart roar in my ears. Hailing from every degree on the compass: millions of acres of ponderosa, aspen, juniper. Slickrock canyons, a sinuous rose gold. And yawning, sagebrush-flecked basins and badlands. I'd been at home with a new baby, locked down in my own mind—so I hadn't really taken in the scope of my new home on the Colorado side of the Four Corners. The panorama unfurls new and hopeful—with a brief burst of June green as bonus before July's dry yellow. In this moment, it's easy to forget how much the West is trending toward more heat, less water. Just as it's easy to forget I'm a mother.

Bess approaches at a lope on a red horse—I don't yet know to call it a sorrel gelding.

"Was that what I think it was?" Bess asks, her face grim as she performs a quick head count on the calves. I nod, wide awake for the first time in nine months—well, seventeen, if you count the bedridden, eight-month pregnancy. My smile is a map spread out across the land— from the winsome, eastern horizon of Colorado's San Juan Range to the western one, my Utah homeland, ninety-nine miles away.

All I can do now, is keep my eye on the glorious back of beyond. To the wider, wilder world into which the black paintbrush tip of a lion's tail just vanished.

Micah shimmies loose the excitement and my body shudders with him. My mind, so muddled by maternity, suddenly sharp as claws.

I know now, what I need, to salvage my own hide.

120. Nucla
from "Dr. Don: The Life of a Small Town Druggist"
by Peter Hessler

*Peter Hessler, who is best known for his four books on China, moved to
Ridgway in 2011 and turned his journalistic sensibilities toward western Colorado. One of the stories he chose to tell (in an article for the
September 19, 2001 issue of* The New Yorker*) focused on a small-town
druggist in Nucla.*

*What holds a small-town community together? Maybe it's a school
or a post office; maybe it's a church or service organization. Maybe
it's a café or a tavern, or some other business. Maybe it has to do with
the mayor or some other civic leader. In Nucla, Don Colcord, who is
affectionately known as Dr. Don (even though he is a pharmacist, not
a physician), has been an important community player for a long time.
Peter Hessler's appreciative profile celebrates the life of a small-town
druggist devoted to his neighbors and his hometown.*

In the southwestern corner of Colorado, where the Uncompahgre Plateau
descends through spruce forest and scrubland toward the Utah border,
there is a region of more than four thousand square miles which has no
hospitals, no department stores, and only one pharmacy. The pharmacist
is Don Colcord, who lives in the town of Nucla. More than a century
ago, Nucla was founded by idealists who hoped their community would
become the "center of Socialistic government for the world." But these
days it feels like the edge of the earth. Highway 97 dead-ends at the
top of Main Street; the population is around seven hundred and falling.
The nearest traffic light is an hour and a half away. When old ranching
couples drive their pickups into Nucla, the wives leave the passenger's
side empty and sit in the middle of the front seat, close enough to touch
their husbands. It's as if something about the landscape—those endless
hills, that vacant sky—makes a person appreciate the intimacy of a Ford
F-150 cab.

Don Colcord has owned Nucla's Apothecary Shoppe for more than
thirty years. In the past, such stores played a key role in American rural

health care, and this region had three more pharmacies, but all of them have closed. Some people drive eighty miles just to visit the Apothecary Shoppe. It consists of a few rows of grocery shelves, a gift-card rack, a Pepsi fountain, and a diabetes section, which is decorated with the mounted heads of two mule deer and an antelope. Next to the game heads is the pharmacist's counter. Customers don't line up at a discreet distance, the way city folk do; in Nucla they crowd the counter and talk loudly about health problems....

Somebody asks about decongestants; a young woman inquires about the risk of birth defects while using a collagen stimulator. A preacher from the Abundant Life Church asks about drugs for a paralyzed vocal cord. ("When I do a sermon, it needs to last for thirty minutes.") Others stop by just to chat. Don, in addition to being the only pharmacist, is probably the most talkative and friendly person within four thousand square miles. The first time I visited his counter, he asked about my family, and I mentioned my newborn twin daughters. He filled a jar with thick brown ointment that he had recently compounded. "It's tincture of benzoin," he said. "Rodeo cowboys use it while riding a bull or a bronc. They put it on their hands; it makes the hands tacky. It's a respiratory stimulant, mostly used in wound care. You won't find anything better for diaper rash."

Don Colcord was born in Nucla, and he has spent all of his sixty years in Colorado, where community-minded individuals often develop some qualities that may seem contradictory. Don sells cigarettes at his pharmacy, because he believes that people have the right to do unhealthy things. He votes Democratic, a rarity in this region. He listens to Bocelli and drives a Lexus. At Easter, the Colcord family tradition is to dye eggs, line them up in a pasture, and fire away with a 25-06 Remington. A loyal N.R.A. member, Don describes shooting as essentially peaceful. "Your arm moves up and down every time you breathe, so you control your breathing," he says. "It's very similar to meditation." He was once the star marksman of the University of Colorado's rifle team, and for many years he held a range record for standing shooting at the Air Force Academy.

Calmness is one reason that he has such influence in the community. He's short and slight, with owlish glasses, and he seems as comfortable talking to women as to men. "It's like Don looks you in the eye and the rest

of the world disappears," one local tells me. Faith in Don's judgment is all
but absolute. People sometimes telephone him at two o'clock in the morning, describe their symptoms, and ask if they should call an ambulance for
the two-hour trip to the nearest hospital. Occasionally, they show up at his
house. A few years ago, a Mexican immigrant family had an eight-year-old
son who was sick; twice they visited a clinic in another community, where
they were told that the boy was dehydrated. But the child didn't improve,
and finally all eight family members showed up one evening in Don's
driveway. He did a quick evaluation—the boy's belly was distended and
felt hot to the touch. He told the parents to take him to the emergency room.
They went to the nearest hospital, in Montrose, where the staff diagnosed
severe brucellosis and immediately evacuated the boy on a plane to Denver.
He spent two weeks in the I.C.U. before making a complete recovery. One
of the Denver doctors told Don that the boy would have died if they had
waited any longer to get him to a hospital.

    At the Apothecary Shoppe, Don never wears a white coat. He takes
people's blood pressure, and he often gives injections; if it has to be done
in the backside, he escorts the customer into the bathroom for privacy.
Elderly folks refer to him as "Dr. Don," although he has no medical
degree and discourages people from using this title. He doesn't wear a
nametag. "I wear old Levi's," he says. "People want to talk to somebody
who looks like them, talks like them, is part of the community. I know
a lot of pharmacists wear a coat because it makes you look more professional. But it's different here."

    … He is, by the strictest definition, a bad businessman. If a customer
can't pay, Don often rings up the order anyway and tapes the receipt to the
inside wall above his counter. "This one said he was covered by insurance,
but it wasn't," he explains, pointing at a slip of paper on a wall full of them.
"This one said he'll be in on Tuesday. This one is a patient who is going on
an extended vacation." Most of his customers simply don't have the money.
Each year, Don writes off between ten and twenty thousand dollars, and he
estimates that he is owed around three hundred thousand dollars in total … .

    "It's just a cost of doing business in a small town," he says. "I don't
know how you can look your neighbor in the eye and say, 'I know you're
having a tough time, but I can't help you and your kid can't get well.'"

121. Paradox
from *One Man's West* by David Lavender

*The Paradox Valley owes its name to the Dolores River. Steep sandstone
walls to the north and south edge in this valley, which runs east-west
for about twenty-five miles. The river provides the geological paradox,
flowing as it does from south to north and carving out a route through
those canyon walls, instead of flowing along the valley's longer edge and
taking the path of least resistance.*

*Growing up in southwestern Colorado, writer and historian David
Lavender knew the Paradox Valley during periodic post-World War II
mining booms, mostly carnotite from which uranium and vanadium are
extracted. He also knew it as a relatively isolated agricultural valley,
where his stepfather wintered herds of cattle that grazed in nearby
mountains during the summer months. It was reasonably good ground
for grazing and for growing corn, wheat, and alfalfa, as long as the irrigation ditches were flowing. But that all changed during times of drought,
as Lavender writes in his autobiographical book,* One Man's West.

The dreary month of April rolled around. The scant snow which winter
had brought was gone. Under the pale, wind-streaked sky the air was raw
and cold. Out in the scattered farm lands which dotted the few choice
sections of West Paradox, Mackinaw-clad plowmen—driving teams
because the valley could not then afford tractors—were turning the red
earth for spring planting. When summer came the cliffs would reflect
the searing sunrays until the great trough simmered like an oven. Corn,
wheat, and alfalfa would grow rich and tall wherever water could be
brought to it through the irrigation ditches that tapped the thin streams of
the La Sal Mountains. But in April there was no hay. Last summer's crop
had been devoured. Gaunt wooden derricks stood useless in the empty
stackyards. Cattle bawled hungrily on the feed lots.

As we had been doing for days now, a long, lazy, horse-faced cowboy
named Mike Gaynor and I loaded hundred-pound sacks of "cotton cake"
on pack horses and rode out to one of the fields. The cattle were clustered
by the gate, waiting for us. They were range stock, white-faced Herefords

and normally wild. But now they sniffed around us like dogs, so close
we had to slap them aside from the sack mouths. We doled the cake out
to them like gold. It had been trucked over snow-choked roads from the
railway at Montrose, and when it was gone there would be no more. We
dribbled it on the ground in long ribbons, so all the animals could get at it.

They couldn't gulp it, though they tried. Cotton cake, a yellow-
ish-gray stuff pressed out of cottonseed into lumps about the size and
hardness of pebbles, takes chewing. It is pure, concentrated food. For
bulk, the animals had to eat brush. Up on the ditchbank we could see the
willow stubs, as big around as our thumbs, which they had gnawed like
beavers, trying to fill the hollow places in their stomachs. It hadn't been
enough for some of them. A couple of dead ones lay near by; we would
have to get a team, drag them off, and dump them in an arroyo. We
stood there shivering in the wind, watching the animals quarrel over the
life-giving cake, hooking one another aside, grabbing a mouthful, and
then running along the line as if they thought there might be tastier bits
at the next place. The best of them looked none too good, their win-
ter-roughened coats all woolly and their backbones sticking out like the
ridgepole of an unguyed tent.

Mike Gaynor swore under his breath. Whether the creatures lived or
died made no difference to him; he drew his wages just the same. But a
cowboy feels far more than impersonal pity for a hungry animal.

He glared at the cold sky. "My God," he said, "won't the grass ever
grow again."

Highway 550

Red Mountain to Ridgway

122. Red Mountain Pass
from "Red Mountain" by Robinson Jeffers

Known especially for his writings about the rugged central California coast, poet Robinson Jeffers established himself as an authentic and original voice in the American literary world of the twentieth century. He wrote passionately about wild places, especially those he witnessed in California and elsewhere. And he railed against cultural indifference to "the astonishing beauty of things." For several years during the 1930s, Jeffers and his family traveled to Taos, New Mexico where they vacationed at the home of Mable Dodge Luhan, a wealthy matron of the arts. It was likely during those summer travels that he noticed Red Mountain (which is actually a set of three peaks between Silverton and Ouray) whose name comes from the reddish iron ore that colors this alpine terrain.

Red Mountain

Beyond the Sierras, and sage-brush Nevada ranges, and vast
Vulture-utopias of Utah desert,
That mountain we admired last year on our summer journey, the same
Rose-red pyramid glows over Silverton.
Whoever takes the rock pass from Ouray sees foaming waterfalls
And trees like green flames, like the rocks flaming
Green; and above, up the wild gorge, up the wild sky,
Incredibly blood-color around the snow-spot
The violent peak. We thought it was too theatrical to last;
But if we ship to Cape Horn, or were buying
Camels in Urga, Red Mountain would not turn pale for our absence.
We like dark skies and lead-color heights,
But the excellence of things is really unscrupulous, it will dare anything.

123. Ouray
from "Toward the Sun" by Kent Nelson

Kent Nelson, a long-time resident of Ouray, is both an accomplished athlete and a prolific author. His passion for sports and writing mesh well in a collection of stories called "Toward the Sun," in which many of his characters run, climb or ski their way into altered states, maybe even moments of transcendence. As reviewer Mary Park says, Nelson's interest lies in "sports as obsession, as a crucible that shapes and deforms his characters' lives." That is certainly true in the title story, about a mountain runner we witness through the eyes of his wife. She wonders about his running habit, why he is so driven to make his miles in the vertical world that surrounds their town (as it does here in Ouray). One might wonder the same about an athlete in any extreme sport, and there are plenty of them—runners, bikers, skiers, climbers— here in the high country of Colorado.

As a veteran of the famous Imogene Pass Race, an annual event that crosses the mountain country between Ouray and Telluride, Kent Nelson knows the lay of the land from a runner's point of view. He draws on that experience in this excerpt from "Toward the Sun," which tells the tale of a hard-core mountain athlete who wants to run himself into a wilder way of being.

Nieman runs in the mountains. He starts from our small house at nearly 7700 feet, and in a few minutes I see his tattered gray sweat suit drifting among the dark spruce on the Twin Peaks Trail. When I return from the garden with the day's pick of beans, lettuce, and squash—we get no to- matoes at this altitude—he will be coming out of the Oak Creek gorge at 8500 feet. I like to watch him there because the trail skirts through scrub oak and along a cliff, and he is in the open for several minutes until he turns the corner and crosses the meadow into aspens.

I lay the vegetables on the porch step, wipe my hands on my blouse, and pick up the binoculars. In the circle of the glass, Nieman's maroon form is muddled by heat waves from the neighbor's roof, but I do not need perfect focus to be absorbed. Against the red sandstone, he holds

his arms perpendicular to his body, as if he were a hawk tilting its
wings to catch the thermals and updrafts which swirl among the crags.
He reaches out with his long legs and steps lightly over the rocky trail,
darting as the path twists along the contour of the cliff....

I can understand the desire to hone the body to a fine edge, to increase the endurance of the muscles, to strive for greater lung capacity.
But those motivations are superfluous to Nieman. His body is already
beyond fitness, past the limits of endurance. He wants to push away the
routine of daily life, to escape. But where? He is in the mountains five or
six hours a day. If he could eat and sleep on his feet, he could run forever.
No one runs like Nieman simply to take his mind off his problems.

He leaves the cliff edge and climbs to the meadow. His brown hair
tufts in the wind, his legs drive effortlessly uphill. His ragged sweatsuit
sways and dances against the pale green. He breaks into the clearing and
crosses suddenly from the sunlight into the shadow of the dark timber....

Once I asked what he thought about when he ran. When he was in the
mountains alone and felt the mist of the clouds on his face, what did he
know? When he skipped over roots and rocks and climbed to the ribbons
of snow, he must have thought something.

"No," he said. "I don't think about anything."

"Your mind is blank? Absolutely blank?"

"Not blank, but I don't think of anything."

Then he was silent. He smiled at my wanting to know and I got angry.
If he didn't want to talk that was one thing, but to smile as though I were
sweet for asking was another. I suppose it angered me that he knew he
did not have to explain himself. I loved him anyway. The more he was
silent, the more I poured myself into his silence....

2. The air has a nick of autumn on the morning. Nieman takes me with
him into the mountains. In the high country, the aspens have already
edged to yellow. Nieman is unusually quiet. Sometimes when we hike
together he speaks of the wildlife or the weather or the history of the
mines, but this day he moves quickly along the trail, waiting at intervals
for me to catch up. Several times I sense he wants to speak to me. In
his face is a strain seldom there. But what he knows he will not tell, and

what he will not tell commits us both to silence … .

Even after we set up our rough camp at the edge of the meadow, Nieman is not at ease. He scans the steep meadows, looking for something, and when I ask what he seeks, he turns away … .

He stares at the rocky scree and the dark timber above us. Seeing what? Knowing what? He looks old. Then he nods and utters an eerie cry. I follow his gaze.

Elk. I find them easily in the binoculars. There are perhaps thirty of them, mostly light-rumped cows moving slowing uphill, grazing the shreds of grass which are invisible to me from such a distance. Two spike bulls with dark manes escort the cows.

I glance at Nieman who crouches stock-still.

Then from below the elk, from the dark timber, comes a huge antlered bull. He climbs to the others, stops, and turns his head toward us.

Nieman starts running. It is astonishing how quickly he moves away from me up the sharp angle of the hill. Within a minute he is into the timber, breaking through brush, leaping fallen logs. I call to him, but he does not hear me, or he hears me and does not answer … .

It takes me half an hour to reach the opening in the trees where Nieman's tracks are. I find the markings on the ground where he had gathered the dirt in his hands. I touch the earth to confirm what I know and lift my hands to my nostrils. The smell is everywhere, sickening, so strong it's horror. The odor is of elk urine and the musk of elk beds recently deserted.

From the cover of the trees I can see nothing, so I move higher, aching, knowing how Nieman smells. The game trails are overgrown, and I fight my way through the underbrush. The branches scrape me, catch my anger, but I gain higher ground. Gray granite peaks surround me, and beneath and across stretch the deep valleys where snow lies in perpetual shadow.

I scan the slopes for several minutes before I see the elk again. They have already moved a mile or more into another drainage. The hills dividing each ravine are lines of yellow and gray, one beyond another, sliding downward toward the stream. The elk skirt these hills, running now, sensing the danger behind them.

Then Nieman appears just below the line of the ridge. In the binoculars I see the thin game trail he follows, and as seconds elapse, he becomes clearer. His stride is forceful, strong yet graceful. The tension in his face is gone ... .

Watching him, I feel a lightness seep into me—weakness and strength. I gaze around: the high country is as foreign as a bleak moon.

The elk run around the base of a huge crag, descend into another valley, then climb higher toward the saddle between the two peaks. For a time Nieman closes the gap, but the elk move faster. After a few minutes, they tire, and Nieman gains.

He holds his head straight. His legs reach out, and his arms churn smoothly. I imagine his body beneath the sweatsuit, the sweat mingling with the urine and musk of elk. I wonder whether our child would have Nieman's body, Nieman's elk body, Nieman's resolve.

The elk ascend the last pitch to the saddle, and in the angle of the sun become part light and part silhouette as they disappear over the pass. I shiver and turn away before Nieman reaches the top.

124. Ridgway
from Old Fences and New Neighbors
by Peter Decker

Peter Decker wore a few different hats over the course of his life: university professor, cattle rancher, Colorado Agriculture Commissioner, director of the Western Stock Show, and author.

In his book Old Fences and New Neighbors, *he offers his perspective on cattle ranching in Ridgway, a vocation that he knew firsthand for twenty-five years. During that time, he witnessed the economic and social transformation of his community.*

Talk at the Ridgway coffee shop had revolved around cattle prices and the weather for as long as I could remember. Ranchers whose livelihood depended on calf prices at the weekly cattle auction in Montrose and timely rains through the summer months were far more concerned about weather patterns off the coast of California and Mexico than they were

with the direction of the Dow Jones average or who won a presidential
debate. By the early 1990s, however, the general subjects of conversation
in the coffee shop had changed.

Tourists filled the shop all summer, asking locals where to fish, what
jeep trails were open in the mountains, how to get to Telluride, and the
average price of a local house lot. An increasing number of new residents
filed into the post office each morning to pick up their mail. The old-timers complained about the newcomers, said they didn't recognize anyone
at the post office anymore, and talked about the damned hunter from
Texas who mistook a pack horse over near the OXO Ranch for a bull
elk."Remember when" stories became very popular. Like the story of old
Jim Harrison, a six-foot-four mule skinner who ran a small herd of cattle
on his homestead at the head of Beaver Creek when he wasn't hauling
ore from the mines. In the midst of the Depression, Jim's cattle loan
came due at the Ridgway bank. After trailing cattle into Ridgway from
his ranch some eight miles away in early November, he walked into the
office of the bank president, Mr. Walther, and asked for an extension of
his loan until spring. "Can't do that, Jim," Mr. Walter said. Looking out
the bank window at his cattle in the street, Jim responded: "Well, there
are your cattle. You feed 'em." Jim got his loan extension, and Marie
Scott helped him with the payoff by buying his homestead; she continued
to look after Jim until he died in the 1960s.

By the 1990s, cattle ranching no longer defined the local economy.
Where in 1975 some nineteen thousand head of cattle were raised in the
county, twenty years later there were fewer than six thousand. Ranchers
realized that their meadows and pastures were valuable homesites, too
valuable, perhaps, for grazing cows. Some of those who continued ranching on their high-priced real estate owned their land free and clear or owed
only a small mortgage, and some possessed considerable off-ranch income
that allowed them the luxury of not having to worry about making a profit
from their livestock. The many ranchers in the area, including myself,
who fell into neither category began seriously thinking about moving our
livestock operations out of Ridgway and into areas where the cost of land
and labor better matched the economics of the cattle business.

It didn't require a banker or an economist with a PhD to understand

that if a cow needed approximately three acres of irrigated meadow
(with a 1996 market value of approximately $4,000 per acre) for herself
and her calf for a year, and if the value of the weaned calf in the best of
times was $500, the return on the rancher's investment was 4 percent
before subtracting expenses. One rancher told me, "Heck, I'd double my
income this year and probably for the foreseeable future if I sold off my
herd and land, paid the taxes, retired my debt, and invested the remainder
in Treasury bills." Unless one married into or inherited a ranch large
enough to support a family and generate a profit (a very unlikely scenario,
given inheritance taxes), it made little economic sense by the 1990s to
buy expensive land in the Ridgway area for a livestock operation, or even
to continue ranching when the incentives to sell were so enticing.

Highway 50
Gunnison to Delta

125. Gunnison
from "Hiking with Hobbes" by George Sibley

Ever since George Sibley started writing for the Crested Butte newspaper in the mid-1960s, he has been a steady presence in the pages of various high country publications, most recently Colorado Central Magazine. *His articles, essays, and books are rooted in his passion for the headwaters country of central Colorado where he has made his home (Gunnison) for many years. There aren't too many trails in the Upper Gunnison River Valley that Sibley hasn't walked or skied, including the Lamphier Lake trail in the Fossil Ridge Wilderness northeast of Gunnison. But even a familiar walk can take a turn into the great unknown ...*

Hobbes, a longtime friend, one with whom I've been hiking for 25 years or so, is a political scientist, a philosopher really; we call him Hobbes because that cranky old medieval philosopher, Thomas Hobbes, was kind of his lodestar—not a hero, just a light to steer by in his own meditations and musings on the future of the species. Hiking with Hobbes is fun because the conversation is always pretty rich, moving back and forth through current events of the past five or six centuries.

Anyway, we decided to hike up to Lamphier Lake in the Fossil Ridge Wilderness .... We've both been to Lamphier Lake before, but never together, and also—not recently. Which is why, as the morning wore out, we both began to think that the trail to the lake had grown steeper since our last trip up, and maybe quite a little longer. We had to acknowledge that this may have been because we have become a little older. I'm only 78, but Hobbes is 83, and has had some serious stresses in recent years, including the loss of his longtime partner.

We were stopping more often to catch our breath, and spending a little more time on Hobbesian questions like—look at this stand of dense and mostly dead lodgepole—is this a happy forest? Contented? Hobbes tends toward "mysterious but ultimately perfect are the ways of Nature," while I think that the condition of a lot of our forests is more akin to the urban slum. We can kill twenty minutes or half an hour easily on something like that.

The upshot of this is that we reached a point where both Hobbes and the day were wearing out, and I asked Hobbes several times if it was time to turn around and head home. Well, he would say, don't you want to get to the lake? Well, I'd like to, of course, I'd say, but—and he'd say, well then, and we'd get back on the trail. Thus do old men enable each other in reenacting youthful folly.

We were having that conversation for about the fourth time, sitting on a big rocky overlook from which we could see all the way to the Continental Divide, when some younger hikers came along, fully equipped with electronic technology, and told us it was still almost half a mile to the lake. Okay, I said, we're eating lunch here, enjoying the view, then heading down, and Hobbes agreed this time. So we ate lunch, which consisted of sandwiches we'd each brought, and sharing some grapes I'd brought and an innocuous little loaf of carrot cake that Hobbes had scrounged out of the fridge before we left his house.

Then we tried to stand up.

Interesting exercise: trying to stand up when you are suddenly two or three feet taller than you remember, with noodle bones, and the planet is gently but insistently rocking you in its cradle. Or maybe not so gently: Hobbes looked like he was trying to stand up in a strong wind. "Whew," he said. "I'm kind of dizzy."

"Can you walk? Downhill?" My razorsharp mind was plodding through stuff.

We started downhill. It was obvious we were both having trouble remembering the basics of walking downhill, or anywhere. "I feel like I'm drunk," he said.

A vagrant thought wandered into my mind. "Hobbes," I said. "That carrot cake … who … what … "

"S---- baked it," he said—his daughter, who had moved up from New Mexico to stay with him through his problems.

My razorsharp mind immediately wandered to a hypothesis. "Could she have used some special ingredient?" (Legal of course.)

"Uh-oh," said Hobbes.

So we began a long trip down the mountain, that was fairly quickly complicated by a side effect of the carrot cake, serious cases of drymouth, and other signs of dehydration like serious leg muscle pains for Hobbes. Being the young guy on the trip, I was doing okay, aside from the constant need for enough water to unglue my tongue from the roof of my mouth. We were both balance-challenged, but leaned into each other as much as away from each other, and only fell a couple times.

But it was very slow going. The situation began to penetrate my mind, and I didn't know whether to laugh or panic: two old farts staggering around accidentally stoned, hilarious. But two-plus miles up a rocky mountainside—not so funny.

Hobbes really was feeling serious pain; but Hobbes being Hobbes, he needed to analyze it, talk through it, and the only way he could do his analysis was by stopping completely in order to expound on it. "What is the mind-body relationship?" he asked. "Am I really in physical pain? Or is this psychosomatic?" He then wandered into a greener field of Shakespearean analysis: "What did that soliloquy mean, anyway?"

"What soliloquy?"

"To be or not to… " Then a pause; then, "I don't think I'm making any sense," he said, with a prim note of discovery.

I, on the other hand, descended into a panicky pedantic state of freeze-dried rationality. "Hobbes," I said, "Hobbes my friend, we have just one thing to think about now, one thing to do, and that's to get down this mountain."

"But my legs, the mind-body issue --"

"Hobbes!" I reiterated. "Getting down the mountain! That is our sole focus now. All questions will be answered, all perspectives considered, and all hypotheses analyzed—at the bottom of the mountain!"

So we staggered on into the disappearing afternoon. It involved frequent rest stops, and occasional philosophy stops—and once Hobbes memorably stopped and broke into song, maybe some old Shakespearean ditty, or his own setting for a poem by Emily Dickinson, his favorite poet.

As I began to come down from whatever had been in the carrot cake, I began to worry that we would actually not get down on our own resources.

"Should I maybe go on down and get some help?" I asked, but Hobbes was adamant: "No! Never!" Exactly the way I would have responded, had it been me in trouble. I'm at an age where I'd rather die on a beautiful mountain than be rescued from it.

The hikers who had passed us going up caught up with us on their way back down, and they opted to stay with us, which was good company, especially since they lived in Mississippi where Hobbes grew up. And more especially since they had some water. Hobbes was not remembering things that well at that point, so that coincidental Mississippi connection was re-established three or four times in the remaining 1.4 miles on their electronic device—each time requiring a delay in forward progress.

I persisted in my stoned mantra: "All questions will be answered and all issues discussed—at the bottom of the mountain!"

Our new companions chuckled the first three or four times I said that—then, as the shadows lengthened, they began saying it too. Their water, along with ours, was mostly gone, but Hobbes became more stable and coherent as we came down (physically and psychically), and when it became apparent that we would make it off the mountain, I went on ahead quickly to bring the car closer to the wilderness boundary. Fifty yards from the trailhead, I met Hobbes's daughter coming up to look for us. I asked her then and there if there'd been anything special in the little carrot cake.

"Oh my god!" she cried. "He knows he's not supposed to touch anything on that shelf!" Hobbes was in trouble. But also out of trouble by then; we'd made it off the mountain. Under our own power, with a little help from friends.

There are undoubtedly sober lessons to be learned from that day—something about old men learning our limits, about listing ingredients in baked goods, about how much water to carry, et cetera. But my main takeaway from it is the image of Hobbes swaying in the rocky trail, singing over and above the pain in his legs. It might have been one of his finest moments.

126. Black Canyon National Park
from *City of Illusions* by Ursula K. Le Guin

"Several canyons of the American West are longer and some are deeper,"
writes Colorado historian Duane Vandenbusche, "but none combines the
depth, sheerness, narrowness, darkness, and dread of the Black Canyon."
Sunlight is a fleeting presence inside of the canyon; Precambrian rock layers
at the bottom live mostly in the shadows. Canyon walls are steep and precar-
ious. It is the kind of place that makes an impression on even a casual visitor.

It certainly made an impression on author Ursula K. Le Guin. Best
known for her speculative fiction, Le Guin was traveling through Colorado
with her family in the 1950s. During a visit to Black Canyon, Le Guin's two
young children wandered off momentarily and, much to her horror, van-
ished over the rim. Her parental nightmare had a fortunate ending when
she found her children resting safely on a ledge beyond her line of vision.

Needless to say, Le Guin never forgot the Black Canyon, images of
which found their way into her novel, City of Illusions. *In that book, she*
imagines a city built across the abyss of the canyon. Known as Es Toch,
this city is inhabited by The Shing, alien conquerors who have subdued
the rest of earth's population. Their city soars into the sky on either side
of the canyon. Le Guin describes it this way:

The City of the Lords of Earth was built on the two rims of a canyon,
a tremendous cleft through the mountains, narrow, fantastic, its black
walls striped with green plunging terrifically down half a mile to the
silver tinsel strip of a river in the shadowy depths. On the very edges of
the facing cliffs the towers of the city jutted up, hardly based on earth at
all, linked across the chasm by delicate bridge-spans. Towers, roadways
and bridges ceased and the wall closed the city off again just before a
vertiginous bend of the canyon ....

Es Toch gave no sense of history, of reaching back in time and out in
space, though it had ruled the world for a millennium .... Es Toch was
self-contained, self-nourished, rootless .... Yet it was wonderful, like a
carved jewel fallen in the vast wilderness of the Earth: wonderful, timeless, alien.

127. Montrose / Uncompahgre Plateau
"Our New Life in the Forest," by Mary Ann Rawlings (Ott)

*About twenty miles directly west of Montrose and a couple of thousand
feet higher—just off the old Roubideau Trail—stands a US Forest
Service facility known as 25 Mesa Guard Station. The Uncompahgre
Forest Reserve was established in 1905 in part to settle disputes between
stockmen and farmers, and also to protect deteriorating watersheds. By
the time Bill Rawlings joined the Forest Service in 1956, relations among
the farmers and cowmen were civil enough and the forest was supplying
Ponderosa Pine for small-scale timber and sawmilling enterprises.*

In a piece that appeared in the Christian Science Monitor, *Mary Ann
Rawlings describes their first impressions of the Uncompahgre Valley in
the summer of 1956. After an eight-day journey from Massachusetts with
three small children and a trailer in tow, the young parents, like many
newcomers, were surprised to find that Colorado is not all mountains
and evergreens. Perhaps the Forest Service had hired them to plant
trees among the conical shale formations called 'dobies? Following
a steep road, Bill coaxed their 1951 Kaiser twenty-five miles onto the
Uncompahgre Plateau, 2,500 feet above the valley floor. At last, they
found the forest and mountain views they'd dreamed of—when in doubt,
go higher!*

When we arrived in Delta, Colorado, it was surely the hottest day in June
and certainly the worst part of our eight-day trip from Springfield, Mass.
We had eaten lunch in Grand Junction and driven on to Delta through the
most barren and unlovely stretch of land that we New Englanders had
ever seen. Where in this brown desert of rocks and unbearable dry heat
could there possibly be timber and green hills?

Our destination was the Uncompahgre National Forest where Bill, my
husband, had been assigned upon completion of his forestry degree at the
University of New Hampshire. The few cars we met seemed to sense the
urgency of getting through this desolate area as quickly as possible. They
whizzed by us as we plodded along at 35 miles per hour with our huge
trailer swaying along behind us. Upon arriving in Delta, we reported

immediately to the Forest Service Headquarters where Bill obtained
directions that would lead us to the ranger station. Then we made a trip
to the grocery store and bought carton after carton of provisions. There
was just enough room left for six-month-old Woody to lie down while I
held two-year-old Jeannie in my lap, and three-year-old Rip sat up in the
car seat. Thus we started off to find the forest.

Soon after we left town, the tarred highway gave way to a rough stony
road which meandered aimlessly among dunes and rubbish heaps. Once it
dipped down into a valley made fertile by a rushing stream. The road then
rose abruptly. Our faithful car, now 2,250 miles into our cross-country trip,
chugged ever upward with the needle on the temperature gauge protesting
violently. We didn't say much. The children were in complete charge of
the conversation, which was dominated by howls from Woody, who felt
righteously indignant at being ejected from the comforts of his front seat to
his present cramped position among the groceries.

The thought uppermost in our minds was, "Where is the verdant
green forest with snow-capped mountain peaks that we had dreamed of
since the arrival of our appointment papers from the Forest Service?"
Nowhere was there a scrap of vegetation to be seen. Soon, however, we
began to see stumpy cactus and dusty sagebrush, and finally, piñon pine
and juniper clinging to the rocky canyon walls. As we bumped along the
road which had been graded down to bedrock and worn into a gigantic
washboard by the heavy lumber trucks, our attention was focused on the
temperature gauge. It was a hot day and the motor was under a constant
strain from hauling the big trailer over these steep grades in low gear.
Bill's eyes switched momentarily to the gas gauge and made the devas-
tating discovery that the gas tank was bordering on empty. It was too late
now to turn back. We had already come 15 miles, and it was undoubtedly
less than that to the ranger station. We just prayed that we would have
enough fuel left to carry us safely to our new home.

On we climbed from canyon to hilltop, one after another. At last, we
came to the sign: "Uncompahgre National Forest." Here we saw scrub
oak and aspen whose white trunks reminded us of our New England
birches. The road hair-pinned up a very steep grade and at last we were
on the Uncompahgre Plateau. Ponderosa pines towered over the aspen.

White-faced cattle lumbered off the road and little calves scampered to
the shelter of the brush. Chipmunks scurried across the road with their
little tails pointing straight up. Mourning doves flitted by. This was our
welcoming committee.

About five miles after we had entered the forest, we came upon a
big Forest Service sign pointing down an old road to "25 Mesa Ranger
Station." The road went straight for about a mile, then made an abrupt
turn and came down into a pretty little clearing dotted by aspen groves
and dominated by a yellow bungalow trimmed with brown, a garage, and
barn. Although the gas gauge read empty, we had made it. With a sigh of
relief, Bill turned off the motor and we all piled out of the car to survey
our new domain.

Alas! We had no key! The doors and windows had been carefully secured. Here we were, 27 miles from town, with an empty gas tank and no
house key. We unsuccessfully tried every key in our possession and then
hurriedly peered in all the windows, examining them carefully to see if
one might possibly have been overlooked. We finally found an unlocked
window, and while Bill unloaded the trailer to get a stool and screwdriver
to move the screen, I ted poor Woody on the lawn, since it was well past
his supper time. Like an accomplished second-story man, Bill succeeded
in breaking in, then flung open the door to our new life in the forest.

128. Delta
from *Chronicles of the Forbidden* by John Nizalowski

*Downtown Delta tells you about itself. As many as twenty murals scat-
tered around town celebrate this town's heritage as an agricultural hub
and business center. Fruit growers, the first hardware store, the old
opera house, a Denver Rio Grande locomotive, a newsboy, an old-timer
enjoying the view from a sidewalk bench—these are a few of the small-
town icons that artists have selected for the walls of various downtown
buildings and businesses. Historic buildings like the Egyptian Theater
have been cared for and renovated over the years to preserve a Main
Street kind of ambiance. Writer, poet, and Colorado Mesa University*

professor John Nizalowski, enjoyed some of Delta's small-town ameni-
ties while he lived there with his young family. He revisits those days
in some of the essays that appear in a collection called Chronicles of
the Forbidden, *including this reflection on the annual Fourth of July*
celebration.

In the final years of my first marriage, I lived with my wife of those
days and our two daughters in a century old house in Delta, a small
Colorado ranching town. Our home was on Delta's outskirts, and just a
few blocks away, the rangelands began, leading up to the faint, far-off
ridge of the Uncompahgre Plateau.

Just south of those same blocks there is a town park with a 60-acre
lake at its heart. This was where every Fourth of July, Delta would
launch its fireworks, affording us a perfect view of this annual display
from our back yard. However, when Ursula, my oldest daughter, was a
young child, she found the fireworks' sharp cracks and massive booms
too frightening to bear. So, every Fourth of July, when the sky would
grow dark, I would take her by the hand and we would walk upstairs
to the attic. There, we would watch the fireworks from the west facing
window.

Like most attics, ours was filled with stuff—a few wooden chairs
with cracked legs, two unneeded kitchen tables, a stack of rolled posters,
and plenty of boxes containing old clothes, receipts, bank statements,
letters, photographs, books, vinyl albums, and the like. Midway, a
cinderblock chimney rose from the floor and vanished into the ceiling. At
the far end, where the window faced the east, I had a desk, a few bookshelves, a space heater for the winter, and a portable swamp cooler for
the summer. But at the west end there was nothing but life's detritus. So,
for the fireworks viewing, I would grab an old stuffed chair cushion, sit
myself down, and place Ursula on my lap. From our floor seat, we would
stare out the fly-specked, dusty window. In order to see the fireworks
better, we left the light off, so the only illumination came up the stairwell
from kitchen below. A bit spookily, the broken chairs and stacked boxes
loomed around us in the hot, attic darkness.

At last, a white flash would throw shadows on the boxes behind us.
Toward the right, through the window, the fireworks with their fountains

of light had begun—the sparkling arcs of light totally silent, the thunders muffled. Ursula, freed from frightful sounds, delighted in the display beyond the glass, cheering for each incendiary umbrella. In the light of the nearby streetlamps, I could see Isadora, Ursula's sister, by the apricot tree below, almost dancing in her joy at the colorful detonations. Her mom stood nearby, pointing out the wonders in the sky.

When the penultimate, frenzied cluster of fireworks faded from the sky, we would sit for a moment to make sure it was truly finished. Then we would stand, brush the attic dust off our clothes, and head downstairs into the bright fluorescent lights of the kitchen. There, Isadora and her mom would join us from outside, and we would finish the night's celebration with chocolate cake and ice cream.

Of course, as Ursula grew older, the day came when fireworks no longer scared her, and she would stand outside in the back yard to view them with everyone else. So, though we didn't realize it at the time, there was one evening when we watched the fireworks from behind the upstairs west window for the last time, and made the final Independence Day descent through the narrow tunnel of the walled attic stairway into the light below.

129. Cedaredge
from *Island in the Sky* by Muriel Marshall

Cedaredge advertises itself as the "Gateway to Grand Mesa." It is located at the southern end of a scenic byway (Highway 65) that crosses Grand Mesa, which is also described as the largest flat-topped mountain in the world.

If flat-topped mountain sounds like an oxymoron, it may be an especially appropriate term for the geographical paradox that is Grand Mesa. Because of the Mesa's elevation relative to the surrounding river valleys—it rises as much as 6,000 feet above the Colorado and Gunnison Rivers—it gathers lots of water from moisture-laden fronts headed east. Even though it is surrounded by arid landscapes, hundreds of lakes are scattered across the mesa as a result. But the depressions that formed these lakes were not scooped out by glaciers as is the case elsewhere in the mountains of Colorado; rather they were formed when slabs of basalt broke away from the resistant cap of the mesa. As these slabs of rock slid downhill, they left water-gathering troughs in their wake.

The lava flow that created that basalt led to another paradox in the Grand Mesa story. The top of the mesa, now the high point relative to the surrounding valleys, was at one time the lowest point in the landscape—a landscape not unlike the Grand Valley where the Colorado and Gunnison Rivers meet today. After slow-moving lava solidified in the lowest points of that ancient valley, water flowing around it eroded softer sedimentary layers and left the harder rock in place. This "topographic inversion" resulted in the Grand Mesa.

Relative to the rest of Colorado, Grand Mesa has an otherworldly quality, as suggested by the Ute word Thigunawat, *which has been translated as "the home of departed spirits."` As author Muriel Marshall demonstrates in a book called* Island in the Sky, *some locals have turned to metaphor in an effort to understand the geography of this place.*

People who live with Grand Mesa cite its brag name: "Largest Flat-top Mountain in the World," then try to bring it down to size by comparing it with something they can get a handle on ... .

Looked down upon from high enough in the air, the flat of Grand Mesa resembles a gigantic prehistoric beast with open jaws, a wriggling tongue that is Kannah Creek, bony spine that is Crag Crest, and a fat, tree-furred body rolling down to bare-belly adobe badlands above the incredibly recent towns and farms that ring it round. One of the beast's hind legs angles off toward Paonia, its tail tilts up Chalk Mountain and the iron-rich core of Electric Mountain that got its name by drawing dragon fire from thunder storms ... .

Grand Mesa, they say, is like a huge ship heading into the prevailing westerlies, riding high above turbulent seas of gray-spume 'dobie badlands.

It is like a fortress castle with rock battlements rising sheer, hundreds of feet high. As a matter of fact, it did share the name "Battlement" with its little sister mesa to the north in early Forest Service annals.

In its flatness it is so like a vast table that an early cartographer gave it the Spanish name for table – *mesa*. The table is always set for company, covered with snowy damask in winter; graced in summer with a cloth of all-over flower embroidery and set with hundreds of crystal-blue lakes. This profligate floweriness has on it another metaphorical nickname: "Roof Garden of the World."

The Mesa, they say, is like an immense layer cake topped with icing of chocolate-dark lava spread on stacked layers of strata, the whole resting on a fluted pewter cake plate of 'dobie-bordered river bottom. In this popular comparison it would be a very crumbly layer cake, held together only by the icing.

Grand Mesa is "like" so many things; but actually there is nothing else like it on earth.

130. Paonia
from "A Newcomer's Old Story" by Paul Larmer

There has always been a transient element in the Western demographic, especially in the high country of Colorado, much of which was developed around mining interests. As Wallace Stegner pointed out, there are boosters—those who are most interested in profiting from a boom, whether it involves gold and silver or real estate, and less interested in sinking down roots—and there are stickers, who are more devoted to cultivating community and a lasting sense of home. In the latter category, there are those who can claim a lifelong relationship with their home ground, and there are those, a much bigger population, who were "born elsewhere but moved to Colorado as soon as they could."

Sometimes, as demonstrated by numerous bumper stickers, "birthright" Coloradans refer to themselves as "native," but that is a problematic term when the difficult history of the Utes and other indigenous people, many of whom were forcibly removed from the state, is taken into consideration. Nevertheless, it names a way of being at home in one's place that a newcomer cannot claim, even though many of those who arrive later on in their lives develop a deep sense of rootedness in their

adapted homes. Paul Larmer, longtime editor, publisher, and now devel-
opment director of the High Country News, *a regional publication based*
in Paonia that covers environmental issues all over the West, explores
the dynamic between natives and newcomers in the following essay.

"I'm a third-generation Coloradoan," the man tells me, leaning in close
across the kitchen table inside his self-built home. "My people settled
country down in Southern Colorado."

I read between the lines: "I belong here. Do you?"

I know the answer. I am a newcomer—only five years in western
Colorado. I own a house, but I hold no title to this landscape.

I could tell him that I am a fifth-generation Californian, born in the
state that my great-great grandfather unluckily settled in the year after
the 1849 gold rush. But people here don't think much of Californians. We
are the latest invaders—and the cause of unaffordable housing and trendy
coffeehouses.

I just nod.

My companion then surprises me. "You know my wife and I are still
considered outsiders, and we've lived here twenty-one years," he says.
"Unless your kids marry into one of the old area families, you'll always
be an outsider."

That's what fascinates me about the West: It's old and new at the
same time, and there are as many shades of nativeness as there are
varieties of broken-down trucks in its weedy backyards.

I remember when rural western counties began passing ordinances
proclaiming that livestock grazing, logging, and mining were their
"custom and culture" and should be preserved no matter how destructive
or uneconomic they might be. These counties were saying "The West is
mine because I got here first."

"First" is a relative term. I loved the editorial a few years ago by a
Native American writer from Wyoming questioning the custom-and-cul-
ture crowd's sense of time. Why, Debra Thunder asked, should society
declare the recent activities of newcomers from Europe the law of the
land, while ignoring the customs and cultures of Native peoples, who
have lived on the land for hundreds of generations?

The truth is that the West has always been a place in motion, cultur-
ally and biologically. Before the mountain men were evicted by settlers,
Native tribes vied for turf and resources, pushing each other in and out of
various valleys and canyons just as surely as real-estate developers and
the people they serve now push around the "old-timers."

The only difference—and it's important—is the scale and speed of
change. Within just one century people from every nook of the United
States and from around the world have reshaped the West, blocking and
rerouting rivers, turning desert into lush agricultural fields, and, most
recently, building sprawling suburbs.

Yet we newcomers still come, drawn to a region that appears wild
and untouched next to the tamed habitats of the East. But it's not untouched. The plant and animal world is experiencing the same kind of
change as the human world. In fact, the two are inexorably linked.

Tamarisk, an Asian shrub that escaped the gardens of southern
California, chokes thousands of miles in the Colorado River drainage,
pushing out native cottonwoods and willows. Spotted knapweed, cheat-
grass, leafy spurge, and a host of other annual grasses and flowering
exotics cover millions of acres of former grasslands. European starlings
and finches dominate my bird feeder, which hangs from a Chinese elm.

I should feel at home among such exotic company, yet part of me
wants to join the loggers and ranchers to fight exotic plants and animals
and even human newcomers like myself. How can the West accommo-
date so many newcomers without losing its identity?

As a child, my family moved every three or four years on the trail of
my father's corporate career. We were American weeds, and we lodged
temporarily in Los Angeles, Chicago, St. Louis, and Philadelphia. Yet
these were never home. Family, not place, defined my home, which is
why I still search for my homeland.

I often take my children to the cemetery on the mesa above my new
town. We look out over the valley and wander among the graves, reading
the names of the families who toiled to become natives of this place. I
recognize a few of the family names, but most of them are gone. I wonder if my children will stay here or whether they, like most of the kids
around here, will drift elsewhere, like windborne seeds in search of new

ground. Will this place eventually seep into my bones, or will I always be an uncomfortable newcomer?

Last spring, a carpet of exotic tulips sprang up in the cemetery, sprinkling rainbow colors on the ground between the stones, beneath the ancient cedars. The living, the dead, the native, the introduced—all together, as if it had always been that way.

Interstate 70

Frisco to Glenwood Springs

131. Frisco / Breckenridge
from "Goldboat" by Belle Turnbull

Belle Turnbull was nine years old when her parents moved to Colorado Springs in 1890. There her father recovered his health and became the principal of Colorado Springs High School. Belle Turnbull graduated from that same high school, went on to college at Vassar, and returned to teach English at her alma mater in Colorado Springs until her retirement in 1937. She then moved to Frisco and shortly thereafter to Breckenridge where she devoted herself to writing about the mountains and the people who inhabited them. In both her poetry and prose, she described her own experiences of the mountain landscape as well as those of the entrepreneurs and laborers who struggled to make a living in nearby gold and silver mines.

As a poet, Turnbull was attentive not only to the details and nuances of mountain life, but also to the emotions that she experienced in the presence of such a landscape. In this verse from the poem, "Mountain Mad," she explores her passion for the mountains: "Timberline and the trees / Wind whipped and the sand between— / Why am I mad for these? / What dim thirst do they appease? / What filmed sense brushed clean?"

In the beginning of a poem called "Goldboat," Turnbull focuses her poetic imagination on a traveler's route through the high country of Colorado and, more specifically, through "Rockinghorse Country," which was her fictionalized name for Breckenridge, the Blue River Valley, the Ten Mile Range, and the old mining scars found there.

Over the Great Divide unrolls the highway
And cars go wagging their tails among the thunders,
Range to range stitching, weather to weather.
In half a day you can hem up the watershed

And rush on the prairie or race on the desert again
Unaware of the infinite clues of legend,
The featherstitching of roads that thread the meadows,
Follow the gulches, follow the mountain pattern.

Or a man may twist his wheel where a wild road feathers
Under a range that marches on a valley,
Turn and be gone away to Rockinghorse country,
Wind through a park beside its swaggering river,
Creep on a shelf around a rocky shoulder,
Check in a pasture, by a waterpit
Under a rocksnake of cold blue cobbles mounded.

Still pond, no moving. And a wooden bird,
A squat hightailing monstrous waterwidgeon
Diving its chain of spoonbills down and under
Red-rusted in the turquoise pit.
No moving. And no sound from the grotesque
Impossible of vision.
Only the wind,
The long, the diamond wind disturbs that water.

132. Vail
from *The Triumph of a Dream* by Peter W. Siebert

In 1957, Pete Seibert and Earl Eaton parked an army surplus jeep on the side of US Highway 6 (I-70 didn't exist at that time), strapped on their skis an hour before morning light, and started climbing. Seibert, who was thirty-two at the time, had already lived a full life. In 1943, at the age of eighteen, he had joined the army and volunteered for the 10th Mountain Division. After training as an elite ski trooper at Camp Hale (see Camp Hale entry), he went on to fight in the Battle of Riva Ridge in Italy, where he was severely wounded and told that he would be lucky to walk again, let alone ski. Several years later he became a ski patroller in Aspen, in

*1950 he made the US Alpine Ski Team, and now he was the manager of
nearby Loveland Ski Area. He was living a good life, but had another
ambition—namely, to start a new ski area. Earl Eaton, who had covered
much of the surrounding backcountry prospecting for uranium, said
he knew just the place. In his book* Triumph of a Dream, *Pete Seibert
describes their exploration on the morning of Tuesday March 29, 1957,
which eventually led to the creation of a new ski area and the adjoining
village of Vail.*

Earl Eaton had confided to me that he had seen this nameless mountain
west of Vail Pass that was rarely visited, except by stray prospectors
and shepherds. He had explored it thoroughly with his Geiger counter
ticking. There was no uranium to be mined, but he told me that it was the
damnedest ski mountain he had ever seen ... .

    Floundering upward in three feet of snow along a faintly visible
logging road, it took us two hours to slog the first two miles. I thought
of the old days in New Hampshire and the round-shouldered mountains
there. Compared to those hills, this was like climbing the Himalaya

    We climbed in soft, knee-deep powder, cutting back and forth
through the woods along a narrow skid road once used by loggers. After
almost two hours in the trees, we broke out into sunny, open terrain and
faced a vast landscape of sun-splashed snowy slopes, dotted here and
there with perfectly sculptured spruce and fir trees, rolling up the hill
almost as far as the eye could see.

    I didn't know it then, of course, but this place would become Mid
Vail, where the ski trails Swingsville, Zot, and Ramshorn would all come
together from the summit where skiers would drift off to Cookshack
Restaurant for lunch or take the Number 4 lift back to the top for another
run; or where they would head to the bottom of the ski area on trails such
as Gitalong Road and Giant Steps.

    We decided to stop for lunch: cheese, salami, good bread, and hot
sugary tea from a Thermos. Everything sparkled in the sun. I envisioned
a line of skiers charging down through the virgin powder, making braid-
ed tracks and kicking up rooster tails of snow as they swooshed past and
disappeared in the woods, doing quick turns through the trees. Across

the valley we could now see the Gore Range, mile after mile of great peaks of rock and snow.

"My God, we've climbed all the way to heaven," I said to Earl.

"It's gets better, Pete."

"From now on, I'll believe anything you say, Earl," I promised.

There was a lot more mountain to climb. The snow lay undisturbed, a peaceful glittering blanket in the noonday sun. But from the moment we stepped into the powder, we found it nearly bottomless. It flowed up to our waists as we fought our way up. We traversed back and forth up the slopes until we reached an open ridge running north-south. Of course, we couldn't know it then, but in a few years this ridge would lead skiers to runs that would become our two most famous trails: Riva Ridge and Prima, both named in memory of the harrowing days I'd spent in Italy with the 10th Mountain Division ....

We finally reached the summit—and wow! Seven exhausting hours had elapsed since we began our ascent in the morning darkness. We had climbed 3,050 vertical feet, probably covering at least eight miles in our crisscrossing back and forth. And here we were at the top—11,250 feet above sea level.

In all our backcountry explorations, we had seen nothing like this. Beneath the brilliant blue sky, we slowly turned in a circle and saw perfect ski terrain no matter which direction we faced. North back down the mountain and off to the east and the west lay miles of terrain, both steep and gentle .... And to the south was the most mind-blowing landscape of all: A series of bowls stretched to the horizon, a virtually treeless universe of boundless powder, open slopes, and open sky .... From the friendly rolling slopes near Vail Pass and Shrine Pass, we turned toward the approximate locations of Camp Hale and Leadville, thirty miles due south. We let our gaze sweep over the Sawatch Range and the majestic silhouette of Mount of the Holy Cross. It was a landscape so vast that it was best described by the name we would later pick for one of the most famous slopes of them all: Forever.

133. Vail
from *In the Shining Mountains* by David Thomson

In the Shining Mountains: A Would-Be Mountain Man in Search of the Wilderness *is a little known and underappreciated travelogue through the contemporary Rocky Mountains. Like so many others who have come west with high hopes for a new life in an idealized Rocky Mountain region, Minnesotan David Thomson embarked on a modern-day odyssey to find a true home in wild country. Steeped in the lore of previous western explorers, specifically early day trappers like Jim "Old Gabe" Bridger, he detailed his travels with a keen eye for the landscape as well as an alter ego ("Old Gabe" himself) who sees the world from an old trapper's perspective. In an odd turn of events following the publication of* In the Shining Mountains *back in 1979, David Thomson disappeared. Last seen in Minnetonka, Minnesota, he was apparently headed back west, perhaps to Montana. We may never know whether he found what he was looking for, but he left his readers an amusing take on the contemporary West as imagined on a previous journey with "Old Gabe," his alter ego. In this passage, "Old Gabe" offers a little commentary on contemporary mountain culture as he finds it in the upscale ski town of Vail.*

Fort Vail was crawling with people; the ski hills above the town looked like white anthills. Expensive cars were pouring into the valley in a steady stream, bumper to bumper. Everywhere you looked they were building new lodges. The deer and elk had to cross the freeway in a big steel culvert—there was no other way for them to get over.

I was hungry. I didn't have no more sausage and I barely had enough plews to feed my mule. I set out hunting, but I couldn't get away from them lodges. They was everywhere. They were shaped like a big "A," and they had lots of glass in the ends and balconies for people to be seen from. They stood up there with drinks in their hands, dressed in fine sweaters and tight red or blue leggings, and glanced down their noses at me with looks that would injure a cactus. I went on down the valley and it was the same everywhere. It was all glass, envy, and lipstick. They all had big champion dogs that cost a fortune and chased deer. When they

came back from killing one of the few deer that were left, the people put
them on leashes, put on their jazzy outfits, and strolled through town,
pretending what a hard time they were having with such a big, handsome,
and extraordinarily stupid pedigree dog. I almost shot one of them to eat
but its owners came out of the store. They walked on down the street,
smiling at the people who obviously had money. At night they murdered
each other in their dreams.

   I was down and out. I kept on hunting. Game was fearsome scarce.
I looked in the aspen groves, up the draws, and over the ridges of low
hills. All I found were the A-shaped lodges, and huge gleaming gas hogs
driving up and down over the hills. One man came out on his balcony
in a silk robe and yelled at me to get off his property. He took off a pair
of twenty-two-dollar fireplace slippers and threw them at me one after
the other, yelling that he was going to call the police. I told him to shut
up; I retrieved the slippers, went into town, and sold them to an aspiring
young hotel clerk for four dollars. I continued hunting. Finally, I caught
sign of some Big Macs. I trailed them across a broad expanse of Formica
counter, and kilt two of them near a painting of a river bordered all
around by plastic elderberry bushes. I hated myself when I killed the Big
Macs. I was convinced they were laced with heroin.

   I had enough. It was no place for a mountain man to be. In the town you
had to have a Master Charge card to take a deep breath. That night I found
a Cadillac parked behind a building and siphoned enough gas to drive to St.
Louis and back. I took off in a snowstorm. The fall hunt was over.

   I went north on the Blue River, then east up the Colorado River and
across the slopes of Shadow Mountain, where the aspen trees stood bare
against the sky. It was growing in me to quit the Colorado territory and
strike out for the Northwest.

134. Glenwood Springs
from *Fire on the Mountain* by John N. Maclean

A sculpture in the middle of Two Rivers Park in Glenwood Springs,
memorializes the wildland firefighters who lost their lives in a fire on
Storm King Mountain west of town. It was especially hot and dry on July
2, 1994, when a lightning strike ignited the fire. One of many burning
in the area, the South Canyon Fire was small at first, allowing district
firefighters to focus on bigger blazes in the Grand Junction district.
But with increasing winds, the fire began to spread. Plentiful fuels and
challenging terrain made it increasingly difficult to contain. By July
5, fifty firefighters were struggling to establish and maintain fire lines.
On the morning of July 6, a helicopter pilot was flying giant buckets in
and dousing the fire from the air. That afternoon, a dry cold front came
through and gusting winds changed direction. Forty-five-mile-an-hour
blasts of wind fanned the flames into an inferno that took fourteen lives.

A trail on Storm King mountain, which is about seven miles west of
Glenwood and just to the north of I-70, is also dedicated to the memory
of those who died that day. In his book, Fire on the Mountain, *John N.*
Maclean tells the story of the South Canyon Fire and helps readers ap-
preciate the great courage and commitment required of those who choose
the vocation of wildland firefighting. Dick Good the helicopter pilot who
was flying buckets of water in that day, thought he might be able to help
evacuate some of the firefighters who were trapped on a ridge after the
wind had suddenly changed direction. But conditions in the air rapidly
deteriorated. His heart-wrenching view of the scene from the air, as
described by Maclean, captures some of the terror that firefighters must
have experienced.

In the few moments it had taken him to jettison the bucket, Hell's Gate
Ridge and its human cargo had disappeared behind a thundering column
of gray-black smoke. The mushrooming cloud blotted out the top of
Hell's Gate Ridge, along with Blanco's firefighters, half the Prineville
Hot Shots, Tyler and Browning and the west-flank line with its smoke
jumpers and hotshots.

The sky over the Colorado River remained a brilliant blue with a few lingering clouds, as though it were nothing but a pleasant summer afternoon. Good could fly toward the river, half-circle Hell's Gate Ridge and come to the ridgetop from the opposite direction, from the East Canyon side. It was the only chance left.

Good turned 93 Romeo away from the erupting smoke column. Once over the Colorado River, he turned into the river gorge in the direction of Glenwood Springs. He flew with the wind at his back, past the stubby outcropping of Hell's Gate Point overlooking the river, past Hell's Gate, where Blanco's crew had started from that morning, until he could look back at the East Canyon.

He flew into the smoke haze over the East Canyon and headed for Hell's Gate Ridge.

Good began calling Tyler and Browning but again heard no answer. The two helicopter crewmen must be somewhere along Hell's Gate Ridge—why didn't they respond?

Above him a curtain of black smoke ran across the sky like a squall line, pouring toward him over Hell's Gate Ridge. Its frontal edge had a curling lip.

Good felt wind pressure build on 93 Romeo as he ascended parallel to and just below the ridgetop, under the roof of smoke. He used plenty of "cross-control" leaning the craft to counter the effect of the wind. Dirt, sticks and leaves blew through his rotor wash and into the helicopter's doorway, stinging his face. Even a momentary lull would set 93 Romeo turning cartwheels, but now he had a clear view along the top of the ridge.

Tyler and Browning were nowhere in sight. Instead, Good saw a "wide, wide flame front" beginning to rise on the far side of the ridge. In seconds a rescue pickup of anyone would be impossible. "Rich, Rob, where are you, guys? Come on!" he called. The radio had become a blare of voices without names shouting orders, questions of orders and reversed orders, but nothing from Tyler or Browning.

Then, as if by magic or theatrical direction, a line of firefighters in anonymous yellow shirts and green pants appeared out of the smoke, running along the ridgetop toward the helispot, H2. They were two hundred yards from H2, then one hundred.

Behind them an enormous wave of flame arose from the western drainage and began to sweep the ridgetop, driving the firefighters before it. It swelled to a height of 50, 100 and then 150 feet. It moved faster than any human could run; everything was happening too fast. The flame wave began to break over the ridgetop, transforming the people into surfers riding the curl of a scarlet-orange wave of fire. One by one they peeled off the ridgetop ahead of the wave, heading into the East Canyon. Good saw small fires beginning to burn in the canyon.

The shouts on the radio died out; there were no orders left to give or reverse. Good heard a click as someone keyed a transmitter, and then a scream, a long AAAAHHHH without identifying name or gender. The scream ended, or more accurately, the transmission broke off, and the radio went silent.

Why the hell didn't someone scream five minutes earlier, when there'd been time to do something? Good thought. He let 93 Romeo slip away from the ridge and instantly lost touch with the wind. He flew out of the East Canyon, over the blue band of the Colorado River, and landed in the meadow at Canyon Creek Estates. One of the helicopter's ground crew, Steve Little, rushed up to 93 Romeo. Good sat slumped in his seat.

"They're gone," Good said. "They're all burned over."

Highway 82
Glenwood Springs to Aspen

135. Woody Creek
from "Tentative Platform, Thompson for Sheriff"
by Hunter S. Thompson

Hunter Thompson (1937-2005), legendary journalist, jester, author, and longtime resident of Woody Creek (and the Woody Creek Tavern), famously ran for sheriff of Aspen in 1970 on the Freak Power Ticket. After getting beat up by the Chicago police at the Democratic convention in 1968, and after Nixon's re-election, Thompson had decided that the kind of political change he wanted was unlikely on the national level, at least in the near future, so he directed his concerns to the local scene, campaigning for a progressive mayoral candidate in Aspen named Joe Edwards. It was during that race that Thompson put forward the term "Freak Power" to help mobilize youthful resistance against the more entrenched conservative forces intent on developing Aspen and the Roaring Fork Valley.

Edwards lost the election by only a handful of votes, convincing Thompson that there really was a viable Freak Power constituency. With that in mind, he decided to run for sheriff on the Freak Power ticket. He shaved his head so that he could refer to the crew-cutted ex-army incumbent as "my long-haired opponent." His antics and the notion of Freak Power got the media's attention. Correspondents from the BBC, New York Times, *and* Time Magazine *showed up in Aspen hungry for the story.*

Thompson's own writings appeared for the first time in a fledgling magazine called Rolling Stone, *which would continue to be a venue for his pioneering style of "gonzo journalism"—an unconventional style to say the least, which incorporated first-person commentary, social critique, and self-satire. Like his platform for sheriff, which was featured in his first dispatch to* Rolling Stone, *his writing combined*

serious and comedic elements. Although he lost his run for sheriff, his
articles and books won him a large and devoted audience. Here is an
excerpt from his now famous political manifesto.

Tentative Platform
Thompson for Sheriff
Aspen, Colorado, 1970

1. Sod the streets at once. Rip up all city streets with jackhammers and
use the junkasphalt (after melting) to create a huge parking auto-storage
lot on the outskirts of town—preferably somewhere out of sight … All
public movement would be by foot and a fleet of bicycles, maintained by
the city police force.

2. Change the name "Aspen" by public referendum, to "Fat City." This
would prevent greedheads, land-rapers and other human jackals from capi-
talizing on the name "Aspen." Thus, Snowmass-at-Aspen—recently sold to
Kaiser/Aetna of Oakland—would become "Snowmass-at-Fat City." Aspen
Wildcat—whose main backers include the First National City Bank of New
York and the First Boston Capital Corp.—would have to be called "Fat
City Wildcat." All roadsigns and roadmaps would have to be changed from
Aspen to "Fat City." The local Post Office and Chamber of Commerce
would have to honor the new name. "Aspen," Colo. would no longer exist—
and the psychic alterations of this change would be massive in the world of
commerce: Fat City Ski Fashions, the Fat City Slalom Cup, Fat City Music
Festival, Fat City Institute for Humanistic Studies … Changing the name of
the town would have no major effect on the town itself, or on those people
who came here because it's a good place to *live*. What effect the name-
change might have on those who came here to buy low, sell high and then
move on is fairly obvious … and eminently desirable. These swine should
be fucked, broken and driven across the land.

3. Drug Sales must be controlled. My first act as Sheriff will be to install,
on the courthouse lawn, a bastinado platform and a set of stocks—in order to punish dishonest dope dealers in a proper public fashion. Each year

these deals cheat millions of people out of millions of dollars. As a breed, they rank with sub-dividers and used car salesmen and the Sheriff's Dept. will gladly hear complaints against dealers at any hour of the day or night, with immunity from prosecution guaranteed to the complaining party—provided the complaint is valid....it will be the general philosophy of the Sheriff's office that *no* drug worth taking should be sold for money. Non-profit sales will be viewed as borderline cases, and judged on their merits. But *all* sales for money-profit will be punished severely. This approach, we feel, will establish a unique and very human *ambiance* in the Aspen (or Fat City) drug culture—which is already so much a part of our local reality that only a Falangist lunatic would talk about trying to "eliminate it." The only realistic approach is to make life in this town very ugly for *all* profiteers—in drugs and all other fields.

4. Hunting and fishing should be forbidden to *all* non-residents, with the exception of those who can obtain the signed endorsement of a resident— who will then be legally responsible for any violation or abuse committed by the non-resident he has "signed for." Fines will be heavy and the general policy will be Merciless Prosecution of All Offenders. But—as in the case of the proposed city name-change—this "Local Endorsement" plan should have no effect on anyone except greedy, dangerous kill-freaks who are a menace wherever they go. This new plan would have no effect on residents—except those who chose to *endorse* visiting "sportsmen." Making hundreds or even thousands of individuals personally responsible for protecting the animals, fish and birds who live here would create a sort of de facto game preserve, without the harsh restrictions that will necessarily be forced on us if these blood-thirsty geeks keep swarming in here each autumn to shoot everything they see.

5. The Sheriff and his Deputies should *never* be armed in public. Every urban riot, shoot-out and blood-bath (involving guns) in recent memory has been set off by some trigger-happy cop in a fear frenzy. And no cop in Aspen has had to use a gun for so many years that I feel safe in offering a $12 cash award to anybody who can recall such an incident in writing. (Box K-3, Aspen). Under normal circumstances a pistol-grip

Mace-bomb, such as the MK-V made by Gen. Ordnance, is more than
enough to quickly wilt any violence-problem that is likely to emerge in
Aspen. And anything the MK-V can't handle would require reinforce-
ments anyway ... in which case the response would be geared at all times
to Massive Retaliation: a brutal attack with guns, bombs, pepper-foggers,
wolverines and all other weapons deemed necessary to restore the civic
peace. The whole notion of disarming the police is to *lower* the level of
violence while guaranteeing, at the same time, a terrible punishment to
anyone stupid enough to attempt violence on an un-armed cop.

6. It will be the policy of the Sheriff's office to savagely harass all those
engaged in any form of land-rape. This will be done by acting, with
utmost dispatch, on any and all righteous complaints. My first act in
office—after setting up the machinery for punishing dope dealers—will
be to establish a Research Bureau to provide facts on which any citizen can file a Writ of Seizure, a Writ of Stoppage, a Writ of Fear, of
Horror ... yes ... even a Writ of Assumption ... against any greedhead
who has managed to get around our antiquated laws and set up a tar-vat,
scum-drain or gravel pit. These writs will be pursued with overweening
zeal ... and always within the letter of the law. Selah.

136. Aspen
from *Notes of a Half-Aspenite* by Bruce Berger

*Poet and nonfiction writer Bruce Berger, who grew up in the suburbs
of Chicago, first came to Aspen in 1952 to visit a sister who had moved
to the Mountain West. At that time, Aspen was still rough enough
around the edges, as would befit a former gold and silver town. For
someone seeking an alternative to the conformist ethos of that decade,
it offered a relatively inexpensive and otherworldly destination, where
it was possible to live a life outside of the mainstream. As Berger's
visits became longer and more frequent, Aspen established itself as a
bohemian stronghold in the midst of the Rockies, celebrating music, the
arts, the great outdoors, and the good life that all of that implied.*

In 1968, he bought a cabin next to his sister's house. After that, he
was an Aspen resident, though not necessarily full time since he also
had a passion for desert places, like the Baja regions of Mexico where
he spent time every year. For that reason, and with the wry sense of hu-
mor that permeates so many of his essays and poems, Berger referred
to himself as a "half-Aspenite." In the following excerpt from the book
Aspen: Notes of a Half-Aspenite, *he offers a few reflections on how the*
town has evolved over the last half century or so.

On learning you are a resident, the visitor automatically asks, "For how
long?" If the figure is substantial, the visitor responds, "You must have
seen lots of changes." The obligatory reply is, "Yes." There follows a pair
of questions, posed in one breath so that you can't answer one and evade
the other. "What are the changes? Are they for the better or the worse?"

Well. Since you ask. Aspen, believe it or not, was once a famously
cheap place to live. It had nature and the arts, and because tourism was
just getting off the ground, there were lots of jobs. As a semi-abandoned
mining town full of old buildings that needed patching, there were also
lots of places to live. In the conformist rat race of postwar America,
Aspen was a target for defection, and more and more people defected.
Ninety percent of the surrounding land belonged, as it still does, to the
US Forest Service, leaving a limited amount of private land—mostly
valley bottom—to live on. Supply and demand was fate. Non-conformist
hordes descended upon limited living space and prices shot up. The
pioneering bohemians, some of them artistic and some merely colorful,
could no longer afford the place and moved out. A few skiers and party-
goers discovered their inner realtor, sold their modest digs for a fortune,
and stuck around to sell other people's digs for a commission. For reasons never wholly clear, rich people were not, socially, as enriching as
the poor people they replaced. Dress codes started stressing respectabil-
ity, regulations curbed spontaneity and architectural dilapidation turned
to spiffiness. Dollar spaghetti became twenty-dollar fusilli.

At this point the visitor, glazing, is sorry to have asked, but the local
is warming to the theme. As prices rose, landlords preferred renting to
wealthy outsiders. The workforce moved down valley, often into trailer

courts that reproduced the crowding and regimentation they had come
to escape. Employees now had to commute, congesting the highway
that the Colorado Department of Transportation wanted to unkink and
reslot through my house. Those who wanted to preserve open land and
those who preferred smooth transportation and affordable housing were
thus pitted against each other, even though each side had worthy goals.
Parking downtown was harder to find, even as downtown lost much of its
attraction. The vacant lots I had known as a teenager had been quickly
filled in, often with structures that were replaced with larger structures.
The first visitor-oriented stores were small and owned by families and
individuals, typified by a French vendor of exotic clothing who enlisted
the town in an annual celebration of Bastille Day. As rents went up,
downtown spaces were bought out by chains: Banana Republic, Eddie
Bauer, The Gap. There was no longer a bar where locals gathered, knowing they would encounter other locals, and bartenders admitted cranking
up the heavy metal so they didn't have to listen to the clientele. When
the formerly despised franchises were eventually replaced by real estate
offices and time-share emporia, downtown merchants protested that
shoppers were fleeing because we were losing all our best chains: Banana
Republic, Eddie Bauer, The Gap...

At this point the visitor is gazing past the local's head, trying to find
some nice fellow tourist to talk to, even as the local is finally coming to
the point. Aspen used to be a single-class town. Lift operators and taxi
drivers and cabinet secretaries met socially as equals, indistinguishable
until someone asked their line of work. Now, beneath a crust that attended
arts benefits in black tie, there is a hierarchy of cliques as clearly defined
in Aspen's tiny glass as a poussie-café. The bed-making and cooking jobs,
once held by American dropouts symbolized by that fantasy hero, the
dishwashing PhD, have been taken over by Latin Americans, mostly from
Mexico and El Salvador. The latter phenomenon adds a new and unhealthy
racial cast to class stratification, and because it came into full force as I
started spending half-years in Mexico, I occasionally found myself at parties where I identified more with the help than the host. But the visitor has
heard enough. The local, seeing his victim is about to dash for a chardon-
nay refill, smiles desperately and blurts, "But don't get me started."

Interstate 70
Parachute to Fruita

137. Parachute
from *Where the Water Goes* by David Owen

"Fracking" is the process of injecting a pressurized fluid into a subterranean rock formation in order to fracture the strata and access reserves of oil and natural gas. Although previous attempts had been made, application of the technique wasn't commercially successful until 1950. Now it is a common practice on the Western Slope and elsewhere in Colorado, much to the dismay of those concerned about limited water resources and their possible contamination.

In 1969, an unusual experiment to improve fracking methodology took place in a mountain valley six miles from Parachute. The goal of Project Rulison was to test the feasibility of using nuclear "stimulation techniques" in the fracking process. In other words, the idea was to explode atomic bombs underground in order to "shake loose" natural gas reserves.

Project Rulison, which was part of Plowshare, a federal program to develop non-military uses for nuclear weapons, took place under the auspices of the University of California and the Los Alamos National Laboratory. In a film released by the Lab to introduce the plan, a narrator described Project Rulison as a "unique experiment" and explained how it would work: "A nuclear explosive, equal to forty thousand tons of TNT, will be used to shake loose a great natural-gas reserve locked tightly in a formation called the Mesa Verde …. The energy released by the nuclear explosion will melt and vaporize nearby rock and will fracture the rock beyond to a diameter of about 740 feet. As the cavity cools, the vaporized and melted rock will collect in a puddle at the bottom, and most of the radioactivity will be entrapped here, as it solidifies."

Most of the radioactivity? Some residents of the Western Slope were understandably concerned. In his book Where the Water Goes: The Life and Death of the Colorado River, *David Owen describes the test and its aftermath.*

Project Rulison attracted protests, but not as many as you would think. The detonation took place on September 10, 1969—three weeks after Woodstock. On the *CBS Evening News* that night, Terry Drinkwater reported that "not everyone was happy" about the test, and that roughly a hundred protesters had "marched on the observation tent" (carrying signs that said, among other things, "Kill Nature for Gas?"). The demonstration was orderly, however, and the blast went off as planned. "The earth shook like jelly, there was a muffled sound, block and dirt shook loose from surrounding mesas," Drinkwater continued. "In Grand Valley, a few bricks fell from a few buildings." Workers with Geiger counters checked the site for contamination—"They found none"—and the crew at the control center celebrated with champagne.

Prematurely, it turned out. The explosion freed what was estimated to be 455 million cubic feet of gas. That was disappointingly less than the experts had predicted, and, worse, the gas was rendered unusable by high levels of tritium, a radioactive isotope of hydrogen ....

Nineteen sixty-nine wasn't that long ago. How could responsible adults so late in the twentieth century have thought that using nuclear weapons to create natural-gas wells could be a good idea?

Given the release of radioactivity in that first experiment, it would be hard to find fault with Owen's critique. And yet, as his retelling points out, there were those in the Atomic Energy Commission who insisted on repeating the test with an even bigger explosion.

Three and a half years later the AEC [Atomic Energy Commission] tried again, thirty miles northwest of Rulison, on the other side of the river at Rio Blanco. This time the principal industrial partner was Continental Oil Company, and there were three nuclear devices, totaling one hundred kilotons. They were placed in a single shaft, separated from one another vertically by roughly four hundred feet, and detonated almost simultaneously. Once again, the liberated gas was radioactive and there was much

less of it than the experts had predicted .... If the AEC's scientists had
believed that increasing the power of nuclear blast by 150 percent would
eliminate the resulting radiation, they were disappointed.

138. Grand Junction
from *Eclipse* by Dalton Trumbo

*If you stroll through downtown Grand Junction, you will find a unique
sculpture at the corner of Main and 7th. The naked man in the bronze
bathtub, with a cigarette in one hand and a cup of coffee nearby, is
screenwriter and novelist Dalton Trumbo, working the way he liked to
work.*

*Born in Montrose in 1905, Trumbo grew up in Grand Junction where
he began his writing life as a cub reporter for the* Sentinel, *covering high
school life, the courts, the mortuary, and civic organizations. By the time
he graduated from high school and went on to the University of Colorado,
he knew the nuances of his town as only a reporter does. Later on, in his
first novel,* Eclipse, *and in* Johnny Get Your Gun, *one of his most famous
screenplays, he would return to his memories of those early years in
Grand Junction.*

*Trumbo faced many challenges along the way to his screenwriting
successes in Hollywood. He spent his first ten years in California working at a bakery to help his family through the depression years. After
he had established himself as a screenwriter, he was found guilty of
contempt for refusing to testify in House of Representative hearings on
communist influences in the movie industry. Blacklisted after a year of
incarceration, he survived by writing under a pseudonym, producing
such screenplays as* Roman Holiday *and* The Brave One *which were honored with Academy Awards. Many years later in 2017, a bio-pic called*
Trumbo, *starring Bryan Cranston, told the story of his Hollywood career.*

Eclipse, *his first novel, described the rise and fall of businessman
John Abbot in the town of Shale City, a thinly veiled version of Grand
Junction. When* Eclipse *was originally published in 1935, some locals
resented his fictionalized version of their hometown. But over time, more*

readers came to appreciate Trumbo's work, which the Mesa County
Library Foundation reprinted in 2005. This description, which follows
John Abbot on a late afternoon stroll through the downtown business dis-
trict, portrays a man who appreciated his hometown, as Trumbo clearly
did, despite his willingness to consider its faults as well.

The day wore on. The sun imperceptibly dipped toward a ragged western
horizon, its blinding white now softened to bloodshot yellows. But still it
hung reluctantly above the mountain tops for a period, whirling insanely,
spinning out great wheels of color before its ultimate surrender to evening.
Shadows struck mightily toward the east, and Shale City gasped with relief.

Main Street took on pleasant, neighborly animation with the six o'clock
closing of its stores. Merchants lingered before their stores gossiping
with last-minute customers. Shoppers with bags suspended limply over
their arms sauntered homeward through a dusty red haze. Boys and girls
strolled together or chattered shrilly in little groups. Children on roller
skates dodged breathlessly in and out of recessed store entrances, pursued
by excited mongrel dogs. The street was filled with automobiles roaring
from the kerb, sparring for position in the sudden flow of traffic. Over the
scene hovered the odour of cooling tar-paper from store roofs, of gasoline
fumes from hot exhaust pipes, of sticky bodies turning dry as the evening
carried a faint, cool smell of sweet clover from the river. It was the good
time of day, the carnival time of day, the restful time of day: there was no
more work to be done, and soon the earth would begin to cool.

John Abbot walked slowly through the middle aisle of the Emporium
nodding benignly to right and left as he bade his clerks good night. He
had to go to the Y.M.C.A. for a banquet which was scheduled to begin at
seven o'clock. That left him an hour to kill. Donna Long had gone home
from the store a few minutes early. He wished she had waited to talk with
him. He felt a little lonely. But he supposed she was exhausted with the
heat … . Poor girl! Poor, tired girl! He wished she had stayed.

In the cauterized outer air he paused a moment, trying to think of
something to do. Then he walked very slowly along the Main Street and
Fifth Street windows of The Emporium. Fred Best had just completed a
new window trim. John Abbot inspected it with careful satisfaction.

He stood at the corner, peacefully aloof from the throng of passers-by,
inflamed in the nimbus of a dying sun. He loved this moment of the day.
People ceased to be workers and miraculously were transformed into free
creatures once again. They were filled with unconscious speculation con-
cerning the idleness of the evening to come. Soon there would be family
reunions across supper tables laden with well-done steak and mashed potatoes and garden salad and rich, home-made cake. And afterwards, would
they go for a ride through the warm twilight? Would they treat themselves
to a movie? Would they walk in that little park which fringed the river near
the bridge? Or would they sit on the screen-porch with their shoes off and
their throats bare, reading *The Saturday Evening Post*?

He sighed a little enviously, and walked across the street towards
Mrs. Alloway's establishment. He was not going to eat, but the old
building which housed the cafeteria offered a front veranda with wicker
rocking chairs, screened by woodbines to furnish a measure of privacy
from the street. He would go over and sit down for the idle hour, watching the people pass by, soaking himself in the heat which, at this time of
day—provided you were in the shade—was tranquil and delicious.

139. Fruita
from a letter by John Otto

*In 1906, an itinerant laborer named John Otto came to the Grand Valley
and took a job on a waterline construction project between Pinon Mesa
and the town of Fruita. The more he became acquainted with the local topography, the more he wanted to stay: "I came here last year and found
these canyons and they feel like the heart of the world to me," he wrote.
"I'm going to stay and build trails and promote this place, because it
should be a national park."*

*There were those who dismissed the "hermit of Monument Canyon."
Some people thought that he was crazy, others said he was just a "be-
nign but enthusiastic eccentric." He was clearly passionate about his
work. Almost single-handedly, he built trails into the canyon country that
he loved, took every opportunity to promote it, and helped to initiate the*

campaign to make it a park. The Grand Junction Sentinel *praised his efforts: "John Otto is a patriot to the core and in his work of making the Monument canyon a place of historic value as well as a scenic resort, he should receive the heartiest support and encouragement of the people of this valley. He is doing for love and public spirit, a work which few men would undertake even for monetary compensation."*

Shortly after Colorado National Monument was established in 1911, Otto was appointed park superintendent, a position that earned him a dollar a month until he left the job in 1929. Throughout his residency in the area, he was a tireless promoter and a prolific letter writer to local papers. The editors readily published his letters, which were often entertaining, if not "enthusiastically eccentric." In this letter, he recalls an early visit to the Grand Valley which is still known for its agricultural abundance.

I doubt if any one loves the Big Red Apple more than I do, and it's the truth, ever since I first came through Grand Valley from California to Denver, and at the time bought apples from the boys in front of the old depot in Grand Junction, while the train changed engines, ever since I came over from Glenwood, (over a year upwards) into the east end of this county and cleared one (just one) acre of sage brush and ever since the time (my fourth time into Grand Valley) when I came over from White River down Salt Creek to the desert and on to Fruita, and there, for the first time picked apples in Grand Valley and then left for Nevada, ever since the time when I returned in the Spring and was there when the mountain road was started, to help drill the first hole, to bust the first big rock, fired there the first shot and stayed with the work to bring the First Mountain water into Grand Valley—ever since then I cease—that is I pray no more "Thy Kingdom Come"— for I know the Kingdom is here: King Apple's Kingdom. The love we have for our country, for our flag, is the same love we have for the Big Red Apple. Of course, anyone who's light is dim can't see that the Kingdom is here. I haven't been in Fruita since last September. I hope I won't "get lost" whenever the time comes that I go there again for they say Fruita is growing fast.

Highway 40

Empire to Kremmling

140. Empire / Berthoud Pass
Notes on Charlie Utter

Charlie Utter may be best known now for his friendship with Wild Bill Hickok, with whom he traveled to Deadwood, South Dakota in the 1870s. But prior to his Black Hills adventures, he had already established his reputation as a trapper, prospector, and guide here in the mountains around Berthoud Pass and north into the Middle Park region of Colorado. On March 23, 1865, the Daily Miner's Register *in Central City offered this description of his activities in the area.*

Mr. Utter has been living secluded in the heart of the unexplored regions of our far western mountain ranges.... Hunting and trapping has been his occupation, and he informs us that it has proved a lucrative one indeed. No other human being is living within miles of him and he reigns sole monarch of all he surveys, capturing the beasts and birds for valuable pelts, quite in an undisturbed and easy manner. He was seven days coming over the mountains to this place and walked 80 miles of the distance on snow shoes.

A few years later, he set up a guide and livery business here in Empire where he apparently cut a striking figure according to the author of an article that appeared in Scribner's Monthly:

Our guide is Charlie Utter, who furnishes the twenty-eight saddle horses and the double wagon required by our somewhat numerous party. Dressed in his trapper-suit, Charlie presents a figure well worth looking at. Buckskin coat and pantaloons—the latter ornamented with a leather fringe and two broad stripes of handsome bead-work; the former bordered with a similar fringe rimmed by a band of otter fur, and

embroidered on the back and sleeves with many-colored beads, the handi-
work of a Sioux squaw, and a wonderful specimen of Indian skill; vest of
buckskin tanned with the hair on, and clasped with immense bear-claws
instead of buttons; pistol, knife, and tomahawk in belt, the belt-buckle of
Colorado silver and very large; a broad-brimmed hat and stout mocca-
sins;—these are the externals of this famous Rocky Mountain guide.

*Samuel Bowles, a newspaper editor from Springfield, Massachusetts
included this account of a trip up Berthoud Pass with Charlie Utter in
his book* Our New West, *which was published in 1869. Thunder and snow
up on Berthoud Pass in August were no longer amusing novelties for
Utter who Bowles described as "a famous mountaineer, trapper, Indian
scout, rover, such a character as only the American border can breed,
small and tough, wiry and witty, intelligent and handsome, alike at home
in your parlor or an Indian hut, and to whom all these mountains and
parks are as familiar as your own paternal acres are to yourself."*

The promised view of park and plains, of range on range was lost; only
thick, dark clouds, hanging over impenetrable abysses, were around and
below us; the storm bit like wasps; beards gathered snow and ice; the
mules and horses winced under the blasts .... But there was exhilaration
in the unseasonable struggle; there was something jolly in the idea
of confounding the almanacs and finding February in August. At the
summit of the Pass—thirteen thousand feet high—the storm abated its
intensity to let us dismount and pick out of the snow the little yellow
flowers that crept up among the rocks everywhere. Then it rolled over
again, and now with thunder and lightning, pealing and flashing close
around us. Here our laggard pack mules and their drivers came hurrying
up and forward. Charlie Utter said, as he spurred them by, that perhaps
we might like it, but for him "hell was pleasanter and safer than a thunderstorm on the range."

141. Granby / Hot Sulphur Springs
from *Colorado: A Summer Trip* by Bayard Taylor

American novelist, poet, translator, and literary critic Bayard Taylor was one of the most accomplished travel writers of his time. Although he was more concerned about his reputation as a poet, his letters from faraway places, many of them published in the New York Tribune, *won him the most notoriety and acclaim. Mark Twain was among his travel companions on journeys that included adventures in Africa, Europe, and Asia. In 1866, Taylor saddled up with a party that included William Byers, editor of the* Rocky Mountain News, *and ventured forth into the high country of Colorado, traversing the Front Range, Middle Park, the Gore Range, the Upper Arkansas River Valley, and then circling back through South Park to Denver. The letters he sent to the* New York Tribune *were gathered into a book called* Colorado: A Summer Trip, *which was published in 1867. In this passage, he describes his ride through Middle Park, passing by the present-day location of Granby (which was established in 1904 along the route of the Denver, Northwestern, and Pacific Railway) and camping across the Colorado River (then known as the Grand) from the hot sulphur springs for which the town is named.*

The animals occasioned us much trouble during this day's journey. Our little black pack-mule, Peter, has a diabolical knack of shifting his load, so that the proper balance is lost, and the pack saddle turns .... We were obliged to drive with us an Arapahoe mare, belonging to the new herd, and a more outrageous creature never grazed. By some sort of animal magnetism, she immediately took command of all our horses and mules, and yet never lost an opportunity of biting, kicking, and driving them from the trail. The more violent her behavior toward them, the more they were fascinated with her. Her vicious eyes were always on the lookout; while we watched her all was quiet, but the minute we became absorbed in the scenery or some topic of conversation, she would dash at one of the animals and break up the line of march. White confessed that she had exasperated him to such a pitch that he shot at her, and was now sorry that he missed.

Gradually, climbing the hills, among beds of crimson and violet lupins, scarlet star-flowers and many showy unknown plants, we came at last to a divide, whence the trail sloped down to the valley of the Grand River at the hot springs, now four miles distant. Mr. Byers pointed out a bluff covered with scattering clumps of red cedar, as the objective point of our day's journey. On our right towered a lofty ridge thrusting out buttresses of perpendicular rock, crowned with pines; and beyond the Grand River arose a similar, but much grander and more abrupt formation. Between the two, the river issued, winding away westward among green interlocking hills, until we could only guess its gateway out of the Park among some snow peaks, thirty or forty miles away.

The prospect of a sulphur bath helped us over the remainder of the way, and in another hour we dismounted in a meadow on the banks of the Grand River, directly opposite to the hot springs. Mr. Byers looked at the stream, and meditated; White did the same thing. It was fluid ice (for coldness), forty or fifty yards wide, swift as an arrow, and evidently too deep to ford. On the opposite bank we saw a rough log-cabin, on a little knoll, and a stream of white, smoking water tumbling down a rock into a smoking pool below. Forms were moving among some cottonwoods on the river bottom; their red blankets announced they were Indians. While we were hesitating, some rheumatic eremite whom White knew, came down to the bank, and with much difficulty shouted across the roar of the water, that it was impossible to cross. . . .

It was finally decided that we should camp where we were, and those who wished to visit the hot springs should swim the river. White and I stripped to our shirts and drawers, mounted our animals bare-backed, and rode down to the water. While we were trying to force them in, they refusing with all their might, we were again hailed from the other side, and warned against making the attempt. A short distance below us the river entered a canyon, and became a cataract. This fact combined with the fearful coldness and swiftness of the current made us pause. It was no doubt well that we did so, well that we silently turned and rode back to the camp . . . .

Fortunately, there was more wind and thunder than rain . . . . We made our bed on the wet earth, expecting to be rained on during the night; but the heavens were merciful and we enjoyed sound and tolerably dry sleep.

I experienced three distinct electric shocks, probably from the fact that
I was insulated by the India-rubber cloth upon which I lay, and touched
the earth with my hand. On the snowy ranges persons are sometimes so
charged that there are sparks and crackling sounds at every movement of
their bodies. Men unacquainted with the phenomenon imagine that bees
have gotten into their hair and that rattlesnakes are at their heels. Many
strange stories are told of the effect … , which seems to manifest itself in
an eccentric but not a dangerous form.

142. Kremmling
from "Mountain Medicine Man" by Evan Edwards

*In 1926, Kremmling, Colorado was still an isolated outpost, but there
were some doctors who preferred such places, perhaps as a matter of
service, but maybe too for the adventure of practicing in a small mountain community. In an article that first appeared in* Empire Magazine
(part of the Denver Post's *Sunday edition for many years), Evan
Edwards offered this portrait of Archer Chester Sudan, MD, one such
mountain medic. It was later reprinted in an anthology called* Rocky
Mountain Empire, *which included many off-the-beaten-path* Empire
features from around the state.

It was the night of September 23, 1926, and in a Philadelphia ring Jack
Dempsey and Gene Tunney were banging away at each other with the
heavyweight boxing championship of the world in the balance.

Up in Grand County, Colorado, a group of men huddled about the
telegrapher in the railroad office, listening intently as he translated the
stutter of the telegraph instrument reporting the progress of the fight
above the din of a raging rain and windstorm. Among the figures in the
smoke-filled little room was a tall, husky chap with sandy hair—Archer
Chester Sudan, M.D., the new doctor—who had been in the community
only a few months.

During the fourth round the door of the depot burst open and a
rain-soaked horseman stumbled in with the news that a rancher living

thirty miles back in the hills needed Doc. The rancher had been hunting that afternoon and had accidentally wounded himself in the thigh with a shotgun. The rancher's wife had gotten him home and was trying to stop the blood with flour and towels while this neighbor rode for the doctor.

In Grand County in those days the roads into the ranches were little more than cow trails. Directions were given by "draws" and "gulches," not by miles and signposts.

Sudan hadn't learned where many of these people lived and he needed a guide. C. C. (Lum) Eastin, the Kremmling druggist, who was born and reared in the Gore Range country, volunteered.

They piled into Sudan's Model-T Ford and plowed mud in low gear until 2 a.m. to reach the wounded man. Sudan administered treatment and then he and the druggist built a stretcher to be placed in the car for the patient. Then Sudan, Eastin, and the rancher and his wife started for Kremmling.

After negotiating several steep hills, the car finally stalled just short of the crest of a particularly bad grade. The gears in the car locked, and there was only one thing to do—go for help. Sudan recalled that a ranch house five miles back had recently installed a telephone. So back he hiked in the dark, cold night, with ten pounds of mud on each foot weighing down his every move.

He called the garage in Kremmling, which promised to dispatch a wrecker immediately to the stalled car. Sudan walked back, at times falling because his numbed legs had no feeling after exposure to the mud, rain, and cold.

He reached the car about daylight, just as the wrecker arrived. Then the car was pulled over the hump, the gears released, and Sudan drove quickly to Kremmling.

There he changed clothes while Mrs. Sudan telephoned a Denver hospital to prepare for the wounded man. Then the doctor drove the hundred and thirty miles to Denver, where he amputated his patient's leg. Sudan saw that the man was under good care and out of danger, and then returned to Kremmling. There he learned for the first time that the great Jack Dempsey had been defeated.

Dr. Sudan couldn't have realized at the time that he would spend twenty-one eventful years in the mountain village, that there would be many more night errands through snow and cold as he served the people of that sprawling country.

The nearest doctor before Sudan arrived was at Steamboat Springs, fifty-seven miles distant over Rabbit Ears Pass. Some of the secondary ranch roads were impassable during part of the year, and heavy snows often halted travel by automobile in the entire area. In fact, for some years the state of Colorado charged residents less than the usual license-tag rate because they were unable to use their cars year around.

Often while on rural calls Sudan shoveled out snowdrifts thirty or forty feet long and three to four feet deep, knowing that upon his return he would have to repeat the job as the wind would have drifted the road full again. He drove thousands of miles each year to reach patients, often traveling in thirty-below weather.

When roads were closed, the ranchers would relay him to a patient by feed sled or on horseback. Traveling those unmarked side roads was hazardous. Chains, shovels, boards, and other paraphernalia constituted standard equipment in his automobile. Once he worked seven hours to move his car sixty feet.

He wore out a car a year—even the big, powerful models equipped with special low gears which he drove in later years. By spring the fenders would be "chewed off" by frozen mud, ice, and snow knocked up under the car as he plowed drifts and bucked soft spots. He can't even estimate how many rear ends and clutches he sent to the garage scrap pile.

Frequently he would have to travel sixty to seventy miles to reach a patient living only ten or twelve miles in a beeline from his office. Dozens of times he bogged down while coming back from a call and walked five or ten miles back home to sleep a few hours before another day.

One winter night he was called to treat a young wife "shot through the chest" in an accident on a little ranch nineteen miles in the hills. The report said she and her husband were target shooting when a .22 rifle inflicted the wound.

The doctor hurried to the mountain cabin. After driving fifteen miles on bad roads, he walked the last four over snowy fields.

"Her color was good," Sudan recalls, "too good for a person shot through the chest. I quickly ascertained that it was a freak wound. The bullet struck a rib, coursed around the body, and came out beneath the other breast, leaving marks which to laymen would indicate she'd been badly wounded.

"When I realized she was all right it made me so happy I could have flown those four miles back to the car.

"I told her she wouldn't die, whereupon she sat up in bed and said she was hungry. We all ate roast beaver and drank tea, then I hiked back to my car."

Once Sudan drove into the Williams Fork country in mid-winter to a rancher who was dying of pneumonia. Arrangements had been made for a "high-geared" Ford and driver to meet him. But Sudan's car got stuck and he started walking. About daylight the driver met Sudan and took him to the rancher in time to make the man's last hours comfortable.

That spring a road crew found a fountain pen near the spot where Sudan's car had been stuck. Without hesitation they took it to the doctor.

"This has to be your pen, Doc," one of them said. "No one else but you would have been back in that damn country in the winter."

WESTERN SLOPE NORTH:
YAMPA, WHITE, AND GREEN RIVERS

Flat Tops Scenic Byway /
Highway 64 Yampa to Rangely

143. Yampa / Flat Tops Wilderness
from *Tales of Lonely Trails* by Zane Gray

Zane Gray, best known as the prolific author of over a hundred adventure novels set in the American West, was also an ardent outdoorsman. He wrote about his hunting and fishing adventures in articles for magazines like Outdoor Life, *some of which he gathered in a book called* Tales of Lonely Trails, *which was published in 1922.*

After growing up in Ohio, and establishing a dentistry practice in New York, Grey moved to California in 1918 to carry on business with the movie industry (many of his books were made into movies) and to be closer to the territory that he loved to explore and write about. Over the years, Grey spent time at various cabins he built in places like the Mogollon Rim in Arizona and the Rogue River country in Oregon. He also frequented other favored locations including the Gore Range and the Flat Top Mountains of Colorado. In Tales of Lonely Trails, *he writes about visits to the Grand Canyon, Rainbow Bridge, and Death Valley among other places. He also describes an extended pack trip from Yampa into the Flat Top Mountains and the headwaters of the White River.*

One more climb brought us to the top of the Flattop Pass, about eleven thousand feet. The view in the direction from which we had come was splendid, and led the eye to the distant sweeping ranges, dark and dim along the horizon. The Flattops were flat enough, but not very wide at this pass, and we were soon going down again into a green gulf of spruce, with ragged peaks lifting beyond. Here again I got the suggestion of limitless space. It took us an hour to ride down to Little Trappers Lake, a small clear green sheet of water. The larger lake was farther down. It was big, irregular, and bordered by spruce forests, and shadowed by the lofty gray peaks...

The fishing was good in the Flat Tops. And it was yet another opportunity for Grey and his brother R.C. to indulge in a lifelong angling rivalry.

In the afternoon R.C. and I went out again to try for trout. The lake appeared to be getting thicker with that floating muck and we could not raise a fish. Then we tried the outlet again. Here the current was swift. I found a place between two willow banks where trout were breaking on the surface. It took a long cast for me, but about every tenth attempt I would get a fly over the right place and raise a fish. They were small, but that did not detract from my gratification. The light on the water was just right for me to see the trout rise, and that was a beautiful sight as well as a distinct advantage. I had caught four when a shout from R.C. called me quickly downstream. I found him standing in the middle of a swift chute with his rod bent double and a long line out.

"Got a whale!" he yelled. "See him—down there—in that white water. See him flash red! ... Go down there and land him for me. Hurry! He's got all the line!"

I ran below to an open place in the willows. Here the stream was shallow and very swift. In the white water I caught a flashing gleam of red. Then I saw the shine of the leader. But I could not reach it without wading in. When I did this, the trout lunged out. He looked crimson and silver. I could have put my fist in his mouth.

"Grab the leader! Yank him out!" yelled R.C. in desperation. "There! He's got all the line."

"But it'd be better to wade down," I yelled back.

He shouted that the water was too deep and for me to save his fish. This was an awful predicament for me. I knew the instant I grasped the leader that the big trout would break it or pull free. The same situation, with different kinds of fish, had presented itself many times on my numberless fishing jaunts with R.C. and they all crowded to my mind. Nevertheless, I had no choice. Plunging in to my knees I frantically reached for the leader. The red trout made a surge. I missed him. R.C. yelled that something would break. That was no news to me. Another plunge brought me in touch with the leader. Then I essayed to lead the huge cutthroat ashore. He was heavy. But he was tired and that gave birth to hopes. Near the shore as I was about to lift him he woke up, swam round me twice, then ran between my legs.

When, a little later, R.C. came panting downstream I was sitting on the bank, all wet, with one knee skinned and I was holding his broken leader in my hands. Strange to say, he went into a rage! Blamed me for the loss of that big trout! Under such circumstances it was always best to maintain silence and I did so as long as I could. After his paroxysm had spent itself and he had become somewhat near a rational being once more he asked me: "Was he big?"

"Oh—a whale of a trout!" I replied.

"Humph! Well, how big?"

Thereupon I enlarged upon the exceeding size and beauty of that trout. I made him out very much bigger than he actually looked to me, and I minutely described his beauty and wonderful gaping mouth. R.C. groaned and that was my revenge.

144. Meeker
from *A Wet Ass and a Hungry Gut* by Danny W. Campbell

In a memoir called A Wet Ass and a Hungry Gut, *Danny W. Campbell writes about growing up in Meeker. As is the case with many mountain town families, hunting season is an important way to bolster food supplies for a long winter. This is an ongoing tradition. Hunting skills are passed along from one generation to the next. And for many lifelong mountain dwellers, the first hunting season, or in this case, the first bull elk, are significant cairns along a trail of hometown memories.*

It was time for hunting season again, and my attention quickly became
focused on that. Mom had saved up enough money to buy Dad and me
new hunting boots, which we really needed. The days seemed to drag,
but finally the last Sunday in September arrived, and we got up early to
drive up the White River Valley to scout our hunting country.

We got to our parking place about 9:00 a.m., and I jumped out of the
pickup to run over to the edge of the knoll and look at the beaver ponds.
The hillsides across from me looked as though they were painted, the
aspens dipped in brilliant orange, yellow, and gold. A few minutes later,
we had packed our lunch stuff and begun the hike back into our hunting
country. Down the hillside and across the beaver dam we went, where
I noticed the animals had chewed down several aspens. A stiff gust of
wind greeted us as we crested the game trail, sending thousands of leaves
showering to the ground.

We arrived at the big meadow, then turned south to walk to another
beaver pond to see if the elk were watering there. We came across some
droppings that were quite fresh, so we knew they were nearby. After
checking around the pond, we headed northeast toward what we called
"the big valley." The White River wound its way down the canyon there,
and we could see quite a distance.

After about an hour, we arrived at the big valley and decided to sit
down, rest, and enjoy the spectacular view. I got a Pepsi out from the
lunch bag and Dad lit his cigar, its smoke trailing off with a slight breeze.
Ooooeeee, uh-uh-uh! I sat up with a start when I heard these sounds
break the silence. I asked Dad what it was, and he said that it was a bull
elk bugling. "It's mating season—called 'rut'—for the elk, and the bulls
bugle to call cows and challenge other bulls," he said. "Sometimes the
bulls fight each other in order to control an entire herd of cows ... Many
bulls lose weight during rut because of having to defend their territories."
He told me that as the bulls age, they get more points on their antlers.
When a bull is three or four years old, he'll usually have six points on
each side, and if they live long enough, even more mass on their antlers,
such as the huge bull that a friend of his had gotten a few years ago. Dad
was a good teacher, and I enjoyed learning about game, elk in particular.

Within minutes, the bull elk let another bugle rip—*ooooeeee, uh-uh-uh!*—and it echoed across the canyon.

I kept watching the valley below us where the sound was coming from, hoping and praying that we'd get to see the bull elk. After watching for about thirty minutes, Dad said, "Look in the meadow, by the dark timber." I quickly picked up the binoculars and started glassing the meadow. I spotted a herd of elk—all cows—and looked hard for the bull. I told Dad there were seven cows, but the bull was missing. He reminded me to be patient—to just keep watching. And all of a sudden, a large blond-colored elk—a big bull elk—walked out into the meadow. He was too far away to count the points, but he had a big rack. My heart was pounding; my first bull elk! He followed the cows across the meadow and they all disappeared into the dark timber.....

When I returned to school on Monday, I told my friends about seeing and hearing the big bull. Each day as I rode my bike to school, there were more leaves that had fallen on the sidewalks; every night, when I went to bed, I'd think about that bull elk, and I was counting the days until hunting season began.

145. Between Meeker and Rangely
from "Dinosaur" by Steve Rasnic Tem

Beyond the ranches and grazing lands in the White River riparian corridor between Meeker and Rangely lies the arid and rocky terrain of the Piceance Basin, a geological region in northwestern Colorado made up of shales and sandstones that contain coal, natural gas, and oil shale. Relatively impermeable layers of rock limited access to some of these resources until recent technological advances changed the equation. But resource extraction is only a thin veneer on the surface of a much deeper geological story in this region, one that included the presence of dinosaurs.

As Colorado author Steve Rasnic Tem suggests in his story "Dinosaur," an awareness of geological history opens up an entirely different kind of relationship with a landscape. For the protagonist in this story, a fascination with dinosaurs and the ancient environment in

which they lived invites a dimension of understanding and appreciation
that might escape the casual visitor. A deeper sense of time that comes
along with a little bit of geological awareness, may liberate or at least
distract us from an obsession with our own personal histories. It may
also be a reminder, as it is in this character's experience, that the
world around us is always in a state of flux.

The pickup slid in gravel, and Freddy fought to right it.

You had to be careful driving the roads out here; they lulled you,
made you careless. The truck seemed so easy to drive, it had so much
power, that sometimes you forgot how dangerous one slip might be. One
of the drawbacks to advanced technology, and to evolution. It made you
reckless; it became too easy to lose control over the power. And that
power could leave you upside down off an embankment.

Dinosaurs used to walk the hills here, but it had been different then.
Freddy thought about that a lot, how things used to be so different.... .
Just before the dinosaurs came, low-lying desert then, the early Jurassic
Period. No animals. Great restless sand dunes towering seven hundred
feet, snaking and drifting like primeval dreams. Fading, dying away in
the distance.

The earliest home Freddy could remember was in an old boarding
house a few hundred yards from one of the early oil rigs. A whitewashed
shack, really, several crate-like rooms strung together. He and his father
had shared one. He couldn't remember his mother, except as a gauzy
presence, more like a ghost, something dead and not dead. He didn't
think she had ever lived with them in the rooming house, but he couldn't
be sure. It bothered him that he could remember so little about her—a
hint of light, a smell, that was all. She had vanished. She left us. She left
me, he corrected himself. His father had always told him that, but it was
hard to believe.

The land sunk. An artic sea reached in. Millions of years passed and
in the late Jurassic it all rose again. The dinosaurs were coming; the land
was readying itself.

He sometimes wondered if he had ever known his mother at all.

Maybe his memories were false. Maybe she had died when he was born. Maybe she'd gone away to die, her time done once she'd given him life.

The land just come from the sea was much more humid. Flat plains. Marshy. Great slow streams loaded with silt flowed out of the highlands to the west to feed the marshes and lakes. Dust floated from the volcanoes beyond the highlands. Araucaria pines towered 150 feet above the forest floor, the tops of ginkos, tree ferns, and cycads below them. Giant bat-like pterosaurs flapped scaly wings against the sky, maintaining balance with their long, flat-tipped tails. Crocodiles sunned themselves by the marsh....

Freddy loved a woman in Rangely. Because of her he allowed himself to stay overnight there on Fridays. But it scared him, loving someone like that. She might leave. She might vanish.... He loved her. He was sure of that. His love filled him and formed one of the three anchors of his life, along with the memories of his father and thoughts of dinosaurs. But lately something felt lacking... It was the same all over. They had friends—lovers and married couples—and all of them seemed to be breaking up. Still loving each other, but unable to stay together.

Sometimes his drives from Meeker to Rangely were specifically to see Melinda, but he almost never thought about her during the trip. He thought about his father, and dinosaurs.

Freddy looked out the window of the pickup. Sagebrush flats, rising sandstone buttes, creek beds turned to sand. Old wrecks out in the fields. Before the oil men there had been cowboys, a few farmers. Before them, the outlaws hiding out.

Before the outlaws, fur traders maneuvering through the canyons.

Before that, Indians trading along the Green and Yampa rivers.

Before that, dinosaurs roaming the hot, wet lowlands.

146. Rangely
from "A Water Tank Turned Music Venue" by Alex Ross

Even the smallest towns often have their secret assets, known only to locals and those who linger long enough to get to know a place. One of Rangely's secrets was revealed to sound artist Bruce Odland during a 1976 artist's residency. Several locals took him to an unusual sonic environment in a massive seven-story water storage tank on a hill above town.

A website for what has since become one of the world's most unique performance spaces fills in some of the Tank's history: "Constructed around 1940 as a railroad water-treatment facility, the Tank was moved by a utility company to Rangely in the mid-1960s for use as part of a fire-suppression system. The plan was never realized, as the underlying shale proved unable to support the weight of the filled tank. However, the bed of gravel upon which the tank was placed bowed its floor into a gentle parabola, giving it its remarkable acoustical resonance." When Bruce Odland was introduced to the Tank's unusual acoustics, he knew that it was something special. Other musicians agreed, as did local residents and members of Rangely and Rio County governments, who rallied to save the Tank when it appeared as though it would be sold for scrap.

Alex Ross has been the music critic at The New Yorker *since 1996. He writes about classical music, covering everything from the Metropolitan Opera to the contemporary avant-garde. He has also contributed essays on literature, history, the visual arts, film, and ecology. Here is an excerpt from his article on The Tank, which appeared in the July 24, 2017 issue of* The New Yorker.

The Tank, as everyone calls it, still looms over Rangely in rusty majesty, looking a bit like Devils Tower. Late one afternoon in June, Odland welcomed me there. He's a wavy-haired sixty-five-year-old, with the sunny manner of an undefeated hippie idealist. In recent years, he and others have renovated the Tank, turning it into a performance venue and a recording studio; it's now called the Tank Center for Sonic Arts, and is outfitted with a proper door. "Go on, make some noise," Odland told me. When my eyes had adjusted to the gloom—a few portals in the roof provide shafts of light during the day—I picked up a rubber-coated hammer and banged a pipe. The sound rang on and on: the reverberation in the space lasts up to forty seconds. But it's not a cathedral-style resonance, which dissipates in space as it travels. Instead, sound seems to hang in the air, at once diffused and enriched. The combination of a parabolic floor, a high concave roof, and cylindrical walls elicits a dense mass of overtones from even a football or a cough. I softly hummed a note and heard pure harmonics spiraling around me, as if I had multiplied into several people who could sing....

In the nineteen-sixties, an electric-power association purchased the structure and moved it to Rangely, planning to use it to store water to fight fires. Once it arrived, however, concerns arose that the hillside underneath it might collapse under the weight of so much water. So it stood unused, its ownership passing from one person to another. Eventually, a friend of Odland's bought it, for ten dollars. Musicians ventured inside to play and record; teen-agers used it as a spooky party pad....

What Odland didn't want was to create an artsy enclave that had no connection to the community around it. "This is the anti-Marfa," he told me, referring to the art-world mecca in Texas, which has been gentrified beyond recognition. In Rangely, locals have embraced the scheme. Urie Trucking built an access road into the site. The W.C. Striegel pipeline company supplied raw materials that can be converted into percussion instruments. Giovanni's Italian Grill created a special Tank pizza. Rangely is a conservative town ... but it has welcomed the incursion of avant-gardists bearing didgeridoos, and some of the most dedicated sonic thinkers are locals. A military veteran finds peace playing violin in the Tank.

"People feel a genuine awe," Odland told me. "They may ascribe it to the Tank, but I ascribe it to the awakening of the ears in a predominantly visual age. Our ears get so abused on a daily basis. Our modern society makes a bad offer to them. We don't use the hearing sense the way we evolved to, as hunter-gatherers interacting with nature. In there, you feel the sound on the skin, you feel it in your gut. What people are in awe of is their own ability to hear properly."

Highway 40

Steamboat Springs to Dinosaur

National Monument

147. Steamboat Springs
from *Headfirst in a Pickle Barrel* and *I Never Look Back*
by John Rolfe Burroughs

Steamboat Springs is a resort town, but it is a resort town with a distinctive Western feel. Every Friday and Saturday evening from mid-June to mid-August, Steamboat holds pro rodeo events at an arena only a few blocks from downtown. As local author and historian John Rolfe Burroughs wrote in his book, Headfirst in a Pickle Barrel, *there were plenty of informal "rodeos" on Lincoln Avenue back in Steamboat's heyday as a cow town.*

Situated at the eastern edge of a vast stretch of range country, Steamboat Springs was a cow town in the classic sense and for several decades it owed its existence exclusively to this juxtaposition. Serving the industry as a supply point, it also was a focal point to which cowboys on those infrequent occasions when the exacting nature of their duties permitted, repaired for the purpose of raising several varieties of hell. . . .

Businesswise, Steamboat always has been a "one street" town. Lincoln Avenue, or "Main Street" as it is known colloquially, parallels the Yampa River on the second bench above that stream . . . . In season (that is to say, during the summer months), Lincoln Avenue swarms with the automobiles of tourists zipping hither and yon; but I well remember the time when citizens stepped indoors for safety as this same thoroughfare filled with a red tide of bawling, wild-eyed dogies—a spectacle so overwhelming that even the more venturesome dogs sought the side streets. There, their tails between their legs, they skulked in a state of agonized uncertainty.

In truth, around the turn of the century, Steamboat Springs was far from dull. For one thing, people were much more intimately involved

with animals in those days than now. Three-fourths of Steamboat's more
provident families kept one or more milk cows; and saddle horses were
to my generation what hot-rods and motor scooters are to today's youngsters. More than a few burros of uncertain ownership roamed the streets.
Nightly, innumerable unconfined dogs more than met the challenge posed
by equally numerous coyotes yawping scornfully from the promontories
which encircle the town. And, always and ever, the unfortunate individuals charged with the maintenance of law and order had to contend with
antic cowboys in a frolicsome mood.

A local item which appeared in the July 17, 1903, issue of the *Routt
County Sentinel* is of interest in this respect: "... Grimsley gave a very
credible ride in front of the First National Bank last Sunday evening,
to which many of the citizens objected, not only because it was on the
Sabbath, but on account of the danger of someone getting run over.... .
The streets aren't the place ... for speeding horses and busting broncos."
Editor Weiskopf wrote: "Those ranchmen, cowboys, and town bronco
busters must cease their wild and reckless driving through Steamboat's
streets hereafter, or expect to be called on the carpet.... . It is absolutely
necessary to make an example of one or more of these reckless riders."

*Steamboat's cowboy roots have also shaped the skiing culture in town.
Billy Kidd, who settled into his long-standing work as ski director at
the Steamboat Resort after winning a silver medal in the 1964 Olympics,
helped cultivate his town's image as both a ranching community and a
world-class ski resort. Images of Kidd in ski magazines, carving turns
decked out in a Stetson and other western gear, were part of that. So was
the annual race he hosted for rodeo rider Larry Mahan and a crowd of
cowboy skiers from the Western Stock Show. But Kidd would likely say
that the out-west skiing spirit of Steamboat Springs began with a local
ranching family who raised three Olympic skiers.*

*Buddy Werner, along with his sister Skeeter and brother Loris, were
those three skiers. Their parents Ed and Hazie, who had deep ranching
roots in the area, provided their kids with skis made out of barrel staves
early on. Later, they took jobs in town and encouraged their kids to
get out on the hill, Howellson Hill that is, a fledgling version of the ski*

scene that would later become such a big part of Steamboat. Soon the
kids were launching themselves off a local ski jump and participating in
various competitions. As Burroughs wrote in a biography called I Never
Look Back, *Buddy Werner established his reputation as a racer later*
on when he broke the record, held by one of Austria's finest skiers at the
time, on one of the World Cup circuit's most dangerous racecourses.

No European had really ever taken an American skier seriously until the
day in 1958 when Werner stood at the top of the Hahnenkamm downhill
course peering into the fog that blotted out the run just a couple of yards
away. A teammate called "good luck." Buddy jabbed in his ski poles,
pulled himself in mid-air into his characteristic streamlined crouch and
almost instantly vanished in the murk.

Far below the Austrian spectators waited staring into the fog. From
the loudspeaker, the announcer's voice traced Werner's plunging race.
Suddenly Werner rocketed out of the mists.

He carved a magnificent, steep last schuss that held the crowd breathless and then swept across the finish line. Excitement rippled through
the crowd when his time of 2 minutes, 43 and nine-tenths seconds was
announced. He had broken the record for the 3,200 meter course."

Buddy Werner never won an Olympic medal. Many thought that 1960
would be his year, but he broke his leg prior to the competition. He was
back in 1964, highly favored for the gold once again, but took an unfor-
tunate fall, in part because of his full-on, push-it-to-the-limit style of
skiing that had electrified spectators all over Europe. But it wasn't just
his skiing prowess that won him so many admirers; he was a gracious
and charismatic sportsman whose determination and work ethic were
well known. In the spring of 1964, after he was killed in an avalanche
while participating in a ski film in St. Moritz, Switzerland, friends
and admirers from all over the world came to Steamboat to attend his
memorial. The mountain that he loved (and helped lay out for the ski
area that put his town on the map as a resort) now bears his name as
does the town library.

148. Hayden
from "The Betrayal of Jack" by Charles Wilkinson

In a book called Heart of the Land: Essays on the Last Great Places, *editors Joseph Barbato and Lisa Weinerman gathered reflections from some of this country's finest writers celebrating our geographical and cultural treasures. Charles Wilkinson, emeritus law professor at the University of Colorado, has written eloquently about Western land and culture. In this essay, he considers the way we perceive landscapes and honors the tenure of the Ute people in this area.*

Morgan Bottoms, much of which is the old Carpenter family ranch, is an eleven-mile stretch in northwestern Colorado just east of Hayden where the banks of the Yampa are dominated by cottonwood forests. These groves cover hundreds of acres of land, mostly along the south bank but sometimes enveloping the river by spreading over areas north of it as well.

Each of the cottonwood groves at Morgan Bottoms is tall and dense. The canopy is multi-tiered, with the upper reaches composed of narrowleaf cottonwood trees, whose thick roots pump up huge amounts of water to keep the giant trees alive. Midway, a graceful story of box elders spreads out its many wings. Lower down, you see red-osier dogwoods, with their brilliant flame-colored bark. Various shrubs and forbs, including serviceberry, hawthorn, squawbush, and goldenrod, form a tangled ground cover, with coyote willows thick near the river. The forest floor is within the Yampa's floodplain and the river waters it during the high runoff in spring and early summer. Gnats, mosquitoes, and other insects swarm in the marshy reaches, as does an unbelievable array of bird life: great blue heron, great horned owls, golden eagles, even an occasional bald eagle; mergansers, wood ducks, mallards. Morgan Bottoms is a crucial place for sandhill cranes, part of their only breeding ground in Colorado and one of the state's three staging areas where they fatten up before migrating south.

Yet this profusion of vegetation and wildlife habitat was alien to my eye. Across the whole arid West, cottonwoods run along nearly every low- and middle-elevation river, stream, and creek, but the trees form thin ribbons, two or three deep, not unlike the buffer strips of Douglas fir or ponderosa pine that the Forest Service so assiduously leaves along highways adjacent to clear-cuts. Out here, cottonwoods come in thin strips, not forest, so Morgan Bottoms takes on a surprising, almost suspicious, cast.

For we all perceive the natural world in layers. We may take in nature in a literal way—vegetation, animal species, waters, soils, land formations—but we overlay those facts with our own memories, imaginations, fears, and dreams, and for us those overlays are as complex and real as the natural facts themselves might be. There are many layers, some personal, some held by the public at large, over this part of Colorado.

To me the most haunting overlay on Morgan Bottoms, on the Yampa and on the White, on the whole Colorado Western Slope, will always be the experience of the Utes, how they lived and loved and worshipped and how these horse people rode this terrain for so many centuries.

The tenure of the Ute people in the region traces back farther than we can fully imagine. Some anthropologists think that they migrated into the Colorado Plateau region between A.D. 1000 and 1300. Others believe that the modern Utes emerged from the Fremont people. The Fremont, whom we date back to about four thousand years ago, lived both in villages and on the move, hunting and gathering, and leaving behind housing sites, baskets, pots, and magical pictograph and petroglyphs. In turn, the Fremont probably evolved from hunters and gatherers who lived on the Colorado Plateau beginning about 10,000 years ago or more.

The Utes themselves seemed disinclined to join the debate of non-Indian scholars. They hold by their own explanation. At the beginning of time, Sinawauf, the Creator, had all of the peoples of the world in a bag. He opened the bag and placed the Utes in their mountain, plains, and desert country. By any account, the current of Ute blood runs very, very deep out here.

149. Craig
from *A Seasoned Life in Small Towns* by Janet B. Sheridan

Author and columnist Janet B. Sheridan has lived in small western towns most of her life. Her observations on rural living are gathered in a book called A Seasoned Life in Small Towns: Memories, Musings, and Observations. *Being part of a small community "where everybody knows your name" isn't for everybody. But in this essay, Janet Sheridan celebrates a considerate neighbor who reaffirmed her belief that Craig was her kind of town.*

Welcome to Craig, where neighbors notice.

The first definition for neighbor in my battered 1964 student-edition dictionary is *a person who lives near another.* The broader, second definition—*fellow man, as in love your fellow man*—is a better fit for Craig, because it allows us to monitor more people.

I decided I wanted to grow old in this inquisitive community when one of its watchful members gave my father a needed assist. My dad, ninety, visited Joel and me in 1999. One morning we went to work before Dad got out of bed, so I left breakfast for him on the counter. The phone rang as I was leaving, and I took time to jot directions to a location where I had a meeting that evening.

When Dad wandered into the kitchen, awake and hungry, he overlooked the food, but saw my scribbled directions sitting on top of the microwave. "Hmm," he thought, "Janet must think I'd like breakfast at this place."

He donned his straw cowboy hat and left, turning west instead of east at the end of our driveway, so he didn't end up in a residential area looking for a non-existent restaurant. Instead, miraculously, my directions, "One block, turn left, two blocks, turn right, straight ahead, white siding," led him to a small cafe.

Full of food and high spirits, Dad decided to take a stroll around town on his way home. Twenty minutes later, he came to a park. Realizing he didn't know where he was, he decided a nap might be helpful; so he snoozed on the grass with his hat shading his face for some time, then sat up. The rest cure had failed. He was still lost. He then felt an elderly parent's common concern—fear that he'd be a bother to his busy child.

Later that morning, I received a call from a mail carrier: "Mrs. Sheridan, I just wanted to tell you that walking my route earlier today, I noticed an elderly gentleman sitting on the grass in the Breeze Park and went to see if he needed help. He told me he was visiting his daughter, Janet Sheridan, went out for a walk, couldn't find his way back, and wanted to get home on his own without bothering her. So I directed him to your house and watched until he turned into the right place. Hope that's OK."

Without hesitating, knowing it was against regulations for a post-office employee to reveal the address of a resident, taking in the age and pride of the gentleman before him, this kind person made a Craig decision. Small towns, with neighbors who know you, are to be prized, praised, and lived in for a long time.

150. Browns Park
from *Riding the Edge of an Era* by Diana Allen Kouris

Browns Park, a remote valley on the Green River near the "three corners" territory where Colorado, Utah, and Wyoming meet, was once a hideout on the infamous outlaw trail. The outlaw trail wasn't a specific trail as much as it was a corridor connecting hideouts in some of the west's most isolated territory. Butch Cassady was among the outlaws who traveled between these hideouts, which covered a long and narrow swath of the west between Mexico and Montana. Stories from this era were part of the family lore that inspired the work of author and historian Diana Allen Kouris, who grew up on the Browns Park Livestock Ranch.

The same isolation that attracted outlaws like Cassady, as well as the spectacular canyons of the Green and Yampa rivers, were also of interest to federal land and wildlife managers. Dinosaur National Monument, which was originally established in 1914 around the fossil beds discovered by paleontologist Earl Douglas and his associates near Jensen, Utah,

grew over time to include the river canyons in this corner of Colorado.
Competing interests in the region included the potential for water stor-
age in Echo Park, a deep canyon in the heart of what had become the
Monument (see Dinosaur entry), as well as providing habitat for migratory
waterfowl and other wildlife species on the northern edge of the Monument.
Some of the lands that the government purchased to establish the Brown's
Park Wildlife Refuge had been part of the Brown's Park Livestock Ranch
that Kouris's family had stewarded for several generations.

The transition from ranch to refuge generated some rancor, which
Kouris discusses in her memoir Riding the Edge of an Era. *Federal land*
managers had their intentions and were determined to purchase the land.
Ultimately, Kouris's family had little choice but to go along with the deal
they were offered. The land set aside to benefit wildlife meant the loss of
her family's livelihood on this remote ranch, where hard work, as well as
play, had always been part of the routine.

Nonie and I turned over in our bed and got a whiff of sauerkraut sizzling
in the skillet, which promised that breakfast would be a family favorite.
Our first hotcake, accompanied by bacon, would be layered with butter,
a fried egg, and homemade sauerkraut, and then topped with ketchup.
Mom would likely say, "This'll stick to your ribs and fill up your hollow
legs. It's going to be a long, tough day in the saddle."

… Mom sometimes helped in the hayfield, running the baler in the
fragrant heat, but remained in her height of happiness when she got the
opportunity to ride after cattle. Trailing behind the herd of red and white
Herefords, she twirled her rope at her side while occasionally letting the
knotted end graze the tail of a cow to urge her to hurry. "Come on, ole
girls, step along," she'd say. Even though she couldn't carry much of a
tune, nothing was more endearing than the sound of her voice serenading
the herd and us with the words to the cowboy ballads "Little Joe the
Wrangler" and "Billy Vanero."

… I thought about the day before when we had gathered and sorted
cattle, getting ready to take the main herd to the summer range in
Colorado on Cold Spring Mountain. We had all been on edge because
Dad had one way of working cows, especially in the corral, and that was

the scary way! He was stern with his orders and expectations. We stayed so poised for action that a friend once said we looked as though our eyeballs could be knocked off with a stick and a tune played on our necks. If told to turn a cow, we knew we'd better do so. Dad didn't have to raise a hand to us because his mere glance of disapproval was thunderous.

Dad was often distant. During meals his worries and responsibilities sometimes overtook him, and with a frown he completely removed himself from our conversation and laughter. But he was not mean.... Put a bat in Dad's hands and he became a kid again. Whenever we formed our teams in the pasture below the house for a game of baseball, Dad stopped whatever he was doing to play with us.... And he was our Easter bunny. Each year he got up very early and hurried outside to hide treats and the dozens of eggs we'd colored the night before. He giggled and his eyes lit up with enjoyment as we dashed in all directions, squealing with the treasures that were filling our baskets....

Dad also took great pleasure in turning water down ditches and watching it spread across the pastures and fields, giving them life. He got so excited during rainstorms that he hurried from window to window to watch it pour down and spatter the earth. If one of us kids made the mistake of getting in his way in front of a window, he'd nearly run us over and never even notice....

During dances at the Lodore School, where families came together to have fun, Dad called the square dances without a microphone, served as the bouncer making sure no liquor was ever brought inside, and danced the two-step with Mom in flawless rhythm. When he chose to play, he played hard and gave it his all. The same was true of his work....

Still lingering in bed that June morning... Nonie and I heard Mom's happy voice call, "Hop up, girls. Hop like a bunny. Time's-a-wastin'. Dad just went out to the bunkhouse to call the boys. If you hurry, you can get dressed in the kitchen where it's warm."

We threw the covers back, jumped from our bed, and scooped our clothes up on the run. We went with the certainty that there was always plenty of good food, warm beds, affection, discipline, hard work, and play to go around. Our parents were cattle ranchers. They were partners. And together, they danced.

151. Cross Mountain Canyon
from *Colorado's Yampa River*
by Patrick Tierney and John Fielder

*The Yampa River gathers waters from the Park Range to the east, the
Flat Tops to the south, and the Uinta Mountains to the west on a
250-mile-long run through northwestern Colorado to its confluence with
the Green River in Dinosaur National Monument. As the only tributary
of the Colorado that is not dammed, the Yampa is a wild and free-flowing
river, nowhere wilder than in Cross Mountain Canyon where it encounters a narrow channel choked off with a chaotic jumble of huge rocks
and boulders that make it virtually un-runnable in high water.*

Nevertheless, there are those who try. In the mid-1980s, ABC's Wide
World of Sports *hired two international kayaking champions and filmed
their high water run through this remote canyon located west of Highway
40 between Maybell and Elk Springs. After hitting a wave in Mammoth
Falls, US champion Eric Evans managed to bust a few rolls in a hole
that would not release him. He finally washed out of the rapid face down,
where he was rescued by an EMT who jumped out of a helicopter, caught
up with Evans, and administered CPR.*

In a book called Colorado's Yampa River: Free-Flowing and Wild
from the Flat Tops to the Green, *produced with photographer John
Fielder, Patrick Tierney tells the tale of a run through Cross Mountain
in lower water which, while not as forbidding as peak runoff, has its
own unique challenges. His boating party was led by three seasoned raft
guides and a very skilled kayaker who came along for added safety in the
event that there were any swimmers. "Little did I know," writes Tierney,
"that a shockingly similar situation to something that occurred here in the
1980s was going to evolve on my trip through Cross Mountain that day."*
Right away one boat got pinned against a rock at the first drop. The guide
pried them free for a moment, but the raft hit another rock, started to
wrap around it, folded in the current, and people were swept out. From
up at the scouting spot, I could not see what happened next, but all at
once the other guides were quickly scrambling over rocks and the kayaker shot over to the raft and then out of sight. A passenger had gotten her

foot caught on the line around the outside of the raft and was stuck under the boat. When two guides quickly pulled her free, she was not breathing. They immediately started CPR, with gurgling sounds coming from her lungs. It was a very long thirty seconds. But then she spit up water and started breathing on her own. YES!

The potential complications from a near drowning required an evacuation. But we were in an extremely narrow canyon without cellular service. One guide raced out of the canyon on foot. Another retrieved a rescue backboard stashed nearby in the rocks for just such a need. The crew carefully placed her on the backboard and tied her securely to it. A combination of twelve crew members and participants lifting her over 15-foot-high boulders and around cliffs, and then guides lining her upstream in a raft on calm sections finally got her out of the canyon. It took two and a half laborious hours. A Flight for Life helicopter, called by the marathon runner guide, swooped down and landed, and the guides carefully loaded her inside. She was flown to the hospital, where thankfully she recovered fully. The rest of us walked out of the canyon, never seeing more than the first rapid, but we were just greatly relieved to see her smiling again that night. The guides went back the next day to recover the boats and gear, and successfully rafted the boats through the rest of the canyon. Despite what happened, the lure of Cross Mountain is just too great. I'll be back to run it again.

152. Dinosaur National Monument
from "The Marks of Human Passage" by Wallace Stegner

In 1955, David Brower and the Sierra Club were intent on preventing the Bureau of Reclamation from building two dams in the heart of Dinosaur National Monument. Two of the West's great rivers—the Yampa and the Green—not to mention all of the biological and archaeological resources in the canyons they inhabit, were in deep jeopardy. Had it not been for the advocacy of conservationists, we would be looking at a severely diminished man-made landscape in the heart of what is still a wild and scenic treasure.

A book called This Is Dinosaur, *edited by author, historian, and conservationist Wallace Stegner, was one of the most effective tools in the effort to challenge the dam projects and to promote the idea that any national monument should be off-limits to this kind of intrusion. The idea of the book was to gather the best writing and photography available to make the case for the rivers and their canyons. "We believed that if the public and the Congress knew what Dinosaur contained, the Congress, under public pressure, would remove the threat to it," wrote Stegner later on. "So we named no enemies. We only tried to describe; and every member of Congress got a copy of our book."*

It was an effective strategy. The book won over its share of hearts and minds and was a useful weapon in the fight to keep the Green and the Yampa flowing freely through the Monument. In the first chapter of the book, Stegner's eloquent presentation of Dinosaur's human history highlighted lingering traces of some of the region's first known inhabitants, archeological evidence that might have been lost had the campaign not prevailed.

To describe Dinosaur, one must begin by summarizing its human history, and human history in Dinosaur is quaintly begun in the completely human impulse to immortalize oneself by painting or pecking or carving one's private mark, the symbol of one's incorrigible identity, on rocks and trees.

The prehistoric people who inhabited the Green and Yampa canyons, and who belonged to the cultural complex known to archaeologists as the Fremont Culture, [were] a laggard branch of the prehistoric Pueblo-Basketmaker group, or Anasazi .... The pictographs and petroglyphs which they painted in red ocher or chipped with sharp stones in the faces of the cliffs mark the northernmost extension of the Anasazi Culture .... These murals, together with the terrace camp sites and middens and the many storage granaries in caves, are among the earliest human marks in the area. To us, the most immediately fascinating of the relics the Fremont people left are these pictures, which record the game they hunted, the ceremonial objects they revered, the idle doodling dreams they indulged in, and—most wistful and most human of all—the painted handprints and footprints, the personal tracks, that said, and still say: "I am."

These are all of Dinosaur's history for a long time; they reflect the period from about A.D. 400 – 800. Some archaeologists believe that on the Uinta and Yampa plateaus there may be evidences of the passage southward, sometime about the year 1000, of the Athapascan hunters who were the ancestors of the modern Navajo and Apache, but the origin of those camp sites is still speculative. Leaving out that possibility, there passed nearly a thousand years after the last of the Fremont people departed during which, as far as history knows, these canyons were only wind and water and stone, space and sky and the slow sandpapering of erosion, the unheard scurry of lizard and scream of mountain lion, the unseen stiff-legged caution of deer, the unnoted roar of rapids in the dark slot of Lodore, and the unrecorded blaze of canyon color darkening with rain and whitening with snow and glaring in the high sun of solstice.

Acknowledgments

The early stages of imagining this project began with a meeting of poets, writers, and editors from all over Colorado. Chris Ransick (1962-2019), the former poet laureate of Denver who convened that meeting, had been a student at the University of Montana while William Kittredge and Annick Smith were assembling an anthology of Montana literature called The Last Best Place. *Shortly after his appointment as Denver poet laureate, he secured a grant from the Humanities Council with the intention of creating a similar anthology in Colorado. He knew that this would be a big project, so he enlisted friends from all over the state to help out. Those early visioning meetings in Denver included Aaron Abeyta (Antonito), Laura Pritchett (La Porte), George Sibley (Gunnison), Jessy Randall (Colorado Springs), Jenny Shank (Boulder), David Rothman (Crested Butte), Tim McAvoy (Denver), and myself (Crestone).*

Slowly, the project began to take shape: we all took responsibility for different parts of the state and some of us began to gather materials. Then Chris and his wife Shannon moved to the lower elevations of the Oregon Coast for health reasons. Without his leadership, the project stalled out for a while, until a remnant of the original group—Laura Pritchett, Jenny Shank, Tim McAvoy, and I—reconvened one summer weekend up near Estes Park. Since there were fewer of us and we were all involved in other endeavors, we envisioned the project on a less ambitious scale, meaning it wouldn't be as comprehensive as the book that Chris had envisioned. In the conversations and correspondence that followed, we imagined the anthology as a literary road guide to Colorado, and shaped a proposal along those lines. By the time we heard back from an interested editor, we were all caught up in other pursuits. Later, when that particular press went out of business, we tabled the project.

But the files of material I had gathered remained on my desktop. A few years later, I wanted to see if our proposal still had legs, so I mentioned it to Caleb Seeling at Bower House. His enthusiastic response was the jumpstart I needed to get back to work on this project. This isn't the comprehensive anthology that my old pal Ransick envisioned, but I hope it carries forward some of the inspirations that we all shared in those early meetings. I know for sure that the suggestions offered by my colleagues along the way made it a better book than it otherwise would have been.

I also want to acknowledge the hard work of other Colorado editors whose previously published anthologies offered guidance and, in some cases, excerpts for this book. Those anthologies are listed in the bibliography as are some other books about Colorado that were helpful in this process, most notably Colorado: A Historical Atlas *by Thomas J. Noel.*

I am grateful for librarians all over the state, including my friends at the Baca Grande Library here in Crestone, who were helpful and enthusiastic about the project. When the Covid pandemic shut down most of those libraries, Adams State librarian Mary Walsh helped me to get the books I needed. Her assistance came at a crucial time, without which I doubt I could have completed the manuscript. The same is true with Cheryl Shroeder, another friend from my teaching years at Adams State, who transcribed all the hard copy I brought home into word files. She was also the first person to read and respond to the materials I chose to include in this book. I am grateful for her help and for our conversations. I am also grateful to Caleb Seeling and Derek Lawrence of Bower House for their support and for their patience when this project took longer to complete than anticipated.

As always, my wife, Grace Anderson, offered her great support in so many ways, not the least of which was reading over the manuscript and making important suggestions before I sent off the last draft. She also contributed a lovely essay about her family and the La Plata Mountains near Mancos, Colorado where she grew up. I am lucky to have such a bright light in my life.

I am also lucky to have landed in this great state. I left the East Coast and drove west to Colorado College in 1974. Other than some years spent in Wyoming and Utah and a few short stints in New England and Indiana, Colorado has been my home ever since. This book is an expression of gratitude for all the good years in Colorado Springs, the Upper Arkansas Valley, the Four Corners region of the San Juan Basin, and now the San Luis Valley. It is good to be here.

BIBLIOGRAPHY

Books on Colorado

Baca, Vincent. *La Gente: Hispano History and Life in Colorado.* (1999, Colorado Historical Society)

Benson, Maxine. *1001 Colorado Place Names.* (1994, University Press of Kansas)

Caughey, Bruce and Dean Winstanley. *The Colorado Guide.* (2005, Fulcrum)

Griffiths, Mel and Rubright, Lynnell. *Colorado: A Geography.* (1983, Westview Press)

Hafen, Leroy. *Colorado and Its People: A Narrative and Topical History of the Centennial State.* (1948, Lewis Historical Publishing)

Hankey, Clyde T.. *A Colorado Word Geography.* (1960, American Dialect Society, University of Alabama Press)

Hughes, Johnson Donald. *American Indians in Colorado.* (1977, Pruett)

Lavender, David. *David Lavender's Colorado.* (1976, Doubleday)

Noel, Thomas J.. *Colorado: A Historical Atlas.* (2015, University of Oklahoma Press)

Wyckoff, William. *Creating Colorado: The Making of a Western American Landscape, 1860-1940.* (1999, Yale University Press)

Wynar, Bohdan. *Colorado Bibliography.* (1980, Libraries Unlimited)

Anthologies on Colorado and the West

Anderson, Peter. *Telling It Real: The Best of Pilgrimage Magazine.* (2009, Pilgrimage Press)

Gehres, Eleanor Mount; Sandra Dallas; Maxine Benson; and Stanley Cuba. *The Colorado Book.* (1993, Fulcrum)

Grimstead, Steve. *Western Voices.* (2004, Fulcrum)

Hemesath, James. *Vintage Colorado Short Stories: Where Past Met Present.* (1997, University of Colorado Press)

Hemesath, James. *Where Past Meets Present: Modern Colorado Short Stories.* (1994, University of Colorado Press)

High Country News. *Living in the Runaway West.* (2000, Fulcrum)

Howe, Elvon. *Rocky Mountain Empire.* (Doubleday, 1950)

Lough, James; Christie Smith. *Sites of Insight: A Guide to Colorado's Sacred Places.* (2003, University of Colorado Press)

Meyers, Stephen. *Trails Among the Columbine: A Colorado High Country Anthology.* (1986, Sundance)

Tem, Steve Rasnic. *High Fantastic: Colorado's Fantasy, Dark Fantasy, and Science Fiction.* (1995, Ocean View Books)

Rinehart, Frederic. *Chronicles of Colorado.* (2003, Taylor Trade Publishing)

CREDITS

1. Excerpt from *An Owl on Every Post* by Sanora Babb. Copyright © 2012. Reprinted by permission of Muse Ink Press (www.museink-press.com).

2. Excerpt from *The Worst Hard Time: The Untold Story of Those Who Survived the Great American Dust Bowl* by Timothy Egan. Copyright © 2005 by Timothy Egan. Reprinted by permission of Houghton Mifflin Harcourt Publishing Company. All rights reserved.

3. "Cowboy Days" in *Rhymes of the Range and Other Poems* by Bruce Kiskaddon (E. Hays, Hollywood CA, 1947); "Ridin' Fence" in *Western Poems* by Bruce Kiskaddon (Los Angeles, Western Livestock Journal, 1935); "Drinkin' Water" in *Cowboy Poetry: Classic Rhymes* (Mason Scoggins, Cowboy Miner Productions, 1987). Floyd Beard's cowboy poetry can be found at floydbeardcowboy.com.

4. Excerpt from *Gasa Gasa Girl Goes to Camp: A Nisei Youth Behind a World War II Fence* by Lily Yuriko Nakai Havey. Copyright © 2014. Reprinted by permission of University of Utah Press.

5. "The Confessions of William Dargy" (*Kiowa County Independent*, 2016) reprinted courtesy of Priscilla Waggoner.

6. *Bent's Fort and its Builders* by George Bird Grinnell (Kansas State Historical Society, 1923).

7. Excerpt from *Sometimes a Great Notion* by Ken Kesey, copyright © 1964, renewed © 1992 by Ken Kesey. Used by permission of Viking Books, an imprint of Penguin Publishing Group, a division of Penguin Random House LLC. All rights reserved.

8. Excerpt from *Butcher's Crossing* by John Williams, copyright © 1960 by John Williams; copyright renewed © 1988 by John Williams. Used by permission.

9. Letters from Captain Silas Soule and Lieutenant Joseph Kramer (US Park Service, Sand Creek National Historic Site).

10. Excerpts from "Flight Pattern" by Joanne Greenberg. Copyright ©1995 from *High Fantastic*, Ocean View Books. Used by permission of Robin Straus Agency, Inc.

11. Excerpt from *Country Editor's Boy* by Hal Borland, Copyright © 1970, (Lippincot, Wilkins, and Williams, 1970). Used by permission.

12. Excerpt from *Limon, Colorado: A Place to Call Home*, by Lyle Miller. Copyright © 2016. Used with permission from Western Reflections Publishing Company.

13. Excerpt from *Tenderfoot Bride* by Clarice Richards (Wordwise, 2017).

14. Excerpt from *The Diary of Mattie Spencer* by Sandra Dallas, Copyright © 1997 by Sandra Dallas. Reprinted by permission of St. Martin's Press. All rights reserved.

15. Excerpt from *East of Denver* by Gregory Hill. Copyright © 2019. Used with permission from the author.

16. Excerpt from "July 21, 1993 Last Chance, Colorado Tornado" by William T. Reid. (http://stormbruiser.com/chase/1993/07/21/july-21-1993-last-chance-colorado-tornado/). Used with permission from the author.

17. Excerpt from *The Boys in the Bar* by Sureva Towler in *The Boys at the Bar: Antics of a Vanishing Breed of Cowboys & Hellions* (Johnson Books, 2006). Used with permission from the author.

18. Excerpt from *Plainsong* by Kent Haruf. Copyright © 1999 by Kent Haruf. Used by permission of Alfred A. Knopf, an imprint of the Knopf Doubleday Publishing Group, a division of Penguin Random House LLC. All rights reserved.

19. Excerpts from *Roughing It* by Mark Twain (Signet, 2008).

20. Excerpt from *Colorado Without Mountains: A High Plains Memoir* by Harold Hamil (Lowell Press, 1976).

21. Excerpt from *Stygo*. By Laura Hendrie (Macmurray & Beck Communication, 1994). Used with permission of author.

22. *The Autobiography of Mother Jones* by Mary G. Harris "Mother" Jones (Bibliotech Press, 2019).

23. Excerpt from *Essays from an American Peasant* by Tomas Mariano. Copywrite © 1992, Tomas Mariano. Used with permission of the Mariano family.

24. Excerpt from *Drop City: The First Hippie Commune and the Summer of Love* by John Curl. Copyright © 2017, John Curl. Used with permission of the author.

25. "Road to the Purgatoire" by Doug Holdread. Copyright ©2019 by Doug Holdread. Used with permission from the author.
26. Excerpt from *Ludlow* by David Mason (Red Hen Press, 2007). Used with permission of the author.
27. *King Coal* by Upton Sinclair (Upton Sinclair, 1917).
28. Excerpt from *The World of Damon Runyon* by Tom Clark (Harper and Row, 1978) used with permission of the Clark family; Excerpt from *A Gentleman of Broadway* by Edwin P. Hoyt (Little Brown, 1964).
29. Excerpt from *Westward to a High Mountain* by Helen Hunt Jackson (University Press of Colorado, 1995). Used with permission from History Colorado-Denver.
30. Excerpt from *Of Time and Change* by Frank Waters (MacMurray and Beck, 1998). Used with permission of the Frank Waters Foundation.
31. Excerpt from *Everybody Welcome: A Memoir of Fannie Mae Duncan and the Cotton Club* by Fannie Mae Duncan with Kathleen F. Esmiol. (Chiaroscuro Press, 2013). Used with permission from Kathleen F. Esmiol.
32. Excerpt from "Yo Soy Joaquín" by Corky Gonzales and "Stupid America" by Lalo Delgado. *Here Lies Lalo: The Collected Poems of Abelardo Delgado,* edited by Jarioca Linn Watts (Arte Publico Press, 2011) and *Message to Aztlan: Selected Writings of Rodolfo "Corky" Gonzales,* edited by Antonio Esquibel (Arte Publico Press, 2001). Used with permission from Arte Publico Press.
33. Excerpt from "Prologue:" to "The First Third" from The First Third & Other Writings by Neal Cassady, Revised and Expanded Edition. Copyright © 1971, 1981 by City Lights Books. Reprinted with the permission of The Permissions Company, LLC on behalf of City Lights Books, citylights.com.
34. Excerpt by *The Ringer* by Jenny Shank. Copyright © 2011. Used with permission from Permanent Press.
35. Excerpt from "Here Is a Land Where Life is Written in Water" by Thomas Hornsby Ferrill (Colorado State Capitol).
36. Excerpt from *The Thunder Tree: Lessons from an Urban Wildland* by Robert Michael Pyle, copyright © 1993, 2011. Reprinted with the

permission of Oregon State University Press.

37. Excerpt from *Red Fenwick's West: Yesterday and Today* by Robert W. "Red" Fenwick (Pruett Publishing Company, 1983).

38. Excerpt from "Rocky Flats: Warring God Charnel Ground" by Anne Waldman found in *Disembodied Poetics: Annals of the Jack Kerouac School,* copyright © 1994. Reprinted with permission of University of New Mexico Press.

39. Excerpt from *Everything That Matters* by Pat Ament (Two Lights Publishing, 2004). Used with permission of the author.

40. Excerpt from *Dream from Bunker Hill* from the *John Fante Reader,* edited by Stephen Cooper. Copyright ©2002 by Joyce Fante. Used by permission of HarperCollins Publishers.

41. From *Wandering Time: Western Notebooks* by Luis Alberto Urrea. © 1999 Luis Alberto Urrea. Reprinted by permission of the University of Arizona Press.

42. Excerpt from *The Four Cornered Falcon: Essays on the Interior West and the Natural Scene* © 1993 by Reg Saner. Reprinted with permission of Harper Collins Publishers.

43. Excerpt from *On the Road* by Jack Kerouac, copyright © 1955, 1957, by John Sampas, Literary Representative, the Estate of Stella Sampas Kerouac; John Lash, Executor of the Estate of Jan Kerouac; Nancy Bump; and Anthony M. Sampas. Used by permission of Viking Books, an imprint of Penguin Publishing Group, a division of Penguin Random House LLC. All rights reserved.

44. *An Overland Journey, from New York to San Francisco in the Summer of 1859* by Horace Greeley (C.M. Saxton, Barker & Co, 1860).

45. *In Search of Centennial: A Journey with James Michener* by John Kings (Visual Books/ Random House, 1978).

46. *In Search of Centennial: A Journey with James Michener* by John Kings (Visual Books/ Random House, 1978).

47. Excerpt from "Wellington's Trial by Blizzard" by Bill Hosokawa published in *Rocky Mountain Empire* by Elvon Howe (Doubleday, 1950).

48. Excerpt from Spanish Peaks: Land and Legends by Conger Beasley, Jr. (University of Colorado Press, 2006). Used with permission of

University of Colorado Press.

49. Reprinted from *Huerfano: A Memoir of Life in the Counterculture* (University of Massachusetts Press, 2013). Used with permission of University of Massachusetts Press.

50. Excerpt from *Westcliffe, Colorado: A Short Sketch of this Most Delightful Resort* by W.O. Mieir (Carson-Harper Co, 1898). Public Domain.

51. "Snake in the Grass" by Hal Walter reprinted courtesy of the author.

52. Excerpt from *Early Ascents on Pikes Peak* by Woody Smith (Arcadia Publishing, 2015) with permission from the publisher.

53. Excerpts from *Beyond the Aspen Grove* by Ann Zwinger (Johnson Books, 2002) reprinted with permission from the Zwinger family.

54. Excerpt from *Good Evening Everybody* by Lowell Thomas (William Morrow, 1976).

55. Excerpt from *Saved in Time: The Fight to Establish Florissant Fossil Beds National Monument, Colorado* by Estella B. Leopold and Herbert W. Meyer (University of New Mexico Press, 2012) reprinted with permission from University of New Mexico Press.

56. Excerpt from Dwellings: *A Spiritual History of the Living World* by Linda Hogan. Copyright © 1995 by Linda Hogan. Used by permission of W. W. Norton & Company, Inc.

57. Excerpt from *My Rocky Mountain Valley* by James Grafton Rogers (Pruett Press, 1968).

58. Excerpt from *Halfway to Heaven* by Mark Obmascik. Copyright © 2009 by Mark Obmascik. Reprinted with the permission of Atria Books, a division of Simon & Schuster, Inc. All rights reserved.

59. Excerpt from *The Long Haul: A Trucker's Tales of Life on the Road* by Finn Murphy. Copyright © 2017 by Finn Murphy. Used by permission of W. W. Norton & Company, Inc.

60. Excerpt from *Dumb Luck and the Kindness of Strangers* by John Gierach. Copyright © 2020 by John Gierach. Reprinted with the permission of Simon & Shuster, Inc. All rights reserved.

61. Quote from *Stephen King: America's Favorite Boogie Man* by George Beahm (Andrews McMeel, 1998).

62. Excerpts from *A Lady's Life in the Rocky Mountains* by Isabella Bird,

75. Excerpt from *Heading Home: Field Notes* by Peter Anderson (Bower House/Conundrum, 2017) reprinted with permission from Bower House Books.

76. Excerpt from *Stretch Marks* by Peggy Godfrey (Media Chaos, 2003) reprinted by permission from the author.

77. Excerpt from *Life with Pickle* by J.C. Mattingly (Mirage Press, 2004) reprinted with permission from the author.

78. "Meditación en Dos Ojos: Garcia Lake at Cumbres Pass" by Reyes Garcia found in *Sites of Insight: A Guide to Colorado Sacred Places* (University Press of Colorado) reprinted with permission of the author.

79. Excerpt from *Letters from the Headwaters* by Aaron Abeyta (Western Press Books, 2014) reprinted with permission from the author.

80. Excerpt from *Alex and the Hobo: A Chicano Life and Story* by José Inez Taylor and James M. Taggart, Copyright © 2003. Courtesy of University of Texas Press.

81. Excerpt from *The Last Ranch: A Colorado Community and the Coming Desert* by Sam Bingham, copyright © 1996 by Sam Bingham. Used by permission of Pantheon Books, an imprint of the Knopf Doubleday Publishing Group, a division of Penguin Random House LLC. All rights reserved.

82. Excerpt from *The Life of an Ordinary Woman* by Anne Ellis (University of Nebraska Press, 1980).

83. "Creede" by Cy Warman from *Mountain Melodies* by Cy Warman (Warman, 1892).

84. Excerpt from *Deep Creek: Finding Hope in the High Country* by Pam Houston. Copyright © 2019 by Pam Houston. Used by permission of W. W. Norton & Company, Inc.

85. Excerpt for "River Driver" by Hank Myers from *Denver Times*, March 3, 1902.

86. Excerpt from *Nothing Here But Stones* by Nancy Oswald (Filter Press, 2014) used with permission of Filter Press.

87. Excerpt from "The Bull of Whitewater Rapids" by S.C. Dubick in *Saga Magazine*, May 1973.

88. Excerpt from *Deep in the Heart of the Rockies* by Ed Quillen (Music

Mountain Press, 1998) used with permission of the Quillen Family.

89. Excerpt from *Under the Angel of Shavano* by George Everett and Wendell Hutchison (Golden Bell Press, 1963).

90. Excerpt from Book 6, *Over Trails of Yesterday* by F. E. Gimlett (Hermit, 1943).

91. "Mountain Mamas Tell Tall Tales" appears periodically in the *Crestone Eagle*. Reprinted courtesy of the author.

92. Excerpt from *Rocky Mountain Letters* by William H. Brewer (James D. Houston, 1992).

93. Excerpted from *Olden Times in Colorado* by Carlyle Channing Davis (Phillips Publishing Company, 1916).

94. Excerpt from *A Victorian Gentlewoman in the Far West: The Reminiscences of Mary Hallock Foote* edited by Rodman Paul (Huntington Library, 1972).

95. Excerpt from *The Making of a Hardrock Miner* by Stephen M. Voynick (Howel-North Books, 1978) reprinted courtesy of the author.

96. Excerpt from *Climb to Conquer: The Untold Story of World War II's 10th Mountain Division Ski Troops* by Peter Shelton. Copyright © 2003 by Peter Shelton. Reprinted with the permission of Scribner, a division of Simon and Schuster, Inc. All rights reserved.

97. Excerpt from *Between Urban and Wild: Reflections from Colorado*. Copyright © 2013 Andrea Jones. Used with permission from University of Iowa Press.

98. Excerpted from *The Incompleat Angler* by John J. Lipsey (Lipsey, 1948). Found in Tutt Library Special Collection. Colorado College, Colorado Springs.

99. Excerpted from *Spring's Edge: A Ranch Wife's Chronicles* by Laurie Wagner Buyer. Copyright ©2008, Laurie Wagner Buyer. Reprinted with permission from University of New Mexico Press.

100. Excerpt(s) from *Angle of Repose* by Wallace Stegner, copyright © 1971 by Wallace Stegner. Used by permission of Doubleday, an imprint of the Knopf Doubleday Publishing Group, a division of Penguin Random House LLC. All rights reserved.

101. Quote and "Spirit that Form'd This Scene" from *Walt Whitman's Western Jaunt* by Walter H. Eitner (The Regents Press of Kansas,

1981).

102. Excerpt from *Timber Times and Tales* by Earlene Belew Bradley
(Earlene Belew Bradley, 2005) reprinted with permission from the
author.

103. Excerpt *The View from the Folding Chairs* by Michala Miller
(Western Reflections Publishing, 2001) reprinted with permission
from Kathy Miller.

104. Excerpt from *Ghost Grizzlies: Does the Great Bear Still Haunt
Colorado?* by David Petersen (David Petersen Books; 2009) reprinted
courtesy of the author.

105. Excerpt from *House of Rain* by Craig Childs, copyright © 2007.
Reprinted by permission of Little, Brown, an imprint of Hachette
Book Group, Inc.

106. Excerpt from *When the Legends Die* by Hal Borland. Copyright ©
1963 used by permission.

107. Excerpt from *A Land Alone: Colorado's Western Slope* by Duane
Vandenbusche and Duane Smith (Pruett Press, 1981).

108. "Across the Great Divide" by Stephen J. Meyers appears in *Telling It
Real: The Best of Pilgrimage Magazine* (Pilgrimage Press, 2009).

109. Excerpt(s) from *Education of a Wandering Man: A Memoir* by
Louis L'Amour, copyright © 1989 by The Louis D. and Katherine
E. L'Amour 1983 Trust. Used by permission of Bantam Books, an
imprint of Random House, a division of Penguin Random House
LLC. All rights reserved.

110. "The Hush" by Grace Katherine Anderson courtesy of the author.

111. Excerpt from *The Professor's House* by Willa Cather (Grosset and
Dunlap, 1925).

112. Excerpt *The Sorrow of Archeology* by Russell Martin. Copyright ©
2005. Reprinted by permission of University of New Mexico.

113. "The Trailers of Montezuma County" in *How Delicate These Arches:
Footnotes from the Four Corners* by David Feela (Raven's Eye Press,
2011). Reprinted here courtesy of the author.

114. Excerpt from *Unforgettable Characters of Western Colorado* by Al
Look (Pruett Press, 1966).

115. "Whispers from the Past" by Regina Lopez-Whiteskunk from *Rock*

Art: A Vision of a Vanishing Landscape edited by Jonathan Bailey (Bower House, 2019). Reprinted with permission of Bower House.

116. Excerpt from *West of the Divide: Voices from a Ranch and Reservation* by Jim Carrier (Fulcrum Press, 1992) reprinted with permission of Fulcrum Press.

117. Excerpt from *Fool's Gold* by Rob Shultheis (Lyons Press, 2001) reprinted with permission.

118. Excerpt from *Tomboy Bride: A Woman's Personal Account of Life in Mining Camps of the West* by Harriet Fish Backus (Westwinds Press, 1980).

119. "Almost Animal" by Amy Irvine, which is from a longer work in progress with the same title, appears here courtesy of the author.

120. Excerpt from "Dr. Don: The Life of a Small Town Druggist" by Peter Hessler.

121. Excerpt from *One Man's West* by David Lavender (Bison Books, 2007) used with permission form the Lavender family.

122. "Red Mountain" by Robinson Jeffers from *The Collected Poetry of Robinson Jeffers, 1928-1938, Volume 2*, edited by Tim Hunt (Jeffers Literary Properties, 1987). All rights reserved. Used with permission of Stanford University Press, www.sup.org.

123. Excerpt from "Toward the Sun" by Kent Nelson in *Toward the Sun: The Collected Sports Stories of Kent Nelson* (Breakaway Books, 1999). Reprinted courtesy of the author.

124. Excerpt from *Old Fences, New Neighbors* by Peter Decker (University of Arizona, 1998). Reprinted courtesy of the author.

125. "Hiking with Hobbes" in the September 2019 issue of *Colorado Central Magazine* (coloradocentralmagazine.com), reprinted here courtesy of the author.

126. Quotes from *City of Illusions* by Ursula Le Guin found in "Rocky Mountain Refuge: Constructing Colorado" by Carl Abbot, in Science Fiction Studies; Volume 39, No. 2 (July 2012).

127. "Our New Life in the Forest" by Mary Anne Rawlings (Ott), *The Christian Science Monitor*, October 17, 1956, reprinted courtesy of the author.

128. Excerpt from *Chronicles of the Forbidden: Essays of Shadow and*

Light by John Nizalowski, reprinted courtesy of the author.

129. Excerpt from *Island in the Sky: The Story of Grand Mesa* by Muriel Marshall (Western Reflections, 1999).

130. "A Newcomer's Old Story" by Paul Larmer from *Living in the Runaway West*, editors of the *High Country News* (Fulcrum, 2000) used with permission of the author.

131. "Goldboat" by Belle Turnbull in *Belle Turnbull: On the Life & Work of an American Master* edited by David Rothman and Jeffrey Villines (Pleiades Press, 2017).

132. Excerpt from *Vail, Colorado: Triumph of a Dream* by Peter. W. Seibert (Mountain Sports Press, 2000) reprinted courtesy of Peter Seibert Jr.

133. Excerpt from *In the Shining Mountains* by David Thomson, copyright © 1979 by David Thomson. Used by permission of Alfred A. Knopf, an imprint of the Knopf Doubleday Publishing Group, a division of Penguin Random House LLC. All rights reserved.

134. Excerpt from *Fire on the Mountain* by John N. Maclean. Copyright © 1999 by John N. Maclean. Used by permission of HarperCollins Publishers

135. Excerpt from *The Great Shark Hunt* by Hunter S. Thompson. Copyright © 1979 Hunter S. Thompson. Reprinted with the permission of Simon and Schuster, Inc. All rights reserved.

136. Excerpt from *Notes of a Half-Aspenite* by Bruce Berger (Graphic Impressions, 1987), reprinted courtesy of the author.

137. Excerpt(s) from *Where the Water Goes: Life and Death along the Colorado River* by David Owen, copyright © 2017 by David Owen. Used by permission of Riverhead, an imprint of Penguin Publishing Group, a division of Penguin Random House LLC. All rights reserved.

138. Excerpt from *Eclipse* by Dalton Trumbo (Mesa County Library Foundation, 2005).

139. John Otto letter from in *John Otto: Trials and Trail* by Alan J. Kania (Xlibris, 2008).

140. Notes on Charlie Utter from the *Daily Miner's Register*, Central City, March 23, 1865; and from *Our New West* by Samuel Bowles

published in 1869; both quotes found in *Colorado Charlie: Wild Bill's Pard* by Agnes Wright Spring (Pruett 1968).

141. Excerpt from *Colorado: A Summer Trip* by Bayard Taylor (G.P. Putnam, 1867).

142. "Mountain Medicine Man" by Evan Edwards found in *Rocky Mountain Empire* by Elvon Howe (Doubleday, 1950).

143. Excerpt from *Tales of Lonely Trails* by Zane Gray (Harper and Brothers, 1922).

144. Excerpt from *A Wet Ass and a Hungry Gut* by Danny W. Campbell (London Publishing).

145. "Dinosaur" by Steve Rasnic Tem found in *Vintage Colorado Short Stories: When Past Met Present*, edited by James B. Hemesath (University of Colorado, 1997). Reprinted courtesy of the author.

146. Excerpt from "A Water Tank Turned Music Venue" by Alex Ross from *The New Yorker*, July 24, 2017, reprinted courtesy of the author.

147. Excerpts from *Headfirst in the Pickle Barrel* by John Rolfe Burroughs (Morrow, 1963) and *I Never Look Back: The Story of Buddy Werner* by John Rolfe Burroughs (Johnson, 1967).

148. Excerpt from "The Betrayal of Jack" by Charles Wilkinson in *Heart of the Land: Essays on Last Great Places* edited by Joseph Barbato and Lisa Weinerman (Pantheon, 1995), reprinted courtesy of the author.

149. Excerpt from *A Seasoned Life Lived in Small Towns: Memories, Musings, and Observations* by Janet B. Sheridan (Outskirts Press, 2013) reprinted courtesy of the author.

150. Excerpt from *Riding the Edge of an Era* by Diana Allen Kouris (High Plains Press, 2009). Used with permission of the author and High Plains Press.

151. Excerpt from *Colorado's Yampa River* by Patrick Tierney and John Fielder (John Fielder Publishing, 2015) reprinted with permission.

152. Excerpt from "The Marks of Human Passage" by Wallace Stegner in *This is Dinosaur: Echo Park Country and Its Magic Rivers* (Lyons Press, 2019).